Havana

timeout.com/havana

Published by Time Out Guides Ltd, a wholly owned subsidiary of Time Out Group Ltd.
Time Out and the Time Out logo are trademarks of Time Out Group Ltd.

Previous editions 2001, 2005

10 9 8 7 6 5 4 3 2 1

This edition first published in Great Britain in 2007 by Ebury Publishing
Ebury Publishing is a division of The Random House Group Ltd,
20 Vauxhall Bridge Road, London SW1V 2SA

Random House Australia Pty Limited 20 Alfred Street, Milsons Point, Sydney, New South Wales 2061, Australia
Random House New Zealand Limited 18 Poland Road, Glenfield, Auckland 10, New Zealand
Random House South Africa (Pty) Limited Isle of Houghton, Corner Boundary Road & Carse O'Gowrie, Houghton 2198, South Africa

Random House UK Limited Reg. No. 954009

Distributed in USA by Publishers Group West
1700 Fourth Street, Berkeley, California 94710

Distributed in Canada by Publishers Group Canada
250A Carlton Street, Toronto, Ontario M5A 2L1

For further distribution details, see www.timeout.com

ISBN 10: 1-84670-014-0
ISBN 13: 978184670 0149

A CIP catalogue record for this book is available from the British Library

Printed and bound by Firmengruppe APPL, aprinta druck, Wemding, Germany

Papers used by Ebury Publishing are natural, recyclable products made from wood grown in sustainable forests.

Hasta la
victoria
siempre

Time Out Guides Limited
Universal House
251 Tottenham Court Road
London W1T 7AB
Tel + 44 (0)20 7813 3000
Fax + 44 (0)20 7813 6001
Email guides@timeout.com
www.timeout.com

Editorial
Editor Lesley McCave
Deputy Editor Daniel Smith
Listings Editor Alicia Padrón
Proofreaders Patrick Mulkern, Tamsin Shelton
Indexer Ismay Atkins

Managing Director Peter Fiennes
Financial Director Gareth Garner
Editorial Director Ruth Jarvis
Deputy Series Editor Dominic Earle
Editorial Manager Holly Pick

Design
Art Director Scott Moore
Art Editor Pinelope Kourmouzoglou
Senior Designer Josephine Spencer
Graphic Designer Henry Elphick
Junior Graphic Designer Kei Ishimaru
Digital Imaging Simon Foster
Ad Make-up Jenni Prichard

Picture Desk
Picture Editor Jael Marschner
Deputy Picture Editor Tracey Kerrigan
Picture Researcher Helen McFarland

Advertising
Sales Director Mark Phillips
International Sales Manager Fred Durman
International Sales Executive Simon Davies
International Sales Consultant Ross Canadé
Advertising Assistant Kate Staddon

Marketing
Group Marketing Director John Luck
Marketing Manager Yvonne Poon
Sales & Marketing Manager, US & Canada Lisa Levinson

Production
Group Production Director Mark Lamond
Production Manager Brendan McKeown
Production Coordinator Caroline Bradford

Time Out Group
Chairman Tony Elliott
Financial Director Richard Waterlow
Time Out Magazine Ltd MD David Pepper
Group General Manager/Director Nichola Coulthard
Time Out Communications Ltd MD David Pepper
Time Out International MD Cathy Runciman
Group Art Director John Oakey
Group IT Director Simon Chappell

Contributors
Introduction Lesley McCave. **History** Christine Ayorinde, Stephen Gibbs, James Mitchell (*Family fortunes* Sue Herrod). **Havana Today** Stephen Gibbs. **Havana Tomorrow** Stephen Gibbs. **Where to Stay** Toby Brocklehurst (*Lobby lounging* Sue Herrod). **Sightseeing Introduction** Lesley McCave. **La Habana Vieja** Juliet Barclay, Lesley McCave (*Walk on* Lesley McCave, James Mitchell). **Centro Habana** Susan Hurlich. **Vedado** Susan Hurlich. **Miramar & the Western Suburbs** Lesley McCave. **Eastern Bay and the Coast** Fiona McAuslan. **Eating & Drinking** Matt Norman, Mark Pinkerton. **Shops & Services** Alexandra Baker. **Festivals & Events** Ernesto Juan Castellanos. **Children** Fiona McAuslan. **Film** Apo Martínez. **Galleries** Paul Greene (*The writing's on the wall* Fiona McAuslan). **Gay & Lesbian** Joseph Mutti. **Music & Nightlife** Apo Martínez, Mariley Reinoso Olivera (*Friday night's all right* Matt Pinkerton). **Performing Arts** Sebastian Doggart, Mariley Reinoso Olivera. **Sport & Fitness** Matt Norman. **Getting Started** Toby Brocklehurst. **Pinar del Río Province** Matt Norman (*What a dive* Adam Coulter). **Varadero** Matt Norman. **The Central Provinces** Matt Norman. **Santiago de Cuba** Matt Norman. **Directory** Paul Greene (*Specialist package holidays* Toby Brocklehurst, Lesley McCave; *US citizens travelling to Cuba* James Mitchell).

Maps john@jsgraphics.co.uk.

Photography by Claire Boobbyer, except: pages 3, 11, 26, 28, 29, 34, 35, 45, 53, 54, 75,87, 91, 92, 98, 100, 101, 106, 118, 124, 131, 137, 150, 151, 153, 155, 157, 165, 167, 168, 171, 189, 190, 195, 196, 219 Lydia Evans; page 12 North Wind Picture Archives; page 14 Underwood & Underwood/Library of Congress; page 17 Bettmann/Corbis; page 20 Rex Features; pages 22, 32 Presna Latina; pages 30, 166, 177 Claudia Daut/Reuters; pages 82, 169 Rolando Pujol/South American Pictures; pages 96, 97 Odyssey/Robert Harding; page 149 Image.net; page 175 AEP/Alamy; page 178 Reuters/Michele Crosera; page 185 Mark Henley/Panos Pictures; page 192 Bruno Morandi/Robert Harding; page 197 Alamy; page 200 Travel Library/Robert Harding; Page 202 George Brice/Alamy; page 214 Ellen Rooney/Robert Harding.

The following image was provided by the featured establishment/artist: page 163.
The Editor would like to thank Alubia Barrios, Claire Boobbyer, Jake Duncombe, Martin Hacthoun, Alfredo Martínez González, Jana Pitlanicova, Theresa Staal, Justin Talbot, Charlotte Tidball and all contributors to previous editions of *Time Out Havana*, whose work forms the basis for parts of this book.

The editor flew from London to Havana with Virgin Atlantic (08705 747747; www.virgin-atlantic.com).

Contents

Introduction

Cuba is undergoing a period of change. The oft-asked, looming question of who will take over from Fidel Castro has been answered, temporarily at least, now that his brother Raúl is at the helm, but new uncertainties have taken its place. Will Raúl stay in power? And, if so, for how long, given that he's in his 70s already? If he goes, who will take over, and what will their ideology be? Will they continue the long-term work of the Revolutionaries, or will they bend to (largely) US pressure to 'reform' and 'embrace democracy'? These are all real issues that will be resolved over time.

However, the pace of change is likely to be slow by international standards – hardly surprising in a place that's almost the dictionary definition of laid-back. But for how long will the Cubans put up with their current standard of living? The shortages (ingredients, car parts, electricity, the list is endless), the blackouts, the crumbling infrastructure – they have had to live with these things for decades.

They've put up with worse – particularly during the harsh Special Period of the 1990s – and show a resolve and adaptability that would put most other nations to shame. But this is the 21st century and they have the internet and television, and they hear from their relatives in Miami: oh yes, they do get to see what their American cousins have. They've even had to endure their hospitals making room for Venezuelans – shipped over as part of an agreement between Fidel and his chum Hugo Chávez – while they wait for their operations on the sidelines. They also see the gringos come in and stay in the posh hotels, lounging in the sun by the pool. These things don't go unnoticed, and the dichotomies will eventually take their toll. Most *habaneros* struggle to get by.

While Cubans might hunger for change, the visitors want the country to stay the same for as long as possible, locked in its picturesque timewarp bubble. Well, luckily for them some things never change – the rum, the weather, the music, the infectious charisma of the locals.

But Havana – and Cuba – isn't perfect. Far from it. As well as the less-than-stellar food, there are the *jineteros* clamouring for your pesos, the transport problems, the under-funded museums. Surprisingly, it's not even cheap. Fortunately, it's also a place for simple pleasures – sipping Mojitos, listening to rumba, watching a cabaret, strolling through Vedado's grand tree-lined streets or along the Malecón (no Starbucks, McDonald's or Coca-Cola billboards here). All clichés, but the very things that help Havana lure the tourists.

And lure them it does: foreigners just can't seem to get enough of Cuba, titillated by its exoticism and intrigued by its eccentricities. Now more than ever, Havana is at a tipping point. Get here while you can.

ABOUT TIME OUT CITY GUIDES

This is the third edition of *Time Out Havana*, one of an expanding series of Time Out guides produced by the people behind the successful listings magazines in London, New York and Chicago. Our guides are all written by resident experts who have striven to provide you with all the most up-to-date information you'll need to explore the city or read up on its background, whether you're a local or a first-time visitor.

THE LOWDOWN ON THE LISTINGS

Above all, we've tried to make this book as useful as possible. Addresses, telephone numbers, websites, opening times, admission prices and, for hotels, credit card details, are included in our listings. And, as far as possible, we've given details of facilities, services and events. However, venues can change their arrangements at any time.

Also, in the whole of Cuba, shops, bars and, in particular, *paladares*, don't keep precise opening times, and may close earlier or later than stated. Similarly, arts programmes are often finalised very late. If you're going out of your way to visit a particular venue, we'd advise you to phone first whenever possible. While every effort has been made to ensure the accuracy of this guide, the publishers cannot accept responsibility for any errors it may contain.

There are two things to remember in Havana: everything will take longer than you expect, and everything will cost more than you expect. The golden rule is to take a sense of humour with you wherever you go.

PRICES AND PAYMENT

The prices given in this guide should be treated as guidelines, not gospel. We have listed prices in Cuban convertible pesos (CUC) throughout,

and also in Cuban pesos where relevant. Credit cards are accepted in some hotels, shops and restaurants in Havana. (Although in practice, credit card machines are often broken.) We have used the following abbreviations: **MC** for MasterCard and **V** for Visa. Note that American Express and cards issued by US banks (or even its subsidiaries outside the US) are not accepted in Cuba.

THE LIE OF THE LAND

To make the book (and the city) easier to navigate, we have divided Havana into areas and assigned each one its own chapter in our **Sightseeing** section (pages 53-100). Although these areas are a simplification of Havana's geography, we hope they will give you a useful means of understanding the city's layout and finding its most interesting sights. The areas are used in addresses throughout the guide. See page 54 for a summary of these areas.

Though distances within Havana can be big, many tourists choose to avoid the hassle and crush of the city buses and opt instead for a taxi (ranging from 1950s 'yank-tanks' to air-conditioned tourist taxis), a pedal-powered *bicitaxi*, or a cheeky little orange three-wheeled *cocotaxi*.

TELEPHONE NUMBERS

Havana's phone system can be extremely frustrating and is prone to breakdown. Phone numbers within the city tend to have either six or seven digits. To call Havana from abroad, dial your international access code, then 53 for Cuba and 7 for Havana. Phone codes for places outside Havana are listed in full (if dialling from outside Cuba, drop the 0), for example, in the **Trips Out of Town** chapters (pages 189-218).

ESSENTIAL INFORMATION

For all the practical information you might need for visiting Havana, including emergency phone numbers and details of local transport, turn to the **Directory** chapter at the back of the guide. It starts on page 219.

MAPS

We provide a map reference for all places listed in central Havana, indicating the page and grid reference at which an address can be found on our street maps. These are located at the back of the book (pages 245-256),include detailed street maps of the city, and pinpoint the specific locations of hotels (❶), restaurants (❶) and bars (❶). To make the maps easier to navigate, there is also a street index (pages 249-251). Street maps for towns in the Trips Out of Town section of the guide (pages 189-218) are included in the relevant chapter.

LET US KNOW WHAT YOU THINK

We hope you enjoy this edition of *Time Out Havana*, and we would like to know what you think of it. We welcome tips for places that you consider we should include in future editions and we take note of your criticism of our choices. You can email us at guides@timeout.com.

Advertisers

We would like to stress that no establishment has been included in this guide because it has advertised in any of our publications and no payment of any kind has influenced any review. The opinions given in this book are those of Time Out writers and entirely independent.

There is an online version of this book, along with guides to over 100 international cities, at **www.timeout.com**.

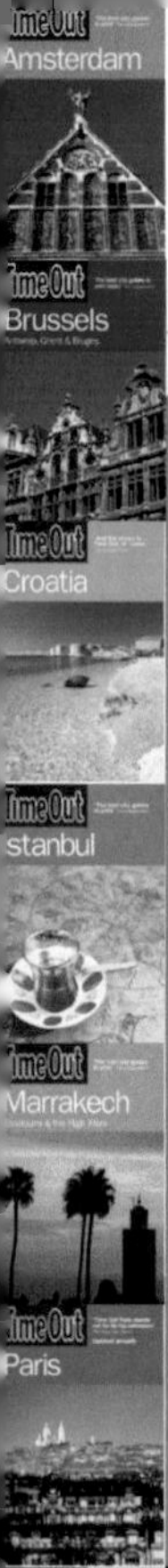

Amsterdam
Brussels
Croatia
Istanbul
Marrakech
Paris

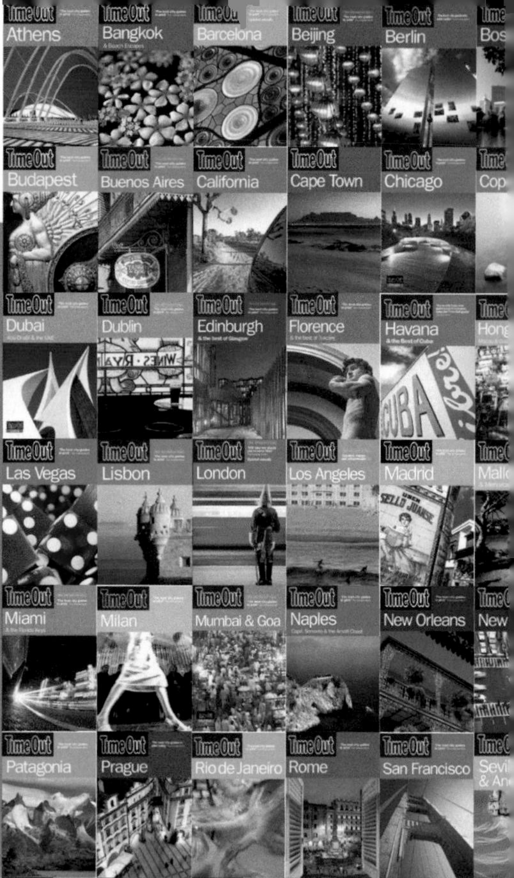

Athens
Bangkok
Barcelona
Beijing
Berlin
Budapest
Buenos Aires
California
Cape Town
Chicago
Dubai
Dublin
Edinburgh
Florence
Havana
Las Vegas
Lisbon
London
Los Angeles
Madrid
Miami
Milan
Mumbai & Goa
Naples
New Orleans
Patagonia
Prague
Rio de Janeiro
Rome
San Francisco

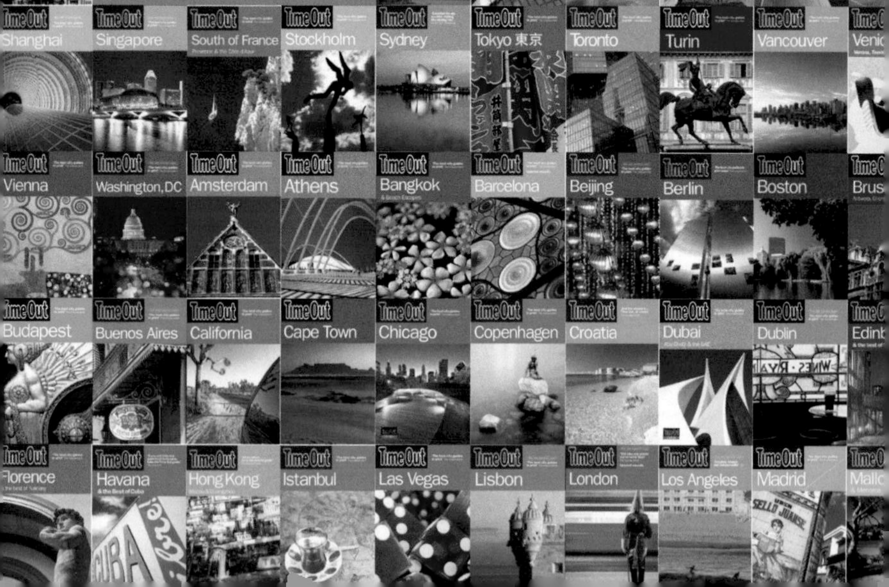

Shanghai
Singapore
South of France
Stockholm
Sydney
Tokyo 東京
Toronto
Turin
Vancouver
Vienna
Washington, DC
Amsterdam
Athens
Bangkok
Barcelona
Beijing
Berlin
Boston
Budapest
Buenos Aires
California
Cape Town
Chicago
Copenhagen
Croatia
Dubai
Dublin
Florence
Havana
Hong Kong
Istanbul
Las Vegas
Lisbon
London
Los Angeles
Madrid

Time Out Miami
Time Out Milan
Time Out Mumbai & Goa
Time Out Naples
Time Out New Orleans
Time Out New York
Time Out Paris
Time Out Patagonia
Time Out Prague
Time Out Rome
Time Out San Francisco
Time Out Seville & Andalucía
Time Out Shanghai
Time Out Singapore
Time Out South of France
Time Out Stockholm
Time Out Sydney
Time Out Tokyo 東京
Time Out Turin
Time Out Venice
Time Out Vienna
Time Out Washington, DC
Time Out Amsterdam
Time Out Athens
Time Out Bangkok
Time Out Barcelona
Time Out Beijing
Time Out Boston
Time Out Brussels
Time Out Budapest
Time Out Buenos Aires
Time Out California
Time Out Cape Town
Time Out Chicago
Time Out Copenhagen
Time Out Croatia
Time Out Dublin
Time Out Edinburgh
Time Out Florence
Time Out Havana
Time Out Hong Kong
Time Out Istanbul
Time Out Las Vegas
Time Out Lisbon
Time Out London
Time Out Madrid
Time Out Mallorca
Time Out Marrakech
Time Out Miami
Time Out Milan
Time Out Mumbai & Goa
Time Out Naples
Time Out New Orleans
Time Out New York
Time Out Patagonia
Time Out Prague
Time Out Rio de Janeiro
Time Out Rome
Time Out San Francisco
Time Out Seville & Andalucía
Time Out Shanghai
Time Out Singapore
Time Out South of France
Time Out Sydney
Time Out Tokyo 東京
Time Out Toronto
Time Out Turin
Time Out Venice
Time Out Vienna
Time Out Washington, DC
Time Out Amsterdam
Time Out Athens
Time Out Barcelona
Time Out Beijing
Time Out Berlin
Time Out Boston
Time Out Brussels
Time Out Budapest
Time Out Buenos Aires
Time Out California
Time Out Cape Town
Time Out Copenhagen
Time Out Croatia
Time Out Dubai
Time Out Dublin
Time Out Edinburgh
Time Out Florence
Time Out Havana
Time Out Hong Kong
Time Out Istanbul

In Context

Features

Memorial a Antonio Maceo. *See p76.*

History

From pirates of the Caribbean to the long goodbye, Cuba's history has been full of drama.

The written history of the Caribbean begins with the arrival of Christopher Columbus (Cristóbal Colón in Spanish). However rich and varied life in pre-Columbian Cuba may have been, there is no evidence that the indigenous peoples possessed a written language. Our knowledge of these times, therefore, is based on archaeological excavations and the writings of early Spanish explorers.

The island was first inhabited by the Siboney and the Guanahatabey, groups that probably migrated (somewhat ironically) from Florida and spread throughout the Caribbean. The archaeological evidence indicates that they were hunter-gatherers, living in small groups near the shoreline or close to rivers and streams. They were followed by the more technologically savvy Taíno, an Arawak people from South America. The Taíno were excellent farmers, boat builders and fishermen. Men cleared forests and defended the village, while women cultivated crops and produced manufactured goods. Seafood was the main source of protein, so most Taíno settlements were located within easy reach of the sea.

COLUMBUS AND CO

Christopher Columbus first set foot on Cuban soil on 27 October 1492. Convinced that he had reached Asia by sailing westwards, he returned home to Spain in the following year, leaving half his men behind on the neighbouring island of Hispaniola. Apart from another fleeting visit by Columbus the following year, Cuba was at this point little more than a staging post for further colonisation as explorers busied themselves discovering other parts of the Caribbean. It wasn't until 1508, when Sebastián de Ocampo circumnavigated Cuba, that the Spanish realised that their new discovery was actually an island.

Life changed dramatically in 1511, when Diego Columbus (Christopher's son) decided to 'settle' the island and appointed Diego Velázquez as its first governor. The new lords of Cuba quickly set about enslaving or killing all but a handful of the indigenous Taíno. One early rebel was Hatuey, a chief from Hispaniola who fled to Cuba where he fought the Spaniards – but unfortunately for him he was captured and burnt at the stake.

Until recently, the conventional view has been that the Spaniards totally exterminated the Taíno in Cuba through the imaginative and diligent application of disease, cruelty (in the form of slavery and torture) and murder. The most recent evidence, while not detracting from the conquistadors' formidable skills as psychopaths, indicates that a few scattered pockets of Taíno society did survive, no doubt overlooked. When the Spaniards began to exploit the island's natural resources, the penny soon dropped that by wiping out the locals, they had also destroyed their only convenient source of labour. This little gaffe was easily remedied, however, when the first African slaves arrived in Cuba from 1513 onwards.

SETTLING IN

The settlement of Cuba was progressing at a frenetic rate. Seven towns were founded across the island (Baracoa, Santiago de Cuba, Bayamo, Sancti Spíritus, Trinidad, San Cristóbal de la Habana and Puerto Príncipe – now Camagüey). Pánfilo de Narváez established the westernmost of these in 1514, and named it San Cristóbal de La Habana (said to be after a prominent local Indian chief, Habaguanex, although this is disputed). Havana was originally located about 50 kilometres (31 miles) south of its current location, near the present-day town of Batabanó, but this region was found to be marshy and plagued with mosquitoes, so the city was relocated to its current home in 1519.

The same year, after setting off from Santiago de Cuba, conquistador Hernán Cortés and his fleet had stopped for supplies in Havana harbour en route to Mexico on his notorious mission to convert the Aztecs into a historical footnote. Havana rapidly became an important hub for Spanish activities in the Caribbean. Its large, sheltered harbour provided an ideal anchorage for vessels en route to Spain, laden with silver and gold plundered from Central and South America.

'A black economy quickly sprang up, and Havana became the smuggling centre of the Caribbean.'

When Spanish galleons opened the Philippines for trade in 1564, Havana's fortune was made. All the riches of the New World and the Orient passed through the city en route for Seville. Havana also developed the drawbacks normally associated with a boom town. It was filthy with sewage and rotten produce; drunks, cut-throats, and whores roamed the mud streets, and during hot weather yellow fever epidemics were frequent. Havana's growing prosperity attracted the attention of English, Dutch and French pirates. The city was extensively plundered or burned with monotonous regularity, until in 1558, the *habaneros* began the construction of the Castillo de la Real Fuerza as a defensive bastion on the edge of the bay (it was completed in 1577). Another two fortresses – Castillo de Los Tres Reyes del Morro and Castillo San Salvador de La Punta – on either side of the harbour entrance, were completed in 1630. A heavy chain was stretched across the harbour mouth and could be lifted into place to block the entrance. The pirates responded by simply plundering Spanish ships on the open seas instead of in the harbour.

By the late 16th century Caribbean piracy was big business. English and French pirates were often licensed by their governments to prey on Spanish shipping, as a means of weakening Spain's hold on the New World. The destruction of the Spanish Armada in the English Channel in 1588 further increased the vulnerability of its colonies to piracy.

Despite these setbacks, Havana grew in power and significance throughout the 16th century. In 1592 Philip II gave Havana its title of 'city'; this was also the year that the Zanja Real, the first aqueduct in the Americas, was built to bring the waters of the Río Almendares to the city. As the 'key to the Indies' Havana became the pre-eminent city of the New World (even though Mexico City and Lima were larger), and the Cuban capital was officially moved from Santiago de Cuba to Havana in 1607. Trade (legal and illegal) made residents rich. Like the nouveaux riches of any era, affluent *habaneros* flaunted their wealth. Stonemasons and craftsmen were brought from Spain to build vast mansions (*palacios*), full of columns and arches, grand staircases and tiled courtyards. In 1674 work began on the massive walls that would take almost a century to build, ultimately enclosing the city within a protective ring of stone ten metres (35 feet) high.

FIRST STIRRINGS OF REVOLUTION

Despite Cuba's growing wealth, political and economic power remained firmly in Spanish hands. This was reinforced by a trade monopoly. When gold supplies began to run down, Spain began to look for other sources of income, and tobacco became Cuba's most important export. In 1717 Spain created an agency known as the Factoría, which purchased all Cuban tobacco at a (low) fixed price and had exclusive rights to sell it abroad. The tobacco growers tried to rebel but were brutally suppressed. In 1740 the Real Compañía de Comercio was founded to control all imports

USS *Maine*: well remembered. *See p115.*

to and exports from the port of Havana. The resulting extortionate customs duties and restricted supply of goods caused great discontent among the populace. A black economy quickly sprang up, and Havana became the smuggling centre of the Caribbean.

This was all to change when a British expeditionary force under the Earl of Albemarle breached Havana's defences in June 1762. The new masters removed trading restrictions and the city prospered under the brief British rule. The British ceded control of the city back to Spain in 1763 in return for Spanish-held territories in Florida, but by that point Cuban landowners and merchants had got a taste of the economic potential of free trade.

After regaining control, the Spanish undertook an extensive programme of renewal and modernisation in Havana: streets were cobbled and gas lighting installed; sewers and drains were built; architectural styles were harmonised; parks and grand avenues were built. Havana was Spain's showpiece in the New World, a great city of 55,000 inhabitants.

In 1791 revolution in neighbouring Haiti destroyed its sugar industry. Cuba replaced it as the region's main supplier and large amounts of capital were poured into creating new production capacity. Trade between Cuba and the newly established United States rapidly became an important source of revenue for the island. Although Spain signed a treaty with Britain to end the slave trade in 1817, Cuba's fast-growing economy was heavily reliant on slave labour. The trade simply moved underground and continued to grow.

A period of relative peace on the European continent after the Napoleonic Wars prompted Spain to lessen the financial drain on its colonies. Discontent over crippling taxation and heavy-handed leadership had been growing for a number of years throughout the New World. In an effort to calm tensions, the Factoría tobacco monopoly in Cuba was abolished in 1817. The gesture was too little, too late. The fires of revolution were already burning throughout Spanish America.

THE YANKS ARE COMING

By 1824 all of Spain's chickens had come home to roost. Years of poor leadership, greed, arrogance and military ineptitude had cost it the bulk of its American empire, which had once spanned nearly all of South and Central America and much of what is now the western United States. All that remained were Puerto Rico and Cuba, and the Spanish were determined to hold on to these vestiges of their greatness. The USA, on the other hand, felt that these islands would make a lovely addition to its young nation. The United States articulated a sweeping policy concerning the Americas that would have repercussions for Cuba up to the present day. The Monroe Doctrine, named after President James Monroe, claimed the western hemisphere as a US sphere of influence and warned Europe not to interfere in the affairs of any of the newly independent American nations.

Meanwhile, revolutionaries from newly liberated Spanish America joined forces with disaffected Cubans in a number of unsuccessful plots aimed at freeing the island from colonial rule. The US feared that independence would end Cuba's participation in the slave trade (a major source of labour for the southern United States). US policy at that time was to try to distance Cuba and Puerto Rico from other Latin American countries, increase their reliance on the US and thereby hasten their ultimate incorporation into the US itself. The policy was very effective; US influence in Cuba grew and it became the island's main trading partner.

After the Mexican War of 1847, the US annexed Texas, California and New Mexico. In 1848 President Polk felt that Cuba had become a US colony in all but name and offered Spain US$100 million for its territory. The Spanish government turned him down. For the next 20 years the US made numerous attempts either to buy Cuba from Spain or forcibly to annex it. Some Cubans regarded this as a better option than a revolution or the untimely ending of the slave trade on which the economy depended. This cat-and-mouse game continued until the end of the US Civil War, when the abolition of slavery diminished Cuba's value to the USA.

By the mid 19th century Cuba's once relatively diversified agricultural base had been almost completely turned over to the production of a single crop: sugar. Whatever the long-term negative economic and political ramifications of Cuba's emergence as a monocrop economy, it led to a short-term period of prosperity in the 1860s, resulting in affluent neighbourhoods springing up outside the city walls. The colonial city centre became a congested slum as Havana's rich fled the old city for leafy suburbs like Vedado. In 1863 the city walls were torn down to accommodate Havana's explosion into the surrounding countryside.

THE TEN YEARS WAR

Spain once again demonstrated its feeble grasp of political reality by failing to respond to Cuban calls for political reform and imposing new taxes in 1866. This was in addition to the extortionate duties already levied on imported and exported goods, which had pushed Cubans to the brink of revolt several times in the recent past. An economic recession followed.

Wealthy plantation owners on the west of the island, who benefited from the huge profits from sugar, were reluctant to rebel against Spain for fear of triggering a slave uprising. Small-scale planters from the east were badly affected by the recession and thus had less to lose. On 10 October 1868 landowner Carlos Manuel de Céspedes issued what was to become known as the Grito de Yara, a proclamation of Cuban independence. The revolutionary war that followed lasted a decade. The Ten Years War officially ended in 1878 when the rebels accepted Spanish peace terms.

While the goal of independence was not achieved, the war had three effects. First, it gave Cuba the revolutionary heroes it needed to rally the populace to the cause of independence. Carlos Manuel de Céspedes, Máximo Gómez and Afro-Cubans Antonio Maceo (known as the Bronze Titan) and Guillermón Moncada have inspired generations of Cuban freedom fighters. Secondly, the war instilled a revolutionary spirit into the Cuban people that they possess to this day. Finally, it destroyed large amounts of agricultural land and bankrupted many Cuban sugar planters, thereby opening the door to a virtual monopoly of the Cuban sugar industry by US interests. These countervailing forces would shape much of the island's later history.

The terms of the treaty signed in February 1878 were hardly satisfactory from the Cuban perspective. The Pacto de Zanjón (Treaty of Zanjón) freed any slaves who had fought on either side during the war, but left the institution of slavery in place. More alarmingly, Cuba would remain subject to Spanish rule, though its people were given limited representation in the Spanish Cortés (parliament). Some of the Cuban military leaders, including General Antonio Maceo, decided to reject the treaty at what became known as the Protest of Baraguá. Fighting continued until they were eventually forced to give up and go into exile.

'José Martí's vision remains at the centre of Cuban political life – though it is yet to be achieved.'

The combination of the war and the ending of slavery in 1886 severely affected sugar production. Competition from European sugar beet caused a fall in world prices and resulted in the loss of some of Cuba's markets. US capital began to flow into the sugar, mining and tobacco industries. By 1884 the United States was buying most of Cuba's exports, increasing Cuban economic dependency on its powerful big brother.

STATE OF INDEPENDENCE

One important figure to emerge at this period was José Martí. He articulated the programme for a Cuba that would be 'economically viable and politically independent'. Responsible for organising Cuban exiles in the US, together with the generals Máximo Gómez and Antonio Maceo, Martí planned an uprising for early 1895. The uneasy peace ended in April with the outbreak of a new War of Independence. Martí was killed in the revolution but his vision remains at the centre of Cuban political life. Unfortunately, it is yet to be achieved.

The War of Independence was brutal and bloody. Once again, the shadow of US interests fell across the proceedings, with American public opinion (and business interests) firmly on the side of the Cuban rebels. When the battleship USS *Maine* mysteriously exploded and sank in Havana harbour on 15 February 1898, it provided a pretext for the US to enter the conflict (under the slogan 'Remember the *Maine*') and signalled the beginning of the Spanish-American War. The war lasted barely three months; just enough time for Havana to be blockaded and the Spanish fleet to be defeated at Santiago de Cuba. With US help, the rebels had won. Cuba was free.

NO SUCH THING AS A FREE COUNTRY

The first hint the Cubans got that they had been conned was their exclusion from the peace table. The United States and Spain negotiated terms for the withdrawal of Spanish forces and agreed the means by which control of the island would pass to the US. For the next four years the island was run by a military government under General Leonard Wood. The US occupation had two principal objectives: firstly to rebuild the physical infrastructure that had been destroyed by the war; and secondly to ensure that the new Cuban political and constitutional framework was shaped in a way favourable to US business interests. This goal was assisted in large part by the imposition of the Platt Amendment, an appendix to the Constitution that gave the US the right to intervene in Cuban affairs if order or stability (in other words, US interests) were threatened. It also granted the leasing of areas of Cuban territory for US military bases (one of which was the now notorious Guantánamo Bay). The first in a long and distinguished line of US laws, this had the effect of making life for Cubans as unpleasant as possible.

In 1902 the Republic of Cuba was created, with the pro-American former schoolmaster Tomás Estrada Palma as its first president. When Estrada was elected to a second term the opposition Liberal Party accused him of fraud and launched a protest in 1906. This ushered in a second period of US occupation. President Teddy Roosevelt appointed Charles Magoon as Governor of Cuba. Hated by Cubans (regardless of political stripe), Magoon served until 1909 when José Miguel Gómez was elected Cuban president. The troops returned twice more (in 1912 and 1917) when it seemed as if outbreaks of unrest might threaten US property.

The early republican period saw huge foreign investment, especially from the US, and also large-scale immigration from the former mother country, Spain. Whole industries were rebuilt and manufacturing output returned quickly to levels reached before the War of Independence. The fact that these revitalised industries were now largely American-owned was not lost on the more alert observers of the time. Renewed industrial expansion fuelled rapid growth in Havana's population (which trebled between 1900 and 1930).

Neo-classical mansions were built along wide avenues in Miramar and other new communities west of the Almendares river. Electrification spread across the extended city. Sewage and drainage systems were modernised, and Havana at last lost its characteristic reek. The goal of all this renewal and expansion was to attract tourism. In the short space of 15 years, Havana transformed itself from a war-ravaged hellhole into an irresistible magnet for foreign visitors.

Outside of the tourist areas and affluent neighbourhoods, however, it was a different story. Housing for lower-income families was generally poor and cramped. Sanitation was non-existent and disease a constant threat. Discontent among the poor and dispossessed, who felt that they had gained little from Cuba's independence, fuelled much of the violence and protest that became an integral part of mid 20th-century political life on the island.

World War I was a time of great prosperity in Cuba. The war destroyed European sugar beet production and the Cuban sugar industry enjoyed enormous profitability. The period was known as 'the dance of the millions' and was accompanied by a building boom in Havana.

Havana's ambition to become the premier tourist destination in the Caribbean was helped immensely in 1919 when the US implemented Prohibition laws. As the Stateside moral crusade gained momentum, holidaymakers flocked to Havana. Sun, sea, sex, drink, drugs, gambling – who could ask for anything more? For those who did ask there was opera, baseball, deep-sea fishing, golf and ballroom dancing.

ECONOMIC GLOOM

As sugar prices began to plummet in the 1920s, the economy fell to its knees. Ever more Cuban property passed into US hands. Nationalism was once again at the forefront of the Cuban political agenda. Gerardo Machado ran for president in 1924 on a nationalist ticket and won easily (he may even have done so without vote rigging). The Cubans thought they had finally elected a president who was committed to real independence. The Americans thought their business interests were at last in safe hands. They were both wrong. Machado's regime set new standards in brutality and corruption, inadvertently giving the Communist Party (founded by Julio Mella in 1925) and other leftist organisations their first significant measure of popular support. The public's loathing of Machado became intertwined with a more general dissatisfaction with Cuba's dependency on the US and the hated Platt Amendment. The Wall Street Crash of 1929 and the subsequent worldwide Great Depression tied a bow on the whole sorry situation.

THE RISE OF BATISTA

Through manipulation of both the Cuban electorate and the US government, Machado managed to get his term of office extended. In 1933 a general strike forced his resignation and flight into exile. The temporary government

Fidel Castro and **Che Guevara**: guerrillas in the Maestra. *See p19.*

that replaced him was ousted in September when a number of non-commissioned officers seized power in the Revolt of the Sergeants. They installed a governing committee chosen by the student movement and with Dr Ramón Grau San Martín as president.

Meanwhile, one of the revolting sergeants (so to speak), Fulgencio Batista, was busy forging the personal and business relationships that were to define the shape of Cuban politics and society for the next 25 years. He formed a friendship with mobster and gambling boss Meyer Lansky, as well as with one of President Franklin Roosevelt's closest advisers, Ambassador Sumner Welles, who became a stout supporter of Batista. The new revolutionary government established fair working practices, granted land to peasant farmers, enfranchised women and denounced the Platt Amendment. The US, predictably, felt that such reforms bordered on communism, and so refused to recognise the new government. In January 1934 there was another coup, led by Batista. Grau was forced to resign and Batista replaced him with the pro-American Colonel Mendieta. The US immediately recognised the new government and acceded to Cuban demands to revoke the Platt Amendment, though it continued leasing Guantánamo Bay.

Although other men held the title of president between 1934 and 1940, it was Batista who held the real power in Cuba. The Batista regime was concerned with creating the appearance of good government, if not its substance. In 1938 the Communist Party (later known as the Partido Socialista Popular) was legalised. After six years as the power behind the throne, Batista had himself properly elected to the post in 1940 and a Cuban constitution was adopted that was a model of social justice. When, in a more-or-less democratic election in 1944, the candidate Batista had groomed for the presidency lost to the veteran politician Grau, Batista graciously took himself off to 'retirement' in Florida.

Behind the scenes, however, it was a different story: political opponents were eliminated, student and labour groups repressed and political dissent harshly punished. It wasn't just Batista, though: the two presidents in power from 1944 to 1952 (Grau and his protégé, Carlos Prío Socarrás) presided over regimes that were, if anything, more corrupt than Batista's. In 1952 Batista reappeared as a candidate for the presidency but, fearing defeat in the elections, he seized power in a bloodless coup. His new government was once again immediately recognised by the US. This launched an era of

Family fortunes

Cuba is home to over 11 million people, two million of whom inhabit the vibrant, chaotic capital city of Havana. But 90 shark-invested miles away, in a parallel world, lies another, smaller Cuba: Little Havana, Miami, USA. The extraordinary history that has both bound together and wrenched apart these two neighbouring yet ideologically opposed countries and cities is the stuff of Biblical parable or Shakespearean drama, featuring a fiercely warring David set against a monolithic and deeply angry Goliath: La Yuma (Cuban slang for the USA).

In Havana you can talk high blood pressure, low blood sugar, the pain in your back, or the heat ('and it's only mid June – if it's like this now, imagine August, *por favor*'). Or how you waited two hours for your bus, or about how *los norteamericanos* are complete lunatics. All of these matters and more will be regularly debated with an expressive vigour, *a lo cubano*. But talk family and separation and the mood changes instantly. The eyes start to water as strained, wistful voices describe sons, daughters, aunts, nieces, mothers, children who are *allá fuera* – that is, outside the country.

Many of those Cubans abroad are living in Miami – an estimated one and a half million mainly white exiles. The long historical chain of white privilege in Cuba meant that whites were the first to leave and settle in the States. Some rise to great heights, others rub along and some never leave their neighbourhood or learn to speak English.

Amarylis's young son left for Hialeah, a Cuban-centric suburb of Miami, six years ago when his father won *el bombo* (the US-organised lottery offering Cubans residency in the States). But this means, under American law, that he cannot return to Cuba for three years. Their bond is as strong as superglue, so can you imagine when he didn't even ring her at Christmas or on Mothers Day? She hears, through a family friend, that he loves his life over there and is doing well at school, but why doesn't he call?

Naty, 22, met a retired US engineer and, while not in love, was desperate for change and to support her family in Havana. They eventually separated and she is now working in tourism in Florida. José Luís's older brother secretly put out to sea in a home-made boat in the 1980s and successfully made the

political authoritarianism and repression during which he suspended the Constitution, stifled the unions and outlawed the Communist Party.

Batista spent most of the 1940s cosying up to US organised crime and big business interests. Cuba quickly became a mecca for gambling, drug trafficking and prostitution. These businesses operated with impunity for a decade (until they were shut down after the 1959 Revolution). By the mid to late 1950s, tourism had done much to eliminate the reliance of the Cuban economy on sugar. Batista was beginning to plough some of this money into urban renewal projects, aimed at improving living conditions in Havana. Unfortunately, his time had nearly run out.

YOU SAY YOU WANT A REVOLUTION

By this point, the Cuban peasantry and working class had endured a bellyful of bad government. For more than 450 years they had been ruled by one mendacious incompetent after another. Worse, their destiny seemed to be as a perennial pawn in someone else's game, whether that of the Spanish, the British, the Americans, or some homegrown despot. The US ownership of many Cuban industries and its domination of the market hindered development and the economy was on a course to total collapse. This deepened a sense of frustration and, from 1953 onwards, various revolutionary groups, including that led by Fidel Castro, opposed the regime. Revolution had twice failed to secure Cuba's independence. Maybe it would be third time lucky.

The Revolution got off to a very bad start. On 26 July 1953 Fidel Castro, a 26-year-old lawyer, led a revolt in which 150 people attacked the Moncada army barracks near Santiago de Cuba. The attack was a failure; Castro and his brother Raúl were arrested, and around 70 followers were killed. During the subsequent trial Castro made his famous 'History Will Absolve Me' speech, outlining his vision for a radically reformed Cuban society. At the end of the trial, Castro was sentenced to 15 years in prison. He was released and exiled to Mexico less than two years later as part of an amnesty instituted by Batista to curry favour with an increasingly hostile Cuban populace. During his exile, a Revolutionary force, named the 26th of July Movement (Movimiento 26 de Julio), was created to mobilise the uprising against Batista.

perilous crossing to Miami. Now, with his US citizenship secure, he is saving up to 'reclaim' José, now 43, and to bring him to Tampa where he works three part-time jobs just to survive. Their mother stays in Havana, in the house where she was born and, she insists, where she will die, *gracias a Fidel*.

Maray's middle daughter, Cristina, a doctor, was on a mission in Venezuela last year when she decided to find a way over the border. There she anxiously waits for the time when she can bring over her mother and younger brother Alejandro to be with her. Maray suffers with the absence of her beloved daughter and says it is only her deep faith in God that keeps her sane.

The millions of dollars of remittances that flow into Cuba from its exiles often help to soften the blow, but the emotional price is high. One is very hard pressed indeed to find a Cuban family that has not experienced this kind of heart-wrenching separation and loss.

The diaspora is not just US- and Miami-based. Cubans are dotted all over the globe and many of these are in Europe – of whom, in comparison, more tend to be Cubans of colour. Anna left for England three years ago to be with an older man she met here while he was on a business trip. But she misses her family and yearns to be back in her own house in a quiet suburb of Havana and working again as a lawyer. Amalia married a young German man she met one day on an east Havana beach. He saw her, fell instantly in love and hired an interpreter so they could speak. She calls every fortnight from Düsseldorf and they come here every summer with their little daughter.

Wherever the destination, the new migration of mainly young Cubans is very often related to economic hardship at home. It is impossible to gauge just how many families are affected by this vast exodus of Cuba's sons and daughters but it is a constant in the lives of most Cubans, emotionally raw and still by far the most explored of themes in numerous plays, books and Cuban films. What is clear is that the seemingly endless standoff between the two nations – the ongoing and increasingly hostile US policy against the island, and Cuba's response to this – have ravaged one of its most sacred institutions.

Ay, mi familia.

Batista soon had cause to wonder if releasing the Castro brothers had been a mistake. Together with 82 men they set off from Mexico on a leaky 60-foot yacht named *Granma* in miserable weather, landing in the eastern Cuban province of Oriente (now renamed, aptly enough, Granma). Fidel and Raúl Castro were back, and this time they had brought with them an Argentinian doctor named Ernesto 'Che' Guevara. Che described the Revolutionaries' arrival as 'less of a landing, more of a shipwreck'. There was worse to come.

'Once again, two foreign powers had decided Cuba's fate without having the decency to include it in the discussion.'

The invasion was intended to be part of a general anti-Batista uprising orchestrated by leftist political parties, student activists and labour unions in Cuba. Unfortunately, Fidel and co landed on 2 December 1956, two days after the planned uprising in Santiago on 30 November. To add insult to injury, Batista's forces were tipped off about the invasion and attacked Castro's small force as it headed for the mountains. In the ensuing firefight, most of the Revolutionaries were either killed or captured, but Fidel and Raúl Castro, Che Guevara and a handful of others managed to escape to the Sierra Maestra. The Cuban Revolution had not made the most auspicious entrance on to the world stage.

Batista was returned for a second term of office in 1954. From their mountain base, the Revolutionaries began to build an army with which they would wage guerrilla war against Batista for the next two years. Against all the odds, Batista was unable to defeat the guerrillas. Their campaign was given new momentum in 1958, when the US government, as if by magic, woke up to the fact that Batista was not a beacon of democracy at all, but a murdering megalomaniac. Worse, he was bad for business. With alacrity, an embargo was placed on arms shipments to Batista's forces, which rather hampered his ability to suppress the Revolution.

Cuban forces successfully repelled the half-hearted **Bay of Pigs** invasion. *See p21.*

In a last-ditch attempt to quieten political opposition, Batista called a presidential election for November 1958. The voters stayed away in droves, the result was clearly rigged, and the US finally withdrew its support of the regime. Ever the astute operator, Batista did not intend to hang around and see how it all turned out, and on 31 December 1958 he beat a hasty retreat to the Dominican Republic.

On 2 January 1959 Che Guevara and Camilo Cienfuegos led their rebel army into Havana. Castro marched his army across the island, entering the city on 8 January. Within a month, the new government had reinstated the 1940 Cuban Constitution. Recognition by the US quickly followed. The Revolution was over and Cuba was finally an independent country. However, it was not to last.

CUBA LIBRE?

What became known as the 'triumph' of the Revolution had been achieved through the combined efforts of a number of movements that apparently had little in common other than a wish to liberate Cuba. But one thing was clear: if Cuba was to be a truly independent country, it would need to eliminate its almost total economic dependency on the United States. Castro's tool for achieving this was simple: he implemented a programme to nationalise key industries and services. An Agrarian Reform Law was passed in May 1959. In 1960 US-owned properties on the island were nationalised. The reaction in the US was one of horror and it retaliated by suspending its sugar quota. The US could see its Caribbean jewel, for so long just tantalisingly out of reach, suddenly disappear over the horizon.

America's hostile stance was driving Cuba firmly into the arms of the Soviet Union. The USSR agreed to purchase five million tonnes of Cuban sugar and in return would supply Cuba with oil, iron, grain, fertiliser, machinery and $100 million in low-interest loans.

In an attempt to destabilise Cuba, the US government launched a large-scale propaganda campaign, embargoed oil exports to the island, indefinitely extended the 1958 arms embargo, and formed a paramilitary army of Cuban exiles, ready to take the island by force. On 19 October 1960 US-Cuban relations had deteriorated to the extent that the US imposed an economic embargo on Cuba that permitted only food and medicine to be imported to the island. On 3 January 1961 Cuba and the US officially broke off diplomatic relations and in April Castro declared the Revolution was socialist. In June 1961 all teaching centres were nationalised and a National Literacy Campaign began. While it may have alarmed the US and members of the Cuban bourgeoisie, the Revolution's commitment to social justice ensured its support by the masses.

It is tempting to argue that, but for a few inflammatory actions by the Revolutionary government and subsequent overreaction by the US, Cuban history in the second half of the 20th century might have been very different. This view, however, ignores the resentment felt by the Cuban people at 60 years of American interference, and the need for Castro's government to maintain popular support by being seen to deliver quickly on its Revolutionary promises.

WORLD ON A KNIFE-EDGE

The open hostility culminated in the 17 April 1961 invasion of the Bay of Pigs (Bahía de Cochinos, or Playa Girón), by US-trained and -supported Cuban exiles. Unfortunately for them, President Kennedy decided not to deploy US air power. Thus, denied significant air or naval support, the insurgents were easy prey for the Cuban Army and Air Force. Of the 1,400 men who landed at the Bay of Pigs, 1,197 were captured, and the rest killed in the fighting.

After the Bay of Pigs debacle, Castro realised that there was little hope of re-establishing normal relations with an increasingly paranoid US. What he urgently needed was a powerful ally who would help him resist US pressure. The obvious candidate was America's sworn enemy and Cuba's most important trading partner, the USSR. In December 1961 Castro became a Marxist-Leninist. His transformation from vaguely left-wing nationalist to committed communist was now complete.

The low point in the tense relations between Cuba and the US began on 14 October 1962, when US Intelligence discovered that the Soviet Union was installing nuclear missile bases in Cuba. Kennedy warned that any missile launched from Cuba at a target in the western hemisphere would be viewed by the US as an attack by the Soviet Union. An intense game of brinksmanship ensued and the two superpowers edged towards nuclear war in what came to be known as the Cuban Missile Crisis. Finally, and without Castro's knowledge, Soviet Premier Khrushchev agreed to dismantle the Cuban missile sites and return all weapons to the USSR on the condition that the United States would guarantee not to intervene militarily in Cuba. Once again, two foreign powers had decided Cuba's fate without having the decency to include it in the discussion.

THE ACCIDENTAL COMMUNIST

Unfortunately, the Cuban government was not in a position to do anything about the situation, as the Soviet Union was the only friend that Castro had. Cuba was driven to replace earlier years of dependence on the US with dependence on the Soviet Union.

Throughout the 1960s the US embargo deepened. All trade between Cuba and the US was banned. America applied pressure to its NATO partners and to Latin American countries to join its embargo, and they obediently complied. In 1963 US citizens could no longer travel to Cuba.

'Between 1961 and 1965 the CIA attempted to kill Castro eight times.'

While there is some evidence that President Kennedy intended restoring normal relations with Cuba (as a precaution against growing Soviet influence on the island, if for no other reason), he was assassinated before he could do anything about it. Some conspiracy theorists assert that the assassination may have been a plot by either Cuban exiles or organised crime bosses opposed to Kennedy's softening approach to the Castro government. Whatever the truth, after Kennedy's death the stalemate inevitably resumed.

Not all US attempts to overthrow Castro were as overt as economic sanctions and amphibious invasions. Between 1961 (after the Bay of Pigs fiasco) and officially 1962 (but in practice it continued until 1965), as part of a destabilisation programme code-named Operation Mongoose, the CIA attempted to kill Castro eight times. On at least one occasion, the Mafia was hired to do the job; other attempts involved poisoned drinking glasses and exploding cigars, but none so much as injured Castro. When they failed to kill him, CIA attention turned to trying to discredit him.

Cuban economic policy during the 1960s was aimed at reducing the country's reliance on sugar. A rapid programme of industrialisation began to build self-sufficient socialism. The programme failed due to a number of factors: economic mismanagement, the exodus of skilled personnel and the embargo. Cuba ended up more reliant on sugar (and on imports from the USSR) than ever, and the basic necessities of life grew increasingly scarce. Rationing was introduced in 1962 and has remained ever since. For many Cubans, the deprivation proved too much and there was a mass exodus; almost 200,000 had left by the end of 1962.

The large-scale migration to the US deprived Havana of many of its professionals. In addition, the Revolutionary government diverted resources away from Havana towards rural areas and the city began to deteriorate. It is estimated that, at the peak of this policy of malign neglect, 150 colonial-era buildings collapsed in the city each year. They were replaced by Soviet-style high-rises of poor design and unsafe concrete construction.

RAPPROCHEMENT... OR NOT

With huge subsidies from the USSR and rises in the world price of sugar, the 1970s saw some improvement in living standards. In 1974 the US government conducted secret normalisation talks with Cuban officials. Apparently, excellent progress was made, but the talks collapsed when Cuba became involved in the Angolan civil war later that year. Cuban foreign policy in the 1970s had shifted from the ideal of exporting Revolution abroad to the more practical goal of offering other third-world countries military and civilian assistance. This further confirmed American opinion that Castro was a loose cannon and must be stopped. Throughout the remainder of the decade, attempts by various Cuban and US politicians to relax the embargo were blocked.

'The Democracy Act would ensure the collapse of Castro's regime "within weeks" – they thought.'

Rapprochements were made from other quarters, however. In 1975 the Organisation of American States voted to end sanctions against Cuba. In 1977 the US travel ban was dropped, the two countries signed a fishing rights agreement and opened Interests Sections (an intermediate step on the way to establishing diplomatic relations) in each other's capitals. In comparison with the previous 15 years, relations were positively balmy.

In December 1975 the First Congress of the Communist Party was held. The following year Cuba adopted a new constitution and a Soviet-style economic system. Later in the year, Castro was elected president of the State Council, consolidating the roles of president, prime minister and commander of the armed forces. In 1980 the Revolution was 20 years old, but for the majority of the population, the hoped-for improvements in living standards had yet to arrive. Many Cubans had had enough and wanted out. Castro responded by allowing free emigration from the port of Mariel, west of Havana. Within days, a flood of migrants was sailing out of Cuba for the US. By September 125,000 Cubans had left.

The improvement in relations with the US came to an end when Ronald Reagan became president in 1981 and instituted probably the most hostile Cuba policy since the early 1960s. Despite conciliatory signals from Cuba, the US administration tightened the embargo, reinstated the travel ban and allowed the 1977 fishing treaty to lapse. Around the same time, Miami exile Jorge Mas Canosa founded the Cuban-American National Foundation (CANF), which quickly emerged as the most powerful anti-Castro pressure group in the US. This group's political lobbying would largely determine US Cuba policy for the next decade.

Castro received Argentinian deputy Miguel Bonasso in September 2006.

Desperate times...

The end of the Cold War may have been welcomed in many parts of the world, but for Cuba it was a disaster. More than 80 per cent of the country's trade disappeared along with COMECON (the Eastern Bloc equivalent of the EEC), and in July 1990 the government was forced to declare a so-called 'Special Period in Peacetime', a polite way of saying that a series of harsh measures would be introduced. Already stretched to the limit after decades of sacrifice, ordinary Cubans were asked to tighten their belts still further. The Soviet Union had supplied two-thirds of the island's food, nearly all its oil and 80 per cent of its machinery and spare parts, and the sudden shortages affected everyone; rationing was extended and the huge drop in fuel imports meant longer waits for public transport as well as frequent power cuts.

To avoid total economic collapse, the government was forced to turn to an old standby, tourism, and it soon overtook sugar as the largest earner of foreign exchange. The desperate attempt to shore up the Revolution created the conditions for a Cuban-style *glasnost*, a tentative and limited opening-up in economic, political and intellectual spheres. Some foreign investment and limited market reforms were permitted; travel restrictions for Cuban citizens were eased and contact with *gusanos* (worms, the word used for exiled relatives) was no longer condemned; and, in August 1993, with inescapable irony, the dollar was legalised in Cuba. Individuals were also permitted to set up small businesses such as *paladares* (private restaurants) or *casas particulares* (rooms to rent).

By the mid 1990s the worst of the crisis was over. But this came at a cost. Mass tourism and the decriminalisation of the dollar led to the re-emergence of a class system, between those who had access to hard currency, and those who did not. The abolition of the dollar as legal tender, and its replacement by the CUC in late 2004, did nothing to alter this painful reality. Social problems eradicated in the early years of the Revolution re-emerged, notably crime (still low by Latin American standards) and prostitution. Even Cuba's achievements in education and health have been eroded by shortages of paper, equipment and medication. Despite the government's expressed determination to cling to a socialist model, the Special Period brought capitalism, albeit in highly controlled form, back to Cuba. Fidel Castro has expressed his determination that as the Cuban economy grows, it will return once more to its state-controlled roots. But can he turn back the clock? Only time will tell.

THE SPECIAL PERIOD

Meanwhile, conditions in Eastern Europe were changing. Perestroika was announced in the Soviet Union in March 1985. In 1989 the Berlin Wall fell and within two years Soviet communism vanished from the world stage. This was a disaster for Cuba. At a stroke, the island lost the subsidies and other monetary support it had previously received from the USSR. The ensuing decade of severe scarcity and deprivation was, with an Orwellian flourish, entitled the 'Special Period' (*see p23* **Desperate times...**).

Of major concern to the Cuban government was the loss of the country's protector. Without the Soviet Union, how would Cuba defend itself against its rapacious neighbour to the north? Reluctantly, Fidel Castro made a dramatic concession that was to have a profound effect on Cuban society. In 1993, in an effort to increase the flow of hard currency into the country (chiefly through remittances), he made it legal for Cubans to possess and spend dollars. (Previously possession of the dollar had been punishable by imprisonment.)

But the United States was at the same time stepping up the pressure. In 1992 Congress passed the Cuban Democracy Act (CDA), also known as the Torricelli Bill after the New Jersey senator who presented it. Designed to 'wreak havoc on the island', the act promised to impose sanctions against any countries found to be 'assisting' Cuba. It further restricted humanitarian aid in the form of food, medicine or medical supplies; it prohibited vessels that had been to Cuba within the previous 180 days from entering any US port; and it banned US Cubans from making remittances to their relatives back home. It was anticipated that the act would bring about the collapse of Castro's regime 'within weeks'. The CDA caused additional hardship to Cubans, but the US had severely underestimated Castro's ability to turn a situation to his political advantage.

In 1994, in response to riots in Havana, Castro again announced an open migration policy, giving Cubans free licence to leave the island if they wished. Almost immediately a new boatlift began and 30,000 migrants left Havana for Florida. This time however, the arms of America were not so welcoming, and the Coast Guard was dispatched to prevent the seaborne immigration. The US had learnt its lesson from the Mariel boatlift and was unwilling to allow more Cubans to arrive unimpeded into Florida. The US policy since this time has been to repatriate any Cubans found at sea or in the air, but to admit those who make it to landfall in the US (after a detailed background check).

In 1996 the US gave Cuba another bloody nose in the form of the Cuban Liberty and Democratic Solidarity Act (better known as the Helms-Burton law). This introduced a raft of measures aimed at tightening the embargo still further. The international reaction was immediate. The United Nations, the European Union, the Organisation of American States, and many other countries condemned it outright. Aside from its manifest shortcomings from a human rights standpoint, the Helms-Burton law walks all over the concept of national sovereignty and gives the United States sole authority to determine other countries' rights to trade with Cuba. Not surprisingly, most nations have chosen to do little more than pay lip service to it, and Canada and Mexico have gone so far as to enact opposing legislation, making it an offence for their residents to abide by any provision of Helms-Burton. It seemed that, at long last, the US had lost international support for its relentless campaign against Cuba.

As the relationship with the US continued to nosedive, Cuba's relationship with religion in general and the Catholic Church in particular began to thaw. The '90s was a period of religious revival in Cuba – perhaps brought on by the hardships of the Special Period. The state responded by allowing freedom of worship for all faiths. In 1991 the Communist Party abandoned its commitment to atheism and admitted believers to its ranks. Pope John Paul II visited in 1998 and in the same year Christmas was restored as a holiday.

END OF AN ERA

US-Cuban relations seemed less tense at the end of the 1990s. In 1998 the Clinton administration lifted its ban on Cubans sending remittances to their families back home, although the amount was limited to a maximum of US$1,200 a year. Clinton also backed the return to Cuba of Elián González – the six-year-old boy picked up in the Florida Straits and 'kidnapped' by his Miami relatives. In October that year the US Senate approved a bill that lifted restrictions on the sale of food and medicine to Cuba. Things took a turn for the worse, however, when George W Bush was inaugurated as President. He categorised Cuba as one of seven 'state sponsors of terror' and during his presidency he has steadily tightened the US embargo. In 2003 he set up the Commission for Assistance to a Free Cuba, a policy group openly designed to hasten 'transition' in Cuba. It has brought about further restrictions on the number of visits Cuban Americans can legally make to see their relatives on the island (to just once every three years), enforced limits on the amount of remittances that can be sent, and made it far more difficult for Americans to obtain a licence to travel to Cuba to attend such things as academic conferences and cultural exchanges.

In April 2003 Cuba played into the hands of those who portray it as a repressive regime by arresting 75 dissidents, declaring them all mercenaries, and sentencing them to lengthy prison terms. Weeks later, in the midst of a spate of hijackings, three men who hijacked a ferry and attempted to sail it to the United States were put on trial, convicted and executed in the space of nine days. International condemnation followed, with the European Union issuing a statement expressing its strong disapproval. Castro responded by describing most European governments as 'lackeys' of the United States. European diplomats found themselves shunned from all contact with the Cuban authorities in Havana. The left-wing Spanish government has led European moves to repair relations, but Cuba has increasingly been more interested in trade and political alliances with Venezuela, China and Iran.

At every turn during his epic leadership, Castro has found a way to defy those who feel he has, surely, run out of options. But in July 2006 he proved that there is one thing that he cannot control: his own physical decline. After delivering two lengthy, rambling speeches in the space of one day to mark the 53rd anniversary of the start of the armed Revolution, Castro, then 79 years old, was taken seriously ill. He underwent an emergency operation to stem intestinal bleeding, and for the first time in his career, delegated his principle powers. His brother Raúl Castro, at that time the world's longest-serving defence minister, became Cuba's acting President. As this guide went to press, the Cuban government's official line was that Fidel was recuperating, and could conceivably return to power. But many doubt it, and suspect that one way or another, Cuba could be at the dawn of change.

Key events

AD 1-1000 Some time during this period, the Taíno replace Cuba's Ciboney inhabitants.

COLUMBUS AND CO
1492 Christopher Columbus lands on Cuba, kicking off a period of Spanish occupation that would last four centuries.
1513 First slaves arrive on the island.

SETTLING IN
1519 San Cristóbal de la Habana officially founded on its present site.
1558-9 Three castles are built in Havana to protect the city from attack, although this does little to reduce piracy in the harbour.
1607 Capital of Cuba moved from Santiago de Cuba to Havana.

FIRST STIRRINGS OF REVOLUTION
1762 British expeditionary force takes control of Havana, although their occupation lasts less than a year: in 1763 they hand the country back to the Spanish.

THE YANKS ARE COMING
1825 First direct intervention in Cuban affairs by the US, when it prevents Mexico and Venezuela from liberating Cubarule.
1848 US President Polk offers to sell Cuba to Spain for US$100 million. The offer is rejected.

THE TEN YEARS WAR
1868-78 Ten Years War: although Cuba loses to Spain, the Cuban people have taken their first steps towards independence.
1886 Slavery formally abolished in Cuba.

STATE OF INDEPENDENCE
1895-8 War of Independence. Spanish rule ends, only to be replaced with interference by the US, who intervene in the war when the USS *Maine* explodes in Havana harbour.

NO SUCH THING AS A FREE COUNTRY
early 1900s Havana prospers, attracting American tourists escaping Prohibition in US. Sugar becomes an increasingly lucrative crop.
1902 Republic of Cuba created. Tomás Estrada Palma elected first president.

ECONOMIC GLOOM
1924 Regime of newly elected President Gerardo Machado represses the working classes and ignites feelings of rebellion in the Cuban population.

THE RISE OF BATISTA
1934 President Batista, endorsed by the US, begins repressive 25-year rule.

YOU SAY YOU WANT A REVOLUTION
26 July 1953 Castro and his army try unsuccessfully to storm the Moncada Barracks near Santiago de Cuba. Castro and his brother Raúl sentenced to 15 years in jail but released after less than two. They go to Mexico, where they plan to overthrow Batista.
1956 Castro, Raúl, Che Guevara and fellow Revolutionaries arrive by boat in eastern Cuba to launch another attack but are forced to hide in the mountains.
31 December 1958 Batista flees. The next day, Guevara marches into the capital, followed six days later by Castro, who declares the triumph of the Revolution.

CUBA LIBRE?
1960 Cuba's relationship with USSR grows, and the two sign a trade agreement. The US imposes a trade embargo with the island.

WORLD ON A KNIFE-EDGE
17 April 1961 Hundreds of US-backed anti-Castro exiles die when President Kennedy aborts an invasion of Cuba at the Bay of Pigs.
14 October 1962 Kennedy discovers that Cuba has Soviet missiles aimed at the US. Nuclear war averted at the last minute.

THE ACCIDENTAL COMMUNIST
October 1965 First official boatlift to the US takes 3,000 Cubans to Miami.

THE SPECIAL PERIOD
1989 Collapse of Soviet bloc shrivels Cuba's economy overnight. The following year, Castro declares the 'Special Period'.
1994 In response to riots, Castro allows people to leave for Florida. 30,000 do so.
1996 Helms-Burton Act imposes rigid conditions on trade by the US with Cuba.

END OF AN ERA
October 2000 Senate approves the easing of certain parts of the US blockade on Cuba. Food and medicine can be traded between the two countries, but with cash, not on credit.
2003 Castro sparks international outrage by arresting 75 dissidents and executing men who attempted to hijack a ferry.
2006 Castro turns 80; the ailing president cedes power to his brother Raúl.

Classic cars outside the **Capitolio**. *See p72.*

Havana Today

The ins and outs and ups and downs of life in the city.

A common first impression of Havana is that of a time warp. On the surface, it's not far off the mark. Wherever you look, you see relics of a bygone era, plodding faithfully on. But *habaneros* would deny that they are stuck in the past. Particularly in comparison with the rest of Cuba, Havana is positively modern. You can get your computer fixed here faster and more cheaply than in most European cities. You can pick up a pirate DVD of the latest US blockbuster weeks before it is released in Miami (that despite the fact that DVD players are, officially, illegal here). The Cuban government is even considering a law that will offer transsexuals free sex-change operations. It is the fact that Havana is not standing still that makes it intriguing. It is the place where all the complex ingredients of contemporary Cuba meet, and where, on every street corner, there is a paradox.

IN THE MONEY

Given that all working Cubans supposedly earn around CUC 15 a month, the queues of locals in the hard currency stores, where everything you don't need, from Christmas lights to Californian apples, is sold at vastly inflated prices, can be difficult to fathom. So is the sight of well-dressed young Cubans downing Bucaneros at the Friday night parties in El Morro, or the *hijos de papá* (children of the well-connected) hanging out at Club Habana on a weekday afternoon, seemingly without a care in the world.

They are the most visible evidence of one reality of everyday life in Havana: that few people here live on their state salaries alone. Almost everyone dabbles in some form of *negocio* – Cuban slang for a whole gambit of black-market enterprises, from selling their state-supplied lunch of a sandwich and a cola to installing illegal TV satellite systems. Add to that the several hundred million dollars that arrives on the island in the form of family remittances from Cubans living abroad, and it is just about possible to square the bizarre circle that is the Cuban economy.

PRIVATE VERSUS PUBLIC

It has been more than 15 years since the break-up of the Soviet Union brought Cuba to near-collapse, and the country has seen several, subtle, pendulum shifts on the government's part in its approach towards private enterprise. The precedent is that in times of economic downturn, private trade has been tolerated, even encouraged, but when the government has felt it can afford it, the free marketers have been reined in, either through heavy taxation or the removal of licences. So while in 1996 there was a total of 210,000 Cubans working for themselves (*cuenta propistas*), by 2006 there were fewer than 150,000.

The reason for the clamping down is that the Fidel Castro has long believed that private enterprise is the economic model of last resort, and that hand-in-hand with it comes inequality. Since the arrival of large-scale tourism in the early 1990s, it has been hard enough for ordinary Cubans to accept the blatant economic divide they see every day between themselves and foreigners. But much more problematic is the sight of some of their compatriots doing conspicuously well, while most feel they are struggling to survive.

BACK TO BASICS

Since 2005 the Cuban central bank has been giving increasingly upbeat reports on the state of the economy. By the end of 2006 it was declared that Cuba was officially booming, with an annual growth rate of 12.5 per cent, the fastest in Latin America. The figures are treated with some scepticism by plenty of observers, but there is no question that healthy nickel prices (Cuba has substantial reserves, mined in Moa, in the east of the island), steady tourism, increasing trade with China and generous help from Venezuela (*see p30* **From Venezuela with love**) have meant that the government coffers are relatively full.

'Cubans might be sociable people, but the housing problem has caused real suffering for many families.'

Habaneros nevertheless complain that they have yet to see much evidence that the good times are back. The reality is that the government has been investing heavily in what sometimes seems like the losing battle of patching up the city's crumbling infrastructure. Across the country, at least US$800 million has been spent on container-size electricity generators, which in Havana and elsewhere have helped reduce the number of power cuts that were once an everyday part of life. Thousands of schools and hospitals have also been refurbished, and there's even some paint being slapped on a few public buildings.

But more noticeable for most Cubans is the other side of the boom. In November 2005 Fidel Castro declared that the 'Special Period' of economic austerity was over, and so was his tolerance of the indiscipline that had flourished within it. The very survival of the Revolution was at stake, he said.

One of the most visible signs of the new order were the troops of young students marching across the city, wearing T-shirts declaring they were 'social workers'. Petrol pump attendants in the capital's service stations were told to go home, as from now on the teenagers would be manning the pumps. For a few months they apparently kept meticulous track of all the petrol that was being sold, and, Cuban media reported, uncovered a major scam. Half all the fuel in the capital, it was announced, was being systematically stolen under the previous system. Then, as quickly as the social workers had appeared, they disappeared.

Since he took over leadership, Raúl Castro has also indicated that he will be taking a hard line against corruption, in all its forms. He is understood to have been behind several unusually blunt articles in the state-run *Juventud Rebelde* newspaper. In the series, entitled 'the great swindle', a team of reporters revealed that their investigations had proved that more than half of all state enterprises were indirectly stealing from their customers.

Private enterprise: the last resort?

Monumento a Antonio Maceo: commemorating the man who survived 24 bullets. *See p76.*

The rip-offs were hardly scandalous, and ranged from bars not filling beer glasses properly to shoe repairers charging double while hiding official price lists. But the message was clear: this has got to stop. Under his watch, General Castro has also informed the managers of state companies that employees had better start turning up to work on time, and, while they are about it, dress properly too.

LA LUCHA

The reality is that most Cubans pay only lip-service to many of the rules and regulations that they have to deal with on a daily basis. They have another, bigger concern, which goes under the catch-all title of *la lucha.* The word is an ironic take on the rallying revolutionary cry of the original *lucha*, or 'struggle', against imperialism.

For most Cubans *la lucha* these days means not a guerrilla war, but the daily, sometimes comic, sometimes tragic, battle to get by. Finding enough food to feed a family is the first struggle. All Cubans are issued with a ration book or *libreta*. But many of the items supposedly provided by the state – such as meat and fish – are not available for months on end. Typically, most *habaneros* can count on six pounds of rice, three pounds of *frijoles* (beans) and a few eggs a month. Most say that is sufficient for around ten days. For the rest of the month they have to turn to the black market, and the *agromercado*. The problem is finding the money to pay for everything.

Given the lack of variety in their diet, Cubans, to an outsider, can seem surprisingly obsessed by food. It is not unusual for a group of *habaneros* to spend what seems like hours discussing their favourite Coppelia ice-cream, or the best way to cook *frijoles*. And be warned if any Cuban recommends a restaurant: quantity not quality will likely be the criteria by which the place is judged. The chances are you will find yourself staring at a large pile of fried meat, and a relatively small bill.

GETTING AROUND

Complaint number two by Havana residents is *el transporte*. Unlike other communist countries, Cuba has always struggled to provide adequate public transport for its citizens. The government says it is importing thousands of new buses from China, but in the meantime those that do ply the streets are few and far between, and horrendously crowded. The converted trucks with two humps, known as *camellos*, are the most uncomfortable. To hitchhike, or *cojer botella*, is the least painful option, which many use to get around. Young women (plenty of whom really are looking for a lift and nothing more) find it the easiest way to get from A to B. Men and older women who want to grab a ride often wait at official hitch-hiking stops, where state cars (recognisable by their blue number plates) are obliged to stop, although they often don't.

> **'It is not unusual to see a family of three aboard a single bicycle, wobbling along the Malecón at night – without lights.'**

Owning a private car is merely a dream for many *habaneros*: both expense and government regulations make it a largely unattainable hope. Loyal party workers and others who have proved their worth to the state might be lucky enough to be rewarded with a regulation Lada, but these cannot be legally sold to another Cuban, and tend to remain in one family. (In recognition of the fact that pre-Revolution cars were legally private property in then-capitalist Cuba, the government does permit them to be sold between Cubans.) This is the reason why so many Detroit classics still ply the streets. Most had their old gas guzzler engines replaced with truck motors years ago, and are seen by their owners as work horses rather than works of art. They are often used as taxis.

Bicycles are also quite a common mode of transport for Cubans. Thousands were imported from China in the 1990s, when petrol was scarce, in an attempt to solve the transport problem. However, Havana is not especially bicycle-friendly: bike lanes seem to appear in the most illogical areas, and are often ignored by drivers. Despite the risks, it is not unusual to see a family of three aboard a single bicycle, wobbling along the Malecón at night – without lights.

HOME SWEET HOME

The third complaint of *habaneros*, and one that the government is finding the most difficult to solve, is that of housing, or *la vivienda*. Homes that were designed for one family are usually crammed with dozens. Decades of zero maintenance, combined with tropical humidity and the occasional hurricane, mean that buildings, particularly in Centro Habana and La Habana Vieja, fall down regularly. If you have noticed how many locals walk in the middle of streets rather than on the pavement, there is a reason.

Moving home is a huge challenge. The only legal way to move is to swap houses or *permutar*. This is an intensely hit-and-miss affair, as it depends on finding someone who has what you want, and wants what you have. The process is further complicated by the fact that advertising is largely prohibited in Cuba. Word of mouth is the traditional way to do a deal, although there is (surprisingly, perhaps, given the lack of internet access for most Cubans), an official website, www.sepermuta.com, which aims to unite swappers. Legally, no money should be exchanged by either party, but, almost always, it is. Anyone who wants to move from the outskirts of the city to Vedado will need tens of thousands of CUCs ready to pass under the table.

As a result, the vast majority of people just stay put, sometimes in complex family arrangements. It is not uncommon to find a divorced couple living in the same house, with their new spouses and just a makeshift cardboard partition separating them. *Barbacoas* (literally, barbecues), additional platforms used to make an extra floor within a single room, are another way *habaneros* adapt to their difficult surroundings. Cubans might be sociable people, but the housing problem has caused real suffering for many families. The pressure, particularly for adolescents, to spend a few hours away from home can be immense. Those young couples sitting on the Malecón are not just looking at the view. They are finding some privacy.

ID CHECK

The housing problem is one justification for another of the dominant experiences of life for many people in Havana: repeated ID checks by the police. The capital is already overcrowded, with 2.2 million inhabitants, and to avoid the situation getting worse the government prohibits people from other provinces from moving to the city without good reason. Those

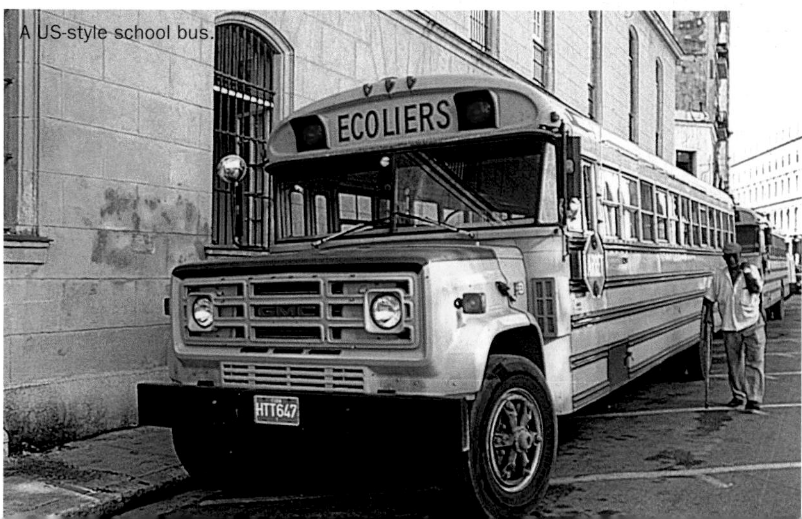

A US-style school bus.

From Venezuela with love

Who's the second most important man in Cuba? Raúl Castro? Carlos Lage? Maybe the correct answer is Hugo Chávez. Venezuela's president has become a vital ally to his northern neighbour. It is an alliance forged on a personal friendship between Presidents Castro and Chávez, and a realisation that each has what the other needs.

Venezuela has potentially the world's largest oil reserves, but not enough doctors to provide for the health requirements of all Venezuelans. Cuba has a chronic shortage of the hard currency needed to buy oil, but tens of thousands of qualified doctors. And both leaders have an equally strong distrust and distaste for most things American. A marriage, it would seem, made in heaven.

By the end of 2006, the Cuban government had sent some 26,000 medical personnel to Venezuela, in return for 92,000 barrels of oil a day – almost enough for its entire needs – at highly subsidised prices. The Cuban doctors in Venezuela often work in the poorest and most dangerous areas, where Venezuelan doctors have in the past refused to go. At the same time thousands more Venezuelan patients (along with many others from the rest of the Caribbean and Central America) come to Cuba every month for free cataract operations, under the Operación Milagro (Operation Miracle) programme. Cuba is also sending teams of experts to Venezuela to teach people in remote regions to read and write. In addition, Cuba and Venezuela have removed most tariffs on trade between the two countries. Venezuela is investing US$400 million dollars in refurbishing an old Soviet oil refinery in Cienfuegos.

Presidents Castro and Chávez believe their deal should be a model for the rest of Latin America, a radical alternative to US-inspired free-trade pacts, an arrangement built on social objectives rather than profit. So far the club, called ALBA (Bolivarian Alternative for the Americas, named after Simón Bolívar), has few members. Only Venezuela, Cuba, Bolivia, and Nicaragua have signed up. Most other Latin American governments, who regard ALBA as more political than economic, have kept their distance.

For Cuba and Venezuela the co-operation works well. But it is not without its problems. Plenty of Cubans grumble about the long queues at hospitals and dentists, which they blame on the fact that most of the staff are in Venezuela. More often than not, the brand-new Chinese buses you see in Havana are taking Venezuelan patients to their lodgings in Tarará or Marina Hemingway, while Cubans are left waiting for public transport in the city to improve. Then there are those who feel that having barely recovered from the collapse of the Soviet Union, Cuba is once again becoming dependent on a rich benefactor. And as Cubans are more than well aware, benefactors tend to come... and go.

who repeatedly offend can be bussed back to their original home, fined or even imprisoned. There are plenty of other reasons, of course, for the police to check people's ID, including an attempt to control prostitution, or simply 'protecting' tourists from meeting chatty, friendly locals. Sometimes it seems to be done just out of curiosity.

Most of the police who work in Havana are themselves from the provinces, typically Oriente, in the east. There is a theory that this strategy of governing one region with the forces from another is a trick Fidel Castro learned from one of his heroes, Julius Caesar. When they know they are not being overheard, plenty of *habaneros* are scathing about the police, whom, like almost anyone from outside the capital, they dismiss as *guajiros* ('peasants') or, more derogatively, *palestinos*. But at the same time plenty of *habaneros* are masters at dealing with the police, quick to shake a hand, explain that today is their daughter's birthday – anything to get off the dreaded *multa* (fine).

POLITICS

An outsider could be mistaken for thinking that Havana, capital city of one of the world's last bastions of communism, where it is not unusual for a million people to line the Malecón shouting 'Down with imperialism', is an intensely political place. The reality is rather different. The vast majority of *habaneros* will be quick to say that politics *no me interesa* (doesn't interest me) if you broach the subject. Part of the reason is fear. Plenty of Cubans believe, with some reason, that talking to anyone, especially a foreigner, about matters political is not a good idea.

But in fact the 'not interested' response might be more honest than it first appears. Cubans have lived with the same rhetoric for so many years that many seem not to bother pondering the issues anymore. Few these days tune into the *Mesa Redonda* ('round table'), Cuba's nightly 'discussion' programme on political issues. Both those who remain fervent supporters of the Revolution and those who wish the country would take a different path tend to feel that things are out of their hands.

Habaneros' political highlights of the year are the mass marches that take place periodically in the capital. But 2000 – when these were almost weekly events, during the campaign to return the shipwrecked young Cuban, Elián González, to his homeland – now seems long gone. In the last few years major rallies have taken place only once or twice a year.

One of the last big rallies to be held before Fidel Castro was taken ill in summer 2006 was to protest the installation from within the US Interests Section on the Malecón of an electronic ticker-tape message board. The sign is an attempt by the US Interests Section to break what it describes as the Cuban 'information blockade', and spells out a combination of news headlines and more provocative critiques of life in Cuba. Days after the sign was installed, the Cuban government began work on a major flag display in front of the building. They were officially installed to commemorate the 3,000-plus 'martyrs' that Cuba alleges have been killed as the result of US-sponsored terrorism. As the flags were inaugurated, no official mention was made of the fact that they also conveniently blocked almost all views of the electronic sign behind.

DIVERSIONS

Habaneros tend to turn to things other than politics when they want a distraction from *la lucha*. Dominoes (often played for money) provide one cheap form of entertainment. The nightly soap operas on TV are also hugely popular. During the summer a trip to the beach to soak in the tepid water with a bottle of rum is a real treat.

'Infidelity has often been described as the national sport.'

But what Cubans love most of all is a party. Birthdays, saints' days, farewells and welcome homes are all seized upon as excuses for spontaneous fiestas. A few bottles of rum, loud *reguetón* on the boom box, and the night is set. Few *habaneros* can afford to pay their own way into the best clubs and discos in the city, which are increasingly geared towards tourists. But when they do, they are determined to make the most of it, and they tend to regard an event that stops at anything earlier than 5am as a bit of a let-down.

Sex is also another free source of distraction for much of the city's population. Cubans are notoriously uninhibited about sex, and spend much of their lives practising it. Infidelity, too, has often been described as the national sport. Cubans certainly regard it as no big deal. Marriage and divorce are also matters to be taken quite lightly in this culture, where living for the moment, ducking, diving, laughing and dancing through the absurdity of it all, is the most important thing. When all is said and done, *habaneros* have a lot to teach the world about taking pleasure in life despite the odds. Hundreds of thousands of them dream of leaving Cuba, and would go tomorrow if they could, but that does not stop them enjoying life with gusto while they can.

Kofi Annan meets Raúl Castro.

Havana Tomorrow

As power passes from one Castro to another, the BBC's Cuba correspondent Stephen Gibbs ponders the future.

What happens after Fidel Castro has gone? It is a question that many have pondered. They have had plenty of time to do so. El Comandante has run the country for close to half a century, making him the world's longest-serving political leader. Queen Elizabeth II and King Bhumibol Adulyadej of Thailand might have sat on their thrones for a few more years, but their role is largely ceremonial. Fidel Castro has never been just a figurehead. An obsessive micro-manager by character, he has directed every aspect of life in this Caribbean island since 1959. Everyone knows it's not going to be the same without him.

But as this guide goes to press, it does seem that the day is drawing near. Although the Cuban authorities have long tried to avoid the issue, claiming in early 2006 that President Castro could easily live to be 140, and putting up posters prior to his 80th birthday declaring '80 more years', even his most loyal followers are beginning to wake up to the fact that not even Fidel goes on for ever.

His health 'accident', as he described it, in July 2006, appeared to mark the beginning of the end. Although almost no details about what the president was suffering from were released, Cubans knew one thing was certain. It had to be serious, or Fidel would never have delegated his powers to anyone, not even his brother. 'Revolutionaries never retire' had long been the veteran president's stock answer to questions about the longevity of his rule. Perhaps not, but sometimes they have to listen to their doctors.

Within the July 2006 announcement that Fidel Castro was, temporarily, standing down were a few clues as to the power structure of a Cuba without him. It was declared that the crucial roles of head of the Communist Party and commander-in-chief of the army would be handed to Raúl Castro. A further six officials were given some of the president's other responsibilities. The anointed few included Carlos Lage, the economics minister (considered a potential moderniser by some) and, from the other end of the spectrum, a few hard-line *históricos* from the early days of the Revolution.

The message being given was that no one person could possibly step into the shoes Fidel leaves behind. The official line is that, overall, the Communist Party of Cuba is the president's natural heir – a strategy that neatly avoids naming a single successor.

But undoubtedly the man to watch, in the short term a least, is Raúl Castro. He has long been something of an enigma in Cuba. In the early days of the Revolution he was portrayed as the more hard-line communist, the enforcer of the Revolution, in contrast to his apparently idealistic brother. But since the early 1990s he has been recast as the pragmatist, the efficient behind-the-scenes administrator.

It was Raúl who is understood to have persuaded Fidel that the only way to save the Cuban economy from total collapse in the dark days of the Special Period was to allow farmers to sell their excess produce in private *agromercados*. More recently he has overseen the Gaviota empire and other army-owned industries and businesses. Headed by ex-soldiers, some of whom are MBA graduates from European business schools, the military-run *empresas* are considered one of the areas of the economy that could be described as efficient.

'Privately, Raúl is believed to be at least sympathetic to the Chinese model of running a country.'

The Cuban government is sensitive to suggestions that Raúl's position as acting president is nepotistic. Officials point to the fact that the younger Castro (he is five years Fidel's junior) participated in the Revolution from its inception, was imprisoned alongside Fidel on the Isla de la Juventud, and has been Cuban defence minister since the early 1960s. All true, but the fact that he is also Fidel Castro's brother is crucial. It enables him, unlike perhaps anyone else in the country, to express openly his differences with *el jefe*. Suggesting that Cuba should pursue a different course to the one that it has been following for the last five decades is a dangerous strategy for any Cuban, but Raúl might get away with it.

So, assuming his presidency becomes permanent, which way will Raúl take Cuba? Most agree that once the aura of Fidel is lifted, the new government will be under more pressure to address some of major causes of discontent among the population. Number one of those is the fact that the basic state salary of CUC 15 a month is blatantly not enough to survive on, and pushes almost everyone to the black market.

In the few months since he became acting president, Raúl, like his brother before him, expressed his determination to clamp down on endemic petty corruption. But, unlike Fidel, Raúl has suggested that corruption is not a symptom of greed but, possibly, the result of a systemic failing in the Cuban economy. 'The Revolution is tired of excuses', he told a meeting of the Cuban National Assembly in December 2006.

Privately, Raúl is believed to be at least sympathetic to the Chinese model of running a country: allowing economic freedom, but under a one-party state. His brother detested the idea. That is not to say that the younger Castro might be about to tear down Cuba's centralised economy, but he might at least begin to allow more autonomy within state enterprises.

Raúl Castro has also indicated that he is in favour of more open debate among Cubans about the problems they, and the Revolution, face. In the months after he took power in July 2006, some unusually critical articles began to appear in Cuban newspapers, exposing the dysfunctional side of state-run enterprises. Furthermore, when he addressed a group of students at the end of that year he urged them to discuss issues 'fearlessly'.

Is this the beginning of glasnost, the spirit of open debate promoted by Mikhail Gorbachev in the dying days of the Soviet Union? It is still too early to tell. Allowing students to express their dissatisfaction is one thing, but would President Raúl Castro allow Cuba's dissidents to participate in the discussion? Fidel has long been notoriously intolerant of opposition, which he regarded as tantamount to treason. Cuba's fragmented dissident movement has had to tread a very delicate line between voicing complaints and facing lengthy prison terms.

Of the few hundred or so Cubans who openly describe themselves as dissidents, perhaps the best known is Oswaldo Paya. Best known, that is, outside Cuba. His existence, needless to say, is not acknowledged in the Cuban state-run media and most Cubans have no idea who he is. Paya, a devout Catholic, first gained international attention in 2002 when he led the Varela Project, a petition of 11,000 names calling for a referendum on reforms in Cuba. The request was promptly turned down, and the constitution amended so that Cuba's socialist system was declared 'irrevocable', whatever the circumstances.

The only regular protest against the Castro government is held every Sunday in Miramar by a group calling itself the *damas de blanco*, or 'ladies in white'. The women are mainly mothers or wives of imprisoned dissidents. Their demonstration amounts to nothing more than a short walk up and down a few blocks of Fifth Avenue, followed by a short call, in unison, for the freedom for their imprisoned relatives. In 2005 the group was awarded the Sakharov Prize for Freedom of Thought by the European Union (Payá too was given the prize, three years earlier).

'Following Fidel Castro's announced illness, there was some expectation that Cuban dissidents would seize the moment. They were nowhere to be seen.'

But none of these dissident groups are expected to be the catalyst for major change in Cuba. Apart from anything else, unlike opposition movements in communist Eastern Europe, they lack the means necessary to make their case heard. Trade unions (which played a crucial role in anti-government demonstrations in communist Poland) are all entirely state-controlled in Cuba. Another possible magnet for dissent, the Cuban Catholic Church, has studiously avoided getting itself involved in politics. In the days following Fidel Castro's announced illness, there was some expectation that Cuban dissidents would seize the moment. They were nowhere to be seen.

Training to be doctors? *See p30.*

The Cuban government has long been warning its people that opposition to the Revolution will come not from within, but from the United States. Plenty of Cubans have a now built-in fear that their houses and futures will be stolen from them by the Miami 'mafia' of Cuban exiles. Undoubtedly there are some exiles with the means, the money and the ambition to take a role in the future of Cuba. But they will face an uphill battle convincing their cousins on the island that they are intending to help, rather than exploit. A few Cuban exiles might cling on to the hope that they might retrieve their pre-Revolution properties and businesses. But many more have set their sights on building a future in the United States, rather than Cuba.

The relationship any post-Fidel government forms with the United States will be crucially important. The US administration has made it clear that it will not lift the trade embargo until fundamental steps towards democracy are met, including the release of political prisoners, multi-party elections and a free press. Raúl has said he is open to negotiations with the US – but only on his terms, which presumably means that the deal, for the time being, is off. Another possibility is that after years of promises, anti-embargo legislators in the US congress manage to get the travel ban on Americans visiting Cuba lifted. What would be the effect on Cuba of millions of American visitors?

Perhaps the biggest threat to a post-Fidel Cuban leadership lies closer to home than anyone at the top of the government might wish to contemplate. For almost five decades all major decisions at national level have been taken by Fidel. Dissent of any kind has not been tolerated. If the irreplaceable Fidel is to be succeeded by a government of committee, that might help preserve his legacy, but it throws up its own problems. Committees are made up of human beings, with human ambitions, disagreements and jealousies. With Fidel Castro's name and blood living on through his brother, it is conceivable that any internal tensions within the government can be contained. But Raúl – born in 1931 – will not be around forever. Should everyone be asking not what happens here after Fidel, but what happens after Raúl?

Where to Stay

Features

Hotel Sevilla. *See p46.*

Where to Stay

From cheap to (increasingly) chic, Havana's hotels and houses cover all the bases.

Tourism in Havana is a considerable cash cow, with accommodation playing a major part in bringing in the revenue. The number of tourists coming to the capital in 2006 exceeded 2.5 million and is set to continue rising. As a result, the number of hotels opening up is also increasing, with new hotel conversions springing up, former hotels coming back to life and existing hotels getting makeovers. Visitors can now choose from a broad range of accommodation for their stay – from a beautifully restored colonial building through to a modern international-style hotel offering better services. While the latter are in no short supply these days, they are generally devoid of character and, more to the point, the former tell fascinating tales of Cuba's extraordinary history. Havana now even has its first bona fide boutique hotel, in the form of the snazzy **Saratoga** (*see p46*).

On the downside, in the past few years the Cuban government has enforced much stricter controls on the tourist industry in a bid to channel more money through government organisations. The number of tour operators in the country has dropped from over 20 to just four (Cubanacán, Cubatur, Gaviota and Havanatur). These companies deal with larger fixed package groups arriving on charter flights (or by coach from other destinations within Cuba) and moving around in buses with official tour guides. These operators tend to use larger hotels in Havana and go to the all-inclusive beach resorts.

But to explore Cuba as an independent traveller is exciting and generally very safe: you just need some guidance.

The best Sleeps

For business travellers
Hotels NH Parque Central (*see p44*); **Saratoga** (*see p46*); **Meliá Habana** (*see p49*); **Meliá Cohíba** (*see p48*) and **Occidental Miramar** (*see p50*).

For gangster territory
Hotel Habana Riviera (*see p47*); **Hotel Nacional de Cuba** (*see p48*).

For peace and quiet
Hostal Los Frailes (*see p41*).

For discerning budgeteers
Casa del Científico (*see p47*); **Hostal Valencia** (*see p42*).

For literary connections
Hotel Ambos Mundos (*see p41*); **Hotel Sevilla** (*see p46*).

For a *casa particular* experience
Casa Belkis (*see p49*); **Casa de Eugenio y Fabio** (*see p44*); **Casa de Évora Rodríguez García** (*see p47*).

For lounging by the pool
Hotel Habana Riviera (*see p47*); **Saratoga** (*see p46*); **Hotel Meliá Cohíba** (*see p48*); **Hotel Meliá Habana** (*see p49*).

NAMES AND CHAINS

Since Cuba started welcoming foreign investment in the early 1990s, many of Cuba's mid-range to upmarket hotels are at least part-owned by foreign companies. The most widespread is the Spanish chain **Sol Meliá** (whose hotels in Havana are the Meliá Cohíba and the Meliá Habana).

Some of the most interesting hotels are in Old Havana, in particular those run by Habaguanex (the commercial division of the City Historian's Office). In the last decade or so, Habaguanex has been restoring delapidated old hotels to their former glory. These characterful, historical small hotels have filled a gap in the market for high-quality, boutique-style accommodation. Many of the hotels are themed to reflect Cuba's historical diversity. Themes include the island's Jewish heritage (**Raquel**), the shipping industry (**Armadores de Santander**) and religious life (**Los Frailes**; for all, *see p41*). Habaguanex offers ten per cent off selected Habaguanex restaurants in Havana, and free entry to some museums in Old Havana.

Otherwise, **Islazul**, **Cubanacán** and **Gaviota** are all Cuban companies offering cheap to mid-range accommodation, as is **Gran Caribe**, which specialises in mid-range and more upmarket hotels. For further ideas about excursions and activities, *see p235* **Specialist package holidays**.

Try Havana biblical style at the **Hotel Raquel**. *See p41.*

KEEPING YOUR COOL

How you react to the inevitable inconveniences that are part and parcel of hotel accommodation in Cuba is entirely up to you. However, as most staff earn very little each month, being short-tempered with them will normally exacerbate the problem. Diplomacy is by far the best way to resolve a situation. Standards vary enormously, but complaints tend to revolve around the same issues: mechanical failures (the air-conditioning or lifts); insipid food; drab decor; slow, inefficient or rude service, and poor communications services. It will be a relief to know that you would be extremely unlucky to come up against all of these problems in one stay but most visitors will encounter at least one. Before kicking up a fuss it's worth remembering that tourism is a relatively new development in Cuba and that the island forms part of the developing world, so resources are scarce. Unfortunately, these factors are not taken into account when prices are set, and the added niggle of having paid hand over fist will do little to increase your tolerance.

CAMPISMOS

Some hotels reserve a set number of rooms for Cuban guests (including honeymooners), who have to get a voucher or win a prize from their

Marble and gold give the **Hotel Armadores de Santander** the wow factor. *See p41.*

work or government to stay in them. Cubans otherwise go to *campismos* – cabin-style accommodation – by beaches or rivers for their holidays. In these places, as a foreigner you will have to pay in CUCs (normally a disproportionately high number), even if you're in the company of Cuban friends. Paying in pesos is no longer a viable option for foreigners, so travellers should drop all hopes of getting bargain accommodation at local rates.

SAFETY ISSUES

Guests in Havana hotels will sooner or later fall prey to the more distasteful side of tourism – the hustlers (*jineteros*) patrolling the streets in search of business. For this reason the security in hotel lobbies tends to be strict; Cubans are questioned on entering a hotel and under no circumstances will they be allowed up to your room. You may not like this policy, often criticised as a form of segregation, but the reality is that Cuba cannot afford to acquire a name for itself as a sex tourism destination: if you want to avoid an unpleasant scene, don't invite a Cuban to your hotel room (*see also p50* **Lobby lounging**).

You may even be asked by various officials to produce evidence that you are a guest, so hang on to your guest card (*tarjeta de huésped*), issued on arrival. You may need it to get in and out of the hotel, to access the dining room or even to ride in the lift.

It's wise to use the hotel safe deposit box for your valuables. (If you are in a *casa particular*, lock them in your suitcase and lock your room). Also, while packing to leave, be sure to check that your cleaner has not 'tidied away' any of your belongings in a place that you are unlikely to check, such as in a drawer or under the bed. But if you feel that staff have provided a satisfactory service, consider leaving a tip, either in the form of cash or some toiletry items; hotel personnel earn extremely low wages.

RATES AND SEASONS

Hotel room rates go up during high season (December to April), in particular around Christmas and Easter (especially during the UK school holidays); the highest rate at hotels is for the two-week period over Christmas and New Year. When we give price ranges such as CUC 80-95/106, the third number signifies this Christmas rate. You should also book in advance if your visit is likely to coincide with a major event in the city, such as the film festival in December. During busy periods it is wise to pay for your accommodation for up to a few days in advance to ensure it is not given to someone else – even after you've checked in! Finally, most hotel rates include breakfast.

THE OFFICIAL WORD

Theoretically, visitors to Cuba are legally required to have two nights' accommodation pre-booked (though in reality you can change your mind after you've arrived, or leave one place and move to another). Always fill in the 'address in Cuba' section of your tourist card when you enter the country, whether it's an official *casa particular* or a hotel. For more on tourist cards and visas, *see p230*.

STAR RATINGS AND CREDIT CARDS

All 'tourist' hotels in Cuba (as opposed to peso hotels) are either state-run or joint ventures with foreign companies, and are classified on a star system from one to five. This is no guarantee of quality, however. Four- and even five-star hotels in Cuba are often only equivalent to three-star hotels elsewhere, although you'll soon notice that the prices are likely to be just as high. Price is normally a more reliable indicator as to how many services the hotel offers.

Note that US credit cards (or even American Express cards issued by a bank outside the US) are not accepted in Cuban hotels, and that *casas particulares* only ever accept cash.

DISABLED VISITORS

People with disabilities are strongly advised to contact their chosen hotel or *casa particular* before going to Havana to find out which, if any, disabled services are offered. It is often better to book through a tour operator with a local office that can give on-the-ground advice.

La Habana Vieja

Expensive hotels

Hostal Conde de Villanueva

Calle Mercaderes #202, entre Lamparilla y Amargura (862 9293/4/fax 862 9682/www. habaguanex.com). **Rates** CUC 80-90 single; CUC 130-150 double; CUC 123-240 suite. **Credit** MC, V. **Map** p256 E15 ❶

This charming former merchant's house, built in the 18th century, has been restored to create a comfortable nine-bedroom hotel set around a central courtyard garden with palm trees and peacocks. The Spanish colonial-style rooms, all with en suite bathrooms, are named after cigar tobacco plantations, and open out on to the first-floor terrace overlooking the garden. The hotel also boasts a cosy bar and restaurant tucked away off the courtyard and, on the mezzanine floor, another bar and a great cigar shop with one of the best tobacco selections in the city. Great location too.

Air-conditioning. Bars (2). Business centre. Café. Internet (pay terminal). Restaurant. Room service. TV.

Hotel Ambos Mundos

Calle Obispo #153, esquina Mercaderes (860 9530/ fax 860 9532/www.habaguanex.com). **Rates** CUC 80-95/106 single; CUC 130-160/182 double. **Credit** MC, V. **Map** p256 E15 ❷

Hemingway fans will know the Ambos Mundos as the place where the writer penned much of *For Whom the Bell Tolls*. His room, No.511, is maintained much as if the writer never checked out, complete with adjustable table at which Hemingway used to write, standing up (admission CUC 1). Ernie aside, the hotel has a lovely lobby, where a pianist tickles the ivories and the waiters mix a decent cocktail; it manages to retain an air of calm despite the bustle on its doorstep. For fantastic views take the cranky old lift up to the roof terrace bar (*see p120*).

Air-conditioning. Babysitting. Bars (2). Conference rooms. Internet (shared terminal). Laundry. Parking. Restaurant. Room service. TV.

Hotel Armadores de Santander

Calle San Pedro #4, esquina Luz (862 8000/fax 862 8080/www.habaguanex.com). **Rates** CUC 80-90/106 single; CUC 130-150/182 double; CUC 105-248 suite. **Map** p256 F15 ❸

It's impossible not to be wowed by Armadores de Santander: a stunning blue and white floor competes with an ornate cream and gold ceiling, and a majestic marble staircase climbs from the lobby flanked by wrought-iron railings… and that's just the entrance. This majestic three-storey building was the headquarters for Havana's main shipbuilders during the 19th century, and has fittingly been restored with a nautical theme. All rooms are palatially furnished, some with spacious terraces (south-facing rooms have the best views of the bay). The 'special' suite, with fine sea views, king-size bed and jacuzzi, is fine territory for a splurge. For the restaurant, Cantabria, *see p106*. **Photo** *p38*.

Air-conditioning. Bar. Internet (cybercafé). Restaurant. TV.

Hotel Florida

Calle Obispo #252, esquina Cuba (862 4127/fax 862 4117/www.habaguanex.com). **Rates** CUC 80-90/ 106 single; CUC 130-150/182 double; CUC 185-214/ 259 triple; CUC 105-285/331 suite. **Credit** MC, V. **Map** p256 E15 ❹

The magnificent entrance of the Florida, which opens directly on to bustling Calle Obispo, draws the gaze of hundreds of passers-by every day. In addition to a striking marble statue of a woman, there are spectacular arches on the upper floors around the atrium, and the staircase is over-arched by a beautiful stained-glass roof created for the hotel's reopening in 1999. The 25 well-furnished rooms have been restored to their original 19th-century charm, with Italian marble floors, high ceilings and balconies. There's a restaurant (*see p108*) and jazz club on the ground floor, with further eating and drinking options right on your doorstep.

Air-conditioning. Bars (2). Business centre. Internet (shared). Laundry. Restaurant. Room service. TV.

Hotel Raquel

Calle San Ignacio #103, esquina Amargura (860 8280/fax 860 8275/www.habaguanex.com). **Rates** CUC 105-115/131 single; CUC 180-200/232 double; CUC 130-250/282 suite. **Credit** MC, V. **Map** p256 E15 ❺

Since it opened its doors in June 2003 following lengthy restoration work by Habaguanex, the Raquel has generated much interest, and deservedly so. Set in a former office building dating from 1908, it is one of the most spectacular hotels in Old Havana, its stunning art nouveau lobby dominated by impressive pillars and a huge stained-glass roof. The 25 rooms (four suites) are tastefully furnished in keeping with the hotel's biblical theme. Right in the heart of what was once the Jewish quarter, the hotel isn't far from Sinagoga Adath Israel de Cuba, Cuba's oldest synagogue (*see p69*). The lobby restaurant and café are good, and the roof terrace offers a picturesque view of the surrounding area. The Raquel is also one of the few small hotels in Havana with a gym; massages and other treatments are offered too. The Jardín del Edén restaurant comes highly rated (*see p108*). **Photo** *p37*.

Air-conditioning. Bar. Gym. Internet (cybercafé). Laundry. Restaurant. TV.

Hotel San Miguel

Calle Tacón #52, esquina Peña Pobre (862 7656/ 863 4029/fax 863 4088/www.habaguanex.com). **Rates** CUC 80-90/106 single; CUC 130-160/182 double. **Credit** MC, V. **Map** p256 D15 ❻

With only ten bedrooms, the appeal of the San Miguel – originally built in the 19th century but modified in the early 1900s – lies in its intimate and hospitable atmosphere. Downstairs is a cosy, atmospheric bar (which would be even more atmospheric if the television were removed), while a grandiose marble staircase sweeps up to the upper floors. The soft beige and pale yellow rooms are furnished in tasteful period style. The third-floor roof terrace and some of the bedroom balconies have unrivalled views over the Bay of Havana, the Morro Castle and La Cabaña fortress.

Air-conditioning. Bar. Internet (cybercafé). Laundry. No-smoking rooms. Restaurant. TV.

Hotel Santa Isabel

Calle Baratillo #9, entre Obispo y Narciso López (860 8201/fax 860 8391/www.habaguanex.com). **Rates** CUC 160-190/211 single; CUC 200-240/282 double; CUC 180-400/442 suite. **Credit** MC, V. **Map** p256 E16 ❼

Originally the palace of the Count of Santovenia, this magnificent 19th-century building is now one of the best hotels in Havana. Photos of the count and his family, together with works of art by top Cuban painters, adorn the walls of the lobby, while the furnishings exude finesse. The 27 rooms (ten suites) are subtly decorated in pastel pink and very comfortably fitted with antique furniture and wrought-iron double beds. Most rooms have their own balcony overlooking the Plaza de Armas, the best of these

being the ones on the third floor. Because of the hotel's discreet nature, many celebrities have stayed here when in Havana, among them former US president Jimmy Carter and Jack Nicholson. The roof terrace also has a great view over Old Havana. Public internet access – from a room on the first floor – is among the fastest in Havana. Despite the hotel's official address, the entrance is actually on the lovely tree-lined Plaza de Armas (eastern side).
Air-conditioning. Bars (2). Business centre. Internet (cybercafé). Laundry. Parking (free). Restaurant. Room service. TV.

Palacio O'Farrill

Calle Cuba #102, esquina Chacón (860 5080/fax 860 5083/www.habaguanex.com). **Rates** CUC 80-95/106 single; CUC 130-160/182 double; CUC 130-200/232 suite. **Credit** MC, V. **Map** p256 D15 ❽
This neo-classical palace, which dates from the 18th century, once belonged to Don Ricardo O'Farrill, a Cuban with origins in – you guessed it – Ireland. And palace is the key word; Don Ricardo was head of one of the most prosperous families in Cuba during colonial times (thanks to the slave trade), and the splendour of this three-storey residence, with its 38 bedrooms, gives an indication of his wealth. The Palacio reopened in 2002 and the design of each floor reflects a different period: the first floor is 18th-century in style; the second incorporates 19th-century elements; and the third-floor rooms have a modern, 20th-century look. The most spacious rooms are located on the second floor. There are also jazz performances in the courtyard on occasional Thursdays, Saturdays and Sundays (very apt as Don Ricardo O'Farrill was the great-great grandfather of the late, great jazz pianist Chico O'Farrill).
Air-conditioning. Bar. Internet (cybercafe). Laundry. Parking (free). Restaurant. TV (cable).

Mid-range hotels

Hostal el Comendador

Calle Obrapía, esquina Baratillo (867 1037/fax 860 5628/www.habaguanex.com). **Rates** CUC 62-72/82 single; CUC 110-130/142 double; CUC 150-170/185 suite. **Credit** MC, V. **Map** p256 E16 ❾
This 18th-century Hispanic-Moorish style residence has an appealing air of tranquillity and seclusion that contrasts with the more ebullient atmosphere of its neighbour, the Hostal Valencia, where the reception desk is located (*see below*). In keeping with Habaguanex's policy of promoting the most valuable historical aspects of its projects, the Comendador has an archaeological excavation site on the ground floor. Human remains found there are thought to have belonged to servants or slaves, since they weren't buried in coffins. The hotel's 14 rooms – including three lovely suites – are decorated in colonial style, with antique furniture. Breakfast is served in the Bodegón Onda (*see p105*), which also offers Spanish tapas.
Air-conditioning. Bar. Laundry. Room service. TV (satellite).

Hostal Los Frailes

Calle Brasil (Teniente Rey) #8, entre Mercaderes y Oficios (862 9383/9510/fax 862 9718/www.habaguanex.com). **Rates** CUC 70-80/83 single; CUC 110-130/142 double; CUC 77-150/172 suite. **No credit cards**. **Map** p256 E15 ❿
Just steps away from the St Francis monastery, the Frailes has become something of a tourist attraction since it reopened as a hotel in 2001, such is the success of its design. A copper sculpture of a hooded friar stands outside the main entrance of what used to be the residence of the Marquis Don Pedro Claudio Duquesne in the 19th century. Inside, the polished terracotta floor, beige leather sofas, stucco walls and stone courtyard (complete with freshwater spring and hanging plants) are awe-inspiring. Staff, dressed as friars, take real pride in the originally decorated 22 rooms (four mini suites), all equipped with antique-style bathrooms, period furnishings and thick wooden beds. As this was a monastery, many of the 22 bedrooms do not have windows; however, this does make it one of the quietest places to sleep in Havana (indeed, although it's just a short walk from the lively Plaza Vieja and Plaza de San Francisco, the hotel prides itself on its quiet, meditative atmosphere.) Breakfast is served in the nearby Café Taberna (*see p106*).
Air-conditioning. Bar. Internet (cybercafé). TV.

Hotel Beltrán de Santa Cruz

Calle San Ignacio #411, entre Muralla y Sol, near Plaza Vieja (860 8330/fax 860 8383/www.habaguanex.com). **Rates** CUC 65-80/83 single; CUC 110-130/142 double. **Credit** MC, V. **Map** p256 E15 ⓫
The neat and colourful exterior of Hotel Beltrán distinguishes it from the sadly dilapidated buildings surrounding it. Hues of blue and yellow predominate throughout this painstakingly restored 18th-century building, which opened as a hotel in 2002. Count Don Juan de Jaruco, the first owner of the building, received some of Havana's most illustrious visitors here, including the esteemed German scientist Alejandro de Humboldt. All rooms have private bathrooms. Breakfast is served in the central courtyard or in the lobby bar.
Air-conditioning. Bar. Internet (cybercafé). Laundry. Parking. TV.

Budget hotels

Hostal Valencia

Calle Oficios #53, esquina Obrapía (867 1037/fax 860 5628/www.habaguanex.com). **Rates** CUC 54-61 single; CUC 85-104 double; CUC 104-125 suite. **Credit** MC, V. **Map** p256 E15 ⓬
This is one of Old Havana's best-kept secrets, although because it's small it gets booked up early. A private home in the 18th century, the Valencia now offers unpretentious *parador*-style accommodation, with 12 simple rooms that open out on to a balcony around a central courtyard garden decorated with with lush tropical plants. The courtyard

always has a buzzy atmosphere with both guests and visitors stopping off for drinks and snacks, while in the Bar Nostalgia, photographs on the walls pay homage to 1950s singers. The hotel's restaurant dishes up a mean paella too (*see p110*). For budget accommodation in the centre of the Old City, this place can't be beat.
Bars (2). Fans. Laundry. Restaurant. TV.

Mesón de la Flota

Calle Mercaderes #257, entre Amargura y Brasil (Teniente Rey) (863 3838/fax 862 9281/www.habaguanex.com). **Rates** CUC 40 single; CUC 60 double. **Credit** MC, V. **Map** p256 E15 13

Every night flamenco brings the crowds to the Mesón, a 19th-century inn that hosted sailors from Spanish galleons during the colonial period (for those worried about the noise, performances end at 11pm). A small hotel with just five rooms, it has conserved the ambience of a Spanish tavern: posters of well-known Spanish bullfighters hang from the original stone walls and wine barrels stand beside the stone arches. The comfortable, nicely decorated rooms are named after ships that once docked at the port, and the reception desk doubles up as a bar serving decent tapas (*see p109*). Great value.
Air-conditioning. Bar. Restaurant. TV.

Hostal Valencia. *See p42.*

Residencia Académica

Convento de Santa Clara, Calle Cuba #610, entre Luz y Sol (861 3335/fax 833 5696). **Rates** (per person) CUC 25 dormitories; CUC 35 suite. Groups CUC 16. **No credit cards. Map** p256 E15 ⓮

Santa Clara was originally Havana's first abattoir. Then, in 1644, it was handed to the silent order of the Poor Clares. These days it offers eight rooms consisting of four-, five- or six-bed dormitories. The management assured us that, while groups are preferred, no one is expected to share a room with strangers. Avoid staying here in summer, unless you've practised sleeping in a sauna.

Bar/café. Laundry. Parking (free).

Casas particulares

Casa de Eugenio y Fabio

Calle San Ignacio #656, entre Jesús María y Merced (862 9877). **Rate** CUC 30. **Map** p256 F15 ⓯

Antique collectors and art enthusiasts will adore this beautifully clean colonial-style home, decorated with precious and delicate objects. The bedrooms lead on to a lovely interior courtyard. English spoken.

Air-conditioning. Fridge.

Casa de Jesús y María

Calle Aguacate #518, entre Sol y Muralla (861 1378/ jesusmaria2003@yahoo.com). **Rates** CUC 25-30. **Map** p256 E15 ⓰

Three modern doubles, all with their own bathroom and an extra single bed, open on to a pretty Andalucían-style tiled courtyard with wrought-iron furniture. A delightful oasis.

Air-conditioning. Fridge.

Casa de Migdalia Caraballo Martín

Calle Santa Clara #164, 1er piso, apto F, entre Cuba y San Ignacio (tel/fax 861 7352/casamigdalia@ yahoo.es). **Rate** CUC 30. **Map** p256 E15 ⓱

Reasonably spacious, clean rooms (one with en suite bathroom) furnished with double and single beds, overlooking the bustling street below. The owner is helpful and enthusiastic. Some English spoken.

Air-conditioning.

Casa de Rafaela y Pepe

Calle San Ignacio #454, entre Sol y Santa Clara (867 5551). **Rate** CUC 30. **Map** p256 E15 ⓲

All rooms have balconies (one has no fewer than three) at this exquisitely preserved colonial-style home, with antique ornaments and mosaic floors.

Air-conditioning. Fridge.

Centro Habana

Expensive hotels

Hotel Inglaterra

Paseo de Martí (Prado) #416, entre San Rafael y San Miguel (860 8595-7/fax 860 8254). **Rates** CUC 75-104 single; CUC 100-160 double; CUC 126-182 triple. **Credit** MC, V. **Map** p256 D14 ⓳

The Inglaterra was founded in 1875, making it the oldest hotel in Cuba. And it's showing in parts; the lobby is in dire need of an overhaul and the rooms are rather tired-looking. On the plus side, the hotel is full of original features: crystal chandeliers, ornate ceilings and intricately designed Andalucían ceramic wall tiles dating back to the 19th century. Plans are afoot to replace the elevators and refurbish the lobby, while leaving these lovely features intact. Café El Louvre, in pole position for people-watching, has tabletops made up of ceramic tiles designed by renowned Cuban artists. The best of the Inglaterra's 83 rooms have good views over Parque Central; 117, 217, and 317 are the best corner rooms. Traditional music is played nightly on the open-air rooftop bar/grill (*see p120*), which has impressive views of Parque Central. The internet café in the lobby often has a queue, but its (relatively) fast and reliable connection makes it worth the wait.

Air-conditioning. Bars (3). Internet (cybercafé). Laundry. No-smoking rooms (2). Parking (free). Restaurants (2). Room service. TV.

Hotel NH Parque Central

Calle Neptuno, entre Paseo de Martí (Prado) y Zulueta (860 6627/6628/fax 860 6630). **Rates** CUC 205 single; CUC 270 double; CUC 335 suite. **Credit** MC, V. **Map** p256 D14 ⓴

For those looking for genuine Western five-star service in a central location, the Parque Central is hard to beat. The hotel was taken over by the Spanish NH group in 2001, and its modern architecture is in stark – and controversial – contrast to many of the colonial-era buildings in the vicinity. But there's lots to recommend it: the rooftop swimming pool, hot tub and terrace restaurant have magnificent vistas, including a bird's-eye view of the Gran Teatro, and the rooms are comfortable and well furnished, albeit in a nondescript corporate manner (ask for one overlooking the park). When it comes to food and drink there are several in-house options to choose from, from the cool lobby bar to the posh El Patio. The Parque Central has one of the best buffet breakfasts in town, with a lavish spread that's worth setting your alarm for. It's also worth mentioning that there are 220 volt European round pin sockets, so do bring an adaptor (most of the electricity in Cuba is flat pin 110 volt).

Air-conditioning. Bars (3) (one VIP). Business centre. Concierge. Disabled-adapted rooms. Internet (cybercafé and in suites). Laundry. No-smoking rooms. Parking (free). Restaurants (2). Room service. TV.

Hotel Plaza

Calle Agramonte (Zulueta) #267, esquina Neptuno (860 8583-9/fax 860 8869/www.gran-caribe.com). **Rates** CUC 80-84/104 single; CUC 110-120/160 double; CUC 161-171/228 triple; CUC 96-160/180 suite. **Credit** MC, V. **Map** p256 D14 ㉑

This hotel was first opened in 1909, and subsequent renovations have aimed at conserving the original feel and decor. To a large extent these efforts have

Home sweet homestay

Cuba's complexities and perplexities are difficult to understand at the best of times, let alone if you're staying in a five-star hotel. One of the best ways to get to know Cubans on their own turf, and get to grips with the realities of daily life, is to stay in a licensed private home, known as a *casa particular*.

HOW IT WORKS

As with the other areas of private enterprise permitted by the state, *casas particulares* are strictly regulated, along similar lines to *paladares* (private restaurants). The *dueño* or *dueña* (landlord or landlady) is required to register with the authorities, rooms for rent have to meet with certain standards and all transactions must be logged with the state.

The first illusion to dispose of is that the Cuban hosts involved are raking it in. The taxes levied are phenomenal: the landlord/lady has to pay around CUC 200-350 per month for every registered room, regardless of whether he or she receives clients. In addition, at the year's end, a further tax deduction is due (25 to 30 per cent), calculated according to business recorded.

PAPERWORK AND ETIQUETTE

When booking into a registered *casa*, you will be required to show your passport and visa and the details will be entered into a register. This procedure is the most certain way of knowing whether your landlord has a licence. There will also be a blue triangle sign next to the front door, which shows they are licensed to rent. Prices vary according to the area and standard of the accommodation but generally fall between CUC 20 and CUC 35 a night. It's well worth trying to negotiate on price, as many owners offer reduced rates for longer stays, or if you pay up front. Most hosts will prepare meals (breakfast is usually a few CUCs extra) and do laundry by arrangement. Many landlords don't speak much English, so have a few relevant phrases to hand. Finally, you should talk directly to the owners unaccompanied by taxi drivers, intermediaries or hustlers. These people will demand to be paid commission, usually CUC 5 per day.

LISTINGS

The *casas* chosen in this guide have been selected on the basis of quality, cleanliness, security and tranquillity, and all are legally registered. A sign with blue and white chevrons saying *arrendador inscripto* is displayed on the doors of these homes. It should be noted that these are by no means typical Cuban homes.

There are various websites that give overviews of *casas* for rent, some of which are able to make the bookings for you; these include Havana Rentals (www.havana-rentals.com) and Casa Particular Organisation (www.casaparticularcuba.org).

been successful, particularly in the vibrant lobby, where guests tread on a colourful mosaic tiled floor and coloured light pours in from the glass roof. It's a different story in the top-floor modern restaurant (where buffet breakfast is served), which suffers from a distinct lack of character. Rooms, some of them noisy, are decorated in a colonial style, but are also looking tatty in parts. They also vary hugely in size, so ask for a bigger one if you're not happy. On the plus side, if you're looking for a central position at a good price, the Plaza is hard to beat.
Air-conditioning. Bars (3). Business centre. Internet (cybercafé). Laundry. No-smoking rooms (10). Restaurants (3). Room service. TV.

Hotel Sevilla

Calle Trocadero #55, entre Paseo de Martí (Prado) y Agramonte (860 8560/fax 860 8582). **Rates** CUC 120-145/176 single; CUC 164-197/241 double; CUC 195-245/294 triple. **Credit** MC, V. **Map** p256 D14 ㉒
The Spanish-Moorish style of the Sevilla's façade is fabulously ornate, in keeping with a hotel that was one of Havana's leading turn-of-the-20th-century hotels. The Moorish style, so prevalent around Andalucía, is continued throughout, with brightly coloured ceramic tiles, intricate mosaics and arches. Refurbishment work to the whole hotel was completed in 2003 (it's now under the French chain Accor) and the standard of accommodation has improved immeasurably. The attractive El Patio Sevillano bar is open 24 hours a day should you need a Mojito at four in the morning, while the fine Roof Garden restaurant (*see p112*) has great views. The hotel pool, one of few in the area, is a pleasant chill-out zone. Graham Greene's *Our Man in Havana* is set here and in the immediate vicinity.
Air-conditioning. Bars (3). Business centre. Gym. Internet (cybercafé, 24hrs). Laundry. Parking (free). Restaurants (2). Room service. Spa. TV.

Hotel Telégrafo

Paseo de Martí (Prado) #408, esquina Neptuno (861 1010/fax 861 4741/www.habaguanex.com). **Rates** CUC 80-90/106 single; CUC 130-150/182 double. **Credit** MC, V. **Map** p256 D14 ㉓
Originally opened in 1860, this historic hotel moved to its present location beside the Hotel Inglaterra (*see p44*) in 1911. In those days it was one of the best hotels in Latin America, and was unique in having telephones installed not only in every room – but at each table in the restaurant. Relics of these antique phones, together with a section of the underwater cable that formed part of the first telephonic link between New York and Havana when it was established in the 1880s, are on display beside the lifts. Telecommunications aside, design is the thing here these days: the ultra-modern lobby leads on to a courtyard bar with ancient half-arch porticoes and sections of the original brick wall exposed. The first two floors are decorated in 19th-century style, while the top floor reflects contemporary tastes. The 63 rooms are unusually spacious, done out in warm colours and equipped with double-glazed windows as well as period shutters (a definite plus, given the busy road below). Of all the newly renovated Habaguanex hotels, the Telegraph has the most contemporary feel.
Air-conditioning. Bars (2). Business centre. Concierge. Internet (cybercafé). Laundry. No-smoking rooms. Parking (free). Restaurants (2). Room service. TV.

Saratoga

Paseo de Martí (Prado) #603, esquina Dragones (866 4317/8282). **Rates** CUC 180-95/210 single; CUC 250-270/280 double; CUC 210-650/670 suite. **Credit** MC, V. **Map** p256 E14 ㉔
Located just south of Parque Central, directly opposite the Capitolio, the five-star Saratoga has been billed as Havana's first genuine boutique hotel, and so far it seems to be meeting expectations. The original hotel was famous back in the 1930s as the place to be seen, but with the Revolution the government moved from its Capitolio headquarters, leaving the hotel without its usual regular mix of ministers. The building later fell into disrepair, until it was taken over, completely regutted, and reopened in 2005. While it may lack the glitz of its former incarnation, it's making waves with discerning travellers, with a high standard of service and impressive attention to detail. There are 96 spacious bedrooms, including seven suites, all decorated with pastel colours and soft furnishings, and all with views over the square or central courtyard. Further bonuses include the rooftop, with gorgeous pool, bar and dining terrace, and views over the whole of Havana.
Air-conditioning. Bars (3). Business centre. Concierge. Gym. Internet (Wi-Fi). Laundry. No-smoking rooms. Parking (free). Restaurants (2). Room service. TV (pay movies).

Mid-range hotels

Hotel Park View

Calle Colón #101, entre Prado y Morro (861 3293/fax 863 6036/www.habaguanex.com). **Rates** CUC 45-50/61 single; CUC 70-80/104 double; CUC 99-114/148 triple. **Credit** MC, V. **Map** p256 D15 ㉕
Built in 1928, the Park View was a pretty prestigious hotel in its day, though it later lapsed somewhat in quality. Now, after a full renovation care of Habaguanex, it's back in business. A quiet, centrally located establishment, with modest-sized but modern rooms, Park View offers excellent value for money. If you want a balcony, ask for a room on the first or fourth floor. The lobby bar, which is decorated in two-tone green, like the exterior of the hotel, is a pleasant spot for a cocktail, though the air-conditioning can be rather fierce. The Prado restaurant on the top floor has an interesting view of the surrounding sadly neglected but beautiful colonial buildings.
Air-conditioning. Bar. Business centre. Concierge. Internet (cybercafé). Laundry. Restaurant. TV.

Budget hotels

Casa del Científico

Paseo de Martí (Prado) #212, esquina Trocadero (862 1604/7/8/hcientif@ceniai.inf.cu). **Rates** *2nd floor* CUC 25 single; CUC 31 double; CUC 37 triple. *3rd floor* CUC 45 single; CUC 55 double; CUC 64 triple. **No credit cards. Map** p256 D14 ㉖

Time appears to have bypassed the Casa del Científico. This hotel was the home of José Miguel Gómez – second president of the Republic of Cuba – between 1914 and 1924, and now offers strictly unrefurbished accommodation. Everything is as it was in Gómez's time, but for some delapidation: these days the marble staircases are worn in places, and the magnificent crystal chandeliers have gathered dust, as has the early 20th-century furniture. Managed by the Cuban company Cientur, the hotel is open to the public, though priority booking is given to scientists attending events in the area (so reserve your place early). Rooms on the second floor have only a shared bathroom with cold water, hence the cheaper prices. The beautiful marble staircase is covered by a stained-glass roof, and leads up to a pleasant restaurant.

Air-conditioning. Bar. Business centre. Laundry. Restaurant. Room service. TV.

Hotel Caribbean

Paseo de Martí (Prado) #164, entre Colón y Refugio (860 8210/8233/fax 860 7994/rel.pub@caribean.hor.tu.cu). **Rates** CUC 33-36 single; CUC 48-54 double. **Credit** MC, V. **Map** p256 D15 ㉗

This modest 38-room hotel has a functional but friendly air, and isn't a bad option for budget travellers. All rooms have en suite bathrooms, and breakfast is served in the snack bar.

Air-conditioning. Bar. Internet. Laundry. Parking (free). TV.

Casas particulares

Casa de Évora Rodríguez García

Paseo del Prado #20 (altos), entre San Lázaro y Cárcel (tel/fax 861 7932/mgilc@hotmail.com). **Rate** CUC 35. **Map** p256 C15 ㉘

A very classy apartment with a magnificent sea view over La Punta, the entrance to the Bay of Havana. The double rooms are well furnished, light and pleasant, each with an adjoining bathroom. Separate entrance.

Air-conditioning. Fridge. TV.

Casa de Gladys Cutiño

Calle Soledad #272 (bajos), entre Concordia y Virtudes (873 7838/renta-gladys@yahoo.es). **Rate** CUC 30. **Map** p254 C12 ㉙

The top two floors in this three-storey home, which is modern and in immaculate condition, have been attractively made over for the exclusive use of guests. Two kitchens, one on each floor, are open to guests. Gladys's endearing personality gives a final touch.

Air-conditioning. Fridge. TV.

Casa de Marcelino y Raúl Díaz Macaya

Calle Marina #113, apto 4F, entre Príncipe y Vapor (878 7075/marcelinodiaz2002@yahoo.es). **Rates** CUC 25-30. **Map** p255 C13 ㉚

The two double bedrooms, adjoining bathroom and lounge have been redecorated in this spotless modern apartment. The experienced and professional owner has rented to visitors for over ten years. The location is very central, and privacy is guaranteed.

Air-conditioning. Fridge. TV.

Vedado

Expensive hotels

Hotel Habana Libre

Calle L, entre 23 y 25 (834 6100/838 4011/fax 833 3141/www.solmelia.com). **Rate** CUC 200 single/double. **Credit** MC, V. **Map** p254 B11 ㉛

After the Nacional, the Habana Libre is probably Cuba's most famous hotel: it towers over Vedado's liveliest junction. Opened in 1958 as part of the Hilton hotel chain, it was nationalised and used as the new Revolutionary government's headquarters for the first three months of 1959. Between 1960 and 1963, Fidel Castro himself stayed regularly in the Castellana suite on the 22nd floor, the only rooms that retain the original '50s furnishings. In 2000 the Spanish Sol Meliá group took over the hotel. Its 572 rooms are remarkable for their spaciousness, and the hotel has a functional, busy feel that won't appeal to all. However, you couldn't want for a better location, on the cusp of lively La Rampa. The Cabaret Turquino nightclub on the top floor (*see p164*) has fantastic views of Havana's skyline (and a retractable roof). The lobby area probably looked great in the '70s but it could maybe do with a facelift now. Note that the air-conditioning is sometimes completely out of action for long stretches, so check before you book. For the restaurants, *see p113*.

Air-conditioning. Bars (4). Business centre. Concierge. Gym. Internet (cybercafé). Laundry. No-smoking floors. Parking. Restaurants (4). Room service. Spa. TV.

Hotel Habana Riviera

Avenida Paseo, entre Malecón y 1ra (836 4051/fax 833 3738/www.gran-caribe.com). **Rates** CUC 74-91/111 single; CUC 106-130/172 double; CUC 137-219/272 triple; CUC 120-140/150 junior suite; CUC 300-317 presidential suite. **Credit** MC, V. **Map** p254 A9 ㉜

The vast reception area of the Hotel Habana Riviera has probably changed little since it was built in the 1950s by Meyer Lansky, as part of a plan to establish a network of casino hotels in Cuba. Those shady days are long gone, and today the Riviera is now a respectable and pleasant place to stay. And yet we can't help feeling that the spirit of the bad old days still resonates in the corridors. The saltwater swimming pool is a big attraction. Curiously, it is coffin-

Hotel Nacional de Cuba.

shaped. One of Meyer Lanksy's architectural suggestions or pure coincidence? The buffet breakfast has one major defect: the coffee is fairly dreadful. The hotel was badly damaged in 2005's Hurricane Wilma, and renovations were ongoing at press time.
Air-conditioning. Bars (2). Business centre. Internet (cybercafé). Laundry. Parking (free). Restaurants (2). Room service. TV.

Hotel Meliá Cohíba

Avenida Paseo, entre 1ra y 3ra (833 3636/fax 833 4555/www.solmelia.com). **Rates** *Standard* CUC 175 single; CUC 225 double; CUC 240-370 suite. *Servicio real* CUC 225 single; CUC 275 double; CUC 365-685 suite. **Credit** MC, V. **Map** p254 A9 ㉝

This imposing tower block hotel was the first real five-star hotel in modern times in Havana, opening in 1995. Facilities and standards of service make it an appealing option for business people, but holidaymakers may find it rather soulless. Guest rooms are comfortable, if rather old-fashioned in decor. If money is no object, try the 'royal' service (*servicio real*). This offers express check-in and check-out, a good all-day buffet (7am-11pm) and an exclusive lift, plus butler service, morning coffee in your room and free use of the gym and sauna. Unlike many hotels in Havana, the lovely swimming pool is only open to guests (and their guests), so it tends to be quieter than is usual. Otherwise, there are no fewer than five restaurants to choose from, although they vary in style and quality (*see p113*); there's also a good cigar bar and jazz club on the first floor, and within a few minutes' walk of the hotel a number of very good music venues, including the Copa Rooms for live salsa, the Jazz Café, and Habana Café for Cuban bands (for both, *see p167*).

Air-conditioning. Bars (5). Business centre. Concierge. Gym. Internet (cybercafé). Laundry. No-smoking rooms. Parking (CUC 8 per day). Restaurants (5). Room service. TV (pay movies).

Hotel Nacional de Cuba

Calle O, esquina 21 (873 3564/7/reservations 855 0294/fax 873 5171/www.gran-caribe.com). **Rates** CUC 120/145 single; CUC 170/220 double; CUC 210/285 triple; CUC 215-1,000 suite. *Executive floor supplement* CUC 21-30 per night. **Credit** MC, V. **Map** p254 B12 ㉞

Havana's most famous hotel, and the only one in Cuba that's a national monument, the Nacional first opened its doors in 1930 and has been frequented by the rich and famous ever since. The hotel has effortlessly withstood the test of time, remaining sophisticated, refined and subtly stylish. Clearly, the marvellous location, twin-towered building, spacious gardens and magnificent views all contribute to the magic; but there's also something about cruising through the lobby in the knowledge that you're following in the footsteps of so many famous names – including Winston Churchill and Al Caopne – that gives the place a special aura. The standard rooms aren't particularly exciting (it's worth seeing several before deciding), but the views over the Malecón or the hotel gardens are impressive. There's even wireless internet access in rooms on the Executive (6th) Floor. Other attractions include the two swimming pools, tennis court, plus good eating and drinking options (*see p113 and p120*; restaurants: Comedor de Aguiar, La Barraca; bar: La Terraza).
Air-conditioning. Bars (5). Business centre. Concierge. Gym. Internet. Laundry. Parking (free). Restaurants (3). Room service. TV.

Hotel Presidente

Calle Calzada #110, esquina Avenida de los Presidentes (G) (838 1801/4/fax 833 3753/ www.hotelesc.com). **Rates** CUC 90 single; CUC 140 double; CUC 200 triple; CUC 130-220 suite. **Credit** MC, V. **Map** p254 A10 ㉟

This seductively elegant and totally tranquil hotel was fully restored in 1999, with subtle 1920s-style decor, care of the Spanish Hoteles C company. The lobby is furnished with antiques and the delicate overhead lighting makes for an intimate ambience. Services have recently been expanded to cater for 21st-century demands, and there's now 24-hour internet and fax access. The two tenth-floor suites, featuring Louis XV-style furnishings, are particularly grand, and there's a lovely swimming pool and bar area at the rear.

Air-conditioning. Bars (2). Business centre. Concierge. Internet (cybercafé). Laundry. Parking (free). Restaurants (2). Room service. TV.

Mid-range hotels

Hotel St John's

Calle O #206, entre 23 y 25 (833 3740/fax 833 3561/www.horizontes.cu). **Rates** CUC 50-56/71 single; CUC 67-80/110 double. CUC 90-108/148 suite. **Credit** MC, V. **Map** p254 B12 ㊱

The Hotel St John's is located in an enviable spot just off La Rampa. It was fully refurbished in the late 1990s, but now it's beginning to weather, particularly in the corridors and the lobby. The modest-size swimming pool on the top floor, beside the café-bar, becomes the Pico Blanco nightclub at 10.30pm. Request a room on the seventh floor or higher for a view of the city (as opposed to the wall of the neighbouring building).

Air-conditioning. Bars (2). Business centre. Internet (cybercafé). Restaurant. Room service. TV.

Budget hotels

Hotel Vedado

Calle O #244, entre 23 y 25 (836 4072/fax 833 4186/www.horizontes.cu). **Rates** CUC 50-63/71 single; CUC 67-80/110 double. **Credit** MC, V. **Map** p254 B12 ㊲

First impressions of the Hotel Vedado – the gloomy, poky lobby area – aren't encouraging. The rooms aren't particularly attractive either. But the big advantage of this hotel is that it's well placed for exploring the area. Request a room on the seventh floor or above if you want a view.

Air-conditioning. Bar. Gym. Internet (cybercafé). Laundry. Restaurants (2). Room service. TV.

Casas particulares

Casa Belkis

Calle 19 #1259, entre 20 y 22 (833 8628/ hostalbelkis@yahoo.com). **Rate** CUC 30-35. **Map** p253 C7 ㊳

This home, which sits nestled in a quiet, pleasant street, is at the upper end of the *casa particular* market. Casa Belkis offers modern and well-equipped double bedrooms, each of which has its own bathroom. Rooms are equipped with comfortable orthopaedic beds and linen sheets. A cosy atmosphere makes it worth the trek.

Fridge. TV.

Casa de Carlos y Julio

Calle E #609 (altos), entre 25 y 27 (832 7203/ carnel@cubarte.cult.cu). **Rate** CUC 30. **Map** p254 C10 ㊴

This period home is beautifully preserved and tastefully furnished. Two doubles (one en suite).

Air-conditioning. Fridge.

Casa de Esther Fonseca

Calle 25 #359, apto A, piso 2, entre L y K (832 0120). **Rate** CUC 20-40. **Map** p254 C11 ㊵

This apartment is in a perfect location, seconds away from La Rampa. It's in pristine condition too, and subtly decorated. Esther offers guests double bedrooms with an en suite or adjoining bathroom. Separate entrance.

Air-conditioning. Fridge. TV.

Casa de Irma

Avenida de los Presidentes (G) #159, piso 2, entre Calzada y 9 (832 7721/2360). **Rate** CUC 30. **Map** p254 A10 ㊶

Don't be disheartened by the slightly dilapidated entrance to this second-floor flat. Inside lie clean, modern rooms. A terrace overlooks the *avenida*.

Air-conditioning. Fridge.

Miramar & the western suburbs

Expensive hotels

Hotel Meliá Habana

Avenida 3ra, entre 76 y 80, Miramar (204 8500/fax 204 8505/www.solmelia.com). **Rates** *Standard* CUC 175 single; CUC 225 double; CUC 265 junior suite. *Servicio real* CUC 225 single; CUC 275 double; CUC 365-525 suite. **Credit** MC, V. **Map** p252 B1 ㊷

This plush hotel, opened in 1998 by Fidel Castro himself, has had a number of heads of state and famous names among its guests. It's popular with business guests, given its location in the hub of business development in Cuba and its vast array of services (leisure facilities extend so far as to include hunting). The impressive cream marble lobby, with its central pool, is an ideal spot to enjoy piano music in the early evening. Restaurants, bars and cafés abound (*see p49*). Don't miss the swimming pools, one of which is reputedly the largest in Cuba.

Air-conditioning. Bars (5). Business centre. Concierge. Gym. Internet. Laundry. No-smoking rooms. Parking (free). Restaurants (4). Room service. Spa. TV (pay movies).

Lobby lounging

Havana hotels and their lobbies hold a particular magical place in the memory and imagination of both Cubans and the visiting tourist. From being the preferred drinking holes of many a 1940s Mafia boss, to the spaces frequented by Hemingway between inebriated fishing trips and typewritten drafts, they now offer visitors an important bolt-hole, a comfortable place to flop, rest and recharge. The sun's too hot and you can't find a cold drink? Lashing down with tropical rain and without a brolly? Look for a lobby.

In the five-star **Meliá Cohíba** (*see p48*), you can sip Mojitos (bar to the right), have a cuppa (left into the lounge) or (straight ahead) sink into enormously comfortable sofas, while enjoying the exquisite flower arrangements.

If you're looking for more action and history, the grand lobby of **Hotel Nacional** (*see p48*), with its spectacular sea-view gardens and patio café, is a must. Equally, drop into the spacious and lively **Habana Libre** (*see p47*), perch on designer bar stools at the sumptuous **Raquel** (*see p41*), or take a lift to the rooftop of **NH Parque Central** (*see p44*), where, over coffee or cocktails, magnificent views of the city await.

A small word of warning: after the first few sun-drenched, salsa-filled days of your stay, you might consider inviting old Cuban friends or your new holiday romance out for a quiet drink. And where more comfortable than in your own or another hotel lounge or bar? Be aware. Doormen are sited at most hotels and it's their job to see who enters and who leaves – and with whom. And so, depending on its exclusivity and location, you may sail through or you may find yourself questioned, and your Cuban friends even refused entry.

The reasons for this apparent prejudice go back a long way. Pre-Revolution, Batista's US-controlled Cuba was both a business, gambling and Mafia centre and a weekend holiday home. Prostitution was rife: in Havana alone an estimated 10,000 of its 1.2 million inhabitants were working the streets. 1959 changed all that, as prostitution was banned and sex shows closed down. Then, in 1991, with the final collapse of the Soviet Bloc and the resulting economic crisis in Cuba, Castro unwillingly legalised the dollar and opened the island up to what he called 'a pact with the devil' – intensive tourism. Inevitably, Cuba was not only flooded with students and curious foreigners, it was also inundated with older European visitors looking for the 'Cuban flavour'. Cubans responded in kind, and by the early '90s prostitution was once again highly visible.

The government had to act. If Cuba were to be seen internationally as, say, another Thailand, its tourism would be deemed tacky and undesirable for the serious business and family market. It would, importantly, also be seen as a grave slur on the Revolution itself, which prides itself on its educational, health and morality. Thus in 1996 Cuban women were officially barred from the guest rooms of tourist hotels, and many Cuban men were also refused entry. In January 1999 further measures were instigated, which saw more than 7,000 women picked up from the streets and many families fined for the dubious deeds of their daughters. Somewhere along the line refusing Cubans entry to hotels became pretty much the norm.

Some say that this segregation also serves to keep foreigners and Cubans a little more separated so there is less exposure to capitalism and perhaps less envy and aspiration generated. Whatever the case, there now, happily, seems to be more flexibility in the doorways of tourist hotels, although the general policy seems to remain the same. While there is still a degree of monitoring, on the whole there is now less attention paid to the many Cubans who now regularly go in and out of hotels – to change money, to make an international phone call or to meet foreign family and friends.

So when in the sun-drenched, salsa-filled days of your stay you think about inviting a Cuban friend or your holiday romance for a quiet drink in a hotel, ask them which hotels you can comfortably go into together. Then order a couple of Mojitos – and relax!

Hotel Occidental Miramar

Avenida 5ta, entre 72 y 76, Miramar (204 3584/ fax 204 3583). **Rates** CUC 100-110 single; CUC 130-150 double; CUC 180-205 triple; CUC 210-300 suite. **Credit** MC, V. **Map** p252 B2 ㊸

A large hotel set on one of Havana's smartest streets, the Occidental is popular with both business travellers and tourists. Rooms are refreshingly decorated with bright Caribbean colours, while the lobby manages to combine comfort and formality. There's a lovely swimming pool, and the restaurant has a reputation for serving good-quality food. And don't

worry about being in a quieter part of town: there's a free shuttle bus service to and from the centre throughout the day.
Air-conditioning. Bar. Internet. Laundry. Parking. Restaurants (2). Room service. TV.

Mid-range hotels

Hotel Comodoro

Avenida 3ra, esquina 84, Miramar (204 5551/ fax 204 2089/www.cubanacan.cu). **Rates** *Hotel* CUC 62-70/80 single; CUC 90-101/110 double; CUC 130-160/180 triple; CUC 130-140/155 suite. *Bungalow apartments* CUC 89-111/248. **Credit** MC, V. **Map** p252 B1 44
This hotel, which opened in 1952, was formerly a school for art instructors and was later used by the central committee of the Communist Party as its headquarters. Today it is an attractively designed Cubanacán hotel with a choice of rooms in the main building or bungalows in the hotel gardens, some with their own kitchen. The hotel also has facilities for scuba diving and will take qualified divers out to the nearest coral reefs. Alternatively, you could go for a dip in one of the nine, yes nine, swimming pools on site. Home to one of Havana's best shopping complexes (*see p123*).
Air-conditioning. Bars (5). Business centre. Concierge. Internet (cybercafé). Laundry. Parking (free). Restaurants (3). Room service. TV.

Budget hotels

Hotel Mirazul

Avenida 5ta #3603, entre 36 y 40, Miramar (204 0045/fax 204 0088). **Rates** CUC 40 single; CUC 50 double. **Credit** MC, V. **Map** p252 B4 45
The charm of this tiny hotel, which is marked only by a blue awning on Quinta Avenida, lies in its quiet, intimate atmosphere. There's no pool, but business people will be attracted by facilities that include three conference rooms.
Air-conditioning. Bar. Business centre. Laundry. Parking (free). Restaurant. Room service. TV.

Casas particulares

Casa de Dr José Mario Parapar de la Riestra

Calle 70 #912, entre 9 y 11, Miramar (203 7269/ jparapar@infomed.sld.cu). **Rates** CUC 30-40. **Map** p252 C2 46
Crossing the threshold of this elegant mansion is like stepping back to 1948, the year it was built. The furniture, decor and even the artwork remain intact, as they were half a century ago, and the owner is attentive yet private. Highly recommended.
Air-conditioning. TV.

Casa de María Rodríguez

Calle 204 #1319, entre 13 y 15, Siboney (271 5904/ 2249). **Rates** vary.
Owned by a friendly family, this spacious house has a pleasant, fresh feel. The well-decorated bedrooms rooms all have en suite bathrooms, and there's a large terrace and garden with a swimming pool for you to enjoy. The owners will prepare meals (including barbecues) to order. A few minutes' drive away is Club Habana (*see p186*), while the best supermarket in town, Palco (*see p125*), is within walking distance. Good English is spoken.
Air-conditioning. Fridge.

Casa de Marta

Calle 28 #106, piso 3, apto 3, entre 1ra y 3ra, Miramar (203 8380). **Rates** vary. **Map** p253 B5 47
A comfortable and modern apartment where the friendly hosts have obviously thought carefully about guests' comfort and privacy. A separate entrance leads into a lounge with adjoining terrace and magnificent sea view.
Air-conditioning. Fridge.

Casa de Mauricio

Calle A #312 (penthouse), entre 5ta y 3ra, Miramar (203 7581/roomsinhavana@gmail.com). **Rates** vary. **Map** p253 A7 48
This stunning 1950s-style apartment, which encompasses the whole top (ninth) floor, boasts a 100-foot balcony running down one side of the building, with views of the sea and river mouth below. The owners, an ultra-friendly couple, go out of their way to make guests feel at home (this is helped by the fact that they get their own key to the lift, which goes directly into the apartment). Good English spoken.
Air-conditioning. Fridge.

Casa de Mayra

Calle 3ra #8, entre 0 y 2, Miramar (209 1947). **Rate** CUC 50. **Map** p253 A7 49
Mayra has two modern en suite doubles for rent in this spacious house. There's a state-of-the-art kitchen and a dining room, together with a lounge and porch that guests are invited to use. The location, close to Vedado and two blocks from the coast, makes this an ideal choice.
Air-conditioning. Fridge. TV.

Playas del Este

Mid-range hotels

Villa Los Pinos

Avenida de las Terrazas, Santa María del Mar (97 1361/fax 97 1524). **Rates** CUC 160 2-room villa; CUC 210 3-room villa; CUC 250 4-room villa. **Credit** MC, V.
A relaxed, relatively upmarket constellation of small villas in a semi-wooded area right next to the beach. Each unit has a bedroom and en suite bathroom, a kitchen and a living room; some also have swimming pools. No visitors are admitted inside the houses, so don't plan on throwing any parties.
Air-conditioning. Bars (2). Internet (cybercafé). Laundry. Restaurant. TV.

Sightseeing

Features

Edificio Bacardí. *See p68.*

Introduction

Havana blast.

The Star and Stripes.

Cuba's sights really are unique. No matter how many photos you've seen of '50s Chevys trundling along crumbling colonial streets, the everyday reality of such a scene is irresistibly charming. Beyond the postcard chic, Havana's fascinating history and culture are given an enormous energy and personality by the city's inhabitants, *los habaneros*. (Though bear in mind that over zealous tourist-guarding police may stop and search any local who tries to have a chat with you.)

Most visitors head straight for **La Habana Vieja** (Old Havana) – the historical core of the city – and rightly so; it has over 500 years of history to offer. Every plaza, street, museum, art gallery and building reveals a secret of Cuba's past – even the ones that are being designed for the future. Since the old city was declared a UNESCO World Heritage Site in 1982, a programme of renovation, co-ordinated by the City Historian's Office, has given parts of Old Havana a much-needed facelift. A word of warning: *jineteros* (hustlers) tend to favour the tourist-intensive arteries in this area, though you're unlikely to suffer anything more than annoying banter.

As too few tourists discover, there is life beyond La Habana Vieja. The capital's various *barrios* (neighbourhoods) all have their own story to tell: **Centro Habana** is a vibrant, urban onslaught to the west of the colonial core, beyond the former city walls; leafy **Vedado**, further west, is a cultural and commercial hub; spacious, sometimes swanky **Miramar** and the western suburbs beyond have few official sights but reveal Cuba's little-seen upmarket side. Across the bay are imposing fortresses, seaside towns and the **Playas del Este** beaches.

TIPS FOR VISITORS

- A small number of museums and historic sites do not charge admission fees (most charge CUC 1-2) but they do appreciate a donation towards maintenance costs.
- If you would like a guided tour in English, it would be wise to call the museum or site beforehand to make a reservation, as bilingual guides may not be available if you turn up on spec. If your guide was informative and

Top five Sights

Museo de Bellas Artes
A beautifully renovated, world-class museum dedicated – in two buildings – to Cuban and international art. *See p72.*

Plaza de Armas
One of Latin America's finest squares – in the heart of Old Havana – should be your first port of call. *See p56.*

Museo del Chocolate
Everyone visits the rum and cigar factories; this lesser-known attraction completes the hat-trick of gustatory delights. *See p65.*

Plaza de la Revolución
If Pope John Paul II thought Cuba's political heart was a necessary stop on the tourist itinerary, it's good enough for us. *See p88.*

Playas del Este
Want beautiful Caribbean beaches but don't want to stray too far? *See p99.*

South parks

Just over 20 kilometres (12 miles) to the south of La Habana Vieja is the city's largest recreational area, comprising the **Jardín Botánico**, **Parque Lenin**, **Parque Zoológico Nacional** and **ExpoCuba**. Take bus No.88 from the Víbora neighbourhood, or hire a taxi (around CUC 15).

ExpoCuba

Carretera del Rocío Km3.5, El Globo, Calabazar, Boyeros (54 9111/2/57 8282). **Open** *Jan-Aug* 9am-5pm Tue-Sun. Closed Sept-Dec, except for special events. **Admission** CUC 1.

25 pavilions at Cuba's largest exhibition area show self-congratulatory displays on the achievements of the Revolution. ExpoCuba also houses a 500-seat amphitheatre, an amusement park and several restaurants.

Jardín Botánico Nacional

Carretera del Rocío Km3.5, El Globo, Calabazar, Boyeros (643 7278/54 9170). **Open** 8am-5pm (last entry 3.30pm) daily. **Admission** CUC 1. Train ride with guide CUC 4 (CUC 3 if in your own car).

Easily accessible from Parque Lenin (*see below*), these gardens feature around 150,000 examples of 4,000 different species of trees and bushes from around the world; the best way to see it all is from the seat of the dinky little 'train'. It's worth sacrificing your street cred for a ride, since it covers most of the garden, way too much to tackle on foot. Don't miss the delightful Japanese garden, situated right next to one of Cuba's best vegetarian restaurants, El Bambú (*see p130* **Living on the veg**).

Parque Lenin

Calle 100 y Cortina de la Presa, Arroyo Naranjo. **Open** *Sept-June* 9am-5.30pm Wed-Sun. *July, Aug* 9am-5.30pm Tue-Sun. **Admission** free.

Spanning 6.7km (3sq miles) this site was conceived by Celia Sánchez, Fidel Castro's close companion, and opened in 1969. Nearly 40 years on, the park is showing its age: as this guide went to press the narrow-gauge railway was out of action, the aquarium virtually fishless and the amphitheatre overgrown. The park is still nice for picnics and the grounds and gardens are well kept. The refurbished amusement park is worth a visit, especially if you have kids in tow, and the equestrian centre is still in business (prices negotiable). The huge and ruggedly beautiful bust of Lenin, carved in 1982 by Soviet sculptor LE Kerbel, is a focal point.

Parque Zoológico Nacional

Main entrance: Carretera de Capdevila Km3.5, Boyeros (44 7613). Alternative entrance: Avenida de la Independencia (Rancho Boyeros), esquina 243, Fontanar, Boyeros. **Open** 9.30am-3.30pm Wed-Sun. **Admission** CUC 3; CUC 2 concessions (incl optional guide).

The national zoo (with its children's zoo) was set up in 1984 on the grounds of 11 abandoned farms, and is now home to 1,000 animals and 110 species. Tour buses wind their way through the 2.43sq km (1sq mile) that have been transformed into African prairie land roamed by giraffe, zebra, antelopes, rhinos, hippos and lions.

pleasant, consider tipping him or her (even though the entrance fee is almost always higher for those who request a guided tour).

- Some sights offer group discounts, so it might be worth investigating.
- Many of the sights listed have special rules for cameras and video cameras, which tend to change often and without notice. Check before you start shooting or snapping, as there may be an extra cost. Some sights, like the cigar factories and the Museo de Bellas Artes, do not allow photography at all.
- Be prepared to be confronted with monolingual (Spanish) explanatory texts in many museums and historic sites. Few places have English translations.
- Children, particularly those under 12, are often allowed free admission.
- During summer months (July and August), the hours of many museums are slightly different. Call ahead to check.
- Cubans, rightly or wrongly, are known for their lack of punctuality, but there tends to be no tardiness when it comes to shutting up shop. Indeed, 5pm may even mean 4.45pm.
- Street names, particularly in La Habana Vieja and Centro Habana, can be confusing. Most people use the old pre-Revolutionary names, while some maps and street signs use a modern name. We have tried to give both in listings; for a selection of the most important old and new street names, *see p224*.

La Habana Vieja

The city's beating heart has one foot firmly in the past.

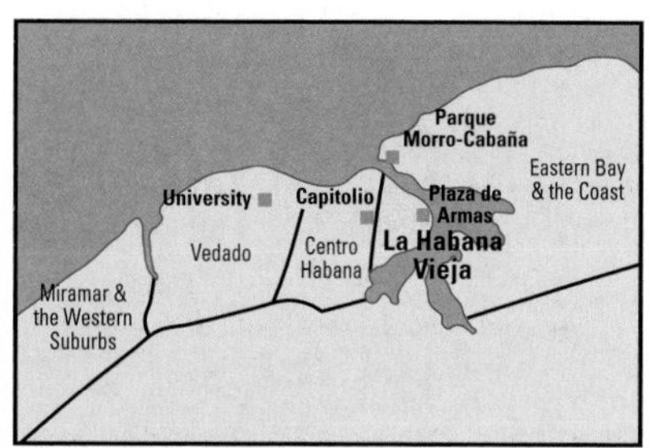

Map p255 & p256

A UNESCO World Heritage Site since 1982 (along with the colonial fortresses), La Habana Vieja, or Old Havana, is usually the first stop on the tourist trail. It's easy to see why: with its rich architectural heritage and an impressively high concentration of museums and galleries – many of which are being restored to their former glory thanks to huge efforts by the City Historian's Office – there's an enormous amount to take in. However, as with many things in Cuba, you'd be wise to lower your expectations somewhat: Havana's traditional 'sights' may be numerous, but few are world class. In fact, visitors are as likely to be as excited by the commotion of daily streetlife as they are by the museums. So, put your walking shoes on and soak it all up… while trying to avoid the seemingly endless stream of *jineteros* (literally 'jockeys'), local touts eager to make a buck by selling fake cigars, guidance to a *paladar* (for a commission) or become your driver for the day.

San Cristóbal de La Habana (1519), one of the first seven towns founded by the Spanish colonisers in Cuba, was service oriented from the start. Tagged the 'Key to the New World and Bastion of the West Indies' because of its strategic location, the port of Havana was a stopping point for all Spanish galleons sailing between Spain and its Latin American colonies. The area now known as Old Havana supplied and repaired boats, and its war ships protected them from pirates who craved their rich cargoes of gold and silver. Later, a large defensive system of colonial fortresses along the northern shore and city walls was built to protect the city and the wealth of passing ships.

Note that this guide defines La Habana Vieja as the area that stood within the old city walls. They occupied what are now **Avenida de los Misiones** (Monserrate) and **Avenida de Bélgica** (Egido), encircling La Habana Vieja in an egg shape along the bay to the east. The street names can often be confusing, as maps and common speech use new (official) names and old (popular) names interchangeably. But within La Habana Vieja, it's not hard, with a good map, to find your way around the grid of narrow streets and small city blocks, nor to get the feel of the early colonial streetscape: a city that radiates out from central squares, characterised by buildings constructed side by side (ventilated mainly through inner courtyards) and an abundance of churches. For more on street names, *see p224*.

Plaza de Armas

The oldest square in Old Havana and the site of the city's foundation, tranquil, palm-filled Plaza de Armas is a good place to begin exploring. It's surrounded by architecture spanning the 16th to the 20th centuries, with a fascinating juxtaposition of building styles.

To appreciate them, stand in **Parque Céspedes** (1834), in the middle of the square, and look around you. To the north-east is the 16th-century, Renaissance-style **Castillo de la Real Fuerza** (*see p57*), the first fortress with triangular bulwarks to be built in the New World; until recently it housed the Museo Nacional de la Cerámica Cubana (*see p64*). The 17th-century school for orphan girls in the south-west corner is now the popular restaurant La Mina (*see p110*). Next door is a curiosity, the **Casa de la Tinaja**, located next to the La Mina restaurant. A *tinaja* is a large jar made of porous stone that is used to filter water for drinking. Since 1544 filtered drinking water has been offered on this spot to passers-by, and the tradition continues to this day. Stop by for a glass of water – but note that there may only be one glass: neck it without the glass touching your lips, like locals do.

Back on the square, the **Palacio del Segundo Cabo** (*see p58*) to the north and the Palacio de los Capitanes Generales (home to the splendid **Museo de la Ciudad**; *see p57*) to the west are stunning 18th-century baroque buildings. **El Templete** (*see p58*), facing the castle, is a 19th-century neo-classical folly marking the legendary spot where Havana was founded. The 20th-century eclectic building that housed the former US embassy, on the plaza's south side, is now the **Museo Nacional de Historia Natural** (*see below*); next to it stands a modern public library built and run by the Office of the City Historian.

In the middle of Parque Céspedes is a white marble statue of Carlos Manuel de Céspedes, Cuban patriot, initiator of the Ten Years War against Spanish colonial rule in 1868 and 'Father of the Nation'. Sculpted by Sergio López Mesa, this replaced a statue of Spanish King Fernando VII, which stood in the square until 1955 (it was moved to the right of the Palacio del Segundo Cabo). From Wednesday to Saturday Havana's largest and best second-hand book market (*see p125*) takes over the park (it's closed on rainy days and during special events or VIP visits).

The east side of the square is dominated by the 18th-century Casa del Conde de Santovenia, renovated in 1867 as a hotel, and again in 1998 as the **Hotel Santa Isabel** (*see p41*).

Castillo de la Real Fuerza

Calle O'Reilly #2, entre Puerto y Tacón (no phone). **Open** 9am-7pm daily. **Admission** phone to check. **Map** p256 D16.

One of the oldest European defensive structures in the Americas, the Castillo de la Real Fuerza (1558-77) was the home of the Spanish captains general in Havana for 200 years, until the new palace – the Palacio de los Capitanes Generales – was built across the square. Heavy-duty this fort may be (its walls are 6m/20ft thick), but it didn't stand up to invasion from the English, who took Havana in 1762. Crowning its cylindrical tower is a small bronze weathervane in the shape of a woman, with one hand on her hip, holding what was once a palm leaf, and the other holding a cross. A replica of the original (now in the Museo de la Ciudad; *see below*), it was cast in 1632 by Cuban artist Jerónimo Martín Pinzón. Called 'La Giraldilla', she is believed to represent Doña Inés de Bobadilla, wife of Hernando de Soto and the first and only female governor of Cuba. The image is now reproduced on the ubiquitous Havana Club rum label.

As part of an ongoing restoration project, parts of the castle were closed as this guide went to press; work was due to finish some time in 2007, with visitors being able to see artefacts recovered from sunken vessels, together with models of ships.

A monument to Cubans who died in World War II stands in the front of the *castillo*. It's not a long list of names – Cuba helped the war effort mainly with sugar and chocolate, having joined the Allies a couple of days after the attack on Pearl Harbor.

Museo de la Ciudad

Palacio de los Capitanes Generales, Calle Tacón #1, entre Obispo y O'Reilly (861 5001/5779 ext 101). **Open** 9am-6pm daily. **Admission** CUC 3; CUC 5 incl guide; free under-12s. **Map** p256 E15.

The Palacio de los Capitanes Generales (1770-91) is now the city's historical museum, and one of Havana's finest sights. To start with, it has without doubt the grandest and most beautiful courtyard in Havana, and rivals the cathedral as the city's finest 18th-century baroque building. Between 1791 and 1898, more than 60 representatives of the Spanish Crown lived here, but it wasn't until the 1999 Ibero-American Summit in Havana that an actual king of Spain visited the palace. The museum houses historical exhibitions, including displays of old horse-drawn vehicles and artillery, plus funerary and religious art. The captain general's apartments are furnished in the sumptuous style of their era and El Cabildo (the room where the town council used to sit) has an 18th-century portrait of Columbus.

Museo Nacional de Historia Natural

Calle Obispo #61, entre Oficios y Baratillo (863 9361/862 9402/www.cuba.cu/historia_natural/general.htm). **Open** 10am-6pm Tue-Sun. **Admission** CUC 3; free under-12s. **Map** p256 E16.

The museum's mammal, bird and reptile exhibitions incorporate a sophisticated video system of animal sounds. Displays also explore the origins of life on Earth and Cuban flora and fauna (though various sections are under long-term renovation). The children's room is a winner, with activities related to nature and prehistory.

Palacio del Segundo Cabo/ Instituto Cubano del Libro

Calle O'Reilly #4, esquina Oficios (switchboard 862 8091/bookshops 863 2244). **Open** *Bookshops* 10am-5.30pm Mon-Sat; 10am-2pm Sun. *Gallery* 10am-5.30pm daily. **Admission** free. **Map** p256 E16.

Originally the royal post office responsible for all postal communication within Spain's Ibero-American colonies, and later the Royal Treasury, the Palacio del Segundo Cabo (1770-91) later became the official residence of the vice-captain general of Cuba. Today the Palacio is the home of the Instituto Cubano del Libro (a state-run institution responsible for the promotion of literature) as well as three bookshops (for all, *see p126*).

Until recently the building was open to the public as a museum; officially it no longer is, but sometimes it is possible to bribe your way in with a few shifty CUCs. If you manage to get in, it's worth trying to get a glimpse of the Moorish details in the balconies and the courtyard, the graceful rooms and the superb *pietra dura* table in the middle of the ballroom. The mezzanine floor of the palace is occupied by Galería Raúl Martínez, which exhibits and sells works by well-known Cuban painters.

El Templete

Calle Baratillo, esquina O'Reilly (no phone). **Open** 9am-6.30pm daily. **Admission** CUC 1 (incl guide); free under-12s. **Map** p256 E16.

The oldest neo-classical building in Havana, the columned El Templete (1828) marks the spot where, under a legendary ceiba tree (an ancestor of the one currently on the site), Havana was founded in its present location on 16 November 1519, with the first mass and town council. (In fact, the city was originally founded several years previously on the south coast of the island, but moved later to this strategically stronger location.) Inside the chapel are three paintings by French artist Jean Baptiste Vermay (whose ashes lie in the middle of the room): two represent the mass and *cabildo* (town council) and the huge middle one shows the inauguration of El Templete. If you're lucky you'll catch one of the friendly English-speaking guides on your visit.

Each year on 16 November, a procession headed by the city's 16th-century maces (which are normally kept in the Museo de la Ciudad) makes its way around the Plaza de Armas to the ceiba to commemorate the city's founding. Superstitious *habaneros* – and that means everyone – queue up all evening to walk around the tree and make a wish. The wishes are only meant to work if you haven't spoken all day, a feat quite beyond the average Cuban, so plenty of money is left between the roots of the tree as an extra insurance policy.

Along Calle Oficios to Plaza de San Francisco

It's only a short three-block walk along Calle Oficios, Havana's oldest street, from the southwest corner of Plaza de Armas to Plaza de San Francisco, but there are plenty of sights along the way. Just a few doors down Calle Oficios is the **Casa de los Artistas** (No.6; *see p151*;

Friends, comrades, countrymen.

Walk on A snapshot of styles

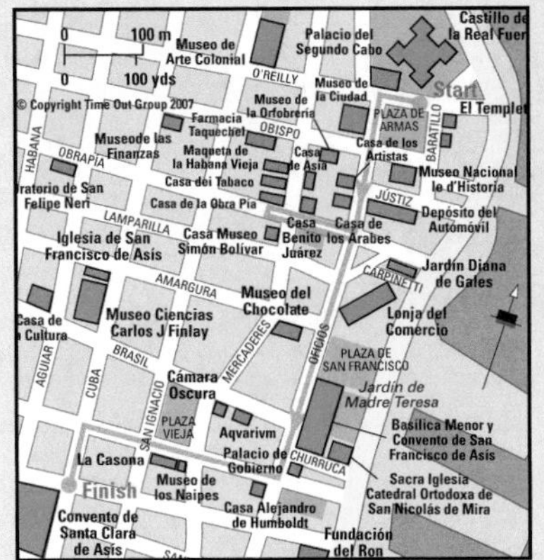

With an architectural heritage spanning more than five centuries, La Habana Vieja is a virtual time machine of styles and techniques. Almost any street offers up a wide range of appealing buildings, some exuberant, others sober, each one with its unique place in the story of the city. The following walk is limited to the highlights of the eastern part of the Old City.

Start off in the **Plaza de Armas**. On the north side of the square stands the **Castillo de la Real Fuerza** (1558-77; *see p57*), one of two fortresses that have guarded the entrance to Havana's harbour for centuries. It was built to a Renaissance plan and is one of the oldest surviving European buildings in the New World. Atop a tower on the north-west side of the castle is La Giraldilla, the symbol of Havana, a weathervane in the form of Doña Inés de Bobadilla, the first and only female governor of Cuba and wife of the explorer Hernando de Soto. This is a replica of the original 1634 statue that was blown down in 1926, and is now safely ensconced in the **Museo de la Ciudad** (*see p57*).

Just south of the Real Fuerza, on the eastern side of the Plaza de Armas, lies **El Templete** (1828; *see p58*), the oldest existing neo-classical building in Havana. It occupies the site where the city was founded in 1519. Across the square from El Templete, the western side of the Plaza de Armas is dominated by the baroque **Palacio de los Capitanes Generales** (1770-91; *see p57*). Housing the Museo de la Ciudad and boasting one of the most beautiful courtyards in Havana, the *palacio* rivals the cathedral as the city's finest 18th-century building.

Leave the square and walk south along Calle Oficios, turning right on Calle Obrapía and you'll come to **Casa de la Obra Pía** (1665; *see p65*) at the corner of Calle San Ignacio. The building is most notable for its curvaceous baroque portico (which was carved in Cádiz in 1686 and shipped across the Atlantic). Today it houses a museum of 18th-century furniture and goods, as well as a collection of objects belonging to Cuban novelist Alejo Carpentier.

Return east on Calle Obrapía, turn right on Calle Oficios and walk to the Plaza de San Francisco de Asís. At the corner of Calle Amargura is the **Lonja del Comercio** (Stock Exchange, 1909; *see p61*). The building was renovated in 1996 to provide rental office space, adding a reflective glass upper floor, and while it's not much to look at from outside, visitors are allowed in to look at the cupola from inside.

Continue along Calle Oficios, turn right on Calle Muralla, and enter Plaza Vieja. On the south-east corner is the **Palacio Cueto** (1908), currently awaiting funds to restore it to its former glory as a five-star hotel. A whimsical building with art nouveau influences, it contrasts completely with the rest of the buildings on the *plaza*.

Across the square to the west sits the **Casa del Conde de San Juan de Jaruco** (1737; *see p62*), notable for its fine *mediopunto* stained-glass windows, which were used to filter the blinding rays of the tropical sun. *Mediopunto*, together with iron grilles and rounded arches, have become hallmarks of 'typical' Cuban architecture.

Continue west on Calle Muralla, turn left on Calle Cuba and walk to the corner of Calle Luz. The huge **Convento de Santa Clara** (1638-48; *see p69*), covering four city blocks, is a pre-baroque nunnery with rammed-earth walls and beautiful cloisters, which incorporates a church. The building looks plain from the outside, so it's worth entering to see the ornate wooden ceiling and lovely courtyards.

From here it's a short stroll back to Plaza Vieja, which has a wealth of various eating and drinking options, including Taberna de la Muralla (*see p110*) for cool pints.

Plaza de San Francisco, with its **Basílica** (*see p62*) and statue of a French gentleman.

look out for the plaster cross over the door, as it can be hard to spot). Across the street at No.13 is the self-explanatory **Depósito del Automóvil** (863 9942, closed Mon) and its collection of beautifully restored vehicles, which dates back to 1905. Halfway down Jústiz, between Calles Baratillo and Oficios, is a late 18th-century house that's now the **Casa de la Comedia** (*see p175*).

Back on Oficios is the former Colegio de San Ambrosio, which provided ecclesiastical studies for children from 1689 to 1774. The building is now the **Casa de los Árabes** (No.16, 861 5868), home to Havana's only mosque (*see p230*) and also to a modest selection of Islamic fabrics, weapons and household goods. Across the street is the Gabinete de Conservación y Restauración department of the City Historian's Office (No.19, entre Obrapía y Obispo, 861 5846), which holds workshops on restoring items such as colonial furniture, statuary, textiles, documents and ceramics. Though it's not a museum, visitors are welcome to check out the excellent 'before and after' photo exhibition in the entrance hall (a good way of getting to grips with the extent of renovation taking place in the area) and the 17th- and 18th-century objects on the patio.

Plaza de San Francisco

Formerly a small inlet covered by the waters of the bay, the spacious, paved Plaza de San Francisco dates from 1628. From the start the square was a commercial centre, and during the colonial period a fair took place here every October with coin and card games, lotteries and cock fights – perhaps an early sign of Havana's future role as a gambling mecca. One of the terminals of the Zanja Real, the first aqueduct in the Americas, the water source in the square helped to supply ships tied up at the wharves that fringed the square. In its day the buildings around the square have been home to some of the city's most wealthy and notable inhabitants, including the governor and mayor; the city jail was also once situated here.

Today the square is dominated by the 18th-century basilica on the south side, with its impressive tower, the Lonja del Comercio (1909) on the north side, and the Aduana (1914, Customs House) and Sierra Maestra cruise ship terminal on the east side. More modern additions include a Benetton, restaurants – whose tables, chairs and umbrellas are gradually sprawling unattractively into the treeless square – and the **Agencia de Viajes San Cristóbal** (*see p234*), which specialises in cultural tourism in Old Havana. In the centre of the square is the Carrara marble **Fuente de los Leones**, sculpted in 1836 by Italian artist Giuseppe Gaggini. The square is frequently used for girls' 15th birthday celebrations, so you're likely to see bevies of crinoline-wearing beauties self-consciously feeding the pigeons for photo opportunities.

The first thing to catch the eye as you enter the square is the 42-metre (140-foot) tower – the tallest colonial structure in Cuba after Trinidad's Iznaga Tower (*see p211*) – topping the baroque **Basílica Menor y Convento de San Francisco de Asís** (*see p62*); the convent houses a small museum containing exhibitions of religious art.

In front of the basilica is the endearing bronze statue **El Caballero de París** (Parisian Gentleman), actually a native of Spain, and Havana's most beloved homeless person, who died aged 85 in 1985. His remains are buried in the church. Touching his beard or fingers is meant to bring you good luck. The statue is by sculptor José Villa Soberón, who was also responsible for the statue of John Lennon in Vedado (*see p85*).

Accessible via the church and also through a gate behind the Fuente de los Leones is a garden in memory of Mother Teresa (who visited Cuba and met Castro in 1986). At the southern end of the garden is the **Sacra Iglesia Catedral Ortodoxa de San Nicolás de Mira** (Calle Churruca, esquina San Pedro (Avenida del Puerto), 862 6710), a tiny but lovely Greek Orthodox church. A Russian Orthodox church is currently being constructed a little way down the Avenida del Puerto; work is expected to be finished sometime in 2007.

A huge chunk of the plaza is taken up by the eclectic **Lonja del Comercio** (Stock Exchange, 866 9587/9588), which was spruced up by the City Historian's Office in 1996 to provide profitable office space for rent. The addition of an upper floor with a reflective glass façade obstructs the view of the beautiful golden dome crowned by a bronze statue of the god Mercury – a replica of the original work by Flemish artist Jean Boulogne (Giambologna) – but visitors can enter the building during working hours to admire the striking cupola (though no photography is allowed).

Exit at the back of the Lonja to see the curious **Jardín Diana de Gales** (Calle Baratillo, esquina Carpinetti), a garden planted in memory of Princess Diana, with two unattractive abstract sculptures by Cuban artists and an engraved Welsh slate plaque donated by the British ambassador.

Continuing south on Oficios, between the short street Churruca and Muralla is the eclectic early 20th-century **Palacio de Gobierno** (No.211, 863 4352). The Republican Chamber of Representatives was housed here until it moved to the Capitolio in 1929, and the Palacio became home to the Ministry of Education. Today the main building is a museum, with documents from the Republican period (1902-59), including the first passports ever issued in Cuba; it also houses the tiny **Museo de la Educación**, focusing on the literacy campaign in Cuba (note that Havana's key museum on education is the Museo de Alfabetización in Marianao; *see p94*) and the municipal government of La Habana Vieja.

Just before you get to the palace you'll see a railway carriage, the **Mambí**, parked incongruously on Churruca. It was used by successive early 20th-century Cuban presidents on their trips around the island and is worth a visit for the inlaid mahogany furniture, specially designed silver and glass and the ingenious early air-conditioning system.

Adjacent to the Palacio's annex is the leafy **Parque Alejandro de Humboldt**, named after the German naturalist considered by many to be Cuba's 'second discoverer' after Columbus. On the other side of Oficios is **Casa Alejandro de Humboldt** (*see p62*), where he worked during his first visit to Cuba. One block east on Santa Clara takes you to Calle San Pedro (Avenida del Puerto) and the **Muelle de Luz** (Luz Dock), which has ferries to Regla and Casablanca. One block north on San Pedro at the corner with Sol is the **Fundación Havana Club** (*see p62*), a museum about rum-making.

Heading back on Oficios and west on Brasil (Teniente Rey) brings you to the **Aqvarivm** (No.9; *see below*), a small freshwater aquarium. Continuing on Brasil, you'll come across archaeological sites that show portions of the 16th-century **Zanja Real** (Royal Canal); it was part of the original aqueduct that provided the city with fresh water from the Río Almendares, and was the first aqueduct to be built by the Spaniards as they settled in the Americas.

Aqvarivm

Calle Brasil (Teniente Rey) #9, entre Oficios y Mercaderes (863 9493). **Open** 9am-5pm Tue-Sat; 9am-1pm Sun. **Admission** CUC 1; free under-12s. **Map** p256 E15.

Set up by the City Historian's Office, this aquarium is a celebration of *habaneros'* obsession with keeping freshwater fish in tanks. Inside is pleasantly cool, and though some of the tanks are a little overcrowded, staff seem to take good care of them.

Basílica Menor y Convento de San Francisco de Asís

Calle Oficios, entre Amargura y Brasil (Teniente Rey) (862 9683/3467). **Open** 9am-6.30pm daily. **Admission** *Church & museum* CUC 2. *Tower* CUC 1; free under-12s. **Map** p256 E15.

Built between 1719 and 1738, this was one of Havana's most modish religious sites in its day. The basilica originally had a dome and crossing at the eastern end, but they were destroyed by a hurricane in 1846. The east wall of the central nave now boasts an arresting trompe l'œil mural of how the perspective of the church would have appeared before the dome's demise. Today the main hall of the church, with its excellent acoustics, is one of Havana's finest concert halls, home to the renowned all-female chamber orchestra Camerata Romeu. Chamber and choral music concerts are held every Saturday night and occasionally during the week.

The crypt of the basilica is the final resting place of numerous 17th- and 18th-century aristocrats. Between them, the basilica and the convent, with its exquisite storeyed cloisters and serene, fern-filled courtyards, house the Museo de Arte Religioso, with paintings by José Nicolás de la Escalera and Vicente Escobar, missals with tortoiseshell, ivory and hammered silver covers, polychrome wooden images and early marriage registries (one for whites and the other for *mestizos* and blacks). The armchairs and lectern used by Fidel Castro and Pope John Paul II during the latter's January 1998 visit to the island are also to be found here, upstairs in the north cloister. The tower is reached via a rickety wooden staircase; brave it for fine views over the city. It is occasionally closed for restoration. **Photo** *p60.*

Casa Alejandro de Humboldt

Calle Oficios #254, esquina Muralla (863 9850). **Open** 9am-4pm Tue-Sat; 9am-noon Sun. **Admission** free. **Map** p256 E15.

In this house, explorer Federico Enrique Alejandro de Humboldt (1769-1859) installed his instruments, and botany and mineral collections, during his first stay in Havana (1800-01). Restored as a museum, there are more than 250 scientific instruments, books, maps and works of art detailing Humboldt's work in Cuba. The museum is also the venue for major cultural, scientific and environmental events.

Fundación Havana Club (Museo del Ron)

Calle San Pedro (Avenida del Puerto) #262, esquina Sol (861 8051/862 3832/www.havanaclubfoundation.com). **Open** *Museum* 9am-5.30pm Mon-Thur; 9am-4pm Fri, Sat; 10am-4pm Sun. *Shop* 9am-7pm daily. **Admission** *Museum* CUC 5 (incl obligatory guided tour); free under-16s. **Map** p256 E15.

This promotional centre houses the Rum Museum. Displays cover the whole production cycle, including the harvesting of the sugar cane, sugar mills (with a tiny working model of a mill and distillery that children will love) and the processes of fermentation, distillation, filtration, ageing, blending and bottling. Tours happily emerge in the tasting room; you can also buy a liquid souvenir in the gift shop (*see p131*; be sure to enter the lottery for a bottle of 25-year-old San Cristóbal rum), and there's also a bar with excellent cocktails (*see p119*). The Fundación is also becoming a popular venue for contemporary art, with a gallery on the second floor.

Plaza Vieja

The 16th-century Plaza Vieja has always been a residential rather than a military, religious or administrative space, and is surrounded by elegant colonial residences, combined with a few very striking early 20th-century art nouveau buildings. Over the past 150 years, Plaza Vieja has played host to an open-air food market, a park, an outrageously misjudged car park built by Batista in 1952 (now demolished) and an amphitheatre. However, restoration is gradually re-establishing Plaza Vieja's original atmosphere; the Carrara showpiece fountain at the centre of the square is a replica of the original 18th-century one by Italian sculptor Giorgio Massari that was destroyed by the construction of the car park; and many of the 18th-century residences around the square are now restored with housing on the top floors and commercial establishments, including several small museums plus art and photo galleries, on the ground floor.

The best place to start is in the north-eastern corner of the square, where the intriguing **Cámara Oscura** (*see p63*), located atop Edificio Gómez Vila (1933), gives a bird's-eye view of Old Havana and the bay.

The oldest and best-preserved structure in the Plaza Vieja is the Casa del Conde de San Juan de Jaruco (1737) on the south side, restored as the **La Casona** art gallery (*see p152*). On the west side, look out for the original small frescoes on the façade of the mid 18th-century **Casa del Conde de Casa Lombillo** (No.364), restored in 1989. The **Centro de Desarrollo de las Artes Visuales** (862 9295, closed Sun, free, closed until mid 2007), on the plaza's north-west corner, was built in 1805 and has some interesting baroque woodwork. On the east side of the square is the 18th-century building that houses the **Fototeca de Cuba** (*see p152*), with photography exhibitions.

The lovely art nouveau **Palacio Cueto** (1908), on the south-eastern corner, is currently in a state of rack and ruin. Differing in style

Plaza Vieja. *See p62.*

from the rest of the square, this building was constructed initially as a hotel, was later converted into apartments, and is now awaiting an investment partner before it can be restored to its original role by the City Historian's Office. (In 1988 its façade featured in the Cuban movie *Vals para La Habana*.) On the south side of the square, the former home of historian Martín Félix de Arrate (No.101) now houses the **Museo de los Naipes 'Marqués de Prado Ameno'** (860 1534), dedicated to the somewhat specialist subject of playing cards.

There are still more sights in the immediate vicinity of Plaza Vieja. An interesting silkscreen workshop is located one block west of Plaza Vieja, on Calle Cuba. Inside the **Taller de Artes Serigráficas René Portocarrero** (No.513, entre Brasil (Teniente Rey) y Muralla, 862 3276, closed Sat & Sun) is a small gallery shop. A block north on Calle Cuba, at the corner of Amargura, is the former Iglesia y Convento de San Agustín, now the **Iglesia de San Francisco de Asís** (861 8490), known locally as San Francisco el Nuevo and not to be confused with the Basílica Menor y Convento de San Francisco de Asís (*see p62*). Built in 1633 by the Augustinians and later transferred to the Franciscans who renamed it, the convent has assumed various identities in its time. The altarpiece and cupola are stunning, but the church is often undergoing restoration. Today the building also houses the splendid **Museo Nacional de Historia de las Ciencias Carlos J Finlay** (*see below*).

Cámara Oscura

Calle Brasil (Teniente Rey), esquina Mercaderes (266 4461). **Open** 9am-5.20pm daily. **Admission** CUC 2; free under-12s. **Map** p256 E15.

Located on the top floor of the Edificio Gómez Vila, 35m (115ft) off the ground, the Cámara Oscura provides a 360-degree panoramic real-time 'moving image' of what's happening in much of La Habana Vieja. The only one of its kind in the Americas, the Cámara Oscura was donated to Cuba by Cádiz, Spain. There are great views from the roof.

Museo Nacional de Historia de las Ciencias Carlos J Finlay

Calle Cuba #460, entre Amargura y Brasil (Teniente Rey) (863 4824/4841/museofin@ceniai.ins.cu). **Open** 9am-5pm Mon-Sat. **Closed** until late 2007/early 2008. **Admission** CUC 2 (incl guide). **Map** p256 E15.

On 14 August 1881, when this former convent was a scientific academy, Cuban scientist Dr Carlos J Finlay presented his ground-breaking work naming the *Aedes aegipti* mosquito as the transmitter of yellow fever. Now a science museum, there are paintings, busts and portraits of erudite scientists from around the world, a panorama of medicine in Cuba and a display of Finlay's work. On the third floor is a restored 19th-century pharmacy. Note that the museum was closed as this guide went to press, but was due to reopen by early 2008 at the latest.

Calle Mercaderes

North of Plaza Vieja, the corner of Calles Amargura and Mercaderes is known as the **Cruz Verde** (Green Cross), due to a green-painted cross fastened to an old cornerstone (on a building now known as the Casa de La Cruz Verde). During the 18th and 19th centuries, this was the first stop for the Procession of the Cross (Vía Crucis) on Good Friday, which made its way from the Basílica Menor y Convento de San Francisco de Asís to the Iglesia del Santo Cristo del Buen Viaje.

Restoration of the building has provided housing for local people, as well as for the scrumptious **Museo del Chocolate** (*see p65*), a fine stop if your energy levels are flagging. Opposite, an 18th-century residence is almost fully restored as the future **Museo de Arte Ceremonial Africano**, but there was no clear opening date as this guide went to press. Likewise, the **Museo de Cerámica** is due to move to its new site here, but plans were still being finalised at press time.

Further north, on the corner of Mercaderes and Lamparilla, sits the tiny but lovely **Parque Rumiñahui**. The centrepiece of the park is a sculpture given to Fidel Castro by Ecuadorean artist Oswaldo Guayasamín. Opposite the park, on the other side of Mercaderes, is the luxury **Hostal Conde de Villanueva** (*see p39*), located in the elegant former home of the Conde de Villanueva (1789-1853), who was a key international promoter of Cuban cigars and a leader of Creole society.

Around Parque Simón Bolívar

Continuing north on Mercaderes, you'll reach **Parque Simón Bolívar** on the corner of Calle Obrapía. In addition to a statue of 'El Libertador' himself, the park has a ceramic mural (1998) by Venezuelan artist Carmen Montilla. South of the park is a small gunsmith's shop, the Armería de Cuba, which played a significant, if unwilling, part in the Revolution. Young Revolutionaries stormed the shop on 9 April 1958, the day of a general strike, to get weapons for the fight in the city. The shop now houses the **Museo Armería 9 de Abril** (861 8080, closed Mon), with displays of old guns.

On the western side of the Mercaderes/ Obrapía junction is **Habana 1791** (*see p132*), a boutique selling Cuban colognes and perfumes. Next door is **Terracota 4**, the studio-galleries of three ceramicists: Amelia Carballo, José Ramón González and Ángel Norniella. The **Casa-Museo Simón Bolívar** (*see p65*), which was inaugurated in 1993 to commemorate the 210th anniversary of the South American liberator's birth – and testament to his enduring popularity in the continent, is next door.

Located next to the park as you head east, is the 1796 building that houses the **Casa Oswaldo Guayasamín** (*see p64*), named

The **Museo del Chocolate** is a real sweet treat. *See p65.*

after the Ecuadorean-born 'artist of the Americas', who died in 1999.

Facing the park to the north on Obrapía is the Mexican-themed **Casa de Benito Juárez**, also known as the Casa de México (*see below*). Across Mercaderes on Obrapía, heading west, is the atmospheric **Casa de la Obra Pía** (*see below*), built in 1665 by a former solicitor general, Captain Martín Calvo de la Puerta y Arrieta. The house (and street) assumed the name Obra Pía (meaning 'pious act') in 1669, when the owner began providing dowries for orphan girls. It was restored as a museum in 1983. On the opposite side of the street, the **Casa de África** (Calle Obrapía #157, entre Mercaderes y San Ignacio, 861 5798, closed Mon), located in a 17th-century mansion, has displays including a large collection of gifts received by Castro from African countries, and a collection of *santería* icons belonging to Fernando Ortiz, the Cuban ethnographer and expert on Afro-Cuban culture.

Back on Mercaderes, the **Museo del Tabaco** (No.120, entre Obispo y Obrapía, 861 5795, closed Mon) offers a modest display of lithographic prints, old pipes and lighters, early cigar boxes and ashtrays, and a Casa del Habano (862 8472; *see p124* **Up in smoke**) on its ground floor. In the same building is the **Taller de Papel Artesanal** (no phone, closed Sun), which makes handmade paper using natural fibres, and recycled, textured paper. A couple of doors down is the fascinating **Maqueta de La Habana Vieja** (*see below*). Opposite is the small **Casa de Asia** (No.111, entre Obispo y Obrapía, 863 9740, closed Mon), which displays collections from different Asiatic cultures on the ground and first floors, including stone from the Great Wall of China.

Casa de Benito Juárez/ Casa de México

Calle Obrapía #116, esquina Mercaderes (861 8166/ mexico@cultural.ohch.cu). **Open** 9.30am-4.45pm Tue-Sat; 9.30am-12.45pm Sun. **Admission** free. **Map** p256 E15.

This pink building has a permanent display on the Aztecs, collections of silver- and copperwork, ceramics and textiles, plus pre-Columbian and popular handicrafts from Mexico. Two rooms feature rotating exhibitions by contemporary Mexican and Cuban artists.

Casa de la Obra Pía

Calle Obrapía #158, esquina Mercaderes (861 3097). **Open** 9am-4.45pm Tue-Sat; 9am-12.30pm Sun. **Admission** free. **Map** p256 E15.

This eye-catching yellow house has a large courtyard, coloured decorative friezes and a uniquely designed baroque portal made in 1686 in Cádiz, Spain. Its interior is filled with colonial furniture and linen goods typical of those that would have decorated the home of 18th-century Havana nobility. A permanent collection of objects belonging to Cuban novelist Alejo Carpentier (1904-80) is also housed here, including the blue Volkswagen he used when he was Cuban ambassador to UNESCO in Paris. The Casa de la Obra Pía is also home to the sisterhood of embroiderers and weavers of Belén, one of the Old Havana guilds that are being revived.

Casa Oswaldo Guayasamín

Calle Obrapía #111, entre Oficios y Mercaderes (861 3843). **Open** 9am-4.30pm Tue-Sat; 9am-noon Sun. **Admission** free. **Map** p256 E15.

Along with work by the late Ecuadorean artist Guayasamín (a close friend of Castro in his time), the upper floor has murals painted by renowned 18th-century Cuban painters José Nicolás de la Escalera and José Andrés Sánchez. A small shop sells Guayasamín silkscreens, lithographs, reproductions and jewellery.

Casa-Museo Simón Bolívar

Calle Mercaderes #156, entre Obrapía y Lamparilla (861 3988). **Open** 9am-5pm Tue-Sat; 9am-1pm Sun. **Admission** free. **Map** p256 E15.

Simón Bolívar, South American liberator, stayed here when he visited Havana in March 1799. The ground floor has detailed displays on his life and work, and there are also three art galleries with works by Cuban and international artists. The upper floor, with its splendid tinted-glass windows and curved iron and marble banister, has contemporary Venezuelan and Latin American paintings, sculptures and literature.

Maqueta de La Habana Vieja

Calle Mercaderes #116, entre Obispo y Obrapía (group visits 861 5001). **Open** 9am-6pm daily. **Admission** CUC 1; CUC 2 incl guide. **Map** p256 E15.

This meticulous and captivating scale model (1:500) of the Old City took three years to build, and shows some 3,500 buildings located within the square mile of the Old City. The experience is enlivened by an evocative sound and light show. Group visits should be co-ordinated through the Museo de la Ciudad on the above number.

Museo del Chocolate

Calle Mercaderes, esquina Amargura (866 4431). **Open** 10am-7.30pm daily. **Admission** free. **Map** p256 E15.

To call it a museum is an overstatement, perhaps, though there are some nice artefacts relating to the history of chocolate in Cuba. In any case, it's a lovely place to stop for a breather, whether you opt for a warming cup of hot chocolate (thick enough to stand your spoon in) or a soothing glass of cold chocolate. You can also watch chocolates being made at the back of the premises. Make sure you buy some truffles to take away. Note that there are often long queues for tables, and that the museum sometimes closes when the chocolate runs out or a VIP turns up for a visit.

Plaza de la Catedral & around

Originally named Plaza de la Ciénaga (Swamp Square) because of its muddy terrain, the **Plaza de la Catedral** – the last square built inside the walls of the old colonial city – became one of Havana's most important squares. Here, the main conduit of the Zanja Real – the city's first aqueduct, constructed between 1565 and 1592 – entered a cistern to supply the Spanish fleet docking in Havana. Once the square had been drained and paved, buildings were constructed around the central space to create a dry square embellished with porticoes, which provide shade and shelter from tropical rainstorms. In addition to the cathedral, which gives the square its definitive appearance, the other three sides are taken up by the façades of 18th-century aristocratic baroque mansions, all built within a 40-year period and showing a strong architectural harmony.

With its curves and flourishes above doors and windows, the **Catedral de La Habana** (*see below*) is Havana's finest example of 18th-century Cuban baroque. Baroque was late to arrive in Cuba, and the porous nature of the locally quarried limestone, which was embedded with coral fossils and seashells, handicapped its ornate style. Even so, Cuban writer Alejo Carpentier described the cathedral as 'music made into stone'. On the south side of the square, across from the cathedral, is the Casa del Conde de Casa Bayona (1720), also known as the Casa de Don Luís Chacón, the oldest house in the area and today the **Museo de Arte Colonial** (*see p67*).

The mid 18th-century **Casa de Lombillo**, on the eastern side of the square, is unusual in having three façades, a main one on Empedrado and the other two facing Mercaderes and the square. Today it houses the City Historian's Office and two galleries: one displaying 19th-century lithographs of Old Havana and the other a changing programme of contemporary exhibitions.

Next door, the **Casa del Marqués de Arcos** (1746) is a mansion that became a post office in the mid 19th century, a role it partially maintains to this day (look out for the unusual stone mask postbox in the wall). Restoration work has been hampered by severe subsidence – the square is still very marshy below the surface. The mansion's imposing main entrance is on Calle Mercaderes; stand here to get a good view of the striking mural by Cuban artist Andrés Carillo on the opposite wall, depicting 67 important artistic, literary and intellectual figures from 19th-century Cuba standing in front of or going into a mirror image of the building, which functioned as the Liceo de La Habana for many years. Further along Mercaderes, tucked away on the right-hand side as you head towards Plaza Vieja, is a lovely public garden, complete with bust of Hans Christian Andersen.

Back on Plaza de la Catedral, facing the Casa del Marqués de Arcos, is the Casa del Marqués de Aguas Claras, now touristy restaurant **El Patio** (*see p110*). Built between 1751 and 1775, it boasts an exquisite inner courtyard and elegant original 18th-century stained glass on its upper-storey windows. Next door, the commercial **Galería Victor Manuel** (*see p153*) occupies the former Casa de Baños (public bath house), which was built over the square's cistern in the 19th century.

The north-west corner of the square is occupied by the 18th-century Casa de los Condes de Peñalver, which has at different times served as a post office, a bank and a school. Today it houses the **Centro de Arte Contemporáneo Wifredo Lam** (*see p152*), one of Havana's best art galleries. Half a block west up Calle Empedrado is **La Bodeguita del Medio** (*see p105*), the renowned Hemingway haunt that today is more likely to be full of camera-wielding tourists than gravelly writers. A few doors further along is the **Fundación Alejo Carpentier** (Calle Empedrado #215, entre Cuba y San Ignacio, 861 5506, closed Sat & Sun), which promotes the work of one of Cuba's most important 20th-century writers. Another block west on Empedrado is **Parque San Juan de Dios**, which has a marble statue of Cervantes (1906).

Catedral de La Habana

Calle Empedrado #156, entre San Ignacio y Mercaderes, Plaza de la Catedral (861 7771).
Open 10.30am-3pm Mon-Fri; 10.30am-2pm Sat; 9am-noon Sun. **Mass** 7.15am Mon, Fri; 8.15pm Tue, Thur; 5.30pm Sat (special mass for children); 10.30am Sun. **Admission** free. **Map** p256 D15.

Construction of the cathedral was begun in 1748 by the Jesuits; though they were expelled from Cuba in 1767, work continued on the building for a further 20 years and in 1787 the Diocese of Havana was established and the church consecrated as the Catedral de la Virgen María de la Concepción Inmaculada. The two towers, which are different in size, continue to puzzle scholars: some say that one is larger to accommodate the interior staircase, while others argue that the other is narrower to avoid encroaching on the street.

The interior embellisment of the cathedral dates from the early 19th century, when the original baroque altars were replaced with neo-classical ones, and the original wood ceilings were plastered over. Its paintings, sculptures and gold- and silverwork were executed by the Italian masters Bianchini and Giuseppe Perovani. The eight large paintings by Jean Baptiste Vermay are copied from originals by Rubens and Murillo. Note that despite the official opening times, the cathedral is often locked, though you can sometimes gain access just before mass.

Museo de Arte Colonial

Casa del Conde de Casa Bayona, Calle San Ignacio #61, Plaza de la Catedral (862 6440). **Open** 9am-6pm daily. **Admission** CUC 2; CUC 3 incl guide; free under-12s. **Map** p256 D15.

This building once accommodated the Havana Club rum company, but became the Museo de Arte Colonial in 1969. Panelled ceilings with elaborate designs complement the collections of opulent colonial art, furniture, glasswork and porcelain.

Calle Tacón & northern Habana Vieja

Walking up from Calle Tacón's southern end (from O'Reilly) takes you past several adjoining houses of note. The oldest is the **Casa de Juana Carvajal** at No.12, dating from the early 17th century. It is named after a liberated slave who was given this building as an inheritance by her former owner, Lorenza Carvajal. Juana enlarged the house in 1725 and decorated the interior with friezes. In 1988 it was restored as the headquarters of the Gabinete de Arqueología, the archeology department of the City Historian's Office. No.4, built in 1759, is where the Havana Architectural Association was founded in 1916. Until recently, the building housed Italian restaurant **D'Giovanni** (*see p107*), but the restaurant has been moved next door because steam from the cooking was damaging the friezes, which were painted in the 17th century by anonymous Italian artists. No.4 might be turned into an extension of the **Gabinete de Arqueología de la Oficina del Historiador** (No.12, entre O'Reilly y Empedrado, 861 4469, closed Mon), which is dedicated to archaeological studies in Old Havana, and has a fascinating and often-overlooked exhibition of pre-Columbian art and objects from the 16th to the 19th centuries Restoration work on the friezes was still ongoing as this guide went to press, but you could still enter the foyer to see the large ceramic mural (a copy of a Klimt).

Back on Calle Tacón is the large and sombre baroque **Seminario San Carlos y San Ambrosio** (862 6989; currently closed for restoration). It was built in 1774 as a Jesuit seminary – renowned Cuban intellectuals José de la Luz y Caballero and Félix Varela were among its alumni – and still functions as such. It boasts one of the most tranquil courtyards in Havana and a magnificent library; visitors are welcome (ring the bell to the right of the entrance). In front of the seminary is the popular crafts market (*see p135*), though the market was due to move some time in 2007 to the newly restored Alamacenes San José on Calle Luz, between Oficios and Avenida del Puerto.

Through the park and over the other side of Tacón is the white Carrara marble **Fuente de Neptuno** (Neptune Fountain), which dates from 1838; beyond it is the bay. North of the Seminario is a small castle, built in 1939 as an imitation colonial fortress to house the police (today it is the General Command of the Policia Nacional Revolucionaria, or PNR). In front of the castle is **Parque Arqueológico de la Maestranza**, which shows the remains of one of the earliest artillery factories in Latin America. To the west is Parque Infantil 'La Maestranza', a small children's amusement area, and to the north is Parque Anfiteatro. Inland is the **Palacio de la Artesanía** (*see p132*), a popular stop for handicrafts, books and music. Housed in the palatial late 18th-century home of Mateo Pedroso y Florencia, one of the city's richest slave traders, the building constitutes a typical example of the spatial distribution common in Havana's 18th-century domestic buildings, with open ground-floor areas suitable for retail, warehousing and stabling, a cramped mezzanine floor for slave quarters and high-ceilinged, airy family rooms.

North of here, where the road curves around into Monserrate, is the handsome Casa de Francisco Pons (1906), which now houses the wonderful **Museo Nacional de la Música** (*see below*). Head south on Compostela to reach the unusual **Iglesia del Santo Ángel Custodio** (861 0469), opposite the Museo de la Revolución (*see p73*). The church's wedding-cake appearance is due to a mixture of 17th-century Gothic and 19th-century neo-Gothic styles. Félix Varela and José Martí were baptised in the church, and renowned 19th-century Cuban writer Cirilo Villaverde used it as the setting for the key scene of his famous romantic novel, *Cecilia Valdés*, when the heroine has her lover stabbed on the steps of the church as he is about to marry another woman.

Museo Nacional de la Música

Calle Capdevila #1, entre Habana y Aguiar (861 9846). **Open** 10am-5pm Mon-Sat. **Admission** CUC 2; free under-15s. **Map** p256 D15.

Displays at the museum of music include an unusual collection of African drums, string instruments, music boxes, old American phonographs, a Chinese organ and one of the first gramophones (1904) made by the Victor Talking Machine Company. A small shop sells CDs, cassettes and magazines.

Calle Obispo & around

One of the first streets to be constructed in La Habana Vieja, and still one of the liveliest in the area, Calle Obispo runs from Plaza de Armas almost as far as Parque Central. This street is great for strolling and bustles with life – courtesy of a blend of tourists and locals (including plenty of hustlers). It's lined with shops offering handicrafts, art and books, plus bars, restaurants and holes-in-the-wall selling cheap pizzas and ice-cream.

The dignified and eclectic 1920s **Hotel Ambos Mundos** (*see p41*) occupies the intersection of Obispo and Mercaderes. Ernest Hemingway stayed here off and on during the 1930s, and began writing *For Whom the Bell Tolls* in room 511. The room has been restored as a mini museum featuring Hemingway's desk and authentic furniture from the period. Across the street is a late 1950s building, notable for being out of character with the surrounding area. An old Dominican convent, which became the Universidad de La Habana in 1728, originally stood on this site, but was knocked down in the early 20th century. In 1958 the present – rather hideous – building of offices and a heliport was constructed and all that remains of the university is the bell. The building was recently re-clad in dark mirror glass, and part of it is a new university college affiliated to the University of Havana, with the rest of the space given over to shops, exhibition spaces, a library and so on.

The **Farmacia Taquechel** (*see p134*) at No.155, with its floor-to-ceiling cedar and mahogany shelves and 19th-century French porcelain apothecary's jars, is worth a browse, as is **Droguería Johnson** (862 0311), two blocks up the street at the corner with Aguiar. Unfortunately, a fire in March 2005 consumed the lovely mahogany interior, but as this guide went to press work was under way to restore it.

On the corner of Obispo and Calle Cuba is the 1907 Banco Nacional de Cuba, one of the first buildings constructed after the Republic was born in 1902. The Ministerio de Finanzas y Precios and the **Museo de las Finanzas** (Calle Obispo #211, esquina Cuba, 867 1800 ext 1007, closed Sun) – check out the magnificent old round vault door – are now located here. In the early 20th century this area was known as Havana's Wall Street because of the high concentration of banks. Francophiles can make a detour from here to Calle O'Reilly: at No.311 is the **Casa Víctor Hugo** (*see below*).

Back on Obispo, at No.305, is the **Museo Numismático** (861 5811/863 5380, closed Mon), which contains an interesting selection of coins dating from the conquest to the present.

Not to be missed nearby is the **Oratorio de San Felipe Neri** (no phone), on the corner of Obrapía y Aguiar. Its opening times are erratic, but it's worth a little detour when walking along Obispo to check for announcements on the façade. A 17th-century oratory converted to a bank in the early 19th century, lyric theatre and song are performed here during music festivals.

On the corner of Obispo and Cuba is the elegant neo-classical **Hotel Florida** (*see p41*). Built in 1836 and a hotel since 1885, it hass kept its beautiful inner patio and arches throughout its life. At the western end of Obispo is a cluster of good bookstores (*see p126*). At the very end, where Obispo hits Monserrate, is the highly popular bar **El Floridita** (*see p108*), where the Daiquiri, king of cocktails, was born. Inside are photographs and a statue of the Floridita's most famous client, Ernest Hemingway.

On the adjacent *plazoleta* (small square) is an exceptionally elegant life-size Carrara marble statue of engineer Francisco de Albear y Lara, sculpted in 1895 by Cuban artist José Villalta de Saavedra. Albear built an aqueduct, still functioning, which was awarded the gold medal for technical and aesthetic excellence at the Paris Exhibition in 1878. Across the street is the luscious, imposing Centro Asturiano (1927), a Spanish Renaissance building, now part of the Bellas Artes complex (*see p72*).

Heading north along Avenida Bélgica (part of the western boundary of Old Havana), at No.261, is the opulent art deco **Edificio Bacardí** (862 9310). Built in 1930 for the Bacardí company, it is topped by the company's bat emblem, which also appears on locks and the Lalique glass lamp fittings you'll find throughout the building. For the best view of the building, go to the rooftop terrace of Hotel Plaza located across the street.

Casa Víctor Hugo

Calle O'Reilly #311, entre Aguiar y Habana (866 7590/1). **Open** 9am-4.45pm Mon-Fri; 9am-1pm Sat. **Admission** free (donations welcome). **Map** p256 D15.

Opened by the Oficina del Historiador in 2005 to mark the bicentenary of the death of Victor Hugo, this neo-classical mansion contains French exhibits such as books, newspapers and other historical documents. Screenings of French films are also held here. Check out the bust of Huge in the courtyard.

Plaza del Cristo

A sleepy little park that you'll find just three blocks south of Obispo on Bernaza, Plaza del Cristo was created in 1640 around the Ermita del Humilladero. The hermitage was the final station on the Vía Crucis (procession of the

In with the old

'One cannot build the future by erasing the past. We are building the Havana that the past – our profound knowledge of it, its ever-present spirit – inspires us to create, but we are making a city of the present that looks towards the future.' These are the words of Eusebio Leal, charismatic head of the Oficina del Historiador de la Ciudad (City Historian's Office) in Havana, the group responsible for much of the restoration work you will see in your walks through Old Havana.

The concept for the funding of this project is simple but effective: all profits earned in the restaurants, bars and hotels of La Habana Vieja are invested directly back into the city's restoration. But in addition to the physical renovation of the buildings, the organisation hopes to bring about a spiritual renaissance in the life of the Old City. Services for visitors are a key financial focus, but the balance between tourism and local rejuvenation is given very careful attention.

Alongside the opening of upmarket hotels within existing historic buildings, new structures have been created from scratch, among them an old people's home and a ay-care centre for children with degenerative illnesses. In addition, housing in less touristy areas of the city – such as a 14-block strip across from the Malecón – has also started receiving the attention it deserves.

Indeed, housing is Old Havana's most pressing problem; the historical centre has more than 70,000 inhabitants cramped closely together in 22,500 'units', most of which are the results of multiple subdivisions of the existing space made over more than a century. These appalling conditions constitute an urgent challenge for the authorities.

In 1981 a planning programme was devised for much-needed restoration work. Each of the 3,500 buildings in the historical centre has been assigned a grade of historical/ aesthetic importance, a proposed end use and a carefully costed restoration schedule. Restorations have already been completed in large sections of the Old City, but the situation is still grave – there's a serious structural collapse about once every three days. You'll notice that *habaneros* instinctively cross to the other side of the street rather than walk too close to a shaky façade or a crumbling balcony.

Furthermore, when the government recently initiated a crackdown on 'corruption' and introduced tighter controls on every remotely entrepreneurial project, the restoration schedule came under threat, slowing to a crawl. It's hoped that it will continue in due course – but while some people may claim that Old Havana will be unrecognisable in two years, our advice is, as with everything else in Cuba: don't hold your breath.

cross; *see also p63*), which took place every year during Lent. The baroque **Iglesia del Santo Cristo del Buen Viaje** (Brasil (Teniente Rey), esquina Bernaza, 863 1767) now covers the site of the old hermitage on the north-eastern side of the plaza. Of the original building, only the enclosure and painted wood ceiling still remain.

A couple of blocks east on Calle Brasil (Teniente Rey), at the corner of Compostela, is **Farmacia La Reunión** (*see p134*), once known as Farmacia Sarrá, and the most beautiful of the old pharmacies in Old Havana. The interiors are extraordinary: one half is Gothic with early Revolutionary decorative additions, the other part is neo-classical. Check out, too, the old surgical and dental instruments lying around the place.

Across the road from the pharmacy on Calle Compostela stands the former **Convento de Santa Teresa**, which is destined to be restored for use as a hotel eventually.

Southern Habana Vieja

A poorer area less frequented by tourists, the southern part of Old Havana offers visitors the chance to enjoy the more natural pace of daily life, and to visit some lovely churches and convents. Three blocks south of Farmacia Sarrá, at the junction of Calles Compostela and Luz, is the 1720 baroque **Convento e Iglesia de Nuestra Señora de Belén** (*see p70*).

Along Calle Acosta, one block west of Calle Compostela, is the orthodox **Sinagoga Adath Israel de Cuba** (Calle Acosta #357, esquina Picota, 860 8242). The synagogue was recently renovated and is open to visitors again, though you should phone to check it's open first. From Calle Compostela, two blocks east on Calle Luz is one of Old Havana's must-see sights: the exquisite 17th-century **Convento e Iglesia de Santa Clara** (*see p70*).

South of here, on the corner of Calles Cuba and Acosta, is the **Iglesia del Espíritu**

Santo (Calle Cuba, esquina Acosta, 862 3410). Claiming to be the oldest church in Havana, the original hermitage, built in 1638 for freed slaves, no longer exists. Elegant and dignified, this simple church contains murals, stained glass and a wooden ceiling. Two blocks further south is the baroque mid 18th-century **Convento e Iglesia de La Merced** (*see below*). Its plain exterior contrasts sharply with its striking interior – well worth a visit.

South-west of here you enter the old working-class neighbourhood of **San Isidro**, one of Old Havana's poorest areas. On the corner of Calle Leonor Pérez (Paula) and Avenida de la Bélgica (Egido) is the **Casa Natal de José Martí** (*see below*), birthplace of Cuba's national hero.

At the eastern end of Calle Leonor Pérez (Paula), overlooking the bay, is the baroque **Iglesia de San Francisco de Paula** (*see below*), unusual for its isolated location in the middle of a busy portside road. The walkway at the front of the church leads to the dockside **Alameda de Paula**, the first promenade to be constructed in La Habana Vieja. Created in 1771, it was originally a dirt track stretching three blocks and bordered by two lines of poplar trees. In 1805 a tiled pavement was added along with some stone seats; later, a fountain with a commemorative column was built in honour of the Spanish navy (only the column survives). One block south on Luz to San Pedro (Avenida del Puerto) takes you to the stately neo-classical **Hotel Armadores de Santander** (*see p41*), built in 1827.

Casa Natal de José Martí

Calle Leonor Pérez (Paula) #314, entre Bélgica (Egido) y Picota (861 3778). **Open** 9am-6pm daily. **Admission** CUC 1; CUC 2 incl guide; free under-12s. **Map** p256 F14.

This modest dwelling, dating from 1810, was where Cuban national icon José Martí was born on 28 January 1853: the Martí family rented the upper storey at the time. Inside are objects relating to Martí's life and work: possessions, manuscripts, photographs and furniture.

Convento e Iglesia de La Merced

Calle Cuba #806, entre Leonor Pérez (Paula) y Merced (863 8873). **Open** 8am-noon, 3-5pm daily. **Mass** 9am Mon-Sat; 9am, noon Sun. **Admission** free. **Map** p256 F15.

Built between 1755 and 1876, La Merced is arguably one of Cuba's most beautiful churches. Its lavish robin-eggshell blue interior has high arches and frescoes covering the chapel and cupola. The Capilla de Lourdes (Lourdes Chapel) has an outstanding collection of religious paintings by renowned Cuban artists: Estéban Chartrand, Miguel Melero, Pidier Petit and Juan Crosa, among others. The other chapel has a peaceful grotto. The convent's serene courtyard features some interesting statuary.

Convento e Iglesia de Nuestra Señora de Belén

Calle Compostela, entre Luz y Acosta (860 3150/861 2846). **Open** 8am-6pm Mon-Fri. **Admission** free. **Map** p256 E15.

Built in 1720 as a Franciscan convent, church and hospital for the poor, Belén was taken over by the Jesuits in the mid 19th century and underwent more than two centuries of renovation and expansion. The unusual vaulted arch, built in 1775 over Calle Acosta to the south, connects the convent with its neighbouring buildings. More extraordinary is the Real Observatorio (Royal Observatory), built in 1858 on top of the tower of the school, and used continuously until 1925. The Jesuits were Cuba's first official weather forecasters and used the observatory for the study of hurricanes and other tropical weather patterns. The observatory was the first of its kind in the Caribbean and, over time, became one of the most important weather stations in the Americas. It's now under restoration for a few years as the future Museo de Meteorología y Astronomía.

Convento e Iglesia de Santa Clara

Calle Cuba #610, entre Sol y Luz (866 3631/861 2877/5043). **Open** 9am-4.30pm Tue-Sat; 9am-12.30pm Sun. **Admission** CUC 2 (incl guide); free under-12s. **Map** p256 E15.

Built between 1638 and 1643, Santa Clara was the city's first nunnery, with its occupants coming from Cartagena de Indias in Colombia. It remained a working nunnery until 1922, when the nuns sold the church and convent and moved to a new site. Apparently, for the next 40 days, people visited the convent continuously to see what was behind its formerly impenetrable walls. The simple, stark exterior of the building and its thick rough stone walls belie the surprising richness of the interior, which features ornately carved wooden ceilings and beautiful leafy patios, open for visits. Two of the three cloisters are fully restored: one houses the Centro Nacional de Conservación, Restauración y Museología (CENCREM), the organisation in charge of restoring artefacts from all over Cuba; the other contains a small free-standing building run as a cheap and moderately cheerful Moorish-style *hostal,* Residencia Académica (*see p44*).

Iglesia de San Francisco de Paula

Avenida del Puerto, esquina San Ignacio (860 4210). **Open** 9am-7pm daily. **Admission** free. *Concerts* (Fri) CUC 5/10. **Map** p256 F15.

In 1664 a chapel and women's hospital were built on this site; both were destroyed in a hurricane in 1730 and, 15 years later, rebuilt in a baroque style. In the 1940s the hospital and part of the church were torn down. It has now been restored as a concert hall; the ashes of famous Afro-Cuban violinist Claudio José Domingo Brindis de Salas are preserved here. Inside is a tiny religious art museum. It is also the base and rehearsal space of Ars Longa, the Office of the City Historian's ancient music group. Note that Mass is not held in this church.

Centro Habana

A no-frills, densely packed part of town, with a distinct character of its own.

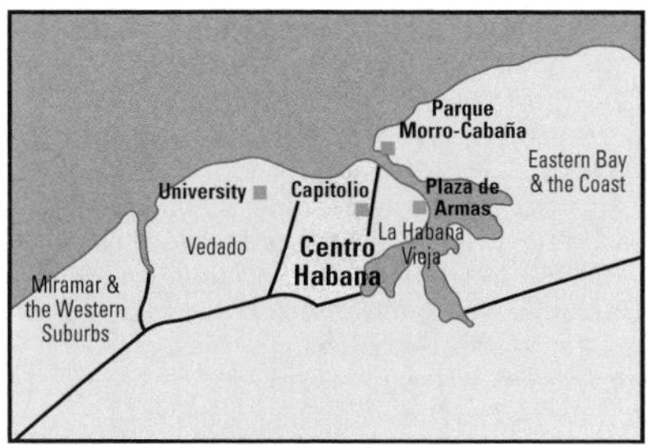

Maps p254 & p255

Known for its crumbling buildings, potholed streets, lack of greenery and people crammed into every nook and cranny, Centro Habana is often overlooked by visitors who prefer the more tourist-friendly areas of La Habana Vieja and Vedado. Yet it would be a mistake to bypass Centro, with its neighbourhoods that throb with life, the city's only Chinatown, and the high-energy commercial streets of San Rafael, Neptuno and Italia (Galiano), which have been springing back to life in recent years.

Much of Centro Habana's history is related to that of the city walls (*las murallas*), built between 1674 and 1797 to encircle the Old City. By 1863 La Habana Vieja had become so overcrowded that the demolition of the walls was ordered, to open up land in the bordering areas. From 1880 on, a huge amount of construction took place, and, in keeping with a period of growth in Havana as a whole, the area soon became more sophisticated, with the construction of sumptuous palaces, and the development of nightlife and culture. Centro Habana's new look, in particular in its eastern reaches, was finished in the 1920s, when French urbanist Jean-Claude Nicolas Forestier was contracted to landscape the area.

These days the area may be somewhat neglected – after all, it is mainly a residential zone rather than one frequented by many tourists – but there are plans to improve the situation. Since 1995, for example, the City Historian's Office has been slowly restoring the buildings along the Malecón, starting with the façades along the oldest and most traditional part of the seafront. Hopefully, the rest of Centro will get the attention it deserves in due course.

From the Capitolio north along El Prado

Paseo del Prado (known as 'El Prado') was the first promenade to be built outside the city walls. Completed in 1772, it was envisaged as a place where locals could stroll and socialise. It became popular with Havana's bourgeoisie, eager to show off their fashionable European gowns and suits. El Prado was remodelled in 1834, and prominent buildings sprang up. By 1928 Forestier had introduced bronze lions, lamp-posts and marble benches to this key artery. These days the shady tree-lined street is an essential attraction for tourists.

The domed **Capitolio** (*see p72*) dominates El Prado's southern end; check it out from the Hotel Sevilla's Roof Garden restaurant (*see p112*). Across the street from the Capitolio to the east is the **Sala Polivalente 'Kid Chocolate'** (*see p185*), an indoor sports arena named after Cuba's second finest amateur boxer (after Teófilo Stevenson), who won two world titles after going pro and moving to the US.

The capital's **Capitolio**. *See p72.*

Capitolio

Paseo de Martí (Prado), entre San Martín (San José) y Dragones (861 5519). **Open** 9am-7pm daily. **Admission** CUC 3; CUC 4 incl guide; free under-12s. **Map** p255 E14.

Look familiar? This smaller clone of Washington's neo-classical Capitol building was built between 1926 and 1929 by Enrique García Carrera. The 62m (207ft) dome was the highest point in the city until 1958, when it was surpassed by the José Martí monument in the Plaza de la Revolución (*see p88*). The steps up from El Prado are flanked by bronze statues from Italian sculptor Angelo Zanelli, who also created the one inside the foyer, which at 17.7m (58ft) tall is the world's third largest indoor statue. The 24-carat diamond embedded in the floor in front of the statue is a replica of the original, which was stolen (and later recovered); it marks point zero of Cuba's central highway network.

The Capitolio is a cache of pleasant surprises, from original fine art and a vast 300,000 tome library with mahogany floor-to-ceiling shelves to the unusual acoustics that reverse the sound of footsteps in the Salón de los Pasos Perdidos (Hall of the Lost Steps). The wings on either side of the entrance hall once housed the ornate Senate and Chamber of the House of Representatives, but now governmental offices are at the Plaza de la Revolución. **Photo** *p71*.

Parque Central & around

Bordered by El Prado, Zulueta (Agramonte), Obrapía and Neptuno, **Parque Central** was laid out in 1877. At its centre is the 1905 statue of José Martí in Carrara marble, by José Villalta de Saavedra – the first monument in the country dedicated to the poet, writer, lawyer and fighter for Cuban independence. He obviously inspires locals, who gather in the park under his gaze to debate passionately about baseball (*see p187* ***Esquina caliente***).

Several key hotels border the park, including the eclectic **Hotel Inglaterra** (*see p44*), whose pavement is paved with tiles glazed with images from contemporary artists. Its café was a popular meeting point for youthful *habaneros* rebelling against the Spanish regime, and is still a good place to watch the action on El Prado. Opposite the north-east corner of the park is the **Hotel Plaza**, and on the Neptuno side is the luxury **Hotel NH Parque Central** (for both, *see p44*), a harsh modern effort that stands at odds with its surroundings. On the corner of El Prado and Obrapía is the neo-baroque **Gran Teatro de La Habana** (*see p174*), with its magnificent interior monumental staircase and exterior decoration. This end of Calle San Rafael (to the right of the theatre as you face it) is the beginning of a five-block pedestrian-only stretch, bordered by shops, restaurants and cafés, that leads towards Chinatown (*see p77*).

Museo Nacional de Bellas Artes & around

The **Museo de la Revolución** (*see p73*) and **Memorial Granma** (behind the museum) are essential visits for anyone wanting to get to grips with the Cuban Revolution. A major overhaul was due for completion some time in 2007, but it is still open for visits. Across from the Granma exhibit is the Cuban wing (Arte Cubano) of the **Museo Nacional de Bellas Artes** (*see below*), which reopened in 2001 after an expensive renovation. It is now easily Havana's most impressive museum.

The **Real Fábrica de Tabacos La Corona** (*see p78*) cigar factory, which used to be across the street from the museum, moved to Cerro at the end of 2005.

Two blocks south of Bellas Artes is the **Museo de los Bomberos** (Firefighters' Museum; Agramonte/Zulueta #257, entre Virtudes y Ánimas, 862 7762, closed Mon & Sun). Located in the fire station (1910), it is easily recognisable by its triumphal arch-like façade. Inside is a small, charming exhibition about Cuba's firefighters, including some old horse-drawn firefighting water tanks.

Museo Nacional de Bellas Artes

Arte Cubano: Calle Trocadero, entre Zulueta (Agramonte) y Avenida de Bélgica (Monserrate) (861 3858/www.museonacional.cult.cu).
Arte Universal: Calle San Rafael, entre Zulueta (Agramonte) y Avenida de Bélgica (Monserrate) (861 3858). **Open** *Both* 10am-6pm Tue-Sat; 10am-2pm Sun. **Admission** *Arte Cubano* CUC 5. *Arte Universal* CUC 5. *Joint ticket* CUC 8. Free under-14s. **Map** p256 D14.

The National Museum of Fine Arts, opened in its current location in 1954, was reopened in 2001 to unanimous praise, following a five-year closure. No expense had been spared on the renovation work, catapulting it straight into the don't-miss category. The art collection – totalling nearly 50,000 works – has been divided into two separate buildings: the Cuban art collection (Arte Cubano), which stayed in the original Palacio de Bellas Artes (1954) on Trocadero, and the international collection (Arte Universal), which was installed in the refurbished Arte Universal wing two blocks down on San Rafael, half a block east of Parque Central in the former Centro Asturiano, a beautiful early 20th-century Spanish Renaissance-style building.

The Arte Cubano building takes in more than 30,000 works organised into sections: colonial, turn-of-the-last-century, modern and contemporary. This collection incorporates the very best of Cuban art, and is by far the most comprehensive in the country, with works by key artists such as Amelia Peláez, René Portocarrero and Wifredo Lam, as well as more recent works by Zaida del Río and Roberto Fabelo.

The international collection (Arte Universal) is a passable survey of world art – divided by country of origin, with pieces ranging from the 16th century to the present – but it blanches when compared to the building itself. Its entry hall is staggering: a cavernous space with a massive staircase crowned on both sides by carved marble lions, while the celestial stained-glass ceiling depicts Columbus's arrival in the Americas. The restoration is the masterpiece of Cuban architect José Linares, a tireless visionary. The largest collections in Arte Universal are Italian, French and Spanish – and these should be the essential stops on any fleeting visit. Those with more time may want to investigate the fourth floor, dedicated to ancient art; it houses mainly Greek, Roman and Egyptian sculpture and artefacts, the most impressive being a Greek amphora from the fifth century BC in remarkably good nick. Other small collections include German, Dutch, Flemish, Latin American and US works.

Museo de la Revolución

Calle Refugio #1, Avenida de las Misiones y Agramonte (Zulueta) (862 4092/3). **Open** 10am-5pm daily. **Admission** CUC 5; CUC 7 incl guide; free under-12s. **Map** p256 D15.

The Museum of the Revolution is located in the elegant Palacio Presidencial, the official residence of 21 Cuban presidents between 1920 and 1965. The Revolutionary government announced its first new laws here in 1959 and continued to use the palace until 1965 when its headquarters moved to the Plaza de la Revolución. In 1974 the building was turned into a museum dedicated to the Cuban Revolution.

The palace was designed by Cuban Carlos Maruri and Belgian Paul Belau, with the interior decoration entrusted to Tiffany of New York. Highlights of the interior include the Salón de los Espejos, which is a replica of the Hall of Mirrors in the Palace of Versailles. The Salón Dorado (Golden Hall) is made of yellow marble with gold embossing on the walls, and there are four canvases by Esteban Valderrama and Mariano Miguel González mounted on 18-carat gold sheets. There are permanent exhibitions on the history of Cuban struggles from the 15th century to the present, including Che Guevara's pipe and the uniform of Cuban cosmonaut Arnaldo Tamayo.

One hall is dedicated to the Special Period (*see p23* **Desperate times...**), the emergency plan taken on by Cuba in the early 1990s when the collapse of the Soviet Union took away 85% of the island's trade, to devastating effect. Bullet holes from a failed coup carried out by students in 1957 are still visible in the palace's main stairway.

Behind the museum (and included in the ticket price) is an exhibit of the *Granma* yacht, in which Fidel and 81 others sailed from Tuxpán, Mexico, to Cuba in December 1956 to launch the Revolution. The boat, displayed behind glass, is surrounded by planes, vehicles and weapons used during the Revolutionary wars against Batista and in the Battle of Playa Girón (Bay of Pigs).

The **Museo de la Revolución**.

The northern stretch of El Prado

The **Palacio de los Matrimonios** (Prado #306, esquina Ánimas, 862 5781, closed Mon) is one of the most popular places to get married in Havana. The 1914 building is a former Spanish social club, and its upper floor is worth a peek for its deliciously ostentatious ornamentation. The *palacio* was closed for renovations as this guide went to press, with work expected to continue throughout 2007. The nearby **Unión Árabe de Cuba**, representing some 8,000 mainly Lebanese Arab descendants, has a small art gallery with rotating exhibitions on Arab-influenced art and ceramics. East along Trocadero is the stunning Moorish-style **Hotel Sevilla** (*see p46*), built in 1908 and now fully restored. Al Capone and his bodyguards are reputed to have taken over the entire sixth floor on a visit here.

North on El Prado, at Trocadero, is the Casa de José Miguel Gómez (1915), once home of the Republic's first president, and now the **Casa del Científico** (*see p47*) – a hotel, restaurant and bar. It has a striking stained-glass window and an observation tower with views of El Prado. The **Escuela Nacional de Ballet** (Prado #207, entre Trocadero y Colón, closed Sat & Sun, visits arranged through CENEARTE – 202 2326) is located immediately north in the first 20th-century palace to be constructed in this area as a social centre. Inside, two mightily impressive monumental staircases lead up to the lavishly decorated upper floors. Further north, at Calle Colón, is the **Teatro Fausto** (*see p176*), with its interesting art deco-inspired exterior.

Fishermen on the **Malecón**.

La Punta & around

Off El Prado's northern terminus is the **Castillo de San Salvador de la Punta** (*see below*), finished in 1600. This castle, and its counterpart El Morro across the bay (*see p95*), was built when the Spanish realised that they had to buck up their efforts to keep out marauders. In 2002 it was impressively restored and opened to visitors.

On the corner of Malecón and El Prado is the **Memorial a los Estudiantes de Medicina**, constructed around the remains of a wall used by colonial firing squads, and built in memory of eight medical students who, on 27 November 1871, were shot here by loyalist soldiers, after being falsely accused of desecrating the tomb of a Spanish journalist who had writtin in opposition to Cuba's independence. Every 27 November medical students and other youths gather at this site to pay homage to their memory.

To the south-east of the memorial is a further reminder of Havana's brutal colonial past: the newly restored remains of the **Cárcel de La Habana** (Avenida de los Estudiantes, entre Paseo de Martí (Prado) y Agramonte (Zulueta)), where many Cuban revolutionaries who fought against Spanish colonialism, including José Martí, were imprisoned. Today it houses small art exhibitions, with a modest display of photos and torture devices. Note that it's only open in the mornings, and is closed all day Monday.

Presiding over the bay is the massive marble and bronze **Monumento a Máximo Gómez**. Designed by Italian sculptor Aldo Gamba and unveiled in 1935, this striking monument honours the Dominican commander-in-chief of Cuba's Liberation Army, a key figure in Cuban independence struggles. A spiralling road leads to the underwater tunnel linking metropolitan Havana with the eastern beaches and bay.

Castillo de San Salvador de la Punta

Avenida del Puerto, esquina Paseo de Martí (Prado) (860 3196). **Open** 10am-6pm Wed-Sun. **Admission** CUC 5; free under-12s. **Map** p255 C15.

The fort of San Salvador was designed by Giovanni Bautista Antonelli, who also created the Castillo de los Tres Reyes del Morro (*see p95*) on the opposite side of the harbour mouth. It was commissioned by Captain General Juan de Texeda, whose name can still be seen cut into a stone in the bulwark to the right of the entrance. Every night for centuries a 250m (820ft) chain boom was raised between the two castles to keep out marauding shipping, and the chain's terminal on the Punta side, three massive upended cannons, can still be seen.

The British invasion in the mid 1700s seriously damaged the fort – walk around to the Morro side to see a British cannonball still embedded in the wall. (If the guards make a fuss, ask to see Señor Echeverría, the director; he'll probably escort you and give you a fascinating lecture in English on Havana's fortifications.) Despite the damage, it continued to be used for defence through the 19th century. By the time the 20th century came around it was anything but a protective bastion, and at one point was even used as a cow barn. Nevertheless, a trophy restoration, finished in 2002, raised the fort to its original height by clearing out its moat, and unearthed relics spanning five centuries.

Initially, the fort housed some of these artefacts, plus a ship gallery with models of historic vessels and a unique collection of riches – gold bars, emeralds, pieces of eight and treasure boxes – from 16th- to 19th-century treasure galleons that sank off the Cuban coast. But the area's susceptibility to flooding caused by hurricanes has resulted in the decision to move these exhibits to the Castillo de la Real Fuerza (*see p57*), which will also house a new scale model of the 17th-century *Santísima Trinidad*, built in Havana. La Punta will be used as a site museum, with displays from the fortress itself. This is scheduled to happen by mid to late 2007, the same time that the exhibitions at the Museo de la Real Fuerza will be available to the public. In the meantime, although you can walk into La Punta, there is little to see other than the structure itself.

Along the Malecón & Calle San Lázaro

The Malecón pedestrian promenade and seawall was constructed between 1901 and 1954 to maximise access to the seafront. No trip to Havana is complete without spending some time strolling and lingering along its seven-kilometre (4.5-mile) arc that anchors Havana's waterfront. Now a 24-hour source of adventure, the Malecón provides vital breathing space for *habaneros*, and the section fronting Centro Habana, with its neo-classical and neo-Moorish buildings – many in a tumbledown state from constant battering by waves and salt water spray – is the most picturesque of all. Walking west along the Malecón from the foot of El Prado, the first building that catches one's eye is the **Centro Hispano-Americano de Cultura** (860 6282/6290, closed Sun). Formerly an exclusive men's club, today it promotes Spanish-American culture through concerts, dance, art, literature and so on.

Inland is the **Casa-Museo José Lezama Lima** (Calle Trocadero #160-162, entre Industria y Consulado, 863 4161, closed Mon), where the prodigious poet, art critic and novelist lived from 1929 until his death in 1976. Inside is his original furniture, books and substantial art collection.

Moving west will bring you to the *barrio* known as **Cayo Hueso**, roughly bordered by Padre Varela (Belascoaín), Zanja, Infanta and Malecón, and the second community to establish itself outside the city walls. It is said that its name comes from the phonetic corruption of the English 'Key West', spoken by returning Cubans who settled in this neighbourhood. Many of these people were former tobacco industry lords who had fled the island in 1857 after the economic crash, but returned after the War of Independence at the turn of the last century.

Street beats

Rumba in Cuba is a dance, as well as a type of music. Confusingly, it has little to do with rumba flamenco, and absolutely nothing to do with Latin ballroom dance. Authentic Cuban rumba is a raw call and response format in song and dance, driven by pulsating African rhythms and tinged with Hispanic influences. A direct legacy of the African slaves brought to Cuba, rumba was born in the docklands of Matanzas and Havana. It incorporates many complex rhythms played out on a range of percussion, including boxes (*cajones*), conga drums and hand-held instruments, among them the all-important *clave* (wooden sticks that beat out the syncopated rhythms). Rumba tended to be played by slaves on their days off, and was a secular manifestation of African religious traditions.

The original rhythms have now been distilled into three main rumba formats, each with its own dance form: *yambú*, the slowest of the three, is a dance for couples in which a game of seduction is acted out; *guaguancó*, the most popular form, is more overtly sexual, an interaction in which the man tries to catch the woman unawares; *columbia*, the most flamboyant form of rumba, is predominantly a display of male virtuosity, either a solo or a gladatorial shoot-out between a succession of male soloists. Within these formats, rumba allows for endless improvisation and other dance elements are often woven in.

Rumba is sometimes an impromptu happening. However, as a visitor, your best bet is to find the regular rumba spots around town, where the event is more formal but does still attract as many Cubans as tourists. The most atmospheric is the **Callejón de Hammel** (*see p163*), where several rumba groups play on the weekends; the best known is Clave y Guagancó, which also performs at the **UNEAC** (*see p167*). Other good venues are **Centro Cultural El Gran Palenque** (*see p165*), the patio of the **Conjunto Folklórico Nacional de Cuba** (*see p173*), where Los Muñequitos de Matanzas, one of the greatest of all rumba troupes, can occasionally be seen. Folkloric troupe Raíces Profundas often plays on the patio of the **Teatro Mella** (*see p176*). Younger rumba troupes Vocal Baobab and Irosos Obbá are also well worth catching. Vast quantities of rum are consumed at rumba gatherings, so things can get rather heated.

Mr telephone man

There's hardly anyone in the world who doesn't know that Alexander Graham Bell invented the telephone. Except that he didn't. In fact, it wasn't even invented in the USA. The basics of the phone were invented in Havana, by an Italian named Antonio Meucci, 25 years before Bell had even thought of it.

The story of Meucci remains largely unknown, but after Christopher Columbus, he is one of the most important Italians ever to have been to Cuba. Born in Florence in 1808, Meucci was invited to Havana in 1835 to become the chief engineer at Teatro Tacón, today the Gran Teatro de La Habana (*see p174*). He and his wife readily accepted, and stayed in Havana for the next 15 years. An engineer and chemist, interested in metals, Meucci was hired in 1844 by Governor Leopoldo O'Donnell to galvanise swords, buttons and helmets for the Spanish troops.

But Meucci was at heart an inventor, and with his electronic equipment he built a medical apparatus, in co-operation with local physicians, for electrotherapy (the application of electric discharges to patients suffering from rheumatism). In 1849, during an electrotherapy session with a patient suffering from head rheumatism, Meucci made a chance discovery. While the patient sat in one room with a copper connection in his mouth, and Meucci in another with the other connection in his hands, an electric shock of 114 volts was applied. Meucci heard a scream 'more clearly than if it had been natural'. When he then placed the connection to his ear, he could hear the patient's voice. Overwhelmed by his discovery, he named it 'the speaking telegraph', thus becoming the first to achieve the electrical transmission of the human voice.

In 1850, the Meuccis emigrated to New York to improve and promote his invention. Antonio successfully designed a telephone instrument with the first known antisidetone circuit to eliminate voice echo and background noise. He was the first to develop basic techniques for the telephone line and the first to file a caveat on the telephone, in 1871, five years before Bell's patent. (Meucci filed a caveat as he couldn't afford the much more expensive patent.)

But in 1871 Meucci was badly scalded in an accident when the boiler of a ferryboat exploded, killing 60 people and wounding over 200. His long recovery took all the financial resources the couple had, forcing them to live on state assistance and the help of friends. Due to lack of resources, it was impossible for Meucci to send the $10 required to renew his third caveat in 1874.

Unfortunately for Meucci, a patent was subsequently issued to Bell, and in 1876 Bell claimed to be the inventor of the telephone. Meucci sued, and in the famous Bell/Globe judgement, the Supreme Court moved to annul the patent issued to Bell on grounds of fraud and misrepresentation. When Meucci died in 1889, the case was discontinued as moot since the Bell patent had expired. Bell thus remained credited in the public eye as the inventor of the telephone and Meucci, together with Havana, was deprived of his fame as being the real inventor.

In 2001, and under pressure from Italian-Americans and historians, the US House of Representatives passed a resolution saying 'the life and achievement of Antonio Meucci must be recognized, as well as his work inventing the telephone'. But, unfortunately, popular perception remains unchanged.

The full story of Meucci, including photos, diagrams and models of his myriad inventions, as well as the story of telecommunications in Cuba, can be found in the **Museo de las Telecomunicaciones** (*see p78*). Also check out the plaque located inside the Gran Teatro de La Habana (*see p174*), placed there in 1997 in Meucci's honour.

The recently restored **Parque Maceo**, by the waterfront at the northern end of Calle Padre Varela (Belascoaín), has new fountains and benches, plus lush Chinese grass. In it stands a majestic monument to Lieutenant-General Antonio Maceo, known as the 'Bronze Titan', who survived 24 bullet wounds before he was killed in action in 1896. At the western end of the park is the Torreón de San Lázaro, the oldest monument in the area, a little circular watchtower built in 1665 to overlook the former cove of San Lázaro (*la caleta*), then a frequent landing site for pirates.

The forge where José Martí was sentenced to hard labour by the Spanish, is located at what is now the **Museo Fragua Martiana** (Calle Príncipe #108, esquina Hospital, 870 7338, closed Sat & Sun), which features some of the national hero's belongings, including a revolver, prisoner chains, jail clothes and texts.

On Infanta and San Lázaro is the concrete **Parque de los Mártires Universitarios**, created in 1967 to honour university students involved in Cuba's independence struggles. On Infanta, between Neptuno and Concordia, lies the baroque **Convento e Iglesia del Carmen** (878 5168); its tower is topped by a gracious 7.5-metre-tall (25-foot) sculpture of *Our Lady of Carmen*, made in Naples in 1886.

Search the streets south-west of the convent for **Callejón de Hammel**, a small pedestrian street one block south of San Lázaro, named after Fernando Hammel, a French-German blockade runner who carried guns to the Confederacy during the American Civil War. He first came to Cuba running away from the coast guard from the north. Its buildings are covered with brightly coloured murals depicting Afro-Cuban *orishas* and allegories by renowned Cuban artist Salvador González Escalona (*see also p154* **The writing's on the wall**). There are also sculptures made from scrap and old bike parts. This is one of the best places to see rumba in Havana (*see p75* **Street beats**). A popular little stand selling medicinal herbs (*yerbero*) is also here.

The only remaining wall of **Cementerio de Espada**, Havana's first cemetery, dating from 1806, can be seen on Aramburu two blocks east of San Lázaro. The outlines of the coffins from wall niches are still clear. Back on San Lázaro, between Oquendo and Marqués González (878 8404), is the **Convento y Capilla de la Inmaculada Concepción**. Visitors are welcome to view the patio and chapel, with a delicate wooden ceiling, stained-glass windows and a painted altar. Ring the bell for entry.

Chinatown

Cuba's Chinatown, or *el barrio chino*, is centred around Calles Zanja and Dragones in the heart of Centro Habana, and was once the largest and most economically important in Latin America. At its height Havana's Chinese community numbered 130,000; for more information, *see also p111* **Chinatown**.

Many Chinese Cubans left the country after 1959. However, the remaining Chinese and their descendants maintain a distinct community and Chinatown is now home to numerous traditional associations, a Chinese-language newspaper, restaurants (*see p111*) and a pharmacy (Zanja, entre Manrique y San Nicola) that, since 1920, has provided natural medicines to the local community. Chinese New Year is celebrated here every year, with traditional dragon and lion dances starting at the large pagoda-style Pórtico Chino, built in 1999 as the Chinese gate leading into Chinatown from Zanja. There is also an exquisitely carved, gold-plated mahogany ancestral altar, brought from China over a century ago, located on the top floor of the Lung Kong Bar-Restaurant on Dragones between Manrique and San Nicolás (862 5388).

In 1995 the government approved the creation of a state business entity with the goal of promoting the recovery of Chinese arts and traditions, resulting in a rejuvenation of the district. On the south-western edge of the *barrio* is the charming **Iglesia de Nuestra Señora de la Caridad del Cobre** (Calle Manrique #570, esquina Salud, 861 0945, closed Mon). Built in 1802 and completely restored in the early 1950s, this church has a gold-plated altar, lovely statuary, stained-glass windows and two grottos. Nearby, on Avenida Reina, at the corner of Padre Varela (Belascoaín), lies the lovely **Convento e Iglesia del Sagrado Corazón de Jesús e Ignacio de Loyola** (862 4979/2149), a Gothic-inspired church built between 1914 and 1922. Its tower is over 77 metres (257 feet) tall and topped by a bronze cross, with 32 gargoyles and a variety of statuettes. The inside is illuminated by 69 spectacular stained-glass windows.

South of the Capitolio

The land immediately south of the Capitolio was originally Campo de Marte, an 18th-century drill square. In 1892 it was renamed Parque Cristóbal Colón to commemorate the fourth centenary of the discovery of America, and in 1928 became the **Parque de la Fraternidad**. The new park was designed, in accordance with Forestier's plans, for the sixth Pan-American Conference, held in 1928. A silk cotton tree, the so-called 'Tree of American Fraternity', was planted in the park's centre with soil from 21 countries of the Americas, and busts were erected of North and South American independence heroes: Abraham Lincoln, Simón Bolívar, Benito Juárez and others. The streets around the park are some of the best spots to see Havana's 'mobile museum' – American cars from the late 1940s and early '50s, now mostly privately operated taxis.

The south-west corner is overlooked by the impressive neo-classical **Palacio de Domingo Aldama** (Calle Amistad #510, entre Reina y Estrella; not open for visits). Constructed in 1844 by prestigious architect Manuel José Carrera, it is actually two large mansions built together to appear as one grand structure. North of here, on Calle Industria, is the stunning neo-baroque **Real Fábrica de Tabacos Partagás** (*see p78*). The **H Upmann** cigar plant on Amistad has moved to Vedado (*see p88*). Two blocks west on Dragones is the

Museo de las Telecomunicaciones (*see below*), located in a building which stands out for its 62-metre-high (203-foot) tower smothered in rich Mozarab and medieval features.

South-east of the Capitolio is the elegant **Hotel Saratoga** (Prado #603, esquina Dragones; *see p46*). Reopened in September 2005 following extensive renovation, the present-day hotel incorporates part of the original neo-classical façade. Nearby is the Asociación Cultural Yoruba de Cuba and its **Museo de los Orishas** (*see below*). Around the corner to the east, on Dragones, is **Teatro Martí**. Built in 1884 (as Teatro Irijoa), it achieved great popularity because of its excellent acoustics and central location. In 1901 the Teatro Martí was the venue for the Constitutional Convention for the new Republic; it was under restoration as this guide went to press (and due for completion in late 2007/early 2008).

Museo de los Orishas

Paseo de Martí (Prado) #615, entre Máximo Gómez (Monte) y Dragones (863 5953/www.cubayoruba.cult.cu). **Open** 9am-5pm Sat. **Admission** CUC 10; CUC 5 concessions; free under-12s; no photos allowed. **Map** p255 E15.

Opened in 2000 by a group of enterprising *babalaos* (experts in divination), this is the first museum in the world dedicated to the *orishas* (gods) of the Yoruba pantheon. Its 31 larger-than-life terracotta *orishas* have large painted backdrops showing the natural environment and attributes connected with each one. Descriptions are (unusually) in Spanish, English and French. Because it's a bona fide NGO (non-governmental organisation), it depends on its income and charges more than state museums. There's also a restaurant on site, serving African and creole food (open noon-10.45pm daily). For more on Afro-Cuban religion, *see p49* **Having faith**.

Museo de las Telecomunicaciones

Calle Águila #565, esquina Dragones (866 4767). **Open** 9am-6pm Tue-Sat. **Admission** free. **Map** p255 E14.

Since its construction in 1927, this building has been dedicated to Cuba's telephone services. Inside the museum, the story of Cuba's telecommunications technology from the end of the 19th century to the 1990s is told through displays of old phones, telegraph equipment, etc. Have fun dialling old phones and seeing how 1910 switchboards actually transmitted the numbers, complete with clicks and clacks. There are also displays about Italian-born Antonio Meucci, who, while living in Cuba, invented the telephone well before Alexander Graham Bell (*see p76* **Mr telephone man**).

Real Fábrica de Tabacos Partagás

Calle Industria #520, entre Dragones y Barcelona (862 0086-9). **Open** 9-11am, 12.30-2.30pm Mon-Fri. **Admission** CUC 10 (incl guided tour); free under-12s. **Map** p255 E14.

This factory has been producing fine cigars for more than 160 years, and offers the most insightful cigar tour in Havana. An English-speaking guide is always available, and the cigar shop is one of the most popular in the city. Visits can be arranged at the nearby hotels Saratoga (*see p46*), Inglaterra or NH Parque Central (for both, *see p44*), but you can also just turn up and tag along.

Confucian in **Chinatown**. *See p77.*

Southern Centro Habana

Officially part of the Cerro district, but on Centro Habana's southernmost boundary, is the **Cuatro Caminos** market. The country's largest indoor agricultural market since 1920, it stands at the juncture of four districts (hence the name, Four Roads). Also in the area is the **Real Fábrica de Tabacos La Corona** (Avenida 20 de Mayo #520, entre Marta Abreu y Línea del Ferrocarril, 879 6596, closed Sat, Sun). Tickets (CUC 10 incl guide) are available from the Hotel Saratoga (*see p46*).

Mercado Cuatro Caminos

Calle Máximo Gómez (Monte), entre Arroyo (Manglar) y Matadero (870 7470/861 4969). **Open** 7am-5pm Tue-Sun; 7am-2pm Sun. **Map** p254 F12.

Full of bustle and ambience, excitement and smells, the country's largest indoor agricultural market makes an interesting detour. Built in 1920 and covering an entire block, it's always packed with *habaneros* buying live goats and hens, takeaway meals and a tantalising array of tropical fruit and vegetables (for more on the city's fruit and vegetable markets, *see p130* **Living on the veg**).

Vedado

'La Habana Moderna' combines elegant, tree-lined residential streets with high-rise buildings, lively clubs and a wealth of museums.

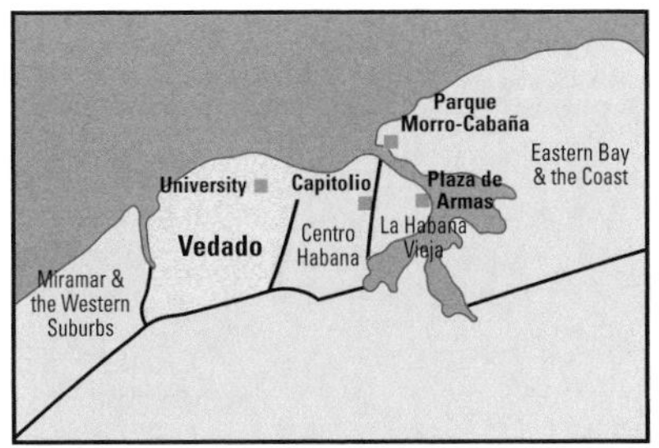

Map p254

With its sumptuous mansions, fine parks, lively music and arts scene and towering hotels, Vedado couldn't be more different from La Habana Vieja. While Old Havana is filled with stunning colonial architecture that demands your attention non-stop, Vedado gives the sense of a cosmopolitan elegance combined with streets that are best explored at leisure. Its grand houses, an eclectic mix, are set back from the road with verandas and gardens, and every now and again you'll stumble across an art gallery, a museum, a nightclub or a restaurant.

Originally an area of dense woods and limestone hillocks, in the 17th century Vedado (meaning 'forbidden zone') became a military area closed to civilians in a drive to defend Old Havana against pirates. By the late 19th century, after the brief Spanish-American War came to an end, Vedado began to enter a new age, financed by US money (some of which came from US gangsters), which led to an explosion in construction – hotels, fancy restaurants, casinos, shops and nightclubs. Soon Vedado became an eclectic showpiece of Havana, with everything from neo-classical to Italian Renaissance, art deco to modern, and was established as the city's key social and cultural hub. Vedado was also the first part of the city to benefit from urban planning: its grids of tree-lined thoroughfares are oriented to catch cooling ocean breezes, there are numerous parks, and lettered and numbered streets make it reasonably easy to navigate.

La Rampa

Vibrant and bustling at any time of the day (or night), La Rampa – the steep stretch of Calle 23 between Calle L and the Malecón – is the best place to start exploring Vedado. In the swinging '50s these five blocks replaced El Prado in Centro Habana as the most popular place for Havana high life. Today La Rampa still buzzes with bars, discos, cinemas, restaurants and hotels, as well as an excellent jazz club, **La Zorra y el Cuervo** (*see p169*), and **Coppelia** (*see p81*), championed by the Revolution as 'the ice-cream parlour of the people'. Nearby is the 27-storey landmark **Hotel Habana Libre** (1958; *see p47*), which was built by an

Coppelia ice-cream parlour. *See p81.*

Walk on Jewish Vedado

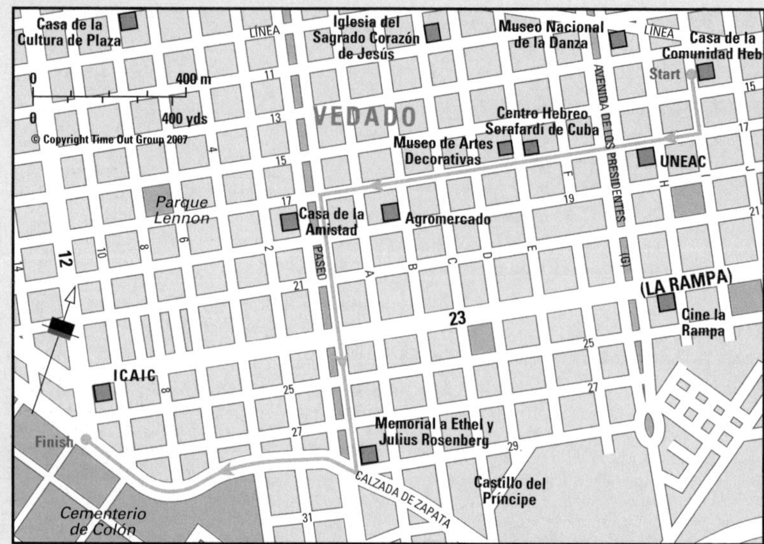

The presence of Jewish people in Cuba dates right back to 1492, when Luis de Torre, a convert, accompanied Christopher Columbus on his trip to the island.

Today Cuba's Jews number 1,300, but the community wasn't always so small. Jewish immigrants arrived from Turkey and the Near East before World War I. With the increase of anti-semitism in Europe, the migratory waves swelled, and by 1925 the Jewish population of Cuba was about 8,000. By 1952 it had doubled to 16,000, 75 per cent of whom lived in Havana. After 1959, however, the changes to the island's social and economic structure (such as nationalisation of private business) led many Jews (and non-Jews) to leave the country. Although most Jewish institutions didn't disappear completely, the Jewish population dwindled rapidly.

The heart of the Jewish community, and a good place to begin a walking tour, is the **Casa de la Comunidad Hebrea** (*see p84*). Locally known as the Patronato, this is also the site of the Gran Sinagoga Bet Shalom (built in 1953 by Ashkenazi Jews), one of the city's three still-functioning synagogues.

The second functioning synagogue in Vedado, the **Centro Hebreo Sefaradí de Cuba** (Calle 17 #462, esquina E, 832 6623), built in 1954 by Sephardic Jews, is an easy walk from the Patronato, south on I and west on 17. The Sephardic ark is the oldest in Cuba; there are also its five Torah books, including the oldest sefer in Cuba.

Five blocks west on 17, and then south on Paseo to Zapata, the **Memorial a Ethel y Julius Rosenberg** (*see p87*) is tucked into a tiny park. Every year, on 19 June – the day of their execution – Cubans gather here for a modest remembrance ceremony.

Continuing six blocks west on Zapata at Calle 12 is the majestic entrance to the **Cementerio Colón** (*see p88*), where several Jews of note are buried. Although Cuban Jewry boasts two cemeteries in **Guanabacoa** (*see p98*), one of the Jews of note buried here in Colón is Frank Steinhart (1864-1938). He arrived in Cuba as part of the occupation army and stayed on to become the first US consul general. In 1907 he became the major shareholder and president of the Havana Electric Railway Company, and later bought the Cuban Light & Power Company. To find the large mausoleum where this notorious magnate and his wife are buried, walk up the main road from the main gate, and when you reach the chapel, look for the elegant grey stone and black granite structure to your left.

American firm as the Havana Hilton just before the Castro regime took over. In 1960 it was nationalised and renamed. In fact, immediately after seizing Havana, Fidel and Che took over a whole floor as a command post, and it remained their HQ for nine months. Over the front entrance is an immense abstract tiled mural by Cuban artist Amelia Peláez. Along La Rampa, you'll find business offices, ministries and international airline agencies (near the Malecón), plus a *feria artesanal* (crafts fair) between M and N; *see p135*). Opposite is the **Pabellón Cuba** (Calle 23, entre M y N, 832 9056/9110, closed Mon), an exhibition hall built in 1963 that hosts cultural activities and exhibitions throughout the year.

Just off La Rampa, with its grand, palm-lined entrance on Calle O, is one of the most celebrated hotels in the city, the **Hotel Nacional de Cuba** (*see p48*). Built in 1930 to accommodate US tourists attracted by Havana's gambling opportunities, it was once the preferred lodging for Winston Churchill and Mafia king Meyer Lansky. The hotel, with its Moorish-influenced architecture, occupies a commanding position on Taganana Hill, the site of the 18th-century Santa Clara Gun Battery. Two cannons – a German Krupp and an immense Ordóñez, once the largest in the world, with a ten-kilometre (six-mile) range – are still here. Non-residents are free to roam the gardens, and its terrace bar is one of the finest places in town to sip Mojitos (*see p120*).

At the bottom of La Rampa, two blocks south of the Nacional on Calle O, is the **Casa-Museo Abel Santamaría** (*see below*), and on the ground floor of the same building is a well-stocked peso bookstore.

Casa-Museo Abel Santamaría

Calle 25 #164, entre O e Infanta (835 0891). **Open** 10am-5pm Mon-Fri; 9am-1pm Sat. **Admission** free. **Map** p254 B12.

Inside apartment 604 (on the sixth floor; there are two lifts), Fidel Castro and Abel Santamaría spent 14 months planning the 26 July 1953 assault on the Moncada Barracks in Santiago de Cuba. The small apartment, still with its original furnishings, seems an unlikely starting point for events that shaped the history of a nation.

Coppelia

Calle 23, esquina L (830 3514/832 7821). **Open** 10.30am-10pm Tue-Sun. **Map** p254 B11.

One of Havana's best-known attractions, this flying saucer-shaped ice-cream parlour, which features in the celebrated Cuban film *Fresa y chocolate*, was built in 1966. Upstairs is a series of glassed-in circular rooms, where service is swift; alternatively, sit outside at one of the three open-air sections in the leafy park. For all of these, you pay in Cuban pesos, and usually have to queue. There's also a CUC section downstairs, as well as takeaway kiosks selling in CUCs (handy if you want to say you've been to Coppelia but don't want to hang around). Before the Special Period of the early 1990s, you used to be able to choose from more than 20 flavours of ice-cream; today the selection is much more limited, but it's still worth a visit nonetheless.

The university & around

On Calle L, three blocks south of Calle 23, is the monumental 88-step *escalinata* (staircase) leading up to the **Universidad de La Habana** (*see p83*), sitting atop Aróstegui Hill like an acropolis. The welcoming Alma Mater sculpture halfway up the 50-metre-wide (164-foot) steps was made in 1919 by Czech artist Mario Korbel. Facing the base of the stairway, in an amphitheatre-like area often used for political rallies, is the **Memorial a Julio Antonio Mella**, which holds the ashes of the young student leader and founder of the University Student Federation (1923) and the Communist Party of Cuba (1925), who was assassinated in 1929 in Mexico City by the Machado regime. At the bottom of the hill is Calle Infanta, which marks the boundary between Vedado and Centro Habana.

Within the tree-shaded campus are two unusual museums: the **Museo de Ciencias Naturales Felipe Poey** and the **Museo Antropológico Montané** (for both, *see p82*),

Universidad de La Habana. *See p83.*

Museo Napoleónico.

which are both located in the Escuela de Ciencias (Science Department), which has a magnificent, leafy inner courtyard.

Two blocks south of the stairway is the eclectic Renaissance-style Casa de Orestes Ferrara (1928), which since 1961 has housed the **Museo Napoleónico** (*see below*), with its extraordinary collection of Napoleonic and French Revolutionary artefacts.

South of the Museo Napoleónico and past the large **Estadio Universitario Juan Abrahantes** (University Stadium) and on to Calle Zapata is a splendid view to the west of the white chalk sides and shady old jagüey trees of Aróstegui Hill.

After Calle Zapata crosses Avenida de los Presidentes (Calle G), you can catch a glimpse of the small 18th-century **Castillo del Príncipe**, built after the British invasion of Cuba in 1762. This fortress (off-limits to the public) is unique in Cuba for its partially vaulted tunnel, which allowed protected movement about the castle.

North of the castle on Avenida de los Presidentes (Calle G), at Calle 27, is the semicircular Italian marble **Monumento a José Miguel Gómez** (1936). Designed by Italian artist Giovanni Nicolini, the monument has bas-reliefs showing important moments in the life of Gómez, who was president of Republican Cuba from 1909 to 1913.

Back at the castle and east along Avenida Salvador Allende (formerly Avenida Carlos III) is **Quinta de los Molinos** (1837), the summer residence of the captains general of Cuba. Máximo Gómez, general-in-chief of the Liberation Army, also stayed here in 1895. The house, named after the two tobacco mills (*molinos*), is now the **Casa-Museo Máximo Gómez** (879 8850). The ornamental tropical gardens that front the house were transplanted from an earlier site on El Prado and contain fountains, artificial hillocks, mini waterfalls, pergolas and grottos. Both the house and the gardens are closed for restoration for the foreseeable future, although it's still business as usual with regards to the *casa*'s function as a music venue (**La Madriguera**; *see p168*).

Museo de Ciencias Naturales Felipe Poey & Museo Antropológico Montané

Facultad de Matemáticas y Cibernética, Escuela de Ciencias, Universidad de La Habana, Avenida de la Universidad, esquina J (both 879 3488). **Open** 9am-noon, 1-4pm Mon-Fri. Closed July, Aug. **Admission** CUC 1; free under-12s. **Map** p254 C11.

Downstairs in the handsome Escuela de Ciencias is the Felipe Poey Museum (1874); named after an eminent 19th-century naturalist (his death mask is on display), this is the oldest museum in Cuba. Displays include 19th-century specimens of Cuban flora and fauna – plenty of stuffed animals – and a fine collection of multicoloured Polymita snail shells, as well as the largest collection of molluscs in Cuba. Upstairs, the Museo Antropológico Montané (1903) has a rich collection of pre-Columbian pottery, carved idols and turtle shells. Another highlight is a tenth-century Taíno tobacco idol that was found in the Guantánamo Province, used to crush tobacco leaves in religious ceremonies.

Museo Napoleónico

Calle San Miguel #1159, entre Ronda y Masón (879 1460). **Open** 9am-4.30pm Tue-Sat; 9am-12.30pm Sun. **Admission** CUC 3; CUC 5 incl guide; free under-12s. **Map** p254 C11.

This is probably the finest collection of Napoleonic and French Revolutionary memorabilia outside of France. Assembled by Orestes Ferrara, adviser to President Gerardo Machado and ambassador to Washington, DC and Rome, the 7,400-piece collection includes the emperor's death mask, his gold-handled toothbrush, a lock of hair, the pistol he used at the Battle of Borodino, his two-cornered hat, Napoleonic artworks by famous European artists and a farewell note written by Marie Antoinette to her children on the day of her execution. While you're there, check out the stunning mahogany-panelled dining room and library.

Universidad de La Habana

Avenida de la Universidad, esquina J (878 3231). **Open** 8am-5pm Mon-Fri. **Admission** free. **Map** p254 C11.

Built between 1906 and 1940 around a central quadrant, this majestic neo-classical walled complex contains numerous interesting buildings. These include the Aula Magna (Main Hall, 1906-11, generally only open for important events), with its seven exquisite murals painted in 1910 by Armando Menocal, and the late art deco library (1937). The tranquil, shady campus is a replacement for the original university in Old Havana, dating from 1728, which was knocked down during Batista's presidency to make way for a helipad. **Photo** *p81*.

Along the Malecón

On the waterfront in front of the Hotel Nacional is the **Memorial a las Víctimas del *Maine*** (**photo** *p85*) dedicated to the 266 sailors who died when the US battleship *Maine* exploded in Havana harbour on 15 February 1898. Sent to Cuba two months earlier to protect US interests during Cuba's independence war with Spain, the Americans blamed Spain for the explosion and used it as the pretext to enter the war under the slogan 'Remember the *Maine*'. (However, the possibility that the US sabotaged its own ship, so as to justify entering the war, cannot be ruled out.) The heavy iron eagle that originally topped the monument was knocked down by jubilant crowds immediately after the 1959 Revolution, who then carried the pieces triumphantly through the streets. Today the segments of the eagle's body are on permanent display in the Museo de la Revolución (*see p73*), while the bird's head is in the Eagle Bar of the US Interests Section, which is open only to American and Cuban staff.

If you continue west along the Malecón you soon come upon the **United States Interests Section** (USINT, 1952; *see also p226*), the closest thing in Cuba to an American embassy. Of little interest architecturally, the American-designed building is significant as a symbol of what Cuba considers to be hostile American policies. East of USINT, facing it in defiance, is the **Tribuna Antimperialista**, a public square inaugurated in April 2000 and remodelled in 2006, which has been the focus for celebrations – such as Castro's delayed birthday fanfare in December 2006 – as well as protests. It's also a venue for music too: in May 2005 American rock group Audioslave played here, with the rare approval of both the US and Cuban governments.

On the south side of the square is the much-photographed caricature of a Cuban Revolutionary yelling at Uncle Sam: '*Señores imperialistas, ¡no les tenemos absolutamente ningún miedo!*', meaning 'Dear Imperialists, You don't scare us at all!'

West around the headland, at the foot of Avenida de los Presidentes, is the **Monumento a Calixto García Iñiguez**, in honour of the 19th-century rebel leader of the Liberation Army in Oriente Province. Made of black granite, its 24 bronze friezes depict scenes from the Wars of Independence. One block south is the beautiful art deco **Casa de las Américas** (*see below*), a cultural centre founded in 1959 to promote and exhibit Latin American and Caribbean literature, history and art. International literary figures such as Gabriel García Márquez are regular visitors. Another block south is the ten-storey **Hotel Presidente** (1927, reopened 1999), which combines Spanish Renaissance architecture with eclecticism; when it was built, it was one of the city's tallest buildings. Across the street is the palatial former Casa de la Condesa de Loreta. Built in 1923 with French-inspired neo-baroque architecture and topped by a large glass dome, today it is part of the Ministry of Foreign Affairs and thus can only be enjoyed from the outside.

A few blocks west along the Malecón is the 22-storey **Hotel Meliá Cohíba** (1994), a Cuban-built, Spanish-run giant whose startlingly contemporary structure stands out from the traditional architectural streetscape of Paseo. The Cohíba dwarfs the nearby ultra-kitsch **Hotel Riviera** (1957), once the world's largest casino hotel outside Las Vegas. Another kilometre west is the mouth of the Almendares river (*see p87* **A river runs through it**) and the tunnel to Miramar.

Casa de las Américas

Avenida de los Presidentes (G), esquina 3ra (838 2706-9/www.casadelasamericas.org). **Open** *Casa* 8am-4.45pm Mon-Fri. *Galería Latinoamericana & Sala Contemporánea* 10am-5pm Mon-Fri. **Admission** *Casa* free. *Galería & Sala* CUC 2; free under-12s. **Map** p254 A10.

The Casa de las Américas collection of over 6,000 works of art are displayed in four galleries. The main building houses the Galería Latinoamericana, which has rotating exhibitions, and the Sala Contemporánea, where Cuban and Latin American photographs and engravings are exhibited and sold. Also under the same wing are the Galería Haydee Santamaría (Calle G, esquina 5, closed for renovation until at least late 2007), located one block south, and the nearby Galería Mariano (Calle 15 #607, entre B y C, 838 2702, closed Sat, Sun & Aug), which houses a popular art collection. The main building also houses Librería Rayuela, which sells books in Spanish and English, records and cassettes. Casa de las Américas is also a publishing house.

Calle Línea & around

Calle Línea was the first east–west thoroughfare through Vedado and one of the main axes along which this part of the city was urbanised. Línea still has a busier, more urban feel than the rest of tranquil, leafy Vedado.

On Calle 17, between M and N, is the unsubtle, 28-storey **Edificio FOCSA** (1956), which used to house Russian bureaucrats and students after the Revolution. When built, the FOCSA building was among the largest reinforced concrete structures in the world. The tower was formerly the exclusive Club La Torre for wealthy owners of large companies. Having reached a sorry state of decay, the FOCSA's 376 apartments, restaurant-bar (La Torre) and exterior were renovated and repainted in late 2003. La Torre (*see p115*), located on the 33rd floor, offers a sensational view of the city. There's a shopping centre here too.

Back on the ground and west on Línea, a small square with an eight-metre-high (26-foot) memorial honours those Chinese who participated in Cuba's independence wars. At the column's base is written, to the eternal pride of Chinese-Cubans: 'Not one Chinese was a deserter, not one Chinese was a traitor.' Two blocks further west is the **Centro Cultural Bertolt Brecht**, although it was closed for restoration as this guide went to press. (Check out the mural painted in honour of Bertolt Brecht, located in the garden of the Teatro Mella at Línea and B.)

Gran Sinagoga Bet Shalom.

Next door is the **Patronato de la Casa de la Comunidad Hebrea** and **Gran Sinagoga Bet Shalom** (Calle I #241, entre 13 y 15, 832 8953, www.chcuba.org), the biggest of the city's three functioning Jewish centres for religious worship, education, social work and recreation, built in the 1950s. A monumental parabolic dome highlights the entrance to the synagogue.

At the corner of Calle Línea and Avenida de los Presidentes is the **Museo Nacional de la Danza** (*see below*), opened in October 1998 to coincide with the 50th anniversary of the National Ballet of Cuba. Two blocks west on Línea, between E and F, is the **Galería Habana** (1962; *see p155*), which was the first of a national network of galleries set up to disseminate and promote Cuban artists, and which today exhibits works by some of Cuba's best-known avant-garde artists.

The Parroquia del Sagrado Corazón de Jesús, more commonly known as the **Parroquia del Vedado** (Vedado Parish Church, Calle Línea, entre C y D, 832 6807) is a couple of blocks further on. Built over 100 years ago as Vedado's first church, it still retains almost all its original features, including the wooden altar, stained-glass windows and a carved wooden pulpit. One of the smaller stained-glass windows was commissioned by María Teresa Bances – the wife of Cuban nationalist José Martí's son. Her former home is nearby on Calzada #807, at the corner of Calle 4, and is now the Centro de Estudios Martianos (Calzada #807, esquina 4, 838 2297/8, open 8.30am-4.30pm Mon-Fri), devoted to the study of Martí. Inside is one of the most beautiful hand-cut Italian chandeliers in Havana. It's not a museum, but visits are allowed during working hours; phone first. Five blocks to the east, at Calzada and D, is **Teatro Amadeo Roldán** (*see p169*), one of the city's finest theatres for classical music.

Museo Nacional de la Danza

Calle Línea #365, esquina Avenida de los Presidentes (G) (831 2198/musdanza@cubarte.cult.cu). **Open** 11am-6.30pm Tue-Sat. **Admission** CUC 2; CUC 3 incl guide; free under-12s. **Map** p254 A10.

Through displays taken mainly from the private collection of Alicia Alonso, Cuba's prima ballerina and the founder of the Ballet Nacional de Cuba, the story of ballet in Cuba is told through photos, costumes, prints, awards, sculptures and sheet music. Treasures, dating from the 17th century to the present, include a signed autobiography of Isadora Duncan that she gave to Alonso and a black fur cape belonging to Anna Pavlova. Future plans for the museum include a documentation and information centre on dance.

The **Memorial a las Victimas del *Maine*.** *See p83.*

Central Vedado

Running south through the heart of Vedado, **Avenida de los Presidentes** and **Paseo** are like two wide ribbons flowing downhill to the Malecón, with large trees on both sides and down their middle, and bordered by some of the most upmarket mansions in the area, in various states of decay or repair. One that has recently been restored is the eclectic early 20th-century residence at Paseo No.304, now the **Museo-Biblioteca Servando Cabrera Moreno** (*see p86*). Cutting across these avenues are key east–west streets such as **Línea**, **17** and **23**.

Cuban writer Alejo Carpentier called Calle 17 'the gallery of sumptuous residences'. Check out the grand house at No.301 (1915), now the **Instituto Cubano de Amistad con los Pueblos** (ICAP), which was designed by American architect Thomas Hastings. Immediately west, at No.354, is the former residence of banker Juan Gelats. This 1920 building, with its white marble spiral staircase and lovely stained-glass window, is now the base of the **National Union of Writers & Artists** (UNEAC). Just around the corner on Calle H is UNEAC's **Galería Villa Manuela** (*see p155*), located in an eclectic 1920s house.

Further west on Calle 17 at the corner of E is the **Museo Nacional de Artes Decorativas** (*see p86*), housed in the beautiful **Casa de José Gómez Mena** (1927). At Calle 19 and B you'll find one of Havana's many typical open-air fruit and vegetable markets (*see p130* **Living on the veg**). A couple of blocks west on 19, at the corner of E, is a splendid mansion, now the **Centro Cultural Dulce María Loynaz** (835 2732-4, promociondml@loynaz.cult.cu). The former home of Loynaz (1902-97), one of the foremost poets of the Spanish-speaking world, the house has been restored to its former glory – complete with period furniture – and is now a centre promoting literature, theatre and music.

Just south of the junction of Calle 17 and Paseo is the Casa de Juan Pedro Baró. In 1995 the house was turned into the **Casa de la Amistad** (831 2823, 830 3114/5). Built in 1926 by Baró for his beloved wife, the mansion combines an Italian Renaissance exterior with a modern art deco interior. Sand from the banks of the Nile, crystal from France and Carrara marble from Italy were used in its construction. The former library, with its wooden bookshelves still intact, is now a restaurant, Primavera (*see p114*), and the lush gardens are one of Vedado's most captivating spots for a wide variety of live music, and, beginning late Sunday afternoon, for dancing (*see p164*).

Three blocks further west on Calle 17, at 6, is a neighbourhood park, **Parque Lennon**. This area was a popular scene for rock and Beatles fans back in the day, and a life-size bronze statue of John Lennon sitting on a bench, by Cuban sculptor José Villa Soberón, was unveiled here on 8 December 2000, the 20th anniversary of Lennon's assassination.

Bordering the park is the **Unión Francesa de Cuba** (Calle 17 #861, esquina 6, 832 4493), a cultural society founded by French immigrants in 1925 and today representing some 600 members. Located in an early 20th-century mansion, the building includes restaurants (*see p115*) and a rooftop with fine views of the area.

Museo-Biblioteca Servando Cabrera Moreno ('Villa Lita')

Calle Paseo #304, entre 13 y 15 (836 0010/835 2027). **Open** 10am-6am Tue-Sat; 10am-1pm Sun. **Admission** phone for details. **Map** p254 B9.

Inaugurated in September 2005, this museum-library is dedicated to the life, works and personal collections of this important 20th-century Cuban artist. Defying categorisation of his style, Cabrera (1923-81) is best known for the intense sensuality and erotic lyricism with which he reflected the human body in his art. In addition to displaying his works, this museum includes Cabrera's family portraits, furniture and personal belongings. Inside is also a library holding an important part of his personal book collection. Outside the house is the Garden of Sculptures, where works of art are presided over by a huge mural by Marta Arjona and a sculpture by Rita Longa.

Museo Nacional de Artes Decorativas

Calle 17 #502, esquina E (830 9848/8037/ artdeco@cubarte.cult.cu). **Open** 10.30am-5.30pm Tue-Sat; 10am-12.30pm Sun. **Admission** CUC 3; CUC 6 incl guide; free under-12s. **Map** p254 B10.

This beautiful museum, equipped with one of the most attractive staircases to be found in Cuban residential architecture, has interior decoration by Jansen of Paris and French mahogany carpentry. The first floor displays rococo Louis XV period furniture, tapestries, paintings, a Regency-style dining room with walls covered in Italian marble, and paintings by Hubert Robert, among others. The second floor has collections of Chantilly, Meissen, Sèvres, Wedgwood and Faenza ceramics, oriental porcelains, in addition to Chinese crystal and decorative folding panels.

UNEAC

Casa de Juan Gelats, Calle 17 #354, esquina H (832 4551-3/www.uneac.com). **Open** 8am-5pm Mon-Fri. *Bookshop* Sept-June 9am-5pm Mon-Fri. July, Aug 9am-5pm Fri, Sun. *Performances* 5pm Wed; 10pm-2am Sat (cabaret; no shorts, no children). **Performances** CUC 5-10. **Map** p254 B11.

UNEAC – the National Union of Writers and Artists – is housed in a beautiful converted mansion set in leafy grounds. The bookstore is a good source of magazines and periodicals on Cuban literature, art and music. Café Hurón Azul and the patio area are meeting places for writers and artists, and a popular venue for bands and soloists, with music ranging from folkloric to trios and quartets to jazz and bolero. *See also p167.* For Galería Villa Manuela, *see p155.*

Calle 23 & around

Stretching across Vedado from east to west, Calle 23 is a defining artery both in terms of geography and character. From the modern-day buzz and '50s high-rises of La Rampa, the street soon enters a mixture of low-rise apartment buildings, parks and commercial areas along its central stretch.

In a small park at 23 and J, Cervantes fans will find an unusual nude and skinny statue by artist Sergio Ramírez of Don Quixote, mounted on his rail-thin steed Rocinante. A few blocks further west is the restored **Casa Ambientada de Arquitectura y Mobiliaria** (Calle 23 #664, entre D y E, 835 3398, casavedado@cultural.ohch.cu), containing exhibits on period architecture and furniture. The façade and interior show striking examples of elaborate moulded wall reliefs dating from the 1920s, when the house was built.

Further west on 23, at the intersection with Calle 12, is Vedado's second vibrating nerve centre (after 23 and L), with restaurants, cafés, peso shops, art galleries, cinemas and the headquarters of the **Instituto Cubano del Arte e Industria Cinematográficos** (ICAIC; *see p146*). Directly across the street from ICAIC is its **Centro Cultural Cinematográfico** (*see also p150 and p165*), with a small café, art gallery and store selling posters of Cuban films, plus videos and DVDs. Or you might want to visit Café Literario, half a block to the west just

Vedado from across the bay.

Sightseeing

A river runs through it

Map p253

Nature hiking, birdwatching and a river environment in the middle of the city? Río Almendares, the city's green lung, is the place to go. The Almendares provided fresh water to colonial Old Havana in the 16th century; along its banks are the ruins of the oldest (1592) Spanish-built hydraulic water system in the Americas.

In the 1920s French landscaper Jean-Claude Nicolas Forestier proposed a large national park for Havana. This dream was never realised, but in 1989 a smaller version took shape: the **Parque Metropolitano de La Habana** (PMH), a project that aims to clean up the river, revitalise agriculture, carry out reforestation and add recreational facilities. And, so far, the results have been tangible.

At the river's mouth is the **Torreón de Santa Dorotea de Luna de la Chorrera**, a tower built in 1762 and now a gastronomic destination, with the Mesón de la Chorrera in the tower itself, and the swanky restaurant **1830** (*see p114*) in the beautifully restored 1920s mansion next door.

Under the PMH project, the delightful **Parque Almendares** (Calle 47 #1161, entre 24 y 26, 203 8535, closed Mon in Jan-June, Sept-Dec) has been revived and the river is regularly cleared of *malangueta*, a voracious aquatic plant. Activities include a playground, pony rides, boating and a small amphitheatre.

From here the road enters the lush and wild **Bosque de La Habana**, 62,000 square metres (15 acres) of forest, criss-crossed with small footpaths. Tiny **Isla Josefina**, still part of the forest, is a protected island-forest that shelters birds, reptiles (mainly lizards) and various insects.

Heading south on Avenida 26, then west on Calzada de Puentes Grandes (Avenida 51), takes you to the **Jardines de La Tropical** (Avenida Tropical, esquina Rizo (881 8767/8745, closed Mon, *pictured*), with its lavish vegetation, grottos, mazes, cascades, pavilions, an unusual open ballroom and a crumbling miniature Swiss chalet.

To find out more about the PMH, meet the specialists and see a scale model (1:2,000), visit the Aula Ecológica (Ciclovía y 26, 881 9979, closed Sat & Sun), and the old Parque Forestal behind. Guides are available for the park's three main trails or can be arranged at the Aula's small Centro de Información y Documentación (205 1558/9) within Parque Almendares, and the Centro de Interpretación del Bosque de La Habana located just outside.

past Calle 12, a charming little café serving coffee and Cuban sweets, which also has a modest stand of Spanish-language books (mainly poetry and literature).

One block south of 23, on Calle 12, is Zapata, where you'll find the main entrance to the **Cementerio Colón** (*see p88*), an extraordinary city of the dead on the southern limits of Vedado. Following Zapata west around the periphery of Colón to Calle 26, between 28 and 33, is the **Cementerio Chino**. Dating from the 19th-century Qing dynasty, this Chinese cemetery has Asian-style lion statues and brightly coloured burial chapels, as well as Western classical and Christian influences. Although it's not usually open to the public, visits can be arranged (groups only) by contacting the offices of the Cementerio Colón.

Following Zapata east to the intersection with Paseo is the often-missed **Memorial a**

Ethel y Julius Rosenberg. Sculpted by Cuban artist José Delarra, it honours the American couple who died in the electric chair in Sing Sing prison, New York, in 1953, after being falsely accused of giving the Russians the secret of the atom bomb (*see p80* **Walk on**).

Back on Calle 23, between 14 and 16, is the famous **H Upmann** cigar factory (835 1371/2), which relocated here from Centro Habana in 2004. Visits (CUC 10), including tours with English-speaking guides, must be co-ordinated beforehand at one of these hotels: Saratoga (*see p46*), NH Parque Central or Inglaterra (for both, *see p44*).

The quieter western end of 23 is a residential neighbourhood of large individual properties, which extends as far as Río Almendares, the boundary between Vedado and Miramar; to the south is Nuevo Vedado (*see p89*).

Cementerio Colón

Calle Zapata, esquina 12 (830 4517). **Open** 9am-5pm daily. **Admission** CUC 1 (incl tour); 50¢ under-12s. **Map** p254 C9.

A dazzling miniature city of creamy marble, glittering bronze, polished granite, angels, crosses and rich symbolism, the Cementerio Colón (officially Necrópolis de Colón) was designed by Spanish architect Calixto de Loira and built between 1871 and 1886, on 550,000 square metres (136 acres) of former farm land. Laid out in a grid divided by *calles* and *avenidas*, with the octagonal Capilla Central (central chapel) at its heart, the cemetery has monuments, tombs and statues by outstanding 19th- and 20th-century artists. Plots were assigned according to social class, and soon became a means for patrician families to display their wealth and power with ever more elaborate tombs and mausoleums.

The main entrance is marked by a grandiose gateway decorated with biblical reliefs and topped by a marble sculpture by José Vilalta de Saavedra, *Faith, Hope and Charity*. Some of the most important and ornate tombs lie between the main gate and the Capilla Central: the Capilla del Amor (Chapel of Love) built by Juan Pedro Baró for his beloved wife Catalina Laza; the exquisite Monumento a los Bomberos (Firemen's Monument) built by Spanish sculptor Agustín Querol and architect Julio M Zapata to commemorate the 28 firemen who died when a hardware shop in La Habana Vieja caught fire in 1890; and probably the most visited grave in the cemetery, La Milagrosa (The Miraculous One), the final resting place for Amelia Goyri de Hoz who died in childbirth in 1901 and was buried here with her stillborn baby at her feet. When her tomb was opened some years later, the dead child was found in Amelia's arms. Ever since, the mother has been the centre of popular myth, and is celebrated as the Miraculous One, symbolising eternal hope.

A huge number of famous Cubans have also found their final resting place here, including General Máximo Gómez, novelist Alejo Carpentier, composer Hubert de Blanck and countless martyrs to the Revolution. Start your visit at the information office (left of the main entrance), where you can enlist the services of an excellent English-speaking guide.

Plaza de la Revolución

Rising above the city on Catalanes Hill, the **Plaza de la Revolución** (until 1959 called Plaza Cívica; **photo** *p89*) is Cuba's political centre. Paseo leads directly south on to this bleak square, a huge asphalt wasteland that lacks shade. Nevertheless, given its political importance – it's a key location for May Day marches and other festivities – it's an essential stop on any itinerary. It was also at this square that Pope John Paul II celebrated a mass during his first visit to Cuba in January 1998.

The first large modern buildings were constructed around the square in the early 1950s under Batista. With the notable exception of the Teatro Nacional and the **Biblioteca Nacional** (1957), they are all government buildings, including the ministries of the Interior (1953), Communications (1954), Defence (1960) and Economy and Planning (1960). Most important is the Palacio Presidencial (1958), on the south side of the plaza, which houses the Council of State, the Council of Ministers, the headquarters of the Cuban Communist Party and Castro's Presidential Office.

The awesome **Memorial y Museo a José Martí** (*see p89*), constructed during the 1950s to designs by Aquiles Maza and Juan José Sicre, is the centrepiece of the square. Looking west from the top of the memorial you can see **Plaza Organopónico**, a 6,000-square-metre (1.5-acre) minifarm with neat rows of seasonal veg. City residents buy the day's harvests at the little stand (open 8.30am-5pm daily) on Calle Colón at the corner with Calle Hidalgo.

Attracting as much attention as Martí's memorial is the bronze silhouette of **Ernesto 'Che' Guevara**, the work of Cuban sculptor Rafael Avila, on the façade of the Ministry of the Interior on the north-west side of the square. The world-famous image – and prime photo opportunity – comes from the iconographic photograph of the Revolutionary by Alberto 'Korda' Gutiérrez. Nearby is **Teatro Nacional de Cuba** (1958; *see p175*), one of the city's most important venues. The glass-plated façade conceals two performance spaces, a piano bar and the animated **Café Cantante** (*see p164*). The theatre is surrounded by abundant gardens, decorated with ponds, winding paths and sculptures by Cuban artists.

In the otherwise monotonous Ministerio de la Informática y las Comunicaciones on the north-east side of the square is the fabulous **Museo**

Hooray for Che, at the **Plaza de la Revolución**. *See p88.*

Postal Cubano José Luis Guerra Aguiar (*see below*), a little-known gem for philately types. Just north is the **Sala Polivalente Ramón Fonst** (1991), a sports centre catering for basketball, volleyball, martial arts and other sporting events, including international ones. From August to November the National Basketball League plays here (*see also p183*). The neighbouring **Museo Nacional del Deporte** is closed for repairs for the foreseeable future, and there are even suggestions that the venue may eventually be relocated: contact it on 881 4696 for more information.

Memorial y Museo José Martí

Plaza de la Revolución (59 2351/2347). **Open** 9am-4.30pm Mon-Sat. **Admission** *Museum* (incl optional guided tour) CUC 3; free under-12s. *Mirador* CUC 5; CUC 2 concessions. **Map** p254 D9.

The heart of this memorial – a gleaming white, 18-metre (58-foot) marble sculpture of a contemplative Martí – was carved on site by Juan José Sicre. The statue sits on a vast base that provides an impressive podium for political rallies, with sweeping staircases either side. Behind the statue is a soaring grey marble tower, 109 metres (350 foot) high, with a star-shaped base. At the top is a lookout – the highest viewing point in Havana – which gives an unrivalled panorama of the city. On the ground floor of the tower is an exhibition devoted to Martí – writer, anti-colonialist thinker and martyr to Cuban nationalism – and the achievements of the Revolution. The exhibits include many original works, engravings, drawings and a large collection of photographic material on Martí's life, plus information and resources on the construction of the square, and the historical events that have taken place on it. One room has rotating exhibitions by Cuban artists, and there's also a small concert chamber in the building.

Museo Postal Cubano José Luis Guerra Aguiar

Avenida de la Independencia (Rancho Boyeros), esquina 19 de Mayo (881 5551/882 8255). **Open** 9am-5pm Mon-Fri. **Admission** CUC 1; CUC 3 incl guide; free under-12s. **Map** p254 D10.

Displays here, with written explanations in Spanish and English, cover Cuba's postal history from 1648 to the present day. Among the highlights: the first books in the world published on philately; a rare 1850 English Penny Black; the first stamp circulated in Cuba, from 1855; the fairly complete remains of the world's first 'postal rocket' – loaded with letters in its nose cone – launched in Cuba in 1939; the first-day cover stamped in space during the 1980 flight of cosmonauts Arnaldo Tamayo (Cuban) and Yuri Romanenko (Russian); plus examples of every Cuban stamp ever printed, displayed in vertical pull-out glass file drawers. The museum's well-stocked shop sells a wide variety of Cuban stamps.

Nuevo Vedado

Nuevo Vedado – stretching south of the Cementerio Colón and south-west of Plaza de la Revolución – developed in the 1950s mainly along Avenida 26. Sprawling post-Revolutionary apartment blocks have diminished the area's appeal, but one of the city's most-visited attractions (by Cubans), the **Jardín Zoológico de La Habana** (Avenida 26, esquina Avenida del Zoológico, 81 8015, closed Mon), is located here. It was founded in 1939 as Cuba's first zoo, and at one point rated among the ten best urban zoos in the world, but these days while the grounds, with their exuberant vegetation, are lovely, the animals are kept in pretty poor conditions.

Miramar & the Western Suburbs

Grand boulevards and even grander mansions – how the other half lives.

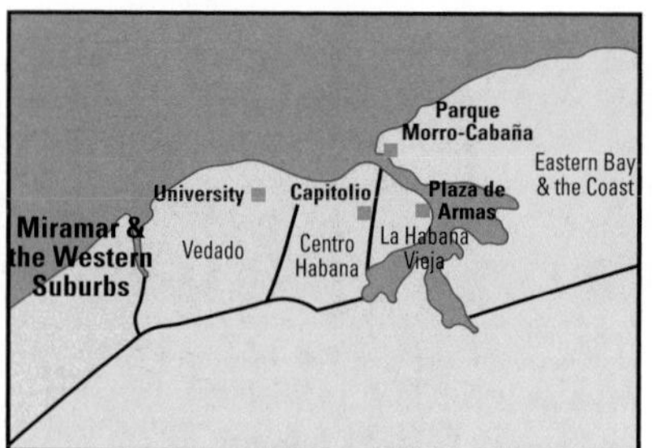

Whereas a wander round La Habana Vieja feels like stepping back in time, a trip to Miramar gives visitors a glimpse of the future. This grand suburb, separated from Vedado by the Río Almendares, is the setting for the city's most recent developments, as trading partners come to do business with Cuba.

In Havana, the political and economic elite have traditionally moved westwards, away from the site where the city was founded in Old Havana, to Centro Habana and then Vedado. By the 1930s, due to the pressure of population growth and an economic upturn, the city jumped the Almendares and expanded into new terrain. The recent arrivals, mainly middle and upper-middle class, were initially forced to use a drawbridge, the Puente de Pote (1924), to commute from their offices in Old Havana to the green and spacious suburbs of Miramar. However, the linking in the 1950s of the Malecón coastal road to the tunnel going under the Río Almendares facilitated the journey.

Until the Revolution Miramar's grandest mansions were the home of the fabulously rich. That changed on 1 January 1959, when wealthy owners opposed to the new Castro regime abandoned the city, many heading for Miami. Most émigrés were convinced that their absence from Cuba would be short-term. They left their servants in charge of their houses, stashed their money away and concealed their treasures – some of which are now national and world heritage pieces – in double walls, gardens and even in the sea, at strategic points off the coast. The properties were used to house students as part of a literacy campaign, but they soon fell into decay as maintenance costs proved impossible to meet. Today many of these houses have been turned into the offices of joint ventures or Cuban enterprises, though others remain as they were on 1 January 1959. A good place to see these mansions is Primera Avenida, which hugs the coast. (Ironically, given that Miramar means 'sea view' in Spanish, this road gives little access to the shore – except for rocky swimming areas at the ends of Calles 16 and 66 – as private houses and buildings reserve this area for their own use.)

Further west of Miramar the upmarket suburbs of Siboney and Cubanacán are proving to be as fashionable as ever, with various Cuban sporting and music celebrities calling them home. Further west is Jaimanitas, where Fidel Castro is said to reside.

Note that the street system in Havana's western neighbourhoods can be rather confusing to visitors: the northern part of Miramar is a fairly straightforward grid, with even-numbered *calles* and odd-numbered *avenidas*, but the roads to the south and west, especially out towards Cubanacán, are winding and the numbering system is harder to follow. Even taxi drivers can have trouble finding addresses around here. If possible, take a decent map with you (*see p234*).

Miramar

Maps p252 & p253

The journey along Havana's seaside Malecón takes you all the way from Old Havana, via Vedado, into the Almendares tunnel, spitting you out on to Miramar's lovely Avenida 5ta, known colloquially as Quinta Avenida, flanked by state-of-the-art offices and spruced-up mansions. The central part of the avenue is a pedestrian walkway landscaped with manicured bushes and other exotic greenery.

As you exit the tunnel, turn your gaze from the picturesque central walkway to the right at the corner of Calle 2. The building you see is

Club Habana. *See p94.*

known locally as the **Casa de Las Brujas** (Witches' House), on account of its unforgiving façade of grey, black and green, and the fact that a couple of elderly sisters lived here until their demise (refusing the state's numerous attempts to buy their home). This sadly dilapidated house, with its fairytale features, is a prime example of Miramar's fading bourgeois past; renovation work had started as this guide went to press, but, this being Cuba, it's a slow process.

Moving down Avenida 5ta, there is increasing evidence of recent economic developments and the emergence of a higher-income professional sector, with foreign company offices, international banks, real-estate offices, embassies in renovated mansions, modern hotels and retail outlets. You'll notice that many of the cars around here have HK registration plates, indicating that their owners are foreign residents. These people are likely to be employees of the foreign companies with the foresight to realise that beyond the beaches, Mojitos and cigars, Cuba is a vast, untapped market. Most investment currently comes from Spain and Canada, with a small group of large companies ploughing money into joint ventures (these include Sol Meliá, Sherritt International, Altadis and Pernod Ricard).

Although the number of foreign businesses operating in Cuba has declined in recent years, reflecting the move by the government to centralise decision-making and trade opportunities, overall exports and production involving foreign participation have gone up (Sherritt, for example, recently invested a further US$500 million in its Cuban operations). In the meantime, American firms, prohibited by the embargo from doing business with their communist neighbour, can only watch as the lucrative market is divided up niche by niche. It remains to be seen how the US

Marina Hemingway. *See p94.*

will approach its main interest in the area – access to potentially important oil deposits off the northern coast of the island.

At the junction of Avenida 5ta and Calle 10 is the **Reloj de Quinta Avenida**, the clock tower that's the official symbol of Miramar, designed by New York architect George Duncan in 1924. Two blocks west along Avenida 5ta is the **Museo del Ministerio del Interior** (*see p93*), housed in an attractively restored building, and a must if you want to see the evidence of a whole range of devious CIA-backed attempts to assassinate Fidel Castro and topple his government.

Two blocks further along Avenida 5ta, at Calle 16, is the **Casa del Habano** (*see p124* **Up in smoke**), a magnificent mansion and one of the best places to buy cigars in the area. Further along, on the corner of 5ta and 30, is **Le Select** (*see p123*) department store.

To get a fantastic overview of demographic and architectural trends within the city, ask for a guided tour of the scale model in the **Maqueta de La Habana** (*see p93*) on Calle 28. Two blocks away from the scale model is the charming **Parque Prado**, set between Calles 24 and 26 and split by Avenida 5ta. The park boasts a statue of the early 20th-century Mexican freedom fighter Emiliano Zapata on its southern side, and a bust of Gandhi on its northern side. Beside it is **Iglesia de Santa Rita de Casia** (*see p93*), the first of three Catholic churches on Avenida 5ta where people still worship. Further along, on Calle 60, is the **Romanesque Iglesia de San Antonio de Padua** (open only for Mass; 5pm Mon, Tue, Sat; 8.30am Wed, Fri; 10.30am Sun), while several blocks west, to the south side, on the corner of 5ta and 82, is the Romanesque-Byzantine **Iglesia de Jesús de Miramar** (*see below*) run by the Capuchin order.

Judging by the largely deserted pews and aisles, it's not the churches of Miramar that draw the crowds; it's more likely to be the aquarium. The **Acuario Nacional de Cuba** (*see below*) is a big hit with locals, especially during the summer school break.

Miramar officially ends at Calle 42 but most people consider that it stretches for an extra kilometre or so along the coast. If you continue along Avenida 3ra, past the sombre tower of the **Russian Embassy** (corner of Avenida 5ta and Calle 62), you reach the heart of recent business developments in the area – the impressive complex of office blocks known as the **Miramar Trade Center**, located between 76 and 80.; it is widely viewed as the future business core of the city.

Acuario Nacional de Cuba

Avenida 3ra, esquina 62 (203 6401-06). **Open** 10am-6pm Tue-Sun. **Admission** CUC 7; CUC 5 under-12s. **Map** p252 B3.

This aquarium was founded during the 1960s and was the first of its kind in Cuba. The collection includes over 3,000 sea creatures, representing around 350 species of marine life. There are sea lion and dolphin shows several times a day (included in the admission price).

Iglesia de Jesús de Miramar

Avenida 5ta #8003, entre 80 y 82 (203 5301). **Open** 9am-noon, 4-6pm daily. **Mass** 9am Mon-Fri; 9am, 5pm Sat, Sun. To visit at other times, enter via the sacristy. **Map** p252 B1.

This is the most architecturally distinguished of the churches located along Avenida 5ta, due to its vast dome, visible for several blocks east and west. Construction work on this, Cuba's second largest church, took five years, and was completed in 1953. Inside, 14 large paintings of the Stations of the Cross by Spanish artist César Hombrados enhance the solemn atmosphere. In one station the artist portrays himself as one of the executioners derobing Jesus; in another his wife is shown as the Virgin Mary. Outside is the 1.8m-tall (6ft) Lady of Lourdes grotto, made of Carrara marble.

Iglesia de Santa Rita de Casia

Avenida 5ta, esquina 26 (209 2298). **Open** 9am-noon, 2-5pm Mon-Fri; 2-6pm Sat; 9am-noon Sun. *Mass* 5.30pm Tue, Thur, Sat; 8am Wed, Fri; 10.30am Sun. **Map** p253 B5.

The church itself is unremarkable, but if you are keen on the work of renowned Cuban sculptress Rita Longa, you will want to see the statue inside, her interpretation of this 14th-century Italian saint.

Maqueta de La Habana

Calle 28 #113, entre 1ra y 3ra (202 7303/7322). **Open** 9.30am-5pm Tue-Sat. **Admission** CUC 3. *Guides* CUC 20-30. **Map** p253 A5.

This is no ordinary scale model. It reproduces all the buildings (and even trees) in the 144sq km (54sq miles) that comprise the metropolitan area of the city on a scale of 1:1,000. Buildings are made out of recycled cigar boxes and colour codes are used to indicate the different historical periods: ochre for the colonial era (16th-19th centuries), yellow for the Republic (1900-58) and cream for post-Revolutionary developments. The model is the work of the Comprehensive Development of the City Group, which has advised city officials on urban planning since 1987. Insightful guided tours are available in English; they are well worth the extra cost, particularly for groups.

Museo del Ministerio del Interior

Avenida 5ta, esquina 14 (203 4432). **Open** 9am-5pm Tue-Fri; 9am-4pm Sat. **Admission** (incl guide) CUC 2; free under-12s. **Map** p253 B6.

This fascinating museum features exhibits ranging from gruesome photos of torture victims of the Batista regime to more recent material on the Elián González crisis. The museum also features a range of explosives and weapons included in plans by Miami groups and the CIA to assassinate Fidel Castro; some of the more intriguing are devices made out of a cuddly toy, a Quaker Oats box and a shampoo bottle. Even without English captions, it is well worth a visit.

Cubanacán

The further west you go, the more magnificent the properties become. So, once you reach the end of Avenida 3ra you are moving into what was almost exclusively millionaire terrain less than half a century ago. Cubanacán is the site of the former Havana Country Club, which became the **Instituto Superior de Arte** (*see below*), Cuba's leading arts academy, thanks to an initiative by Che Guevara.

Slightly west, alongside impressive mansions, is the **Palacio de las Convenciones** (Calle 146 #1107, entre 11 y 13, 202 6011), built in 1979 for the sixth Summit of the Non-Aligned Nations. It becomes the focus of a very tight security operation twice a year when the National Assembly meets here.

Instituto Superior de Arte (ISA)

Calle 120 #1110, entre 9 y 13 (208 8075).

Built between 1961 and 1965 on the grounds of the old Country Club golf course, the Higher Institute of Art is considered to be one of the major architectural feats of the Revolutionary era, and is a work of extraordinary beauty and complexity. Its domed halls, like gigantic mushrooms amid this vast woody landscape, will catch your attention immediately; they form part of the ISA's five schools, incorporating Catalan vaulted arches, cupolas, inner courtyards and curved passageways. African, Asian and Spanish elements also feature in the design, as do symbols of masculine and feminine sexuality.

Project co-ordinator Ricardo Porro, a Cuban architect, designed the visual arts and modern dance schools, while plans for the rest of the complex were undertaken by the Italian architects Vittorio Garatti (ballet and music) and Roberto Gottardi (dramatic arts). Sadly, only three of the five parkland pavilions are completed, and areas of it are in a state of neglect. Californian architect John Loomis put the spotlight on the ISA in a fascinating book, *Revolution of Forms: Cuba's Forgotten Arts Schools*, in 1999. Castro has since invited the three original architects to help complete the project; as this guide went to press work had started on the visual arts building. Though overgrown, this awe-inspiring complex stands as a symbol of a period of great energy and optimism in the early days of the Revolution.

Instituto Superior de Arte.

Sightseeing

Siboney & Jaimanitas

To the west of Cubanacán is the district of Siboney, the heart of scientific research in Cuba in the spheres of pharmaceutics, genetic engineering and biotechnology. Remarkable progress has been made here in the 30 or so years since the initiative was set up, and Cuba has now come up with vaccines against meningitis B and C, and hepatitis B, while producing serious work on AIDS.

Back down on Quinta Avenida and westwards in the direction of Jaimanitas, between Calles 188 and 292, you'll see another reminder of the good old, bad old days: **Club Habana** (*see p186*), previously known as the Havana Biltmore Yacht and Country Club. Opened in 1928 for refined El Laguito residents, this club was so exclusively white and upper class that even dictator Fulgencio Batista was judged not to be 'the right sort'. The club now belongs to the coastguard and the former golf course is its training camp. The plush clubhouse and its private beach are now frequented by foreign diplomats, and entrepreneurs.

About a kilometre further along Avenida 5ta is the village of Jaimanitas, famously home to José Fuster, an astonishingly prolific ceramicist, painter and engraver. **Casa-Estudio de José Fuster**, his eccentrically decorated home/studio and garden is probably Fuster's best piece of work. *See also p155.* Jaimanitas is also, in a manner of speaking, Fidel Castro's home, since this is the closest you will come to the *punto cero*, the military zone where all roads leading in are blocked and guarded, so don't come expecting photos or sightseeing tours.

About 300 metres (984 feet) along from the main entrance to Jaimanitas, on the north side of Avenida 5ta, is **Marina Hemingway** (*see p188*). The marina dates to pre-Revolutionary days, when it was known as Barlovento. It has potential, but due to shortage of initiative or resources a lacklustre atmosphere hangs over the place. There's nothing for Hemingway fans here, but scuba divers should check out **La Aguja** diving centre (*see p188*), one of the few diving centres in Havana. There's also a branch of bakery chain Pain de Paris (*see p129*).

Marianao & La Lisa

These two working-class municipalities border Playa to the south and are characterised by generally poor-quality housing and appalling roads. Nevertheless, if you want to get away from swanky hotels and spruced-up World Heritage Sites to get a glimpse of life as it is lived by the majority of *habaneros*, Marianao and La Lisa certainly offer that.

Art deco fans should seek out **Plaza Finlay** (also known as El Obelisco), at the junction of Avenida 31 and Calle 100. On this well-designed art deco square-cum-traffic roundabout, there's also a 32-metre-high (107-foot) syringe-like obelisk in the centre – a tribute to Dr Carlos J Finlay, who discovered that yellow fever was transmitted by mosquitoes. Four curved-façade buildings complete the architectural harmony of the square. For more art deco, stroll another eight blocks along Avenida 31 to the **Hospital Materno Eusebio Hernández** (1938), also known as the Maternidad Obrera. This maternity hospital is one of the most interesting buildings of its genre in Havana. Hundreds of thousands of babies have been born in this hospital; from the air it resembles a vast womb.

Also of interest in Marianao is the immense Ciudad Escolar Libertad educational complex, established on the site of the old Columbia Military Camp, which Fulgencio Batista flew out of in a tremendous hurry in the early hours of 1 January 1959. Located among the schools on the site is the **Museo Nacional de Alfabetización** (*see below*), created in homage to participants in the massive 1961 literacy campaign. Those with even a smattering of Spanish will find the displays compelling.

After dark, Marianao is the place to be if you want to satisfy your curiosity about the legendary **Tropicana** (Calle 72 #4504, entre 43 y 45, 267 1717) cabaret. Opened over 70 years ago, Tropicana is still as ostentatious as ever.

To the west, Marianao is bordered by the municipality of La Lisa. The area is seriously run-down and has little to offer tourists. Those keen to see the MI-4 helicopter used by Castro and the Cessna plane piloted by Che Guevara in the early years of the Revolution should visit the **Museo del Aire** (*see below*).

Museo Nacional de Alfabetización

Ciudad Libertad Escolar, Avenida 29E, esquina 76, Marianao (260 8054). **Open** (phone first to check) 8am-3pm Tue-Fri; 8am-noon Sat. **Admission** free.

Exhibits include photos, documents, film footage, personal belongings and letters, which form a testimony of the most successful literacy campaign in history: these days Cuba's literacy rate is estimated at 96%, the highest in Latin America. The museum sometimes closes at short notice.

Museo del Aire

Avenida 212, entre 29 y 31, La Coronela, La Lisa (271 0632). **Open** 10am-5pm daily. **Admission** CUC 2; CUC 3 with guide.

This open-air exhibition of combat planes, helicopters, rockets and documents charts the history of Cuba's air defence from the early days of the Revolution. Also of interest are personal belongings of the first Cuban cosmonaut and a planetarium.

Eastern Bay & the Coast

Cross the bay and see Havana from a different perspective.

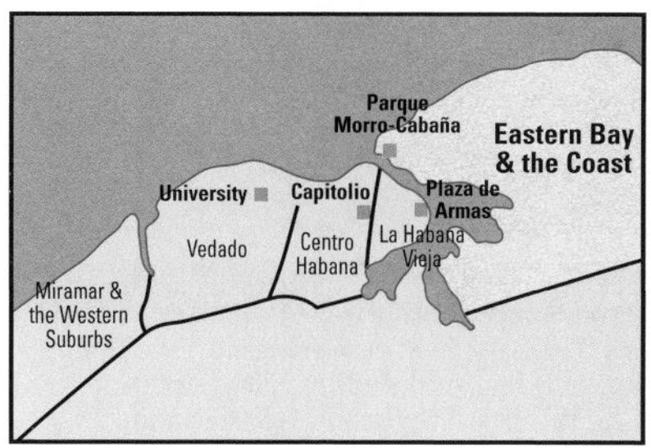

The beacon of the Eastern Bay is the lighthouse visible from the Malecón, which forms part of the immense castle and fortress. Originally built to guard the mouth of the harbour, they are a reminder of Cuba's colonial past. Nowadays they mark the gateway into sleepy villages and residential areas that are well worth exploration. Deeper east, glossy palms provide welcome shade on Havana's radiant Playas del Este.

Parque Histórico Militar Morro-Cabaña

Dominating the north-eastern side of the harbour, overlooking La Habana Vieja, are the two fortresses of the Parque Histórico Militar Morro-Cabaña. Key defenders of the colonial city, these fortresses are now among Havana's most impressive, but lesser visited, sights.

The **Castillo de los Tres Reyes del Morro**, known simply as El Morro, is the oldest structure on the eastern side of the bay, erected in response to the constant threat of pirates. It was designed by Italian military engineer Juan Bautista Antonelli (who was also responsible for the Castillo de San Salvador de la Punta on the other side; *see p74*) and built between 1589 and 1630 by slaves. El Morro sits on a steep rocky outcrop, which helped the canted structure withstand siege by the British for several weeks in 1762. The fortress only succumbed when a mine was eventually set off beneath one of the ramparts; the ravine it made is still visible.

Along with a deep moat and two batteries, additional defence was originally provided by an ocean-side tower, replaced in 1844 by a lighthouse called the **Faro del Morro**. Now a symbol of Havana, it offers one of the finest views of the city, especially at sunset. The history of the lighthouse and castle is explored in the Sala de Historia, while the Sala de Cristóbal Colón charts the history of Columbus's journey to the Americas. Another interesting historical feature of the castle is the prisons, which have holes in the back walls through which prisoners were fed to the sharks.

In 1763, at the end of the British occupation, construction began on the **Fortaleza de San Carlos de la Cabaña**, a 15-minute walk south-east of the Morro castle. This 700-metre-long (2,297-foot) fortress is the largest in the Americas and has never been attacked – less because of its indomitability and more for the fact that takeover invasions had dissipated by the time it was completed. It cost so much that King Carlos III of Spain – after whom the fortress is named – is reputed to have asked for a spyglass to see it, claiming that such a pricey project could surely be observed from Madrid.

Less visited than the Faro del Morro, the fortress's expansive grounds are often virtually devoid of visitors and those who do visit are rewarded with a tranquil setting and panoramic views over the bay. It has a luxurious covered

El Morro.

entrance leading to cobbled streets, a chapel and various military structures, many of which are now museums, restaurants or shops. There is a historical display with gruesome torture devices and a collection of colonial military paraphernalia. The **Comandancia de Che Guevara** displays objects Guevara used in his military headquarters in the fortress just after the Revolution's triumph.

Nearby is the baroque **Capilla de San Carlos**, a bijou chapel where soldiers worshipped San Carlos, patron of the fort. On the eastern side of the complex is the **Foso de los Laureles** (Moat of the Laurels). This is where, during the 19th century and under the Batista regime, dozens of prisoners faced firing squads. (The tables were turned after the Revolution, with the execution of counter-Revolutionaries ordered by Guevara.) There are bullet holes and a plaque in the wall behind the palm tree. The area beyond the moat is where Soviet missiles were stored during the Cuban Missile Crisis of October 1962; disarmed examples are on display.

In the early colonial period, a flagship in the harbour fired regular cannon blasts in the morning and at night to signal the opening or closing of the city gates. Today a squad attired in 19th-century uniforms continues to perform the Ceremonia del Cañonazo (cannon-firing ceremony; *see p138*) at 9pm every evening. It's worth timing your visit to coincide with this explosive attraction.

Parque Histórico Militar Morro-Cabaña

Carretera de la Cabaña, Habana del Este (863 7941). **Open** *Fortaleza* 10am-10pm daily. *Castillo* 10am-7pm daily. *Faro* 9am-8pm daily. **Admission** *Castillo & Fortaleza* CUC 4 before 6pm; CUC 6 after 6pm; free under-12s; camera CUC 2. *Faro* CUC 2; free under-12s. **Map** p255 C16 & D16.

Bayside Havana

As Havana spread out in concentric circles, it swallowed surrounding villages such as **Casablanca**, **Regla** and **Guanabacoa**.

The first two communities have always had a close link with the industrial area of eastern and south-eastern Havana Bay, and been inhabited by less well-off *habaneros* dependent on the sea and harbour for their living.

Casablanca

South-east of La Cabaña is Casablanca, a village that climbs out of the sea to a weather station and the **Estatua del Cristo de La Habana** (CUC 1, free admission for Parque Histórico Militar Morro-Cabaña ticket holders).

Known by some as the 'Christ with sensuous lips', this 20-metre-high (70-foot) marble statue was sculpted in 1958 by Cuban artist Jilma Madera following a commission by Marta Batista – the wife of the former dictator. The statue can be reached by car but it is more interesting to take the 20-minute climb up a staircase from the little park north of the ferry dock, or the road that winds up the hill to the west. It's a contemplative spot with a panorama sweeping from the industrial spires ringing the southern part of the bay to the peaks and domes of Old Havana in the east.

The picturesque **Tren Eléctrico de Hershey** (**photo** *p100*), Cuba's only electric train, has its western terminus in Casablanca. Built in 1920 by US chocolate magnate Milton Hershey, this line linked Havana to the Hershey sugar mill in Matanzas, part of the sprawling Hershey estates, which covered a huge tract of land in Matanzas Province. The dinky trains depart from Casablanca at 4.10am, noon, 8.30pm and 9.10pm daily for the pleasant 90-

Religious festivals in **Guanabacoa**. *See p98.*

kilometre (56-mile) trip through scenic farming communities. Tickets (CUC 3 for tourists) can be bought at the station at Casablanca. Casablanca's Casa de la Cultura is housed in an evocative 18th-century building, the only structure in the town to feature intricate wrought-iron balconies and arabesque tiling.

Regla

The old town of Regla on the south-eastern side of the bay has always been a major fishing and boat repair hub and port for Havana, and was one of the first suburbs established outside the city walls. Founded in 1687, by the mid 19th century it was the city's most important economic centre, with the largest sugar warehouses in the Caribbean. The many slaves who settled here bequeathed to the area a strong Afro-Cuban religious culture.

As you exit the ferry at **Muelle de Regla** on to Calle Santuario, you'll see the neo-classical **Iglesia de Nuestra Señora de Regla** (*see below*). Opposite the green in front of the church the colourful mural combines elements of *santería* with pop art and Cuban imagery.

A few blocks up, on Calle Martí, is the **Museo Municipal de Regla** (*see below*). Further up Martí, between Ambrón and La Piedra, is the **Casa de la Cultura** (97 9905), home to the Guaracheros de Regla, one of the famous *comparsas* (carnival dance troupes). **Parque Guaicanamar** is Regla's shop-lined central park. A short walk south-west of the park leads to a high metal staircase, which provides quick access to the **Colina Lenin** (*see below*), a tribute to the Soviet leader.

Colina Lenin

Calzada Vieja, entre Enlace y Rotaria (97 6899). **Open** *Exhibition* 9am-6pm Tue, Thur-Sat; 1-8pm Wed; 9am-1pm Sun. **Admission** CUC 2.

Offering a panoramic view of the harbour, this, along with the impressive marble sculpture in Parque Lenin (*see p55*), was one of the first memorials outside the USSR to the communist leader, originally consisting of an olive tree planted by Regla workers in 1924. The poor tree has had to be replaced several times due to its struggle with the tropical climate. An immense bronze relief portrait of Lenin's face, surrounded by cement figures, was installed in 1984. There's a small exhibition hall with photos of Lenin, and commemorative ceremonies are held here every 21 January and 22 April, the dates of his birth and death respectively.

Iglesia de Nuestra Señora de Regla

Calle Santuario #11, entre Máximo Gómez y Litoral (97 6228). **Open** 7.30am-5.30pm daily. **Admission** free.

Built in 1818, this church has a Mudéjar panelled ceiling and is the sanctuary of the Virgen de Regla, Havana's patron saint. This black figure, although ostensibly Christian, was used by the slaves to veil their worship of the Yoruban deity Yemayá, the goddess of the seas.

Signs on the noticeboard inside, which advise church-goers that Christians shouldn't solicit the services of soothsayers or worship more than one god, indicate that the Church's attempts to combat such practices continue into modern times. There are two *santería* museum halls adjacent to the church (free admission). For more on Afro-Cuban religions, *see p99* **Having faith**.

Museo Municipal de Regla

Calle Martí #158, entre Facciolo y La Piedra (97 6989). **Open** 9am-6pm Tue-Sat; 9am-1pm Sun. **Admission** CUC 2; CUC 3 incl guide; free under-12s.

A small but inspiring museum with exhibitions on the history of Regla, the most important gods in Afro-Cuban religions and the history of the War of Independence, along with numberous objets d'art. Exhibits include books, maps, photos and artefacts, and staff are keen to be helpful.

Guanabacoa

Inland from Regla is Guanabacoa, once a pre-colonial community and later a centre for the slave trade. It's a lively town, just within the city boundaries, and is the heart of Havana's Afro-Cuban religions: Regla de Ocha, Palo Monte and Abakuá (*see p99* **Having faith**). The town's historical centre was declared a National Monument in 1999.

Guanabacoa is best reached from Havana by car, on the Vía Blanca highway then the Carretera Vieja, passing the **Ermita de Potosí**, on the old cemetery. One of the oldest churches in Cuba (1644), it has a Mudéjar panelled ceiling and an original stone floor.

Guanabacoa is also home to two Jewish cemeteries, located on the old highway about three kilometres (two miles) south-east of Potosí: the Ashkenazi **Cementerio de la Comunidad Religiosa Hebrea Adath Israel** (97 6644) and the Sephardic **Cementerio de la Unión Hebrea Chevet Ahim** (97 5866). Both have memorials to the six million Jews who perished in Nazi concentration camps, and are open from 7am to 6pm daily.

On one side of the Parque Martí in the city centre is the 1721 **Iglesia de Nuestra Señora de la Asunción** (Calle División #331, entre Martí y Cadenas, 97 7368), locally called Iglesia Parroquial Mayor. It's worth seeing for the exquisitely painted altar.

North-east of the park on Calle Santo Domingo and Lebredo is the **Iglesia de Nuestra Señora de la Candelaria y Convento de Santo Domingo** (97 7376, closed Mon), a beautiful baroque church built in the mid 1700s, whose convent was used as a barracks during the British occupation in 1762.

Half a block from the park on Calle Pepe Antonio is the **Teatro Carral**. Opened in the early 1800s as a dance hall (and now a cinema), it has a lovely Moorish arch over its entrance. One block west of Parque Martí on Calle Martí is the town's **Museo Histórico de Guanabacoa** (97 9117, closed Mon), where the Festival de Raíces Africanas 'Wemilere' is held every November (*see p139*). The **Bazar de los Orishas**, two blocks further west (97 9510, closed Sun), has handicrafts from local artists and hosts monthly Afro-Cuban dance shows.

Habana del Este

Moving east you will pass the first of a series of commuter belts: the Ciudad Camilo Cienfuegos, built in the 1960s in response to serious housing shortages. Like Cojímar and Alamar on the coast, the Ciudad is a somewhat dismal place. The most imposing construction along this stretch of coast is the now sadly run-down **Estadio Panamericano** (*see p185*), built for the 11th Pan-American Games in Cuba in 1991. Its adjacent **Villa Panamericana** was once housing for athletes, but was later given to the voluntary workers who had built the stadium.

Cojímar

Set in a little cove at the mouth of the Río Cojímar is a small village of the same name, the shoreline of which still retains the air of a traditional fishing community (in spite of ugly apartment buildings built here in the 1970s to deal with population overspill). The village was made famous by the fact that Ernest Hemingway docked his boat *Pilar* here and could often be found at his favourite local, **La Terraza de Cojímar** (*see p118*).

In 1962 locals erected the **Monumento a Ernest Hemingway** on the north-western corner of the cove. According to local lore, fishermen melted down their propellers to make

Playa **Santa María del Mar**: king of the eastern beaches. *See p100.*

Having faith

The most widely practised religion in Cuba is *santería*, known also as the *regla de ocha* or Yoruba religion after the *orishas* or gods from western Nigeria. *Orishas* represent forces of nature and archetypal human qualities: **Changó** is the god of thunder, **Yemayá** the goddess of the sea and motherhood, and **Ochún** the goddess of love and fresh water. Most *orishas* have Catholic saint equivalents: Yemayá is also known as the Virgen de Regla; Ochún is the Virgen de la Caridad del Cobre, the patron saint of Cuba. Curiously, Changó, the womanising macho man, is linked with Santa Bárbara, the virgin martyr.

Those who wish to initiate into the *regla de ocha* must first consult a *babalao* – an expert in divination – to discover which *orisha* is their 'guardian angel'. Some devotees simply receive the *collares*, a set of coloured beaded necklaces. Others are recommended to enter into a deeper relationship with one *orisha* by taking an initiation called *santo*. Initiations are costly – up to two years' wages – and most people take them for health reasons or in the hope of improving their material circumstances. During the ceremonies in honour of the *orishas*, each one is invoked by using his or her distinctive drum rhythm and dance. Some of the initiated participants may appear to become possessed and assume certain aspects of the *orisha*'s personality.

The annual festivals of the most popular *orishas* draw huge crowds. On 16 December, eve of the **feast of San Lázaro** or **Babalú Ayé**, hundreds of thousands of pilgrims make their way to the sanctuary at **El Rincón** in southern Havana. Some of the more devout drag themselves along on their hands and knees, often with large stones tied to their legs.

Membership of Afro-Cuban religions crosses race and class boundaries. Even Fidel Castro is linked in the popular imagination with Changó. Many believe that this accounts for his nearly 50-year reign and miraculous escapes from CIA-backed assassination attempts. Widely practised throughout Cuba, the *reglas congas*, known also as *palo monte*, originated among the Bakongo peoples of West Central Africa. The term *palo* (stick) refers to the ritual use of trees and plants, which are believed to have magical powers.

A *prenda* or *nganga*, normally a three-legged cauldron, is filled with natural elements such as sticks, seeds and earth to create a permanent fixture akin to an altar in an initiate's home. It also contains the spirit of a dead person and is used by *paleros* to control supernatural forces. Ritual written symbols called *firmas* are drawn on the ground, walls or clothing to call down spirits. Because *palo* is more closely associated with magical practices than the *regla de ocha*, *paleros* tend to be more reticent and it is rare for outsiders to be invited to attend ceremonies.

Abakuá is an all-male secret society that came from eastern Nigeria. Ceremonies, called *plantes*, enact the myth of the African princess Sikán, who discovered the secret of the sacred fish Tanze; drummers evoke the mystical voice of the fish and masked figures or *íremes* represent the ancestors. A system of writing known as *anaforuana* uses symbols to embody religious powers and mark ritual objects. Abakuá members' first loyalty is to their brother members and they are required to be *chévere* or brave and defiant; however, it is an erroneous belief that a new initiate has to kill the first person he meets.

the bronze bust commemorating their legendary visitor. It consists of a pseudo-Greek rotunda, sheltering a bronze bust of the author, grinning and gazing out to sea. Across the street is the old Fuerte de Cojímar fortress,the site where the British landed on their way to conquer Havana in 1762; it's now under military jurisdiction.

Alamar

On the other side of the Cojímar river's drawbridge is Alamar, often attacked as a soul-destroying city of concrete. Housing reforms in Cuba since the 1960s improved living conditions for many, but in some areas – and this is one – 'improvements' meant throwing aesthetic harmony to the wind. Nevertheless, this universe unto itself provides housing for 96,000 inhabitants and is the unlikely birthplace of some of the city's hottest culture. Its active **Casa de Cultura** (Avenida 5ta, esquina Avenida de los Cocos, 65 0624) is an energetic affair, while the affiliated **Fayad Jamís Centro de Arte y Literatura** is a gallery showing digital, erotic and graphic art and installations. The **Mundo de Gallo** (Calle 196, esquina 3ra, 65 6270) is a humorous and eccentric collection of welded art in an

Sightseeing

Sweet like chocolate: the **Tren Eléctrico de Hershey**. *See p96.*

apartment block garden, created and overseen by resident 72-year-old Revolutionary hero and artist Héctor Gallo Portieles. The place is difficult to find, so be prepared to ask for directions. The **Cinema XI Festival** (Avenida de los Cocos #16228, 65 1378), in the centre of Alamar, is one of the headquarters for the **Festival Internacional del Nuevo Cine Latinoamericano** (*see p142*) held in Havana every December, while the amphitheatre on the western end is the site of the yearly **Festival de Rap Cubano Habana Hip Hop** (*see p140*). Behind it is a huge swimming pool.

Playas del Este

Although they're frequently overlooked by tourists, the sugary-white sands at Playas del Este more than hold their own against those at the slicked-up resorts elsewhere in the country, and have the added advantage of buckets of atmosphere. They're just a 20-minute jaunt (by car) from Old Havana: to reach them, follow the (sometimes confusing) signs from the Vía Monumental and Vía Blanca, or take a cab (CUC 10-15 each way).

The Playas del Este are really a single, eight-kilometre (five-mile) stretch with changing names (from west to east): Tarará, El Mégano, Santa María del Mar, Boca Ciega and Guanabo. Several large resort hotels – mainly ghastly 1960s and '70s structures – are scattered between Tarará and Guanabo, with the majority at Santa María del Mar. Furthest west is **Tarará**. The spacious, partially wooded beach with a residential complex was previously used for foreign business men and women but is currently being used to house people involved with the Milagros eye operations project. Close by is the now severely dilapidated Marina Puertasol.

Playa Mégano, with coarser sand backed by pine trees and a long-abandoned, rather ugly domestic tourism complex, is the next along. But easily the most popular of the eastern beaches are Santa María del Mar, Boca Ciega and Guanabo, a trio of creamy sands and crystalline turquoise waters, backed by coconut trees, pines and grassy dunes reaching up to 80 metres (262 feet).

The most honky-tonk of all the eastern beaches is **Santa María del Mar** (**photo** *p98*), whose busiest stretch is in front of the Hotel Club Tropicoco. Being a more touristy area, it has lodgings, restaurants, watersports hire, grocery stores and a pharmacy. Next along comes Havana's gay, lesbian and transvestite beach, **Playa Mi Cayito** (*see also p158*). Then you reach **Boca Ciega**, a lengthy strip with particularly soft white sand stretching from the dilapidated wooden bridge crossing the Itabo river to Guanabo. Quieter than Santa María del Mar, it is popular with Cuban families.

Last but not least is **Guanabo**, also popular with Cubans. Perhaps more interesting than the slightly poorer-quality sand is the strip of shops and snack bars (Avenida 5ta), which are far more varied (and less touristy) than those on the other eastern beaches. There are also plenty of good-quality *casas particulares* in the area, plus fast-food outlets, an ice-cream parlour, an Infotur office and a photo shop.

The **Museo Municipal de La Habana del Este** (Calle 504, esquina 5ta C, 96 2247/4184, closed Sun) is a run-down wooden building at the eastern end of town, with an old whale skeleton and a few aboriginal relics. This neglected collection is saved only by a firm commitment to **Sibarimar**, the area's environmental watchdog project, currently administering 11 endangered areas. The environmentalists who run the project also manage the **Rincón de Guanabo** (to arrange visits call 65 0830), a tiny ecological haven for crabs and birds on a cove east of Peñas Altas after Guanabo, with a visitor centre and café.

Eat, Drink, Shop

Features

Café del Oriente. *See p106.*

Eating & Drinking

Bored of pork, plantain, rice and beans yet? You will be. But it is just about possible to find some flavour in Cuba's cooking.

Food is often the number one complaint of visitors to Cuba. In a country where rations still dictate people's diets and centralised control is paramount, this should come as no surprise. If you're staying in an all-inclusive hotel, there is little you can do to escape the standardised unexciting fare. Independent travellers, however, should be able, with a little effort, to enjoy some memorable meals.

In terms of quality, it all boils down to who owns the restaurant. Private restaurants (*paladares*) offer some great dining experiences, but with the exception of a dozen or so more established places (which are so good they count as proper destination restaurants), they are mostly small-scale operations, which, while authentic, tend to serve bland overpriced dishes. State restaurants, likewise, are a mixed bag. Expensive, swanky restaurants aren't hard to come by these days in Havana's hotels and wealthier districts, but in hotels at least they often lack Cuban charm. And if you think that paying through the nose will secure you decent food or efficient service, think again: in most of these government-run places, the premium is for the location.

Most places will try to encourage you to buy their lobster and will lack condiments like ketchup and fresh pepper, while waiting staff can be inflexible and refuse to take responsibility if something goes wrong. However, *paladares* tend to have a better track record in this regard.

CUBAN DISHES AND INGREDIENTS

Cuban food is hearty and uncomplicated, not as spicily hot as other Latin American or Caribbean fare. Ingredients such as orange and lime juice, olives, peppers, cumin, bay leaves, garlic and lots of onion are evidence of the mix of Spanish, African and Chinese influences that have created a vibrant, earthy cuisine.

Sometimes, though, you'd be forgiven for thinking that Cuban cuisine consists solely of rice and beans, with the odd bit of chicken or pork thrown in. But if you look hard, you may find the occasional traditional Cuban dish on the menu, such as *ajiaco* (stew), *tasajo* (dried cured beef) or *ropa vieja* (a kind of beef stew; the name means 'old clothes' because of how the shredded beef looks). Other typical ingredients to try are *yuca* (cassava), *plátano* (plantain) and *malanga* (taro). *See also p104* **Menu reader**.

STATE RESTAURANTS

The service culture has still some way to go in all Cuban restaurants, but especially state-run ones. Scratch below the surface and you will generally find a great individual serving you, but this will prove of little consolation as he skulks out of sight as you wait for drinks. While the average salary is very low (translating to only US$15 per month), because of their access to CUCs (in the form of tips), waiters actually do much better than the average surgeon, which explains the fierce competition for restaurant jobs. Still, there's no getting away from the fact that waiters tend to rely on tourists' goodwill rather than viewing tipping as a reward for work. If you come across appalling service (or food) in a state-run restaurant, ask to speak to *el gerente* (the boss). The personal touch is more likely to be found at a *paladar*.

PESO RESTAURANTS

These are few and far between, as Cubans simply cannot afford to eat out – the average Cuban will eat in one of the cafeterias or buy pizza from street stands. But they're worth trying for the experience – just set your standards low and see it more as a cultural than culinary experience. Some peso restaurant proprietors will claim it is illegal for them to serve tourists. In fact, if the restaurant doesn't have a specific menu in convertible pesos (CUCs), you should by rights be charged in Cuban pesos like the locals; however, the restaurants often get around this obstacle by offering a tailor-made menu priced in CUCs ('just for you'). If you're not strapped for cash, pay the extra with a smile; the food served to you will usually be better than the peso fare and you'll be helping the waiters supplement their pitiful wages. If you're on a tight budget, stand your ground, agree on a Cuban peso price and check the bill carefully. As a tip, pizza is usually the cheapest option.

PALADARES

Cubans started welcoming paying diners into their houses to enjoy home-cooked food in the mid 1990s, as part of the government's introduction of limited private enterprise. Family members are (in theory) the only employees at *paladares*, so there are usually plenty of dramatic domestic outbursts for you to enjoy while you eat.

The food served at *paladares* is, on the whole, home made, fresh, tasty and filling. That said, quality does vary, and prices aren't always as low as you'd expect. There are at least a dozen excellent *paladares* in Havana (listed in this chapter), so try these first. Indeed, the best *paladares* have evolved into high-quality restaurants, which seem to operate outside of the petty restrictions suffered by smaller, more basic places. *Paladares* come and go all the time, either by choice or because they are closed down for violation of the rules. In theory, *paladares* can only seat 12 customers at a time and they are not officially allowed to serve shellfish or steak. However, a number of owners ignore these rules, so it's worth asking whether these items are available. *See also p112* **Size matters**.

SELF-CATERING

For vegetarians, Havana's *agromercados* (*see p130* **Living on the veg**) are a useful resource (they also sell meat – both cured and fresh, although chicken is a rarity). On the street, stalls sell everything from pizzas to sandwiches to Cuban pastries, and while most kitchens are clean, visitors with delicate stomachs would do well to steer clear. This is also true of ice-cream sold from kiosks, where the milk isn't always pasteurised.

For our selection of the best bread and cake shops in Havana, *see p129*.

JINETEROS

A phenomenon that has grown in line with the increase in the number of visitors to Havana is that of the *jinetero/a*. Literally jockeys, they make their dollars in a variety of ways, ranging from prostitution to 'helping' tourists by 'guiding' them to *paladares* for the 'best meal in Havana'. *Jineteros* will have made a previous arrangement with the *paladar* owners (often their relations), in return for commission. You may get a decent meal by using the services of a *jinetero*, but bear in mind that the city's best *paladares* don't operate in this way and always agree on prices first: many an innocent tourist has parted with CUC 40 per person for rice and beans in granny's kitchen. With all *paladares*, advise management if you're unaccompanied by a guide, as the menu prices drop.

The best Places

For gourmet *paladar* cuisine

La Cocina de Lilliam; **La Esperanza** (for both, *see p117*).

For interesting decor

Doña Juana (*see p115*); **La Esperanza** (*see p117*); **La Guarida** (*see p113*); **Primavera** (*see p114*).

For fine views

Hotel Habana Libre (*see p113*); **Roof Garden** (*see p112*); **La Torre** (*see p115*).

For splashing out

La Finca (*see p116*); **La Guarida** (*see p113*); **El Tocororo** (*see p117*).

For seafood

La Fontana (*see p117*); **El Templete** (*see p110*); **La Terraza de Cojímar** (*see p118*).

For reliable food at good prices

La Casa Julia (*see p111*); **Doctor Café** (*see p117*); **Los Nardos** (*see p110*); **Unión Francesa** (*see p115*).

OPENING TIMES

Opening times and days should be taken with a large pinch of salt. Though the city is becoming more and more used to the demands of overseas visitors, *paladares* in particular can close on a whim. So, if you're going out of your way to visit any of the places listed in this chapter, call ahead beforehand and make sure you go armed with a sense of humour as well as an appetite.

PRICES

Most restaurants and *paladares* in Havana charge in CUC. Be wary of those mystery menus with prices that alter as if by magic as soon as a foreigner enters the room. If anything on the menu is unclear, or if there isn't a menu at all, clarify all the prices in person (unless you like paying CUC 6 for bread and butter). You could also apply the 'Cristal test' to give you a quick indication of how hard the bill will bite when it arrives. In a cheap restaurant a local Cristal beer should cost about CUC 1, rising to CUC 2 in mid-range places and higher if it's an expensive restaurant. Ultimately, though, only the bill will tell you whether you've been ripped off, so scrutinise it very carefully. Note that service charges are beginning to creep on to bills in the most tourist-frequented places.

Menu reader

BASICS
Carta/menú menu; **la cuenta** the bill; **desayuno** breakfast; **almuerzo** lunch; **comida** dinner; **entrante** entrée; **dulce/postre** dessert; **pan** bread; **agua** water (**con gas** fizzy; **sin gas** plain); **vino** wine (**tinto** red, **blanco** white, **rosado** rosé); **cerveza** beer; **café** coffee; **saladito** savoury snack; **trago** alcoholic drink or cocktail; **refresco** soft drink; **jugo de frutas natural** natural fruit juice; **guarapo** sugar cane juice; **limonada** lemonade; **bocadito** sandwich.

COOKING STYLES AND TECHNIQUES
A la parilla grilled; **asado** roasted; **frito** fried; **en cazuela/estofado** stewed; **rebozado** dipped in batter and deep-fried; **empanizado** coated in breadcrumbs and fried; **aporreado** shredded and stewed meat or fish; **fricase** stewed; **escabeche** pickled; **enchilado** stewed in wine and tomato sauce; **potaje** bean stew; **tortilla** omelette

MEAT AND POULTRY
Pierna de puerco pork leg; **jamón** ham; **chuleta** chop; **perrito** sausage/hot dog; **bistec** steak; **carnero** lamb; **chorizo** pork sausage seasoned with paprika; **conejo** rabbit; **pollo** chicken; **guanajo/pavo** turkey; **lechón** suckling pig; **tasajo** jerked beef; **pato** duck; **butifarra** white pork sausage; **res** beef; **palomilla de res** beef steak; **picadillo** minced beef; **chicharrones** fried pork skins and fat.

FISH AND SHELLFISH
Langosta lobster; **camarones** king prawns; **bacalao** salted cod; **atún** tuna; **pargo** red snapper; **cherna** grouper; **pulpo** octopus; **calamar** squid; **pez espada** swordfish; **cangrejo** stone crab.

VEGETABLES, RICES, PULSES AND CEREALS
Viandas refer to vegetables (often root vegetables) that are generally fried or boiled and seasoned with a garlic and lemon sauce. The following are considered *viandas*: **plátano** banana; **plátano macho** plantain; **yuca** cassava; **malanga** taro; **boniato** sweet potato; **papas** potatoes; **calabaza** pumpkin. **Quimbombó** okra; **frijoles** beans (**negros** black, **blancos** white, **colorados** red); **maíz**

Eat, Drink, Shop

CREDIT WHERE CREDIT'S DUE
Cash is king in Cuba and only the top hotels and government-run restaurants accept plastic. And to be perfectly honest, even if they do, they would much rather you paid in cash. Always double-check credit card-friendliness before you consume anything: although many places display MasterCard and Visa stickers, these are often misleading, and even if the place does accept plastic the waiter may still go into a coma if actually asked to settle a bill with a credit card. Besides you may have to wait for 30 minutes while the telecommunication lines deal with your card. Therefore, always take enough cash with you to cover the cost of your meal, and remember that no US credit cards, or even those issued by a bank associated with a US bank, are accepted.

Eating

La Habana Vieja

Old Havana has, in theory, the greatest variety of foreign cuisine restaurants in the city, with Jewish, Vietnamese, Lebanese, Irish in addition to the more widespread Italian, Spanish, Chinese and French cooking all represented. However, in practice the better food is generally found in the Cuban cuisine restaurants where they stick to what they know best.

Location is less of a problem and you can more often than not eat your meal in charming colonial surroundings. Nearly all restaurants in Old Havana are operated by Habaguanex (www.habaguanex.com), the tourist company attached to the City Historian's Office that is responsible for restoring the city. We list two notable ones that don't come under the Habaguanex umbrella: **El Floridita** (*see p108*) and **La Bodeguita del Medio** (*see p105*).

Restaurants

Al Medina

Calle Oficios #12, entre Obispo y Obrapía (867 1041). **Open** noon-midnight daily. **Main courses** CUC 7-23. **Credit** MC, V. **Map** p256 E16 ❶

A former boys' school, this 17th-century building displays a Moorish influence so often found in colonial architecture – apt enough for a Middle Eastern restaurant. The menu is mainly Lebanese, with a large collection of meze dishes, plus grilled chicken and meat to follow if you have room. Like so many foreign cuisine restaurants in Cuba, Al Medina falls

corn; **arroz** rice; **garbanzos** chickpeas; **harina de maíz** cornmeal; **ajo** garlic; **pimiento** bell pepper (**maduro** red, **verde** green); **habichuelas** string beans; **pepino** cucumber; **aguacate** avocado; **tomate** tomato; **rábanos** radishes; **lechuga** lettuce; **col** cabbage; **cebolla** onion; **remolacha** beetroot; **acelga** swiss chard; **zanahoria** carrot; **berenjena** aubergine; **berro** watercress; **frijolitos chinos** soya bean sprouts.

FRUITS

Coctél de frutas fruit salad; **piña** pineapple; **limón** lime; **naranja** orange; **toronja** grapefruit; **fruta bomba** papaya; **guayaba** guava; **melón** watermelon; **plátano** banana; **coco** coconut; **maní** peanuts; **caña de azucar** sugar cane.

DESSERTS

Dulce de coco grated coconut cooked in syrup; **cascos de guayava en almíbar** guava halves cooked in syrup (this dessert is also prepared with orange or grapefruit skins); **pasta de guayaba con queso** guava fruit paste with cheese; **helado** ice-cream; **flan** caramel custard; **panetela** sponge cake; **señorita** millefeuille; **flan de calabaza** squash pudding; **arroz con leche** rice pudding; **buñuelos** fritters.

LOCAL SPECIALITIES

Ajiaco/caldosa pot au feu or stew; **congrí/arroz moro** rice cooked with black or red beans; **mojo** sour orange, garlic and oil sauce served with boiled tubers, like cassava and taro, and meats; **fritura** fritters (**de malanga** taro, **de maíz** corn, **de calabaza** squash); **tostones** fried plantains, **chicharritas de plátano** plantain chips; **croquetas** croquettes; **langosta mariposa** unshelled and grilled lobster; **enchilado de langosta/camarones** lobster/prawns in a wine and tomato sauce; **arroz con pollo a la Chorrera** rice cooked with chicken, peas and beer; **tamal en hojas** corn cakes; **tamal en cazuela** corn soup or purée; **masitas de puerco** fried pork squares; **picadillo a la habanera** stewed ground beef seasoned with raisins and olives; **ropa vieja** boiled, shredded and stewed beef; **aporreado de tasajo** boiled, shredded and stewed jerked beef; **pierna asada** roast leg of pork.

short in the authenticity of its food, and while dishes such as falafel are more or less spot-on, the houmous isn't the best. Eat in the canopied courtyard or the atmospheric cellar-style dining room.

El Baturro

Calle Egido #661, entre Merced y Jesús María (860 9078). **Open** 11am-11pm daily. **Main courses** CUC 2.25-23. **No credit cards**. **Map** p256 E14 ❷

You may never see the cheaper of the two menus at this taverna-style restaurant, as the waiters like to claim that the more expensive one (the one you will inevitably be given), which features combination platters at CUC 16 and upwards, is the only one there is. In fact, there is a cheaper à la carte menu, with seafood, beef and chicken dishes starting at around CUC 2 or 3, which tends to only make an appearance when Cubans in the know ask for it. Nevertheless, the set-meal platters are pretty hearty, including soup, salad, a main dish of lobster, shrimp or meat (and rice and potatoes).

Bodegón Onda

Calle Obrapía #53, esquina Baratillo (867 1037). **Open** 7-10am, noon-6pm daily. **Main courses** CUC 6-25. **Tapas average** CUC 1.50-3. **Credit** MC, V. **Map** p256 E16 ❸

On the surface a plain, corner restaurant, this is actually an authentic tapas bar owned by two Spanish women, serving at least 15 types of tapas for just a few CUCs, plus a few expensive main courses. If you're hungry, go for the *churrasco*, a huge platter of beef with salad and fries (CUC 25). A favourite with the lunch crowd from the Lonja del Comercio business office next door, Onda is a real sleeper at night, as it's more or less hidden away from the rest of Old Havana. A decent mid-range restaurant.

La Bodeguita del Medio

Calle Empedrado #207, entre San Ignacio y Cuba (866 8857/867 1374/5). **Open** *Bar* 10.30am-midnight daily. *Restaurant* noon-midnight daily. **Main courses** CUC 9-16. **Credit** MC, V. **Map** p256 D15 ❹

Most *bodegas* (local grocery stores) in Cuba are on street corners for easy accessibility, but this one, opened by Ángel Martínez in 1942, is in the middle of the street, hence '*del medio*'. This is an obligatory stop for most visitors, its international renown – largely due to the fact that Ernest Hemingway used to drink Mojitos here – reflected in the walls covered in photos and signatures of the rich and famous. However, although it has retained an alluring ambience and everyone can find their own little corner in the labyrinth-layout of small rooms, the quality of the food has fallen behind its reputation. With jerk beef (CUC 9) and swordfish (CUC 15) on offer, the menu does at least promise rarely seen alternatives to most other restaurants round here, but for top-quality cooking go elsewhere. **Photos** *p121*.

Reason to be cheerful: **La Taberna de la Muralla** serves excellent draft Pilsen. *See p110.*

Cabaña

Calle Cuba #12, esquina Peña Pobre (860 5670). **Open** 10am-midnight Mon-Wed; 10am-2am Thur-Sun. **Main courses** CUC 2-18. **No credit cards.** **Map** p256 D15 ❺

Don't make a special effort to dress up in order to come here, but if you're over on this side of Old Havana it's worth popping in for a simple, good-value lunch in one of the few easy-to-find eateries near the entrance to the bay. Ask to be seated upstairs, where you'll be given the cheaper of the two menus, featuring sandwiches for CUC 1.50, burgers for CUC 2 and *platos combinados* for CUC 5 (these come with fries, a drink and a dessert). You'll need to take a table right next to one of the low windows to get any kind of worthwhile view of the fortifications on the other side of the Canal de Entrada, but the interior is sufficiently pleasant to provide a welcome escape from the street and heat.

Café del Oriente

Calle Oficios #112, esquina Amargura (860 6686). **Open** 8.30am-midnight daily. **Main courses** *Lunch* CUC 8-30. *Dinner* CUC 12-30. **Credit** MC, V. **Map** p256 E15 ❻

This is one of the fanciest state-run restaurants in town, with food, service and prices to match. There is a slightly cheaper lunchtime menu, with pasta dishes for around CUC 8, but the real delights are served up for dinner, when the lavish main courses include the likes of rabbit with dried fruits in a port sauce for CUC 18. The food is prepared and presented with considerable flair, in keeping with the tuxedoed waiters and the elegance of the surroundings featuring Greek pillars, plush wallpaper and a grand piano. It's also a lovely place for a drink, especially outdoors, where large tables are the ideal spot to appreciate the view of the square without (for some unknown reason) being approached by hustlers. The upstairs has views of the Plaza de San Francisco, though it can often be booked for large groups so call ahead to check.

Café Taberna

Calle Mercaderes, esquina Brasil (Teniente Rey) (861 1637). **Open** 7am-10am, noon-midnight daily. **Main courses** CUC 4-25. **Credit** MC, V. **Map** p256 E15 ❼

Located on a corner of the Plaza Vieja, this restaurant's theme pays homage to revered musician Benny Moré with its seven-piece band and photos of 'El Benny' plastered over the back wall. The staff here know how to, er, make the most of their customers: don't be surprised if they claim that the menu is currently under review and that for now they will have to deliver it verbally. If this does happen, you will most likely be offered one of the set meals, usually a mixed meat or seafood grill for CUC 20. On the plus side, one of these is enough for two people, and although it's standard Cuban cuisine, it can work out quite economical. The music is more straightforward, with the in-house ensemble providing some of the liveliest and loudest performances of all Havana's restaurants.

Cantabria

Hotel Armadores de Santander, Calle Luz, esquina San Pedro (862 8000). **Open** *Lobby bar* 24hrs daily. *Restaurant* 7am-10pm daily. **Main courses** CUC 4-25. **Credit** MC, V. **Map** p256 F15 ❽

In its attempts to remain faithful to the Basque country, this restaurant serves several typical Cantabrian dishes, such as a grand seafood platter (CUC 23), consisting of lobster, shrimp, fish, squid and mussels. On the whole, though, the food is more Cuban than Basque, but there are some welcome departures from the standard Creole fare, such as Solomillo al Oporto, sirloin steak flambéed with brandy and served in a mushroom and port sauce (CUC 14). The restaurant is tucked away on the first storey of a colonial conversion hotel, the view of the bay providing a very pleasant backdrop, framed by the floor-to-ceiling windows and arches outside. There's a good wine list that is strongest on Spanish varieties.

El Castillo de Farnés

Avenida de Bélgica (Monserrate), esquina Obrapía (867 1030). **Open** *Bar* 24hrs daily. *Restaurant* noon-midnight daily. **Main courses** CUC 3.50-15. **Credit** MC, V. **Map** p256 D14 ⑨

This at-times over-chilled Spanish restaurant – hidden behind the busy bar that's open 24 hours a day – is decorated with photos of Fidel, his brother Raúl and Che Guevara eating here just after they occupied Havana in 1959; it was reputedly one of Fidel's preferred hangouts. There's nothing revolutionary about the place today, the menu consisting of all the usual *comida criolla* dishes and one or two Spanish-influenced alternatives, such as hake *a la gallega*, but there are some good deals including paella for CUC 6.50 and lobster for CUC 14. Fine for a cheap lunch.

D'Giovanni

Calle Tacón #4, esquina Empedrado (867 1027). **Open** 10am-midnight daily. **Main courses** CUC 5-22. **Credit** MC, V. **Map** p256 D16 ⑩

This former Italian favourite has reopened after a lengthy refurbishment, in the courtyard next to its former site. There are plans to reintroduce the old menu of Italian classics such as lasagne and cannelloni, so it's worth a look if you're in the area.

Café del Oriente, for food with flair (and prices to match). *See p106.*

Eat, Drink, Shop

La Dominica

Calle O'Reilly #108, esquina Mercaderes (860 2918). **Open** noon-midnight daily. **Main courses** CUC 5-30. **Credit** MC, V. **Map** p256 E15 ⓫

A convent dining hall, then a meeting spot for Spanish politicos in the 19th century, Dominica is now an Italian restaurant, and one of Habana Vieja's best. Choose from the pavement café in the shadow of the elegant Palacio de los Capitanes Generales or the formal interior, where the menu is the same but you'll dine under chandeliers and over polished floors. The pizzas are good value and come in two sizes, with the smaller (*argento*) starting at just CUC 4.50. The generous portions of pasta, priced from CUC 5, break out from the spaghetti-dominated menus of many Cuban Italian restaurants, with linguine, fettuccini and cannelloni offered (in theory, at least). Seafood is available, too, with a predominance of squid and shrimp dishes.

La Floridana

Hotel Florida, Calle Obispo #252, esquina Cuba (862 4127). **Open** 7am-10pm daily. **Main courses** CUC 6.50-27. **Credit** MC, V. **Map** p256 E15 ⓬

The plush restaurant in this fabulously restored colonial mansion looks out on to the high arches of the hotel's enchanting patio, and with most dishes hovering around the CUC 10 mark, it's unlikely you'll find such affordable eating in these kinds of surroundings anywhere else. Punctuating an otherwise ordinary (though well-prepared) selection of traditional Cuban dishes are some pleasant surprises, such as the Bitoque Caribeño, a beef dish with bacon and fruits cooked in wine, and the Pollo Egipcio, chicken in wine, onion, mushroom and tomato. The menu also has a few vegetarian dishes.

El Floridita

Calle Obispo #557, esquina Bélgica (Monserrate) (reservations 867 1299/switchboard 867 1300). **Open** *Bar* 11am-midnight daily. *Restaurant* noon-midnight daily. **Main courses** CUC 15-42. **Credit** MC, V. **Map** p256 D14 ⓭

This elegant throwback to another era has a bar up front with the cordoned-off seat of former regular customer Ernest Hemingway. The occasional camera flash punctuates what is otherwise very subdued lighting. Unfortunately, the same restraint has not been used in the pricing of the menu, which offers thermidor lobster for a whopping CUC 42. More of a monument than a place to eat, the ambience is nevertheless good, the place smells of class and there are some eye-catching dishes, like flaming shrimp in rum, eye-catchingly priced at CUC 27.

Hanoi

Calle Brasil (Teniente Rey) #507, esquina Bernaza (867 1029). **Open** noon-midnight daily. **Main courses** CUC 3-12. **No credit cards. Map** p256 E14 ⓮

This claims to be a Cuban-Vietnamese restaurant. Frankly, it's nothing of the sort, but who cares when you can get a chicken, fish or pork set meal for CUC 3, paella for CUC 4.25 and extras, like rice and *viandas*, for upwards of 30¢? Haute cuisine it ain't, but you won't fill your belly for much cheaper round these parts.

Los Nardos. See p110.

El Jardín del Edén

Hotel Raquel, Calle Amargura, esquina San Ignacio (860 8280). **Open** 7am-10am, noon-11pm daily. **Main courses** CUC 8-18. **Credit** MC, V. **Map** p256 E15 ⓯

It's easy to get blasé about all the restoration work that has transformed Old Havana, but the Jewish-themed Hotel Raquel really is one of the must-sees, particularly its fantastic lobby, which also houses this restaurant. Included in the mainly Jewish menu are Hungarian goulash and Israeli salad. Kebabs also feature heavily, with Shashlik del Edén (CUC 12), a combination of plainly cooked fish, chicken, tomato and cucumber, among the specials.

El Mercurio Café

Lonja del Comercio, Lamparilla #2, Plaza de San Francisco (860 6188). **Open** 7am-midnight daily. **Main courses** CUC 7.50-18. **Credit** MC, V. **Map** p256 E16 ⑯

This place is somewhere between a classy restaurant and a cafeteria, the gleaming hard woods and mirrored columns mixing with cheap metal chairs and a door leading through to the lobby of the Lonja del Comercio office building. Seafood predominates, and dishes are generally not for the faint-hearted: among the house specials are the Sonata Mercurio – lobster and salmon with cream – while the six meat options include a filet mignon in a mushroom and chocolate sauce. There are plenty of more familiar options, though, such as squid rings, and a seafood paella for CUC 15.50. Call before arriving, as the upstairs room is often booked by large groups.

El Mesón de la Flota

Calle Mercaderes #257, entre Amargura y Brasil (Teniente Rey) (863 3838/862 9281). **Open** noon-midnight daily. **Main courses** CUC 5-18. **Tapas** CUC 1-5. **No credit cards**. **Map** p256 E15 ⑰

After dark, El Mesón de la Flota becomes one of Havana's livelier and more atmospheric restaurants. Live music and dance literally take centre stage, as a programme of flamenco dancers and amped-up musicians perform from a raised platform in the middle of the room, offering more of a show than the usual amateur strummers you'll find everywhere else. Tortilla, spicy potatoes, chorizo and shrimps in garlic sauce feature on the succinct tapas list, while highlights from the rest of the Cuban-Spanish menu include the 'drunken lobster' with tropical fruits (CUC 12) and Catalonian-style shrimps (CUC 7.50). *See also p162.*

La Mina

Calle Obispo #109, esquina Oficios (862 0216). **Open** *Bar & café* 24hrs daily. *Restaurant* 10am-midnight daily. **Main courses** CUC 4-28. **Credit** MC, V. **Map** p256 E16 ⓲

Situated on one of Old Havana's loveliest squares, the Plaza de Armas, La Mina complex – a sweet shop, bar, café, ice-cream parlour and restaurant – has an inside patio populated by roving peacocks, and pavement tables for a view of the square. The usual trilogy of pork, fish or chicken are all competently prepared for less than CUC 8 and accompanied by *congrí* rice and chips. House bands rotate throughout the day.

Los Nardos

Paseo de Martí (Prado) #565, entre Brasil (Teniente Rey) y Dragones (863 2985). **Open** noon-midnight daily. **Main courses** CUC 3-15. **No credit cards.** **Map** p256 E14 ⓳

This is a very popular place worth the wait outside in distinctly insalubrious surroundings (bookings aren't taken). The restaurant has a curious status, being neither fully private nor fully state run. Rather, it is promoted as an Asturian cultural centre and is decorated accordingly, complete with football memorabilia. The wine rack is impressive, although, sadly, not always fully stocked. The tasty food comes in large portions at excellent prices: try the lobster thermidor (CUC 9.50). Service is also pretty good – once you actually get seated. Enjoy the views of the Capitolio as you queue outside as the inside is windowless. **Photos** *pp108-109.*

La Paella

Hostal Valencia, Calle Oficios #53, esquina Obrapía (867 1037). **Open** noon-11pm daily. **Main courses** CUC 8-28. **No credit cards.** **Map** p256 E15 ⓴

The trademark, namesake dish at this intimate and charismatic restaurant has won a string of awards at the annual International Paella Conference in Valencia, but although by Cuban standards it might be better than most, it's still likely to be a bit too basic in flavour for the liking of most visitors. There are also lobster, shrimp, chicken and beef dishes, but if you lower your expectations slightly the paella is probably still your best bet.

El Patio

San Ignacio #54, Plaza de la Catedral (867 1034/5). **Open** *Café* 24hrs daily. *Restaurant* noon-midnight daily. **Main courses** CUC 9-28. **Credit** MC, V. **Map** p256 D15 ㉑

This 18th-century colonial palace is one of Havana's most picturesque, with stained-glass windows, large arches and a pretty central courtyard. These days it's probably the best place in Old Havana for people-watching, and there's usually an excellent band playing (supplemented by impromptu contributions from seasoned deadbeats). The restaurant inside is on two floors and serves Cuban classics. Lowest prices are on the higher floor, an elegant 120-person grill restaurant (try to bag a table on the tiny terrace overlooking the square). But wherever you savour the atmosphere, the food, unfortunately, is unlikely to match the surroundings or the prices (a pepper steak is a staggering CUC 20).

Santo Ángel

Calle Brasil (Teniente Rey), esquina San Ignacio (861 1626). **Open** *Café* 9am-noon daily. *Restaurant* noon-midnight daily. **Main courses** CUC 8-28. **Credit** MC, V. **Map** p256 E15 ㉒

A classy restaurant on the north-west corner of the beautifully restored Plaza Vieja. The café outside has cheapish sandwiches; inside there's a beautiful terrace and several large dining rooms. The above-average prices here are justified by the unusually imaginative and original takes on Cuban cuisine, such as almond chicken in a sherry sauce or tenderloin of beef with pepper sauce on toast. Good-quality food from starter to dessert.

La Taberna de la Muralla

Calle San Ignacio, esquina Muralla, Plaza Vieja (866 4453). **Open** noon-midnight daily. **Main courses** CUC 2.25-13.50. **Credit** MC, V. **Map** p256 E15 ㉓

This bar is a joint venture with an Austrian beer company, which explains the excellent draft Pilsen and Munich beer (both brewed on the premises). The bar has been beautifully restored as part of a wholesale renovation of the square, a sight best appreciated from the outside tables. Inside, long wooden tables bring to mind a revamped London pub. The food is pretty decent, and cheap too (burgers start at CUC 2.50, while charcoal-grilled meat and kebabs go from CUC 3.50). **Photo** *p106.*

El Templete

Avenida del Puerto (Carlos Manuel de Céspedes) #12-14, esquina Narciso López (866 8807). **Open** noon-midnight daily. **Main courses** CUC 8-30. **Credit** MC, V. **Map** p256 E16 ㉔

The location of this seafood restaurant – right on the edge of the bay but also next to a busy road – is something of a double-edged sword, but there's no two ways about it: the food is simply fantastic. Unlike at so many Cuban restaurants, the menu really does deliver on its promises, with an impressive set of starters such as beef and liver carpaccio, and fried *manjúas* (small, almost transparent Cuban fish), plus varied main dishes like Biscayan cod and red snapper in green sauce with clams. All stand out from the rest of the fare offered elsewhere in Havana. Yes, there are plenty of places where you can eat for less, but when it comes to real value for money, El Templete wins hands-down.

La Torre de Marfil

Calle Mercaderes #115, entre Obispo y Obrapía (867 1038). **Open** noon-midnight daily. **Main courses** CUC 3.50-15. **Credit** MC, V. **Map** p256 E15 ㉕

Red Chinese lanterns hanging outside mark the entrance to this restaurant. Originally opened in 1983 a block away, La Torre de Marfil has been in its current spot since 1990. Inside, the decor is attractive, with lovely lacquered tabletops and massive wood beams. Otherwise, there are a few tables out front, a table for eight under a pagoda in the back, and a small interior courtyard. The Chinese food isn't bad, and the prices are reasonable (if your budget is especially tight, ask for the set menu). The absence of a house band and smoke-free air will be definite pluses for some, but service can be slow, even when it's fairly empty.

La Zaragozana

Calle Monserrate #357, entre Obispo y Obrapía (867 1040). **Open** noon-midnight daily. **Main courses** CUC 4-27. **Credit** MC, V. **Map** p256 D14 ㉖

This upmarket Spanish football bar comes complete with flags, scarves and pictures of players. Happy hour (4-7pm) offers cheap food and drink specials every day; later on, exotic dishes such as salmon, squid and frogs' legs go for hard-to-justify prices.

Paladares

La Casa Julia

Calle O'Reilly #506A, entre Bernaza y Villegas (862 7438). **Open** noon-11pm daily. **Main courses** CUC 8-10. **No credit cards. Map** p256 D15 ㉗

Opened more than a decade ago, the granddaddy of Old Havana *paladares* is still kicking. The delicious large meat portions all come with rice and beans plus fried or boiled veg and salad. The decor is typically kitsch, with plastic and dried flower arrangements, and the original velour artwork of the topless jungle goddess with her lion and tiger still hanging on the wall. Service is friendly.

Don Lorenzo

Calle Acosta #260A, entre Habana y Compostela (863 4402). **Open** noon-midnight daily. **Main courses** CUC 12-30. **No credit cards. Map** p256 E15 ㉘

The food here is unusually pricey for a *paladar* (à la carte dishes between CUC 15 and CUC 20), but it's worth it, as it goes beyond the basic meat and fish on offer at most places. In contrast to the relative sophistication of the cooking, the neighbourhood, which could easily serve as a 'before' shot for Old Havana's restoration work, is on one of the more run-down backstreets.

La Moneda Cubana

Calle San Ignacio #77, entre O'Reilly y Empedrado (867 3852). **Open** noon-midnight daily. **Main courses** CUC 8-10. **No credit cards. Map** p256 D15 ㉙

Well-established as one of Old Havana's original *paladares*, this tiny place owes its longevity both to its reasonably priced Cuban meals (served in big portions) and its enviable location in between the Plaza de Armas and the Plaza de la Catedral, at the very heart of the tourist circuit. The walls are covered with banknotes from around the world and footie scarves from Spanish teams. Furthermore, it claims to do the best Mojitos around. There's only one way to find out…

Chinatown

The first Chinese immigrants arrived in Cuba in 1847 to work on the island's sugar plantations after the African slave trade ended. At the end of the 19th century thousands more arrived from California and created Havana's very own Chinatown (*el barrio chino*), with a further wave of immigrants arriving in the early 20th century following the establishment of a republic in China.

The *barrio* was not set to thrive, however. Most of the city's Chinese business community moved to San Francisco after the 1959 Revolution and Chinatown ground to a halt. Restaurants were allowed to open again in 1996 as a move to improve relations with communist China – and to create a tourist attraction.

The main strip of Chinese restaurants is located just off Calle Zanja on the **Bulevar del Barrio Chino** (or Cuchillo), which is decorated with Chinese lanterns. Restaurants are packed every night; waiters in smart silk uniforms beckon customers, menu in hand.

Cubans and foreigners flock here in great numbers to enjoy cheap, tasty meals. The best of the bunch are **Los Dos Dragones**, **Tien Tan** and **Tong Po Laug** (for all, *see p112*). Over in Marina Hemingway, **Pabellón del Tesoro** (*see p116*) is also worth considering. For more on Chinatown, *see p77*.

Centro Habana

In addition to the following selection of the area's restaurants and *paladares*, Centro Habana includes the city's **Chinatown** (*see above*).

Restaurants

A Prado y Neptuno

Paseo de Martí (Prado), esquina Neptuno (860 9636). **Open** noon-midnight daily. **Main courses** CUC 4-12. **Credit** MC, V. **Map** p256 D14 ㉚

Conveniently located near Parque Central (but be careful crossing the road), this neo-classical building was restored as a restaurant in 1998, complete with a snazzy interior, care of Italian architect Roberto Gottardi. The pizza (from CUC 5) is reliably good, while the pasta dishes are worth a try too. The waiters are authentically snooty, and the diverse clientele makes for interesting people-watching.

Size matters

The rules seem clear enough. A *paladar* should have no more than 12 diners at any one time, and should employ only family members. So why, given these regulations, which many of the smaller *paladar* owners are obsessive about enforcing, and paranoid about not breaking, do a select number of the best, longest-established *paladares* continue to operate as restaurants with many more than 12 seats?

The answer depends on who you speak to. Conspiracy theorists will point out that there is something of a trade-off for *paladar* owners and that you should consider the fact that your partner may not be the only person listening to your fascinating anecdote of what you did or where you went last night.

Perhaps the authorities and the inspectors who make frequent checks simply do not notice that a place has grown beyond its official parameters. But in a country where everything seems to be known before it has even happened, this is rather hard to believe, especially as some of the smaller *paladares* have been forced to close precisely for breaking such rules.

In fact, it may simply be a question of natural evolution: some former mom and pop shows were so successful they grew to cope with demand, and having established a fine reputation they have become essential stops on the itinerary of the rich and famous visiting the country – as well as perfect places to demonstrate to visiting overseas politicians that there is such a thing as free enterprise in Cuba... and that it's alive and kicking. So it's more likely that the inspectors and/or authorities are simply turning a blind eye – after all, there might be concern at a high level that diplomats would desert en masse from Cuba if their eating options were limited.

But while the reality may be rather more mundane than the theory, the moral of the story is: there are some great *paladares* in Havana – catch them while you can.

Los Dos Dragones

Calle Dragones #311 altos, entre Rayo y San Nicolás (862 0909). **Open** noon-10.30pm daily. **Main courses** CUC 1.50-8. **No credit cards.** **Map** p255 D13 ㉛

On a backstreet one block from Zanja, this Chinese cultural association is also known as Chung Shan. The spacious restaurant has great service, and is always full of Cubans. Good-quality dishes – all the Cuban favourites, as well as a few Chinese classics.

Roof Garden (Torre de Oro)

Hotel Sevilla, Calle Trocadero #55, entre Prado y Agramonte (860 8560). **Open** 7-10am, 7-10pm daily. **Main courses** CUC 6-29. **Credit** MC, V. **Map** p256 D14 ㉜

This Spanish-Moorish-style hotel has one of Havana's most spectacular rooftop restaurants. If you want to enjoy breathtaking views over the city, go for breakfast in the magical light of morning, or show up early for dinner before the sun sets. Prices are on the high side, the atmosphere can be a bit formal, and it isn't always top quality, but the views make it an unforgettable experience all the same.

Tien Tan

Bulevar del Barrio Chino (Cuchillo) #17, entre Rayo y San Nicolás (863 2081). **Open** 9am-midnight daily. **Main courses** CUC 2.50-17. **No credit cards. Map** p255 D13 ㉝

Whether it's all down to the two chefs from Shanghai, the ingredients imported from China or the perennially present owner, this is *the* place for Chinese food in Havana. The menu is extensive, if a little more pricy than some of the alternatives, service is excellent and the ambience good, so look no further. It recently opened for breakfast, too, and also does takeaway.

Tong Po Laug

Bulevar del Barrio Chino (Cuchillo) #10, entre Rayo y San Nicolás (no phone). **Open** noon-1am daily. **Main courses** CUC 2-12. **No credit cards. Map** p255 D13 ㉞

Popular with both locals and tourists, this place has some of the lowest prices in the *barrio chino*. The good and cheap Chinese dishes include chop suey for CUC 2, noodles for CUC 3, and a variety of grilled meats. Vegetarians will also find some decent options, as in-season vegetables are used in abundance. There's a nice seating area outside, and two air-conditioned rooms inside.

Paladares

Amistad de Lanzarote

Calle Amistad #211, entre Neptuno y San Miguel (863 6172). **Open** noon-midnight daily. **Main courses** CUC 7-12. **No credit cards. Map** p255 D14 ㉟

The simplicity of this basic *paladar* is compensated for by the friendliness of its staff (who love to practise their English). Fish, chicken and pork are the main dishes along with the usual side orders of salad and *congrí* in large quantities.

Bellomar

Calle Virtudes #169A, esquina Amistad (861 0023). **Open** noon-11pm daily. **Main courses** CUC 10. **No credit cards. Map** p256 D14 ㊱

Situated in the midst of Centro Habana's considerable bustle, this authentic *paladar* is cramped but makes up for it by being friendly and spotlessly clean. The tables are laid out in a corridor in a train-like fashion, and the decor is Cuban kitsch. Still, the dishes are substantial, with CUC 10 getting you a main course plus bread, salad, rice and beans and fried plantains.

La Guarida

Calle Concordia #418, entre Gervasio y Escobar (866 9047/www.laguarida.com). **Open** noon-4.30pm, 7pm-midnight daily. **Main courses** CUC 15-20. **Map** p255 D13 ㊲

Havana's most famous *paladar* is an absolutely essential stop on your-visit. Entering the crumbling mansion – the setting of the 1995 film *Fresa y chocolate* – and climbing the marble staircase through what is today an apartment building, you may wonder if you came to the right address. Ring the third-floor doorbell, though, and you're welcomed into a trendy, dimly lit restaurant, crowded with foreigners. The food is so good they haven't changed the menu in years – for example, tuna in coconut sugar cane sauce (CUC 13) and roasted chicken with balsamic sauce (CUC 12). It's on the pricey side, but well worth it. The service is fast and professional too. Be sure to book in advance.

La Tasquita

Calle Jovellar (27 de Noviembre) #160, entre Espada y San Francisco (873 4916). **Open** noon-midnight daily. **Main courses** 80-130 pesos. **No credit cards. Map** p254 C12 ㊳

This is a tiny classic-style *paladar* offering authentic charm in a particularly Cuban kitsch kind of way. Main dishes are comparatively overpriced – and only *moneda nacional* is accepted – but the owner is ultra-friendly, and it's worth going to see the inside of a normal house.

Vedado

Restaurants

El Conejito

Calle M, entre 17 y 19 (832 4671). **Open** noon-11pm daily. **Main courses** CUC 3.50-20. **No credit cards. Map** p254 B11 ㊴

If you get a sudden urge to eat rabbit, this is the place to go. The exterior is 1960s red brick, but inside it's a replica of a 17th-century Tudor mansion. During the first couple of years after the Revolution, Fidel and his personal secretary Celia Sánchez used to frequent the place; she conceived the idea for the restaurant's style. Most of the dishes are good quality: particularly recommended is the mushroomy Conejo Financiera (CUC 8).

Hotel Habana Libre

Calle L, entre 23 y 25 (838 4011/834 6100). El Posino **Open** noon-3pm, 7-10pm daily. **Main courses** CUC 8-20. *La Rampa* **Open** 24hrs daily. **Main courses** CUC 1-12. *Sierra Maestra* **Open** noon-3pm, 7-10pm daily. **Main courses** CUC 12-25. **Set menu** CUC 18. *El Barracón* **Open** noon-3pm, 7-10pm daily. **Main courses** CUC 12-20. *All* **Credit** MC, V. **Map** p254 B11 ㊵

This huge hotel – which began life as the Havana Hilton – boasts no fewer than five eating options. It's worth giving El Polinesio (specialities are barbecued chicken cooked on an open wood-fired grill plus oriental fish and meat dishes) a miss, and instead opting for either the brightly lit cafeteria overlooking the popular Yara cinema, which is a great place for a quick cheap bite, or, at the other end of the scale, the formal rooftop restaurant, La Sierra Maestra, the ideal setting for a romantic dinner, with stunning views over the brightly lit city. Back on ground level there's also a good if unspectacular Italian restaurant, El Barracón, which offers decent pasta dishes.

Hotel Meliá Cohíba

Avenida Paseo, entre 1ra y 3ra (833 3636/834 4555). El Gran Añejo lobby bar **Open** 7.30am-11pm daily. *Habana Café* **Open** 8.30pm-2.30am daily. **Main courses** CUC 11-20. *La Piazza* **Open** 1pm-midnight daily. **Main courses** CUC 7.50- 23.50. *El Abanico de Cristal* **Open** 7-10pm Mon-Sat. **Main courses** CUC 8-28. *Restaurante Plaza Habana* **Open** 7am-10am, 12.30-3pm, 7-11pm daily. **Main courses** CUC 15 buffet breakfast, CUC 23 lunch, CUC 25 dinner. *All* **Credit** MC, V. **Map** p254 A9 ㊶

This huge imposing hotel offers a smörgåsbord of eating options. La Piazza has a standard Italian menu; El Abanico de Cristal serves up an international à la carte menu; and the ground-floor El Gran Añejo does breakfasts, sarnies and tapas. Next door (but part of the hotel) is Habana Café, a Hard Rock-style place with efficient service and a US-themed menu featuring good-quality burgers, nachos, ice-cream sundaes, cocktails and more (worth a look if all that rice and beans is getting you down).

Hotel Nacional

Calle O, esquina 21 (873 3564/7). Comedor de Aguiar **Open** noon-4pm, 7pm-midnight daily. **Main courses** CUC 11-36. *Buffet Veranda* **Open** 7-10am, noon-3pm, 7-10pm daily. **Main courses** CUC 13 breakfast; CUC 20 lunch; CUC 20 dinner. *Cafetería El Rincón del Cine* **Open** 24hrs daily. **Main courses** CUC 6-30. *La Barraca* **Open** noon-11.30 daily. **Main courses** CUC 11-30. **Set menu** CUC 11. *All* **Credit** MC, V. **Map** p254 B12 ㊷

You can spot this landmark monument from almost anywhere in Havana. Inside are four restaurants, offering food in different price brackets, but note that drinks prices are in keeping with the surroundings (CUC 2.50 for a Cristal).

The Comedor de Aguiar is built on the site where Don Luis José Aguiar kicked the Brits' butts during the 1762 occupation. It's so elite that there seems to

If you're on a budget – or just sick of rice – pick up a roadside snack for a few pesos.

be hardly anyone in it; this is possibly something to do with the slightly intimidating, immaculately dressed waiters carefully guarding the doors. Starters, such as smoked salmon with capers and onions, cost from CUC 6, while mains (butterfly lobster, for example) almost hit the CUC 40 mark on occasions. Drinks add a further ouch factor. The quality is generally good, and the service slick.

The downstairs buffet is probably worth avoiding as is the Cafetería el Rincón del Cine unless you have an urgent desire to watch sports on a very large TV played at full volume. If the urge does overwhelm you, you can munch on sandwiches, pizzas and burgers from around CUC 4. A much more appealing option, especially on a hot day, is La Barraca, set in the hotel's picture-perfect gardens. This coolly shaded traditional *ranchón* (ranch) with a rustic feel serves drinks in ceramic mugs and big portions of chicken, pork, fish, seafood, steaks, and occasionally pig-on-a-spit, cooked in an outside clay oven. The wine list is pretty impressive too. For the terrace bar, *see p120.*

1830

Malecón #1252, esquina 20 (838 3090-92). **Open** noon-midnight daily. **Main courses** CUC 6.95-30. **No credit cards. Map** p253 A7 ㊸

Old-world opulence meets Hollywood glamour in this Spanish colonial house. Guests are led down the red carpet to the two ornate dining rooms, one of which opens on to the sea. The ambience is stiff and formal, with waiting staff to match (on a quiet night, you might feel a little lonely). The Cuban food has an international touch, with dishes such as beef in blue cheese sauce (CUC 17.95), and there's an excellent choice of international wines starting at good prices. Visit the elegant stained-glass Bar Colonial for a pre-dinner cocktail. Dinner guests can enjoy an open-air show (11pm Tue-Sun) free of charge.

Monseigneur

Calle O, esquina 21 (832 9884). **Open** noon-1am daily. **Main courses** CUC 6-25. **Credit** MC, V. **Map** p254 B12 ㊹

Monseigneur is an ice-cold, dimly lit world of fake marble, artificial flowers, kitsch statues, plus grand piano with friendly pianist (who welcomes requests). Food is average and averagely priced and service is somewhat uninspiring, but you could do a lot worse.

Primavera

Casa de la Amistad, Calle Paseo #406, entre 17 y 19 (831 2823/830 3114). **Open** 11am-midnight Mon-Fri; 11am-2am Sat. **Main courses** CUC 4-10. **No credit cards. Map** p254 B9 ㊺

Located in the Casa de la Amistad – an exquisite mansion built in the 1920s – Primavera exudes an air of opulence. You can eat at the marble table that's literally built into the room, or simply admire the marble floor, central fountain, mirror wall and intricate iron-grill windows. The food is pretty standard fare (and inexpensive if you steer clear of the lobster), but the wine list is good, with plenty of choice for under CUC 20. Make a night of it and enjoy traditional Cuban music on Tuesdays and Thursdays from 9pm (CUC 5 cover charge). You don't have to eat – it's also a lovely place to come just for a drink and a dance on those nights.

La Roca

Calle 21 #102, entre L y M (834 4501). **Open** noon-midnight daily. **Main courses** CUC 3-18. **No credit cards**. **Map** p254 B11 ㊻

Extremely popular with Cubans and foreigners in equal measure, La Roca offers great cocktails at excellent prices in an art deco setting. The food is of the cheap 'n' cheerful variety (largely consisting of lots of fried chicken and pork, plus some pasta dishes). At 11pm a Cuban comedy set starts up, for which there is often a long line of *habaneros* keen to see the latest in Cuban humour. You're welcome to stay and enjoy the show, although you'll need a superb level of Spanish to make sense of it (for more on comedy, *see pp172-81*). Dress for the cold, as the air-conditioning is intense.

La Torre

Calle 17, esquina M, Edificio FOCSA (838 3088/ 9/832 7306). **Open** noon-midnight daily. **Main courses** CUC 10-25. **Credit** MC, V. **Map** p254 B11 ㊼

Both the bar and restaurant at this recently renovated space offer unmatched views across Havana – which isn't surprising, given that the building is 35 storeys high. The food isn't bad, either and at CUC 15 for a steak this is a good choice of venue if you want to eat in style.

Trattoria Marakas

Calle O #206, entre 23 y 25 (833 3740). **Open** noon-midnight daily. **Main courses** CUC 1.80-8. **No credit cards**. **Map** p254 B12 ㊽

Heavy glass doors lead into this loud and bright pizzeria, done out in the style of an American 1950s diner, complete with small round tables, pistachio-coloured chairs and hanging garlic bulbs. There are more than 20 types of pizza on offer, the cheapest coming in at just under CUC 5. Service varies, but is generally efficient.

Unión Francesa

Calle 17 #861, entre 4 y 6 (832 4493). **Open** noon-midnight daily. **Main courses** CUC 2-7. **No credit cards**. **Map** p254 B9 ㊾

Situated in a lovely corner mansion just across from the John Lennon park, this laid-back restaurant is popular with both Cubans and foreigners. The first floor offers decent pastas and pizzas at bargain prices, but the place to be is on the spacious roof terrace surrounded by plants; kick off with starters such as the cheese plate before moving on to the Pollo al Tropico (grilled chicken with tangy lemon sauce) or the deliciously barbecued *langosta*. Even the salads are good, a rarity in Cuba, and the set menus come with potatoes.

Paladares

La Casa

Calle 30 #865, entre 26 y 41, Nuevo Vedado (881 7000). **Open** noon-midnight daily. **Main courses** CUC 6-10. **No credit cards**. **Map** p253 D7 ㊿

This premium *paladar* really does merit the trek out to Nuevo Vedado. Faux waterfalls provide a pleasant background and the well-oiled kitchen produces excellent grub. Dinner generally doesn't come out too cheap (CUC 15 per head) but the experience is worth it. You can't miss the esteemed owner enthroned in his ever-present seat keeping an eye on all that goes on.

Casa Sarasua

Calle 25 #510, apto 1, entre H y I (832 2114). **Open** noon-11pm Mon-Sat. **Main courses** CUC 4-8. **No credit cards**. **Map** p254 B10 51

If you want an opportunity to have a relaxed chat with an interesting *paladar* owner, look no further than this friendly and welcoming place, which overlooks leafy Calle 25, near the university. The decor is provided by an impressive weapons collection, which is the key to a long and interesting family history. Traditional Cuban fare is the order of the day – *frijoles*, *tostones* and big pork chops. Special menus are offered to students.

Decameron

Linea #753, entre Paseo y 2 (832 2444). **Open** noon-midnight daily. **Main courses** CUC 7-18. **No credit cards**. **Map** p254 B9 52

In this particular case appearances do lie, so don't let the ugly brown brick exterior put you off. Inside is a cosy *paladar* with soft lighting and a collection of grandfather clocks (mercifully unwound), contemporary Cuban paintings, antiques and ceramic objects. The chef adds flair to tired old Cuban dishes (try one of the fantastic steaks), and care is taken in everything, from the smartly dressed tables to the polite service and the French-style presentation. The family that owns it is weird and wonderful.

Doña Juana

Calle 19 #909, entre 6 y 8 (832 2699). **Open** noon-midnight daily. **Main courses** CUC 3-13. **No credit cards**. **Map** p254 B9 53

This friendly *paladar* hides out in a crumbling Vedado building. Make your way up to the first floor, traipse across the living room, down a long gloomy corridor to the kitchen and up to the roof terrace on a pretty steep spiral staircase. When you eventually get there, it's all worth it for the kitschly lit, quirkily decorated rooftop dining area. As for the food, traditional Creole dishes abound in hearty, tasty portions.

El Gringo Viejo

Calle 21 #454, entre E y F (831 1946). **Open** noon-11pm daily. **Main courses** CUC 6-12. **No credit cards**. **Map** p254 B10 54

This is a reliably good restaurant that has stood the test of time for nearly a decade. International food, attentive service and a constant flow of clients make it a great choice if you're in the area, but make sure you reserve ahead if you want to avoid a long wait. Try the Cuban speciality *ropa vieja* (meaning 'old clothes'; it's better than it sounds) for CUC 8.

El Hurón Azul

Calle Humbolt #153, esquina P (879 1691). **Open** noon-midnight Tue-Sun. **Main courses** CUC 8-16. **No credit cards**. **Map** p254 B12 55

This is a good *paladar* near the Hotel Habana Libre with a loyal clientele. Recently refurbished, it still feels a little claustrophobic, but this is more than compensated for by the attentive staff and good food. The speciality of the house is grilled pork – no surprises there, so try to save room for one of the desserts, such as chocolate mousse or fresh fruit ice-cream, which are a bit more imaginitive.

Las Mercedes

Calle 18 #204, entre 15 y 17 (831 5706). **Open** noon-midnight daily. **Main courses** CUC 10-17. **No credit cards**. **Map** p253 B8 56

This small cosy *paladar* has a something of a local feel, and the Cuban dishes it serves are prepared with flair. However, given some of the prices on the set menu (CUC 15 for chicken), you might need to develop a good relationship with the jovial owner to discuss credit terms. The garden is lush, but the fish pond had been drained when we last stopped by – but this place is still worth a try.

Miramar & the western suburbs

Miramar and the suburbs further west are the closest thing Cuba comes to an upper-class area, home to diplomats, expats and well-placed government types. The upmarket restaurants in the area reflect this, and tend to cater to the capital's more demanding diners. In addition to the restaurants listed below, **Club Habana** (*see p186*) has a sophisticated restaurant as well as a grill, while the **Hotel Meliá Habana** (*see p49*) and **Hotel Occidental Miramar** (*see p50*) each have an array of decent eateries.

Restaurants

El Aljibe

Avenida 7ma, entre 24 y 26 (204 1583/4 ext 104 or 114 for reservations). **Open** noon-midnight daily. **Main courses** CUC 12-25. **Credit** MC, V. **Map** p253 B5 57

El Aljibe is one of Cuba's best restaurants, which explains the heavy attendance by expats and nouveaux riches Cubans, especially at lunchtime. The real treat is the house speciality – roast chicken with sour orange sauce served with masses of rice and creamy black beans, salad and fried plantains (portions are unlimited, so go with an appetite). The main seating is in a *ranchón*; if you want to eat in the air-conditioned dining room, it carries a 20% surcharge and has to be booked in advance.

La Cova de Pizza Nova

Avenida 5ta, esquina 248, Marina Hemingway (209 7289/204 1150 ext 2899). **Open** noon-midnight daily. **Main courses** CUC 3.75-10.85. **Credit** MC, V.

Marina Hemingway used to be a top-end place for yachtie-types and others seeking to escape the Cuban grit and grime. In the past couple of years it has been occupied mostly by impoverished Venezuelans who have come to Cuba to receive free medical treatment, so the atmosphere has changed somewhat. Pizza Nova is located alongside one of the marina's canals and has a charming outdoor patio with a huge rubber tree and a bar with a fresh ocean breeze. The pizza, served on a thin crust with plenty of sizzling cheese, comes with a choice of toppings, including lobster. The atmosphere is pleasant and the Mojitos are excellent.

La Finca

Calle 140, esquina 19, Cubanacán (208 7976). **Open** noon-midnight Mon-Sat. **Main courses** CUC 14-30. **Credit** MC, V.

Feel like a splurge? The Farm should be able to help out. It's run by Cuba's gastronomic guru Tomás Erasmo, who, after opening El Tocororo (*see p117*) and El Rancho Palco (just across the street from La Finca), moved on to this more ambitious project. The atmosphere is elegant and romantic, but not overly formal and, best of all, you feel as though you are in a tropical paradise, surrounded by lush plants and trees. All dishes are beautifully presented, from the lobster thermidor or grill to the fresh fish or the sizzling beef platter. Erasmo offers to make almost any dish you fancy if the ingredients are there; they're all fresh (except the beef, which is imported from Chile). Exclusive – and expensive.

Pabellón del Tesoro

Avenida 5ta, esquina 248, Marina Hemingway (204 11500). **Open** 11am-4pm, 7-11pm daily. **Main courses** CUC 6-12. **No credit cards**.

This is a great Chinese option if you're in the area. Located at the end of one of the jetties, the restaurant offers an excellent alternative to Chinatown, especially if you value peace and quiet over the hustle of Centro Habana. Prices are higher than Chinatown, but generally worth it.

Pan.Com

Calle 7ma, esquina 26, Miramar (204 2328). **Open** 10am-midnight Mon-Thur; 10am-2pm Fri-Sun. **Main courses** CUC 1-5. **No credit cards**. **Map** p253 B5 58

In a country where ham and cheese sandwiches are the only meal you can buy involving bread, clean, efficient Pan.Com (meaning Bread.Com) successfully breaks the mould. With three types of bread, fillings that include turkey breast, cream cheese and spiced sausage at reasonable prices, it's hardly surprising that this joint has become a favourite hangout. For a simple meal Pan.Com is hard to beat.

Rancho Palco

Calle 140, esquina 19, Cubanacán (208 9346).
Open noon-11pm daily. **Main courses** CUC 6-26. **Credit** MC, V.
Another of chef Tomás Erasmo's creations, this is a favourite with large groups of diplomats and visiting Americans. With an outside eating area surrounded by lush vegetation, it almost feels like you're eating in an upscale jungle (don't forget the insect repellent). There's also an air-conditioned area, live music and excellent food – fish is especially good, as is the Cuban fare. It all comes at a price, mind, and it can be noisy, so probably not the best place for a quiet romantic dinner.

El Tocororo

Calle 18, entre 3ra y 5ta, Miramar (204 2209/ 202 4530). **Open** noon-midnight Mon-Sat. **Main courses** CUC 12-40. **Credit** MC, V. **Map** p253 A5 (59)
Once Cuba's only sophisticated restaurant, El Tocororo was opened by Tomás Erasmo at a time when pork, rice and beans were all you could get. The decor has a distinct pre-Revolution bourgeois flavour, but lately the place has become more accessible. The speciality is meat and live lobster. Service is excellent, and the food well presented and delicious, but there's no menu: you may have to struggle with the waiters' often-broken English. At night an excellent jazz and Cuban music band entertains while you eat. Alternatively, check out the tapas bar (with live music open until 3am) or Tocororo's Japanese restaurant, the only one of its kind in Havana, serving delicious sushi, sashimi and tempura. T-shirts and shorts are frowned on.

Yasmín

Calle 152, entre 3ra y 5ta, Náutico, Playa (208 7606/7). **Open** noon-11pm daily. **No credit cards**.
The only truly authentic Arabic restaurant in Havana, serving good-quality dishes prepared from imported ingredients by Syrian chefs. Prices are very reasonable, from houmous at just CUC 2 to kebabs from around CUC 7. On the downside, the atmosphere can be lacking, but the food more than compensates. For something a bit different, this place is highly recommended.

Paladares

La Cocina de Lilliam

Calle 48 #1311, entre 13 y 15, Playa (209 6514).
Open noon-3pm, 7-10pm Mon-Fri, Sun. Closed 1st 2wks Aug, last 2wks Dec. **Main courses** CUC 8.50-12. **Map** p252 C3 (60)
This is where the rich and famous (Jimmy Carter, the Rothschilds) go when in Cuba – though you don't have to be either to come here. What started as a humble family-run restaurant has gone upmarket with an intercom entry system and electronic door. Inside, Lilliam's beautiful garden restaurant shines, with the tables set in intimate corners of a large patio filled with tropical plants. The food is excellent: try the chicken mousse, *ropa vieja* (here made with lamb) or stewed lamb. Portions are huge so you may want to share. There's a small, air-conditioned (to Arctic levels) eating area upstairs. Unlike most state-run restaurants, the service is friendly, efficient and in most cases bilingual. If you show up without a booking, you'll be lucky to get a table.

El Diluvio

Calle 72 #1705, entre 17 y 19, Playa (202 1531).
Open noon-2pm, 6.30pm-midnight daily. **Main courses** CUC 7-10. **Map** p252 D2 (61)
One of a set of good-quality Miramar *paladares*, El Diluvio ('the flood') is truly Italian and has one of Cuba's only traditional clay ovens, which explains why the pizzas are so good. Real Italian flavour is also provided for a range of pastas. Service is excellent and the chef very friendly, as well as talented.

Doctor Café

Calle 28 #111, entre 1ra y 3ra, Miramar (203 4718/892 2584). **Open** noon-midnight daily. **Main courses** CUC 5-15. **No credit cards**. **Map** p253 A5 (62)
Occupying a small space in a suburban street, this busy café is friendly and efficient. You can choose to sit under the pergola filled with tropical plants or in the small air-conditioned room. Food is healthy and delicious, and prepared mostly on the large BBQ. The menu changes according to season, featuring seafood, fish and sometimes lamb or beef. The wine list is worth a look, too, with bottles starting from around CUC 12.

La Esperanza

Calle 16 #105, entre 1ra y 3ra (202 4361).
Open 7-11pm Mon-Sat. **Main courses** CUC 10-13. **Map** p253 A5 (63)
This fine *paladar* is like a quaint English drawing room that's been given art deco-meets-baroque touches. There is no menu, which means that one of the two owners will lovingly or brusquely (depending on their mood) recite the options for you. It also means that the final bill will generally not be cheap. Nevertheless, food is prepared with care and the overall experience is usually a very good one. Highly recommended – and popular, so book.

La Fontana

Calle 46 #305, esquina 3ra, Miramar (202 8337).
Open noon-midnight daily. **Main courses** CUC 8-15. **Map** p252 B3 (64)
This long-established, upmarket *paladar* has a steady clientele. There's space to sit at the pleasant terrace, at the *ranchón* out back and in the inside air-conditioned area. Grilled meat and seafood, includ-

ing octopus, snails and fish, are the speciality, and you can see your food being prepared on the large open grill. The fish and seafood kebabs are outstanding; grilled, boneless chicken is lip-smackingly juicy. The wine list is small but adequate. If only the music trio didn't always turn up next to you in the middle of an interesting conversation.

Eastern Bay & the Coast

Restaurants

Los XII Apóstoles

Below Castillo del Morro, Parque Histórico Militar Morro-Cabaña (863 8295). **Open** *Restaurant* noon-11pm daily. *Bar* 11pm-2am daily. **Main courses** CUC 4-28. **No credit cards**. **Map** p255 C16 65

For trad Creole food and a fine view of the Malecón, the Twelve Apostles, situated at the foot of the lighthouse by the Morro Castle, is a good bet. A terrific meat platter, including beef, is yours for around CUC 15, though half a chicken will only set you back CUC 5. At 11pm the place turns into a karaoke bar.

La Tasca

Complejo Morro-Cabaña, Carretera Monumetal, Habana del Este (860 8341). **Open** noon-11pm daily. **Main courses** CUC 5-28. **Credit** MC, V. **Map** p255 C15 66

This snack bar/grill has all the views of the nearby higher-priced Divina Pastora restaurant, but lower prices. The food is similar, too, with fish and seafood the specialities, plus grilled meat and combos (CUC 5.50 for chicken, CUC 9.95 for pork, chicken and fish) and combo grills. A traditional music group plays in the evenings.

La Terraza de Cojímar

Calle Real #161, esquina Candelaria (93 9486). **Open** *Restaurant* noon-midnight daily. *Bar* 10am-midnight daily. **Main courses** CUC 6-35. **Credit** MC, V.

This is a pleasant restaurant despite the tour groups. The walls are lined with black and white shots of Hemingway, many by famous Cuban photographers Raúl Corrales and Alberto 'Korda' Gutiérrez. Included are several images of Gregorio Fuentes – the model for the fisherman in *Old Man and the Sea* – who died in 2002 at the ripe old age of 104. Today it's a seafood restaurant with a beautiful view overlooking the river (bring a sweater: there can be a strong breeze). Try the Paella Terraza (CUC 7) or the *ranchito de mariscos al horno* (CUC 13), like a paella but with more meat and seafood, and cooked in an earthenware bowl.

Paladares

Piccolo

Avenida 5ta #50206, entre 502 y 504, Guanabo (96 4300). **Open** noon-midnight daily. **Main courses** CUC 4-9. **No credit cards**.

The open kitchen at the Piccolo, complete with wood-fired oven, turns out a fine pizza. In fact, nearly all the food is very good, very Italian (even though the owners are actually Greek) and very good value. The huge fruit and veg arrangement at the entrance is impressive, and the vegetable garden makes for a pleasant stroll.

Drinking

Tourists inspired by Ernest Hemingway, Graham Greene and Havana's legendary decadence of long-gone decades are often disappointed by the drinking scene in the city. Periodic police crackdowns on undesirables and an emphasis on upmarket tourism, with prices that keep Cubans away, have not helped to create bars with real atmosphere.

The classic Hemingway haunts – **La Bodeguita del Medio** (*see p105*; **photo** *p121*) and **El Floridita** (*see p108*) – are particularly under-patronised by locals, and have become little more than photo opportunities. It is telling that on some nights, while the tourist bars in

Dos Hermanos. *See p120.*

Eat, Drink, Shop

Old Havana are deserted at midnight, the Malecón is packed six deep with locals and there are large queues outside some nightclubs.

What Havana does have is a number of European-style patio bars in settings with rich architectural heritage. In Old Havana, each of the main squares (Plaza de la Catedral, Plaza de Armas, Plaza de San Francisco and Plaza Vieja) has bars providing a colonial-style ambience that's hard to beat for an afternoon or early evening drink. It's later on in the evening that Old Havana struggles to find a beat.

Where do normal Cubans go for a drink? In general not to the same bars as tourists – unless they want to meet said tourists, of course. Young Cubans with money will go to Friday night parties, to watch comedy at **La Roca** (*see p115*), or will simply hang out with their particular crowd – artsy types at concerts in the cinema, bohemians at concerts in the park and heavy metallers at concerts on the Malecón.

Pure drinking is generally reserved for middle-aged Cubans who sip rum and beer in outdoor cafeterias or dismal peso bars. The latter are worth a look to see a different side of Cuba, but don't stay around to use the toilets. There are plenty of peso bars dotted around Calle Neptuno in Centro Habana.

Drinks are priced pretty universally at CUC 1-2 for a beer (imported beers can cost more) and CUC 2-5 for a cocktail (Mojito, Cuba Libre and Daiquiri are the most common). Cristal – a light lager – is the most-served Cuban beer, while Bucanero and Mayabe are darker.

The best Places

For soaking up the atmosphere

La Terraza del Hotel Nacional (*see p120*) positively oozes history.

For mixing with the locals

Castropol is always packed with Cubans, while **La Fuente** has a more attractive Vedado vibe (for both, *see p120*).

For getting away from it all

Café La Barrita in the Bacardí building (*see below*) offers peace and quiet by the bucketload.

For celebrity graffiti

Yes it's touristy, but there aren't many places apart from **La Bodeguita del Medio** (*see p105*) where you get a permanent marker with your cocktail.

La Habana Vieja

See also p106 **Café del Oriente** *and p110* **La Taberna de la Muralla**.

Bar Chico O'Farrill

Palacio O'Farrill, Calle Cuba #102, esquina Chacón (860 5080). **Open** 10am-11pm daily. **Credit** MC, V. **Map** p256 D15 ❶

One of the better bars among those found in Habana Vieja's *hostales*, this place serves as a relaxing hideaway by day or by night. Bands perform on Thursdays, Fridays and Saturdays.

Bar Havana Club

Museo del Ron, Calle San Pedro #262, esquina Sol (861 8051/862 3832). **Open** 10am-midnight daily. **No credit cards**. **Map** p256 E15 ❷

The Rum Museum in the Fundación Havana Club is an apt setting for a bar, but unfortunately its museum location generally renders it a vacuum at night. Even during the day it's not exactly overrun with punters, although at lunchtime things usually pick up a bit thanks to the reasonable food available. Whatever time you visit, there's an excellent cocktail selection to choose from.

Bar Monserrate

Avenida de Bélgica (Monserrate) #401, esquina Obrapía (860 9751). **Open** 11am-midnight daily. **No credit cards**. **Map** p256 E14 ❸

Still one of the most consistent venues on the Old Havana bar scene. While maintaining much of its nostalgic appeal – multiple ceiling fans whir, surly waiters strut – Bar Monserrate is probably not the best place for a quiet drink. A phalanx of Cubans tends to descend on unsuspecting newcomers with offers to take them to the best disco in town/sell cigars/teach them tiddlywinks (you get the picture). The bands that play here are pretty good.

Bosque Bologna

Calle Obispo #460, entre Villegas y Aguacate (no phone). **Open** 11am-midnight daily. **No credit cards**. **Map** p256 D15 ❹

One of the few leafy spots on Calle Obispo and, accordingly, one of the more attractive and tranquil looking places for a drink. Like all bars and cafés on this bustly street, however, there's still a sense of commotion here, particularly when a band is playing (which is often).

Café La Barrita

Edificio Bacardí, Avenida de Bélgica #261, esquina San Juan de Dios (862 9310). **Open** 9am-9pm daily. **No credit cards**. **Map** p256 D15 ❺

This relatively unknown café-bar beyond the lobby of the magnificent Bacardí building is a real treat. Its classic art deco interior makes it unique among Old Havana's bars, and the mezzanine location somehow adds to its classy yet down-to-earth feel. Kick back on the leather sofas or sip cocktails at the window seats. One of the best places in La Habana Vieja to get away from it all.

Café O'Reilly

Calle O'Reilly #203, entre Cuba y San Ignacio (no phone). **Open** 9am-midnight daily. **No credit cards. Map** p256 E15 ❻

Located only a block away from the restlessness of Calle Obispo is this relaxing, rustic two-floor café. Climb the cast-iron spiral staircase and try to squeeze yourself on to the balcony up above, a perfect spot for a bit of people-watching. It's also good for a light snack too.

Café París

Calle Obispo, esquina San Ignacio (no phone). **Open** 8am-1am daily. **No credit cards. Map** p256 E15 ❼

One of the busiest bars in La Habana Vieja, although it has sadly become overrun with hustlers. Live music is provided every night until midnight by an excellent band (oddly enough, however, dancing is generally prohibited). For newcomers the attraction really is to bar-perch, and take in the comings and goings over a drink.

Dos Hermanos

Avenida del Puerto (San Pedro) #305, esquina Sol (861 3514). **Open** 10am-midnight daily. **No credit cards. Map** p256 E15 ❽

This port-style bar is a little off the tourist track and, as such, is a refreshingly straightforward place to neck back a beer. No house band, no hoards of loitering hustlers, just a traditional watering hole. Worth a visit, but maybe not a detour. **Photo** *p118.*

Hotel Ambos Mundos

Calle Obispo, esquina Mercaderes (860 9529-31). **Open** 24hrs daily. **Credit** MC, V. **Map** p253 E15 ❾

The elegant lobby bar of this hotel can have its ambience thrown out of sync by visiting tourist groups. Instead, head up to the rooftop bar, which is close to the action below but far enough away to enjoy your drink in peace. Gorgeous views too.

La Lluvia de Oro

Calle Obispo #316, esquina Habana (862 9870). **Open** 10am-midnight daily. **No credit cards. Map** p256 E15 ❿

Big on wood and space, this is the best bar on Calle Obispo on aesthetic grounds. But somehow it seems to miss out in the atmosphere stakes when there's no band playing. Nonetheless, it's a good place to meet people, Cuban and foreign alike.

Centro Habana

Castropol

Malecón #107, entre Genios y Crespo (861 4864). **Open** noon-midnight daily. **No credit cards. Map** p256 C14 ⓫

This social club is set in a marvellous (if rundown) building right on the Malecón. The upstairs has been turned into a restaurant (open noon-midnight, main courses CUC 3-12) serving Cuban, Italian, Chinese and international cuisine, which has slightly relegated the downstairs bar to the poor relation. However, that hasn't stopped this venue rapidly becoming a local Cuban favourite: it's worth keeping an ear out for the parties that often take place at Castropol.

Hotel Inglaterra

Paseo de Martí (Prado) #416, esquina San Rafael (860 8595/7). **Open** 24hrs daily. **Credit** MC, V. **Map** p256 D14 ⓬

The veranda bar is a great spot for a pre-theatre drink, with the Gran Teatro next door. The roof bar (La Paradilla) has a wonderful view of Parque Central, but is more geared to copious drinking than to savouring the vista. The band, typically good, is very loud – too loud to have a conversation. The only real solution here is to get up and dance.

Vedado

Primavera (*see p114*) and **La Roca** (*see p115*) are also prime spots for a drink.

Cafetería Sofía

Calle 23 #202, esquina O (832 0740). **Open** 24hrs daily. **No credit cards. Map** p254 B12 ⓭

This is the local that everyone loves to hate. On quiet nights it may be the only bar in town that is really busy, which, given its unattractive decor and lack of sophistication, may come as a surprise. Its interest lies more in the tide of people drifting in and out.

La Fuente

Calle 13, entre F y G (no phone). **Open** 11.30pm-midnight Mon-Thur; 11.30am-1.30am Fri-Sun. **No credit cards. Map** p254 B10 ⓮

One of Havana's best bars, with greenery on all sides and a lovely fountain as the focal point. This is residential territory, so don't come expecting wild salsa dancing on tables, but rather to get an authentic look at neighbourhood life. Shots and beers are cheap.

Opus Habana

3rd floor, Teatro Amadeo Roldán, Calle Calzada #512, esquina D (836 5429). **Open** 3pm-3am daily. **Map** p254 A10 ⓯

A wonderfully kitsch 1970s joint (actually quite modern by Havana standards), where couples sit holding hands on the comfortable leather seats enjoying the happy tunes and fine view. Drinks are good and the service excellent. Food on offer is limited, but if you're hungry at 1am there are certainly worse options.

La Terraza del Hotel Nacional

Calle O, esquina 21 (836 3564/873 3564). **Open** 24hrs daily. **Credit** MC, V. **Map** p254 B12 ⓰

The Hotel Nacional conjures up images of grandeur that – with a palm-lined, spotlit driveway and smart doormen – are not far from being delivered. The magnificent terrace (straight through the lobby) is a perfect place for a pre-dinner drink – it's one of the very few places in Cuba with comfortable lounge seats and sea views and, if you're assertive, slick service. *See also p113.*

Trading (successfully) on the Hemingway connection: **La Bodeguita del Medio**. *See p105.*

Shops & Services

No overdraft necessary.

Let's get one thing straight: Havana is no shopper's paradise. There's very little of what you can't get elsewhere, and because of the embargo even basics can be hard to come by.

The city does at least provide an interesting selection of local arts and crafts, plus the occasional vintage find. In addition, imported clothes, jewellery, perfumes and electronics can be bought at an increasing number of shopping centres and boutiques. Just don't expect the latest trends – or bargain prices. If you see something you like, buy it – you're unlikely to find exactly the same item elsewhere and prices don't vary much across town. Not surprisingly, good-quality products sell out fast. (And 'good quality' is a relative term in Cuba.)

WHERE TO SHOP

Havana's pre-1959 shopping streets – Calle Obispo (in La Habana Vieja), Calle San Rafael and Avenida de Italia (Galiano) (both in Centro Habana) – with their once grand and stylish shops and department stores, haven't quite been revived by the renovation works, but have a reasonable selection. Most better-stocked shops are found in hotels and the Miramar suburbs. One option is to root around the drab peso stores, which will give you an idea of what shopping is like for the locals – but little else.

MONEY MATTERS

Almost anything of interest to visitors to Havana will be charged in CUC (*pesos convertibles*). The more adventurous traveller may want to obtain some Cuban pesos (*moneda nacional*) from the CADECAs (exchange kiosks) scattered around town. Cuban pesos will buy you flowers, toasted peanuts from street sellers, produce at the local fruit and vegetable markets (*see p130* **Living on the veg**), Cuban-style fast food in 'corner shops', Cuban cigarettes and dubious-looking street rum (only of real interest to the self-harming). Cuban pesos will also get you second-hand clothes and shoes (or ones that are long out of fashion or of very poor quality), and a limited selection of household goods in the Cuban peso shops and department stores found in Avenida de Italia (Galiano) in Centro.

Also, don't rely on credit cards: because of the embargo, those issued or backed by an American bank are invalid in Cuba. Other credit cards are accepted in a limited number of establishments, but as phone lines and credit card machines can be out of order, cash is usually best. Try to carry small denomination notes: larger bills (CUC 50 and 100) must be accompanied by a passport and the shop may not be able to change them. For more on currencies and credit cards, *see p230*.

RULES OF ENGAGEMENT

In many places you're required to deposit your bag in a *guardabolso* (deposit box); if so, keep your money and passport. Hold on to your receipt, as guards at the door are obliged to check it against the goods as you leave. The concept of refunds and exchanges is a fledgling one in Havana; exchanging some electrical goods with guarantees shouldn't be a problem, but getting a refund is very hit and miss.

Cubans are only just learning to serve customers with the international standards of etiquette, they are unmotivated and a competitive job market is not really an issue. However, you may encounter professionalism that will make you wonder if you are in the same country. Finally, try not to continually compare things to back home.

One-stop shops

Department stores

La Época

Calle Neptuno #359, entre de Italia (Galiano) y San Nicolás, Centro Habana (866 9423/9692). **Open** 10am-6.30pm Mon-Sat; 10am-1.45pm Sun. **Credit** MC, V. **Map** p255 D14.

A rather tired-looking department store in the heart of Centro Habana. It offers toiletries, fashion clothing, footwear, electrical goods, children's clothes and cosmetics. It also has a relatively good sports clothes shop, and a supermarket and hardware store.

Harris Brothers

Avenida de Bélgica (Monserrate) #305, entre O'Reilly y Progreso (San Juan de Dios), La Habana Vieja (861 1644/1615). **Open** 10am-9pm Mon-Sat; 9am-6pm Sun. **Credit** MC, V. **Map** p256 D14.

This department store stocks fashion, sportswear, children's clothes and toys, a variety of downmarket toiletries, household items and furniture.

La Maison

Calle 16 #701, esquina 7ma, Miramar (204 1543/1585). **Open** 10am-10pm Mon-Sat; 10am-3pm Sun. **Credit** MC, V. **Map** p253 B6.

Let your nose guide you to **Habana 1791**. *See p133.*

This collection of shops is famous for holding fashion shows. Inside you'll find a good jewellery store, clothing outlets with reasonable prices, and shops selling home accessories, sportswear, footwear and cosmetics. The gift store has an excellent selection of traditional Cuban *guayaberas* (*see p129* **Get shirty**), in both cotton and linen. The complex also houses a registry office, where foreigners can marry.

Le Select

Avenida 5ta, esquina 30, Miramar (204 4098). **Open** 10am-6pm Mon-Sat. **Credit** MC, V. **Map** p253 B5.
This complex is set in a beautiful colonial building. There are a couple of boutiques for men and women, and a toiletries shop. On the downside, staff are often busy chatting or simply 'out', and the once well-stocked delicatessen seems at times like a neglected corner shop, with some items past their sell-by date.

Shopping centres

See also p125 **Centro Comercial Palco**.

Casa Bella

Avenida 7ma #2603, esquina 26, Miramar (204 3566). **Open** 10am-7.30pm Mon-Sat; 10am-3pm Sun. **Credit** MC, V. **Map** p253 B5.
This palatial house contains a pharmacy, perfume and shoe shop (for men and women), plus clothes boutiques upstairs, including one for children.

Centro Comercial El Comodoro

Avenida 3ra, esquina 84, Playa (204 6178/9). **Open** 10am-7.30pm Mon-Sat; 10am-3pm Sun. **Credit** MC, V. **Map** p252 B1.
Once an aristocratic club, this is arguably the best shopping complex in Havana. It offers quality products, good customer service and a comfortable environment. Stores include a supermarket, perfumery, jeweller's, a photo developing outlet, a pharmacy, and shops selling children's and electronic goods, sports equipment, shoes and bags. A cigar shop is also on the premises. For beauty, *see p132*.

Centro Comercial La Vigía

Avenida 5ta, esquina 248, Marina Hemingway, Barlovento (204 1151/1156). **Open** 10am-7pm Mon-Sat; 10am-3pm Sun. **Credit** MC, V.
Fear of boat thefts has led to an intensive security presence at the Marina, where shops and restaurants cater for yacht owners, diplomats and expats. There are fashion boutiques, good perfumery and cosmetics shops, footwear and three sportswear stores.

Centro de Negocios Miramar

Avenida 3ra, entre 76 y 80, Miramar (204 4437/8 ext 114). **Open** 10am-6pm Mon-Sat; 10am-1pm Sun. **Credit** MC, V. **Map** p252 B2.
This smart trade centre hosts several boutiques, plus a sportswear store, a photo developing shop, a shoe shop, a jewellery shop, a small supermarket, a mobile phone store, a post office with internet facilities (204 5181), and a bank with a cash machine.

Galerías Amazonas

Calle 12, entre 23 y 25, Vedado (831 9598). **Open** 10am-7pm Mon-Sat; 10am-3pm Sun. **Credit** MC, V. **Map** p253 C8.
This set of shops, near the Chaplin cinema and the Cementerio Colón, has fresh flowers and potted plants for sale in Cuban pesos, a delicatessen, men's and women's fashion, shoe and luggage shop Peletería Claudia and a drinks bar. Opposite is a well-stocked sports shop and a good toiletries store.

Galerías Cohíba

Hotel Meliá Cohíba, Avenida Paseo, entre 1ra y 3ra, Vedado (833 3636). **Open** 10am-7pm Mon-Sat; 10am-2pm Sun. **Credit** MC, V. **Map** p254 A9.

Up in smoke

Cuba is the country that historically produces the best tobacco in the world; and Cuban cigars reel in millions of tourists each year. Of the major cultivating areas, Vuelta Abajo (Pinar del Río Province) and Vuelta Arriba (Villa Clara Province) are considered to have the best *vegas* (small plots). Havana, however, is cigar city, home to the *habano*. This is where the *torcido* (rolling) takes place, transforming the tobacco leaves – already dried and aged – into *habano* cigars. Of the guided tours, the **Partagás** factory (Calle Industria #520, entre Dragones y Barcelona, Centro Habana, 866 8060, tour CUC 10) is the best. For La Corona, *see p78*; for H Upmann, *see p88*.

TIPS ON BUYING CIGARS

- There are two ways to know if a cigar is hand-rolled: the higher price tag and the inscription on the bottom of the box that says *totalmente hecho a mano* (totally hand-rolled).
- Every cigar box has a code stamped on the bottom that indicates the factory where it was made. Factory of origin is important with some brands, such as **Cohíba**, where the best cigars are rolled at the **El Laguito** factory. In addition, the date of packaging is stamped at the bottom of the box – older packing can sometimes be a quality guarantee as the tobacco will be better aged.
- Choosing the size and flavour of a cigar is a matter of personal preference. The most prestigious brand of cigars – as the name suggests – is **Cohíba Espléndidos**. It was the first brand created after the Revolution and all its tobacco comes from the best *vegas* of Vuelta Abajo. More recent brands include **Cuaba**, **Vegas Robaina**, **Vegueros** (made in Pinar del Río), **San Cristóbal de La Habana** and **Trinidad**. Pre-Revolutionary brands still going strong include **Partagás**, **Montecristo** (the top-selling brand), **H Upmann**, **Romeo y Julieta** and **Punch**.
- Each box of cigars must carry the government stamp, the *habanos* stamp and a holographic stamp. To take the cigars out of the country you need the purchase invoice.
- Black market cigars are usually fake and although they sell at half the price or less, they don't offer even half the pleasure (unless, of course, you like smoking banana leaves). The best places to buy real *habanos* are the Casa del Habano shops that are dotted throughout the city. The nicest branches are at the Partagás cigar factory (*see p78*) and at the corner of 5ta and 16, Miramar (204 7975). All accept credit cards.

The Hotel Meliá Cohíba's lobby has a range of shops, including a luxurious deli, fashion boutiques, a perfumery and a sports equipment shop. Cigar, souvenir and jewellery shops are further inside.

Galerías de Paseo

Calle 1ra, entre Paseo y A, Vedado (838 3475/ 833 9888). **Open** 9am-9pm daily. **Credit** MC, V. **Map** p254 A9.

The three floors of shops here include one of the better supermarkets in town, furniture stores, fashion boutiques, shoe shops, and photo developing, as well as stores selling electrical goods, toys, and home accessories. You can relax in the Jazz Café on the top floor. Pretty good shopping – for Cuba.

Galería de Tiendas Internacionales

Hotel Habana Libre, Calle 25, esquina L, Vedado (838 4011). **Open** 9am-6pm Mon-Sat. **Credit** MC, V. **Map** p254 C11.

This centrally located arcade attached to the Hotel Habana Libre includes a pharmacy, a music store, several fashion boutiques and sports shops, a shoe shop, a shop selling hair products, and toy stores. You can also find a jewellery and small cosmetics shop and a hairdressing salon, plus outlets selling souvenirs, liquor and perfumes by the entrance.

Plaza de Carlos III

Avenida Salvador Allende (Carlos III), entre Retiro y Árbol Seco, Centro Habana (873 6374-8). **Open** 10am-7pm Mon-Sat; 10am-2pm Sun. **Credit** MC, V. **Map** p254 D12.

The design of this well-known shopping centre in Centro Habana can induce a sensation of being trapped in a spin dryer. It's very popular among Cubans, featuring clothes stores, a photo developer, sports, cigar and shoe shops, a supermarket, a food court and several 'everything for CUC 1-10' shops.

La Puntilla

Avenida 1ra, entre A y B, Miramar (204 5209/4634). **Open** 9am-6pm Mon-Sat; 9am-2pm Sun. **Credit** MC, V. **Map** p253 A7.

This four-storey shopping centre in Playa has a grill restaurant, a snack bar and fantastic view point. Shops include a supermarket, clothes boutiques, shoe, sportswear and children's clothes shops, and a section of household goods. A photo shop is on the first floor, a hardware store in the basement.

5ta y 42

Avenida 5ta, esquina 42, Miramar (204 7070/2601). **Open** 9am-8pm Mon-Sat; 9am-3pm Sun. **Credit** MC, V. **Map** p252 B4.

Part of the Cubalse chain of shops, this centre has a large array of shops selling all manner of items: food, sportswear, clothing, kids' stuff, shoes, toiletries, beauty products, electricals, fabrics and hardware. **Other locations**: throughout the city.

Supermarkets

Some say Havana is one huge supermarket, and that's not a compliment. To fill your shopping basket, it's almost compulsory to visit most shops in town. The majority of the local grocery stores sell the basics – eggs, flour, sugar, rice, tinned food, UHT or condensed milk, frozen chicken, drinks and toiletries – but often have a limited selection of other items. In addition to the following, other options include **5ta y 42** (*see above*), **Centro Comercial El Comodoro** (*see p123*) or **La Puntilla** (*see above*).

Centro Comercial Palco

Calle 188, esquina 5ta, Playa (273 2168). **Open** 10am-9pm daily. **Credit** MC, V.

Havana's best-stocked supermarket, El Palco has the largest selection of mostly imported groceries, frozen goods, soft and alcoholic drinks, bakery items, cleaning products and toiletries. The growing complex also includes shops selling hardware, shoes, pharmacy items, linen and fabrics.

Supermercado 3ra y 70

Avenida 3ra, entre 68 y 70, Playa (204 4034/6117). **Open** 10am-7pm Mon-Sat; 10am-2pm Sun. **Credit** MC, V. **Map** p252 B2.

This is, by size, the most impressive food store in the city, though long shelves often display the same item for metres. A hardware store is attached.

Antiques

Antiques shops are a rarity in Cuba. You're most likely to see the relics of the country's bourgeois past in government-owned mansions in Vedado and Miramar. However, there is one delightful store, **La Vajilla** (*see below*).

There are strict laws governing the export of items deemed to be of national heritage, so buy from an authorised source. Official shops will provide a receipt and a confirmation for customs (*sello oficial*). If you're not given an export certificate when you buy the item, take it (or a photo if it's too large) to the **National Heritage Office** (Registro Nacional de Bienes Culturales, Calle 17 #1009, entre 10 y 12, Vedado, 833 9658/831 3362) between 8.30am and noon from Monday to Friday. Classic cars and old paintings are the most strictly controlled, but furniture, stamps, coins, books and porcelain may also be restricted. At the time of writing, tourists could only export contemporary art and items purchased at artisan markets but those rules may change.

Havana has a regular Saturday flea market, but the location keeps shifting. Ask around, but remember the restrictions.

La Vajilla

Avenida de Italia (Galiano) #502, esquina Zanja, Centro Habana (862 4751). **Open** 10am-5pm Mon-Sat. **No credit cards**. **Map** p255 D13.

Stock at La Vajilla can be erratic: on the one hand there are excellent examples of late 19th- and early 20th-century furniture and household items, including some superb chandeliers and stained-glass lampshades; other items are grotty and not worth much. This is an official antiques shop, but not everything on sale has a certificate for export.

Books

Antique & second-hand

You need to obtain special permission to take some older books out of the country. Bear in mind that the vendor may not know, or may tell you that you don't need permission regardless.

Librería Anticuaria 'El Navío'

Calle Obispo #119, entre Oficios y Mercaderes, La Habana Vieja (861 3187). **Open** 9am-7pm daily. **No credit cards**. **Map** p256 E15.

El Navío sells antique, new, second-hand and collectable books, plus stamp collections, old photos, postcards, cigar bands and reproductions of Cuban bank notes. The shop was built in the mid 16th century: a portion of the original wall, in the attached courtyard, is protected by glass and parts of the shop's wall reveal original frescoes. **Photo** *p126*.

Plaza de Armas book market

Plaza de Armas, La Habana Vieja (no phone). **Open** 9am-6pm Wed-Sat; closed when raining/overcast. **No credit cards**. **Map** p256 E16.

This book market (*mercado de libros*) has numerous political tracts, books on the Cuban Revolution, Márquez novels, plus atlases, encyclopaedias and the odd book in English. You can find some wonderful old books and some great bindings, but also junk. Feel free to bargain as the prices can be high.

General

International press is almost impossible to get hold of, though you'll sometimes find Italian or Spanish newspapers in hotels.

Centro Cultural Cinematográfico ICAIC

Calle 23 #1156, entre 10 y 12, Vedado (833 9278). **Open** 9am-5pm Mon-Sat. **No credit cards.** **Map** p253 C8.

If you don't make it to the cinema while you're in Havana, you might want at least to stop by the Cuban Film Institute for Cuban films on video (some with English subtitles) and DVD. There's a bar on site too (*see p150*).

Instituto Cubano del Libro

Calle O'Reilly #4, esquina Tacón, La Habana Vieja (863 2244). **Open** 10am-5.30pm daily. **Credit** MC, V. **Map** p256 E15.

The Cuban Book Institute houses three bookshops. Gribaldo Mondadori stocks non-fiction and modern fiction, while La Bella Habana covers guidebooks, music and some political-historical books in English. Librería Fayad Jamis sells books in Cuban pesos.

Librería Ateneo Cervantes

Calle Bernaza #9, esquina Obispo, La Habana Vieja (862 2580). **Open** 9am-9pm daily. **No credit cards.** **Map** p256 D14.

A Cuban peso bookshop selling new and second-hand children's books, a selection of international literature and Cuban poetry.

Librería La Internacional

Calle Obispo #526, esquina Bernaza, La Habana Vieja (861 3283/863 1941-4). **Open** 10am-5.30pm daily. **No credit cards.** **Map** p256 D14.

A reasonable range of fiction and non-fiction books, CDs, cassettes, office supplies and postcards.

Librería Rubén Martínez Villena

Paseo de Martí (Prado) #551, esquina Brasil (Teniente Rey), Centro Habana (861 5849). **Open** 10am-5.30pm Mon-Sat; 10am-1pm Sun. **No credit cards.** **Map** p255 E14.

A mixture of science, education, fiction and political publications, mainly in Spanish. Cuban and some international literature (including a very small selection in English) is also available.

La Moderna Poesía

Calle Obispo #527, esquina Bernaza, La Habana Vieja (861 6983/6640). **Open** 10am-6pm daily. **Credit** MC, V. **Map** p256 D14.

This spacious shop specialises in Spanish-language editions of fiction and non-fiction (including Cuban short stories and poems), posters, magazines, stationery, music, videos and CDs. Books in English can sometimes be found too. Reprographic and binding services are also offered.

Children's clothes & toys

Crafts markets (*ferias*) often stock interesting handmade toys. The department stores are also a good bet, in particular **Centro Comercial El Comodoro** (*see p123*). If you're after

Book some time into your schedule to visit **Librería Anticuaria 'El Navío'**. *See p125.*

clothes, shoes and accessories visit Miramar's **5ta y 42** (*see p125*), **La Puntilla** (*see p125*) or **Harris Brothers** (*see p122*).

Muñecos de Leyendas

Calle Mercaderes #26, entre Empedrado y O'Reilly, La Habana Vieja (no phone). **Open** 10am-6pm Tue-Sun. **No credit cards**. **Map** p256 D15.

A charming – if rather twee – little shop stocking elves, dwarfs, gnomes and fairies, most of which are inspired by Scandinavian mythology.

Design & household goods

It's unusual to find much in the way of tastefully designed items in Havana. Of the department stores, **Centro Comercial El Comodoro** (*see p123*) generally offers the best selection of quality housewares. For fabrics and trimmings, *see below*. Calle Obispo in Old Havana has a few stores stocking household goods – among them are **La Francia** (Obispo esquina Aguacate) and **La Distinguida** (Obispo 110, entre Bernaza y Villegas). For furniture, try the department stores or shopping malls, especially **Galerías de Paseo** (*see p124*).

Artehabana (Plaza Cultural)

San Rafael #10, esquina Industria, Centro Habana (860 8403). **Open** 11am-7pm Mon-Sat; 11am-2pm Sun. **Credit** MC, V. **Map** p255 D14.

Movies, music and musical instruments, stereos, Cuban arts and crafts, books, stationery and shoes are sold at this multi-storey shop.

Colección Habana

Calle Mercaderes, esquina O'Reilly, La Habana Vieja (861 3388). **Open** 9am-7pm daily. **No credit cards**. **Map** p256 D15.

A variety of reproduction items, mostly imported from Spain. Choose from china, glass, furniture, jewellery (some vintage or second-hand), pottery, silk scarves, screens and Cuban artworks.

Galerías Manos (Asociación Cubana de Artesanos y Artistas)

Calle Obispo #411, entre Aguacate y Compostela, La Habana Vieja (866 6345/acaa@cubarte.cult.cu). **Open** 10am-5pm daily. **No credit cards**. **Map** p256 E15.

A Cuban arts and crafts shop selling hand-woven tapestries, lamps, handmade furniture, wooden carvings, paintings, musical instruments, shoes, bags, and jewellery. The attached courtyard hosts a small art market three times a week (*see p135*).

Mercado del Oriente

Calle Mercaderes #109, entre Obispo y Obrapía, La Habana Vieja (no phone). **Open** 10am-5pm daily. **Credit** DC, MC, V. **Map** p256 E15.

This Aladdin's Cave of a shop usually has a tempting array of oriental-style bedspreads, costume jewellery, carvings, tapestries and some clothing.

Electronics

Many items for sale in electronics outlets in Havana are not normally available to Cubans; locals are forced to buy them second-hand and/or on the black market. These goods include microwaves, computers, air-conditioners, freezers, video cameras and DVD players. In addition to the shops listed below, also consider the **Hotel Comodoro** (*see p123*), **Galerías de Paseo** shopping complex (*see p124*), **5ta y 42** (*see p125*) or **Artehabana** (*see p127*).

Casa Panasonic (Jardines de 5ta Avenida)

5ta Avenida, entre 112 y 114, Playa (204 8506). **Open** 10am-6pm Mon-Sat; 10am-1pm Sun. **Credit** MC, V.

TVs, cordless phones, cameras (and memory cards), CD players, radios, music systems, vacuum cleaners, microwaves and more, all by Panasonic.

Centro Video

Avenida 3ra, entre 12 y 14, Miramar (204 2469). **Open** 10am-5pm Mon-Sat. **No credit cards**. **Map** p253 B6.

This chain sells electrical equipment and videos, and also offers video rental and photocopying services. **Other locations**: throughout the city.

Dita

Calle 84, entre 7ma y 9na, Playa (204 5119). **Open** 10am-6pm Mon-Sat; 10am-1pm Sun. **Credit** MC, V. **Map** p252 C1.

Stock includes kitchen items, lighting, hi-fis, TVs, computers and computer components, phones and fax machines. Some items are only available to diplomats or foreigners with special permission, but there's still a wide choice for ordinary customers. **Other locations**: Miramar Trade Center, Avenida 3ra, entre 76 y 80, Miramar (204 0632).

Fabrics & trimmings

Dressmaking is very popular in Cuba, so fabric shops are common. As well as the following, **Centro Comercial El Comodoro** (*see p123*) has a branch of Revert; also try **La Puntilla**, **5ta y 42** or **Centro Comercial Palco** (for all, *see p125*).

Bisart (Teniente Rey)

Calle Brasil (Teniente Rey) #10, entre Oficios y Mercaderes, La Habana Vieja (862 0161). **Open** 10am-5pm Mon-Sat; 10am-2pm Sun. **No credit cards**. **Map** p256 E15.

A spacious, reasonably well-stocked fabric shop. It also sells souvenirs and a good range of T-shirts.

La Muñequita Azul

Calle Obispo, esquina Mercaderes, La Habana Vieja (no phone). **Open** 9am-7pm daily. **No credit cards**. **Map** p256 E15.

There's not much in the way of material here, but the Little Blue Doll does excel at broderie trimmings, satins, zips and cotton thread.

Revert

Calle Obispo #403, entre Aguacate y Compostela, La Habana Vieja (no phone). **Open** 10am-7pm Mon-Sat; 10am-1pm Sun. **No credit cards**. **Map** p256 E15.
Imported fabrics, towels, sheets and bed linen are sold in this operation overseen by the children of the late Mr Revert, whose photo is displayed in the shop.

Fashion

The price of clothing in Havana tends to be high, so *habaneros* have been forced to improvise in order to meet the high standards they set themselves in terms of appearance. Visitors on a budget could also root around some of the fashion boutiques for reductions.

Places worth checking out for decent clothing include **Le Select**, **Tierra Brava** at **Galerías Amazonas** and **Galerías Cohíba**, and **Centro Comercial El Comodoro** (for all, *see p123*). It is also worth browsing **La Época**, **La Maison** and **Harris Brothers** (for all, *see p122*), but apart from these three outlets you'll have to search hard to find anything of outstanding quality.

Benetton

Calle Amargura, esquina Oficios, La Habana Vieja (862 2480). **Open** 10am-7pm Mon-Sat; 10am-1pm Sun. **No credit cards**. **Map** p256 E15.
The world-famous Italian brand also has a concession at the Centro Comercial El Comodoro (*see p123*). Don't expect to come across the up-to-date stuff you find back home, though.

Guayabera Habanera

Calle Tacón #20, entre O'Reilly y Empedrado, La Habana Vieja (no phone). **Open** 9.30am-6pm Mon-Fri; 9am-1pm Sat. **No credit cards**. **Map** p256 D16.
No prizes for guessing what's on sale here – *guayaberas* (*see p129* **Get shirty**), of superior quality, cotton, cotton mix or pure linen, in a good choice of shades. There are women's versions too.

Novator

Calle Obispo #365, entre Compostela y Habana, La Habana Vieja (no phone). **Open** 10am-7pm Mon-Sat; 10am-7pm Sun. **No credit cards**. **Map** p256 E15.
Hats, handbags and scarves are the deal here. The majority of hats are handmade straw varieties.

Paul & Shark Yachting

Calle Muralla #105, entre San Ignacio y Mercaderes, Plaza Vieja, La Habana Vieja (866 4326). **Open** 10am-7pm Mon-Sat; 10am-1pm Sun. **Credit** MC, V. **Map** p256 E15.
In Havana terms, this boutique is exclusive, expensive – and usually empty. It offers a selection of yachting clothing for men and women, including a select range of shoes. Boogie-boards also available.

El Quitrín

Calle Obispo #163, entre San Ignacio y Mercaderes, La Habana Vieja (862 0810/6195). **Open** 9am-5pm Mon-Sat; 9am-3.30pm Sun. **Credit** MC, V. **Map** p256 E15.
Home to handmade Cuban clothing in cotton and linen fabrics. The quality's better than you'll find at the markets, and reflected in the higher prices. *Guayaberas* are a must for men; women will find some dresses. Staff will make curtains to order.

Jewellery

Look out for fine handmade jewellery in most hotel shops. There are also very cheap pieces to be found at the city's crafts markets (*see p135*).

Casa de la Orfebrería

Calle Obispo #113, entre Mercaderes y Oficios, La Habana Vieja (863 9861). **Open** 9am-1pm Mon; 9am-5pm Tue-Sat. **No credit cards**. **Map** p256 E15.
The displays of silver walking sticks, swords and other items of metalwork at this two-storey museum are fairly prosaic, but it's worth stopping by for the attached jewellery shop, which sells some pretty pieces made by local artisans. It's also known as the Casa de la Plata (*plata* meaning silver).

La Habanera

Calle 12 #505, entre 5ta y 7ma, Miramar (204 2546/2648). **Open** 10am-6pm Mon-Fri; 10am-2pm Sat. **Credit** MC, V. **Map** p253 A8.
This very private jewellery store, neatly tucked away, has some fantastic pieces, including vintage and antique (all with export licence; *see p125*). It also sells costume jewellery, watches and silverware. The setting is hush-hush and conservative, and prices range from CUC 50 to exceedingly expensive.

Shoes & leather goods

The best selection of shoes and leather items can be found at the **Centro Comercial El Comodoro**, **Galerías Amazonas**, **La Vigía** (for all, *see p123*) and **La Maison** (*see p122*) shopping centres. The choice for children can be limited, though. For handmade leather accessories, try the local crafts markets (*see p135*), though be aware that the dye used on leather handbags at these markets is not top quality and may run. Shoe repairers can be found in the streets in La Habana Vieja and Centro Habana; otherwise, there's a repair shop at the corner of Calle 16 and Calle 23 in Vedado (if asking for directions, say it's near 'La Infancía', a children's shop).

La Habana

Calle Obispo #415, esquina Aguacate, La Habana Vieja (no phone). **Open** 10am-7pm Mon-Sat; 10am-1pm Sun. **No credit cards**. **Map** p256 D15.
This atmospheric shop, dominated by a fountain, stocks mainly Brazilian-made handbags and shoes.

Get shirty

Nothing else says Havana quite like the *guayabera*. Originally and traditionally made of cotton, these men's shirts, characterised by four pockets on the front, can be long-sleeved or short, and worn loose and untucked. Practical yet smart, they're perfect for the intense tropical heat.

Like so much involving Cuba, the shirt has a long and controversial history. For a start, the Mexicans are known to contest the fact that this is a Cuban shirt at all. Indeed, the *guayabera* is as much a Latin symbol as anything else – Mexicans, Panamanians and Colombians among others have all traditionally worn and crafted the shirt.

However, most agree that the *guayabera* originated in Cuba about 200 years ago, when it was sewn either by a) a poor rural wife for her husband, adding extra pockets so he could carry guavas, or *guayabas* (hence *guayaberas*); or b) a rich landowner's wife, who added extra pockets for her husband so he could carry various sundries while checking out his estate by the River Yayabo (hence *yayabera*). What is true, regardless of the confusion surrounding its origins, is that it has been seen as working man's attire and, later, as casualwear.

The classic *guayabera* is white, but today it comes in all shades and colours, in polyester, cotton or linen (or a mix). They're sold at shops around town – and there are now women's versions too. Across the water in Miami, where the *guayabera* has become a symbol of Latin chic, there are numerous factories turning out all kinds of *guayabera*, including – for those really special occasions – versions to wear with your tuxedo.

Vía Uno

Calle Oficios, esquina Obrapía, La Habana Vieja (866 3785). **Open** 10am-7pm Mon-Sat; 10am-1pm Sun. **Credit** MC, V. **Map** p256 E16.

A pretty good selection of Brazilian-made shoes and handbags at reasonable prices. If you've forgotten to pack your flip-flops, this is the place to come.

Flowers & plants

It's only in the past few years that peso flower stalls and flower carts (*floreros*) have become widely seen in Havana. Try the stall opposite Galerías Amazonas on the corner of Calle 23 and Calle 12 (near the Cementerio Colón), which also sells potted plants, or the one at Calle D #406, between 17 and 19 in Vedado. Great flower arrangements are available at the **Cuatro Caminos** market (*see p78*).

Flor Habana

Calle 12, entre 23 y 25, Vedado (830 5121/831 7651/florhabana@enet.cu). **Open** 24hrs daily. **No credit cards. Map** p253 C8.

This flower shop is the only one in town connected to Interflora. Roses, carnations, lilies, chrysanthemums and other varieties are generally available.

Jardín Wagner

Calle Mercaderes #113, entre Obispo y Obrapía, La Habana Vieja (866 9017). **Open** 9am-6pm Mon-Sat; 9am-2pm Sun. **No credit cards. Map** p256 E15.

You're unlikely to miss the window at Jardín Wagner, which has water cascading down it. The shop stocks fresh flowers and house plants (including gorgeous roses), plus artificial flowers.

Tropiflora

Calle 12 #156, entre Calzada y Línea, Vedado (830 3869/lineay12@ceniai.inf.cu). **Open** 8am-8pm daily. **No credit cards. Map** p253 B8.

This shop sells a wide range of flowers, plus vases, some outdoor furniture and decorations. It's responsible for the fantasy arrangements that decorate the Tropicana cabaret. A delivery service is available within Havana. Note that the Miramar branch is closed on Sunday.

Other locations: Calle 32, entre 5ta y 7ma, Miramar (204 6247).

Food & drink

Most of Havana's department stores and shopping complexes house supermarkets stocking essential provisions (*see p122*). There are also small grocery sections in most petrol stations, selling snack food, drinks and sweets. For fresh fruit and vegetables, *see p130* **Living on the veg**.

Bread & cakes

As if to remind you that sugar is Cuba's main crop, excessive amounts of the stuff are used in cakes and pastries, and locals love it. The quality of a standard Cuban loaf of bread is quite poor, but the buns (*pan suave*, or soft bread) are reasonable. There are also small bakeries scattered around the Old Town.

Pain de Paris

Calle 25, entre Infanta y O, Vedado (836 3347). **Open** 24hrs daily. **No credit cards. Map** p254 B12.

Living on the veg

Many Cubans find the concept of being vegetarian hard to digest. Indeed, as a foreign vegetarian you are likely to cause some consternation among the locals – they simply cannot understand why anyone would willingly abstain from eating meat. The majority of the population considers animal protein an essential part of any meal, and all important occasions in Cuba are celebrated with the slaughter of a pig.

Despite health statistics – heart disease is a major killer – Cubans are stubbornly resistant to change in their eating habits. Advising them to eat more greens is often dismissed with 'I am not a rabbit/goat', or protests that fruit and vegetables are too expensive for the average person. Cubans do buy vegetables on a regular basis. It's just that preferences in this respect may be a bit limited (tomatoes, lettuce, green beans, cabbage, beets, cucumber, avocado). It's hard to find a Cuban table without a salad and a root vegetable or plantains. But the price argument is not entirely unfounded if you take into consideration that at the *agromercados* (farmers' markets; often shortened to *agro*) the cost of ingredients for a modest salad can add up to well over a day's wages. This is a problem that the government has sought to address by providing an alternative source of veg in the shape of community market gardens.

MARKETS

A trip to the *agro* can be one of the simplest and cheapest pleasures of a stay in Havana. It's essential to have some local pesos (*pesos cubanos*, or *moneda nacional*) when you visit: although you can pay in CUCs (*pesos convertibles*), you're far less likely to get ripped off if you pay in *pesos cubanos*, the way the prices are marked up. (Mixing and matching between the two is also quite acceptable.) Local pesos can be obtained from a CADECA kiosk (normally located in or near the entrance). Don't forget a plastic bag (*jaba*), or look for the person selling them near the entrance.

Produce varies hugely according to season and the vagaries of distribution. However, you'll usually find onions, cucumbers, cabbage, tomatoes, chillies, peppers, garlic and green beans, as well as seasonal produce like yucca or taro. Sweet potatoes are easier to find than the humble potato, which is only sold direct to ration-book holders or on the black market. Note also the difference between sweet bananas and plantains (both called *plátanos*): the latter, used only for cooking, generally come in singles (*c/u*, or *cada uno*), while the fruit is usually sold '*la mano*' (in a bunch, literally a hand). When it comes to checking prices, always note whether the item is priced in pounds (*libras*) or singly (*cada uno*).

Other fruit that you might find can include oranges, pineapples, papaya (*fruta bomba*), watermelon, passion fruit, mamey and guavas; mangoes are found in season, from May to September. There's never much in the way of greens. You may find what is called spinach (*espinacas*), but is actually more chard (spinach is virtually impossible to find), while Cuban lettuce can be a depressing item and is usually not worth the bother.

This chain is pretty expensive, and some of the products can look better than they taste. Still, they often have a decent selection of cakes and a few types of bread products, including croissants.
Other locations: throughout the city.

Panadería San José

Calle Obispo #161, entre Mercaderes y San Ignacio, La Habana Vieja (860 9326). **Open** 24hrs daily. **No credit cards**. **Map** p256 E15.
This bakery in the heart of La Habana Vieja is open 24 hours a day. The choice of cakes is pretty good, and there's a coffee shop upstairs.

Pastelería Francesa

Paseo de Martí (Prado) #410, entre Neptuno y San Rafael, Centro Habana (862 0739). **Open** 8am-11pm daily. **No credit cards**. **Map** p256 D14.
Good quality bread, croissants and sandwiches – plus tasty coffee and cakes – are served at this bakery-cum-café, which is located very close to the Hotel Inglaterra.

Chocolate

Museo del Chocolate

Calle Mercaderes #255, esquina Amargura, La Habana Vieja (866 4431). **Open** 10am-7.30pm daily. **No credit cards**. **Map** p256 E15.
This perenially popular shop-cum-museum displays chocolate moulds, jars, cups and saucers, but the real reason to visit is for thick hot chocolate, chocolate milk and chocolate bonbons, which are made on the premises and sold to take away.

Agromercados are open from 7am to 6pm from Monday to Saturday, and 7am to 2pm on Sundays. The city's best and largest is the not-so-central **Cuatro Caminos** (*see p78*). In Vedado, check out **Calle 19 y B** or the smaller **Calle 17 y G**. In Centro Habana, try **Compostela**, between Luz and Acosta. In Miramar, head for **Calle 19 y 68** or **Calle 42 y 19**. A large market is held on the last Sunday of the month at Plaza de la Revolución.

RESTAURANTS

There is a handful of vegetarian restaurants in Havana, most of which are part of the state-run Vergel chain. Try **Biki** (Calle San Lázaro, esquina Infanta, Vedado, 879 6406), **El Carmelo** (Calzada, esquina D, Vedado, 832 4495), **Ecocheff** (Avenida 3ra, esquina 86, Miramar, 206 1663, which was closed at press time) and **Pekín** (Calle 23 #1221, entre 12 y 14, Vedado, 833 4020); all are open noon-10pm daily, and charge in Cuban pesos, meaning that a filling meal for two can be very cheap. There are plans afoot to expand the Vergel menu, but it currently relies heavily on textured vegetable protein, and dishes often lack imagination. Ingredients change with the season, but are always pretty extensive.

Outside the Vergel umbrella, **Eco-Restorán El Bambú** (aka El Bambú; Jardín Botánico, Carretera El Rocío Km3.5, Calabazar, Boyeros, 643 7278/54 9159) is worth the schlep to the southern suburbs, although it's only open from 1pm to 3pm Wednesday to Sunday. Its all-you-can-eat buffet (CUC 12) is excellent – and highly popular with Cubans, who pay in *moneda nacional*. Meanwhile, **El Romero** in Las Terrazas (*see p193*) is in a league of its own both in terms of its eco setting and its delicious food.

Coffee

Casa del Café

Calle Baratillo, esquina Obispo, La Habana Vieja (866 8061). **Open** 9am-5pm Mon-Sat; 9am-1pm Sun. **No credit cards**. **Map** p256 E16.
It's hard to spot this place (look for the hanging sign), but it's worth seeking out: inside you'll find a variety of Cuban roasts and grinds. There's also an original bar from the early 20th century.

Rum

Aside from Bacardí, which was first made in Cuba but is now produced in the Bahamas, the most famous brand of Cuban rum is Havana Club; Matusalén is also often recommended by connoisseurs. Three-year-old rum is used for the famous Mojito and Cuba Libre, while seven-year-old *añejo* is a fine digestif.

For rum or wine, *see also p123* **Galerías Amazonas**; for cigars, *see p124* **Up in smoke**.

Fundación Havana Club (Museo del Ron)

Calle San Pedro #262, esquina Sol, La Habana Vieja (861 8051). **Open** *Museum & gallery* 9am-5.30pm Mon-Thur; 9am-4pm Fri, Sat; 10am-4pm Sun. *Bar* 10am-midnight daily. *Shop* 10am-9pm daily. **Credit** MC, V. **Map** p256 E15.
The Rum Museum has an adjoining bar and shop stocking Havana Club products, including glasses, T-shirts, caps and gift sets. *See also p119 and p62.*

Taberna del Galeón/Casa del Ron

Calle Baratillo, esquina Obispo, La Habana Vieja (866 8476). **Open** 9am-5pm Mon-Sat; 9am-1pm Sun. **Credit** MC, V. **Map** p256 E16.

A brass galleon hanging in the entrance welcomes visitors into this old beamed building for free rum tasting and a good selection of bottles for sale.

Gifts

Apart from rum and cigars – de rigueur purchases for visitors to Cuba (for which, *see p124* **Up in smoke** *and p62* **Fundación Habana Club**) – there's a growing crafts industry offering alternative souvenirs. The big hotels have shops selling gold and silver jewellery, T-shirts and posters. The iconic black and white shots of Fidel, Che and the Revolutionaries in the mountains also make good souvenirs; **ICAIC** film posters (*see p146*) make striking gifts. Some museums have tasteful gift outlets selling silk scarves, CDs or books; the shops in the **Museo Nacional de Bellas Artes** (*see p72*) are particularly good. For design and household goods, *see p127.*

Casa del Abanico

Calle Obrapía #107, entre Mercaderes y Oficios, La Habana Vieja (863 4452). **Open** 9.30am-5pm Mon-Fri; 8.30am-noon Sat. **No credit cards. Map** p256 E15.

A beautiful shop full of fans, where you can have one hand-painted to order by the team of skilled fan-painters. Prices start from just a few CUC.

Hermandad de Tejedoras y Bordadoras de Belén

Calle Mercaderes #122, esquina Obrapía, La Habana Vieja (861 7750). **Open** 10am-5pm daily. **No credit cards. Map** p256 E15.

This workshop, run by the Federation of Cuban Women (FMC), was founded in the early 1990s with the aim of rescuing dying traditions. Items on sale include brightly coloured handmade quilts, bags, clothing and tapestries.

Palacio de la Artesanía

Calle Cuba #64, entre Cuarteles y Peña Pobre, La Habana Vieja (867 1118/866 8072). **Open** 10am-7pm daily. **Credit** MC, V. **Map** p256 D15.

A great one-stop shop for gifts, this complex, located around a colonial-style courtyard, sells cigars, rum, coffee, Cuban music and art, plus fashion, sports clothes and T-shirts, jewellery, watches, shoes, hand-painted fans and books.

El Soldadito de Plomo

Calle Muralla #164, entre Cuba y San Ignacio, La Habana Vieja (866 0232). **Open** 9am-6pm Mon-Fri; 8.30am-noon Sat. **No credit cards. Map** p256 E15.

This sweet little shop specialises in miniature lead models of Spanish colonial policemen, soldiers and armies of the Cuban Independence War.

Health & beauty

Beauty salons

Cuban women place a great deal of emphasis on their appearance and pay particular attention to their hands and feet. Unpainted nails are frowned upon by men and women alike. If you want a wider range of treatments in more comfortable surroundings, head for the salons at **Centro Comercial El Comodoro** (*see p123*), **Palacio de la Artesanía** (*see p132*) or at one of the larger hotels – the best are those at the **Galerías Cohíba** (*see p123*), **Meliá Habana** (*see p49*), **Nacional** (*see p48*) and **Habana Libre** (*see p47*). For a different experience, *see p134* **Groom with a view**.

Centro de Belleza 'Kalinka'

Avenida de Italia (Galiano), entre San Rafael y San Martín, Centro Habana (862 6951). **Open** 8am-6pm daily. **No credit cards. Map** p255 D14.

Hairdressing, facials, massages, pedicures and manicures for Cuban pesos. No appointment necessary.

Salón Estilo

Calle Obispo #510, entre Bernaza y Villegas, La Habana Vieja (860 2650). **Open** 10am-7pm Mon-Sat. **No credit cards. Map** p256 E14.

This cosmetics shop and beauty salon provides facials, massages, waxing and other hair-removal techniques, as well as pedicures, manicures and hairdressing. Prices are very reasonable.

SPA Club Comodoro

Hotel Comodoro, Avenida 3ra y 84, Playa (204 5049/5752/spacomodoro@sermed.cha.cut.cu). **Open** 8am-8pm Mon-Sat. **No credit cards. Map** p252 B1.

A well-equipped beauty parlour offering sophisticated techniques in massage therapy, facials, hair removal, manicure, weight reduction and chiropody.

Suchel

Calle Calzada #709, entre A y B, Vedado (833 8332). **Open** 8.30am-4pm daily. **No credit cards. Map** p255 A9.

This place has a gym, steam bath and hairdresser's, but the real bonus is that it does facials, massages and other treatments, with prices in Cuban pesos. Be prepared to queue, especially after mid morning.

Cosmetics & perfumes

Cosmetics are sold in all the large hotels, and perfumeries can be found in all the shopping centres, including **Centro Comercial El Comodoro** and **La Vigía** (for both, *see p123*). The shop in the lobby of the **Hotel Nacional** (*see p48*) has a decent selection of basics too. *See also above* **Salón Estilo**. If you're looking for something special, **La Maison** (*see p122*) has a wide selection of perfumes and cosmetics, but they might be close to their sell-by date. Don't assume you can try products in the shop: they are luxury items for locals.

Casa Cubana del Perfume

Calle Brasil (Teniente Rey) #13, entre Mercaderes y Oficios (866 3759). **Open** 10am-6pm Mon-Sat. **No credit cards. Map** p256 E15.
This lovely museum-salon cross, with a stained-glass skylight, sells colognes and perfumes in beautiful old-fashioned flacons. Book in for a full body massage or aromatherapy session.

Habana 1791 (Aromas Coloniales de la Isla de Cuba)

Calle Mercaderes #156, entre Obrapía y Lamparilla, La Habana Vieja (861 3525). **Open** 9.30am-6pm daily. **No credit cards. Map** p256 E15.
Recognisable by the wafts of fragrance coming out of the door, this beautiful shop sells around ten varieties of cologne; custom-made scents can also be created. The finished product is packed into a bottle, sealed with wax and sold in an attractive linen bag at reasonable prices. *See also p64.* **Photo** *p123.*

Opticians

Óptica El Almendares

Calle Obispo #364 & 359, entre Habana y Compostela, La Habana Vieja (860 8262). **Open** 10am-6pm Mon-Sat. **Credit** MC, V. **Map** p256 E15.
These opticians have two shops in Calle Obispo (almost opposite each other), one selling a selection of fashionable and reasonably priced frames, plus repair services, the other concentrating on contact lenses and accessories. Eye tests are available.

Óptica Miramar/Casa Matriz

Avenida 7ma, entre 24 y 26, Miramar (204 2269/2990). **Open** 9am-5pm Mon-Fri; 10am-2pm Sat. **Credit** MC, V. **Map** p253 B5.
The friendly and professional Óptica Miramar sells a wide range of frames, contact lenses (plus fluids) and sunglasses. No appointment is required for the on-site optician (test CUC 5).
Other locations: Calle Neptuno #411, entre San Nicolás y Manrique, Centro Habana (863 2161); Plaza de Carlos III, Avenida Salvador Allende (Carlos III), entre Retiro y Árbol Seco, Centro Habana (873 6370).

Pharmacies

Local pharmacies do not offer much choice and are often lacking in what would be considered basics in your home country.
If your ailment can be treated by natural remedies, the pharmacist (in peso outlets) will provide you with what you require from Cuban-made products. For international pharmacies, which stock a range of conventional medicines, *see p227*. For further information about medical issues, *see p226*.

Shiny, happy souvenirs at the **Feria**. *See p135.*

Farmacia La Reunión (Sarrá)

Calle Brasil (Teniente Rey) #41, esquina Compostela, La Habana Vieja (866 7554). **Open** 9am-7pm daily. **No credit cards. Map** p256 E15.

A grand, beautifully restored pharmacy, with a wonderful skylight and originally fitted mahogany furniture. Once the largest pharmacy in Latin America, it now specialises in natural health and beauty products, but also sells reproductions of pharmacy jars and some books on Havana. **Photo** *p135.*

Farmacia Taquechel

Calle Obispo #155, entre Mercaderes y San Ignacio, La Habana Vieja (862 9286). **Open** 9am-6.30pm daily. **No credit cards. Map** p256 E15.

Though nowadays it is more like a museum than a health shop, this lovely building was opened as a pharmacy in 1898 by Francisco Taquechel, and restored to its former glory before reopening in 1995. The interior is beautifully decorated with intriguing gadgets, such as a century-old French porcelain water filter. The shop sells a selection of natural products. *See also p68.*

Laundry & dry-cleaning

Most hotels offer dry-cleaning and laundry services; to do it more cheaply (yourself) try one of the numerous launderettes around the city.

Groom with a view

Although it was established nearly a decade ago, this funky hairdressing salon-cum-museum has somehow managed to stay a well-kept secret among the locals. Located in a small street in La Habana Vieja, just off the Malecón, with stunning views of the castle of El Morro, **Arte Corte** is run by Gilberto Valladares, originally from Cienfuegos and nicknamed Papito (daddy).

Papito is a barber who loves to paint – not an artist who cuts hair – but he clearly has a passion for both professions. The brightly painted salon is decorated with antique and vintage hairdressing equipment and furniture, as well as a variety of paintings. These are both Papito's own works – typically on a dark background, full of what he describes as 'barbers' dreams' – and those donated by other artists and friends.

Papito is also a director of a cultural project, which organises an annual exhibition and festival, uniting hairdressers and barbers with painters and sculptors, designers and historians, all attracted by the art and history of *barbería* (hairdressing).

Papito welcomes curious visitors with a warm smile and is happy to talk to interested passers-by. He and his friendly team do a decent haircut too: prices are, by European standards, very reasonable – CUC 10 for wash, cut and dry, or CUC 25 including colouring (highlights are also available). Book a few days ahead.

Arte Corte

Calle Aguiar #10, entre Peña Pobre y Avenida de las Misiones, La Habana Vieja (861 0202/ artecorte@yahoo.es). **Open** noon-6pm Mon-Sat. **No credit cards. Map** p256 D15.

Farmacia La Reunión. *See p134.*

Aster Lavandería

Calle 34 #314, entre 3ra y 5ta, Miramar (204 1622). **Open** 8am-5pm Mon-Fri; 8am-noon Sat. **No credit cards. Map** p252 B4.

Offers a very good, cheap and efficient dry-cleaning service. There are also self-service washing and drying machines available at reasonable prices.

Markets

Given the paucity of choice and quality you'll often come across in Havana's shops, markets can offer you some real value for money.

Crafts markets

Feria

Calle Tacón, entre Empedrado y Chacón, La Habana Vieja (no phone). **Open** 10am-6pm Wed-Sat. **No credit cards. Map** p256 E15.

The city's largest crafts market is the ideal place to find souvenirs and presents. Highlights include hand-woven hammocks, papier mâché toys, masks, hardwood sculptures, paintings and handmade jewellery. Also keep an eye out for *guayaberas*, embroidered cotton outfits for children. There's something for everyone, although that includes pickpockets, so be alert. As this guide went to press, the market was due to move to the Almacenes de San José on the Avenida del Puerto down near the Iglesia de San Francisco de Paula. **Photo** *p133.*

Feria Obispo

Calle Obispo, entre Aguacate y Compostela, La Habana Vieja (no phone). **Open** 10am-5pm Fri-Sun. **No credit cards. Map** p256 E15.

The artists and artisans at this *feria*, which is located right next to Galería Manos (*see p153*), sell their products to the passing public. Standout products on offer include painted tiles, silver jewellery, leather products and ceramics.

Feria Variedades Galiano

Calle Galiano, entre San Miguel y San Rafael, Centro Habana (no phone). **Open** 10am-6pm Mon-Sat; 9am-noon Sun. **No credit cards. Map** p255 D14.

This aged department store block now houses, on its first floor, a much smaller and calmer version of the *feria* in La Habana Vieja (*see above*). Feel free to browse the clothing, jewellery, leather goods, wood carvings, papier mâché, and painting. Before the Revolution the Variedades chain used to be a Woolworths chain and is still referred to by its previous nickname – *tencen* (from 'ten cents').

Feria de 23

Calle 23, entre M y N (La Rampa), Vedado (no phone). **Open** 10am-5pm daily. **No credit cards. Map** p254 E11.

A small crafts market, selling a similar selection of goods to the other tourist markets.

Food markets

See p130 **Living on the veg.**

Music

The best-known Cuban sound is salsa, but here you'll have access to other typical musical styles. You're also likely to be offered bootlegs or 'homemade' CDs at just about any restaurant, but quality isn't guaranteed.

Casa de la Música de Centro Habana

Avenida Galiano #255, entre Neptuno y Concordia, Centro Habana (862 4165). **Open** 10am-midnight daily. **No credit cards. Map** p255 D14.

The shop is adjacent to a music club, where Cuba's top salsa bands perform. You can buy their music here, as well as an excellent selection of rhythms by other Cuban artists. A selection of musical instruments is on sale, too.

Casa de la Música de Miramar

Calle 20 #3308, entre 33 y 35, Miramar (204 0447). **Open** 11am-11pm daily. **No credit cards. Map** p253 C6.

Musical instruments and a wide variety of Cuban music in the form of CDs, tapes and sheet music is on offer here. The Casa also houses a club for live music (*see p170*).

Habana Sí (Artex)

Calle 23 #301, esquina L, Vedado (838 3162/ habanasi@artex.cu). **Open** 10am-9pm Mon-Sat; 10am-7pm Sun. **Credit** (over CUC 50) MC, V. **Map** p254 E11.

Part of the government-owned Artex group, this specialist music shop sells mainly Cuban music CDs and tapes – jazz, salsa, troubadours, *chachachá* and mambo. Very helpful and friendly staff.

Longina

Calle Obispo #360, entre Habana y Compostela, La Habana Vieja (862 8371). **Open** 10am-7pm Mon-Sat; 10am-1pm Sun. **No credit cards. Map** p256 E15.

This beautiful shop has a wide choice of Cuban music, percussion instruments, cassettes and classic Cuban films on video. Service is good too.

Photographic services

Many hotels and shopping centres offer photo developing services, among them the **Nacional** (*see p48*), **Habana Riviera** (*see p47*), **Comodoro** (*see p123*), **Galerías de Paseo** (*see p124*) and **La Puntilla** (*see p125*).

Foto Habana (Fotografía Luz Habana)

Calle Tacón #22, entre O'Reilly y Empedrado, La Habana Vieja (863 4263). **Open** 9am-7pm daily. **No credit cards. Map** p256 E16.

An attractive shop near the cathedral, selling a variety of cameras, accessories and binoculars. It also operates a one-hour film processing service.

Foto Obispo

Calle Obispo #307, entre Habana y Aguiar, Habana Vieja (no phone). **Open** 9am-6pm Mon-Sat; 9am-1pm Sun. **No credit cards. Map** p256 E15.

A reasonable stock of cameras, films, batteries and photo albums can be found in this conveniently located store, which also does passport photos. Fast turnaround service.

Foto Prado

Paseo de Martí (Prado), esquina Virtudes, Centro Habana (863 4186). **Open** 9am-6pm Mon-Sat; 9am-noon Sun. **No credit cards. Map** p255 D14.

Sells film and offers developing and photocopying.

Sport

You can buy most sports clothes in Havana if you know where to look. Most of the city's department stores and shopping centres have a sports section. There's also a sports shop selling baseball gear at the back of the **Estadio Latinoamericano** (*see p183*).

Adidas

Calle Neptuno #460, entre Campanario y Manrique, Centro Habana (862 5178). **Open** 10am-6pm Mon-Sat; 10am-1pm Sun. **Credit** MC, V. **Map** p255 D14.

This shop, still referred to by many locals as Miami, its former name, sells a range of men's and women's sportswear, running shoes, bags and a small selection of other accessories.

Other locations: Calle San Rafael, esquina Industria, Centro Habana (863 2693); Avenida 78, esquina 7ma, Villa Panamericana (95 4750).

D'Primera

Calle 1ra, esquina B, Vedado (no phone). **Open** 10am-7pm Mon-Sat; 10am-3pm Sun. **No credit cards. Map** p254 A9.

Clothes, sports shoes and other accessories by Puma, Fila, Nike, Reebok and more are sold in this tourist-oriented chain of Caracol shops.

Other locations: Manzana de Gómez complex, Calle Obispo, entre Agramonte (Zulueta) y Avenida de Bélgica (Monserrate) (no phone).

Stationery & supplies

Papelería O'Reilly

Calle O'Reilly #102, esquina Tacón, La Habana Vieja (863 4263). **Open** 8am-6pm daily. **Credit** MC, V. **Map** p256 E15.

A decent-quality stationery store, stocking pens, folders, diaries and all types of paper (fax, wrapping, printer). Photocopying services are also available.

Taller de Papel

Calle Mercaderes #120, entre Obispo y Obrapía, La Habana Vieja (861 3356). **Open** 8.30am-5pm Mon-Fri; 8.30am-2pm Sat. **No credit cards. Map** p256 E15.

A tiny little workshop selling a selection of handmade recycled paper and related products.

Arts & Entertainment

Features

Cinecito. *See p148.*

Festivals & Events

Dance, film, theatre, music, books and cigars – the Cuban calendar has a treat for everyone.

You probably don't need telling, but Cuba is a lot of fun. The country's vibrancy of life, borne of a unique culture that blends Spanish traditions with African roots, translates to a schedule of events that is packed year-round. Whatever time of year you visit, there will always be something going on. Some major events, such as the international film or ballet festivals, more than justify a trip in themselves.

LISTINGS AND INFORMATION

Although finding reliable information can be tricky, mass tourism means that most major festivals have become much better organised over recent years and generally do take place at the projected times. However, it's always best to confirm details before making special plans as details can change at the last minute. This is especially true if you are basing your whole trip around a particular event (although it's rare for a major festival to be cancelled outright).

The **Ministry of Culture** (Calle 2 #258, entre 11 y 13, Vedado) has a good website, www.cubarte.cult.cu, with daily updates on what's going on in every theatre, gallery and museum in town. But don't expect to find places like Tropicana or the Casas de la Música there. If you want to spend your evening in a cabaret enjoying a good Cuban salsa band, then this is not the best place to look. *Cartelera*, a bulletin published weekly in English and Spanish, which you can pick up free of charge at hotels, concentrates mostly on events of interest to tourists. *Granma* (*see p228*) also sometimes publishes information about upcoming events.

The **Buró de Convenciones**, based in the Hotel Neptuno-Tritón (Calle 3ra, esquina 74, Miramar, 204 8273), has its own website, www.cubameeting.org, where you can find anything from book fairs or fishing tournaments to neurosurgery symposiums. Note that it's only in Spanish, however.

In addition, there is a popular programme on national television, **Hurón Azul**, that gives a rundown of the most important upcoming cultural events, while **Radio Taíno** (in both Spanish and English) broadcasts listings for upcoming live music events. Bear in mind, though, that most publicity in Havana still travels by word of mouth, so be sure to ask at your hotel or *casa particular*.

For a list of public holidays, *see p236*. For more film festivals, *see pp146-50*; for performing arts festivals, *see pp172-81*. Note that venues listed within this chapter are also listed in the index (*see pp240-44*).

Regular events

The programme of the **Casa de las Américas** (*see p83*) is always worth a look, as there is a steady stream of exhibitions, concerts and Latin American/Caribbean literary and cultural events. Its major event, **Premio Literario Casa de las Américas**, held every January, is one of the oldest and most prestigious literary awards in the continent, and gathers some of the best writers and critics from the region.

Cañonazo

Information: Jorge Forniet Gil, Casa de las Américas (838 2706/cil@casa.cult.cu). **Venue** Fortaleza de San Carlos de la Cabaña. **Date** 9pm daily. **Map** p255 D16.

In memory of the curfew reminding citizens to return inside the (now-demolished) city walls, a cannon shot is fired from the ramparts of the castle across the bay from Old Havana at 9pm each night.

Top five Festivals

Carnaval de La Habana
See p140.

Festival Nacional del Humor 'Aquelarre'
See p140.

Feria Internacional del Disco 'CUBADISCO'
See p139.

Festival Internacional del Nuevo Cine Latinoamericano
See p140.

Feria Internacional del Libro de La Habana
See p142.

Arts & Entertainment

The soldiers dress up in full 18th-century costume and march solemnly along in a torch-lit file. It's a popular show, so get there early for a good view, but don't stand too close or you'll be deafened by the explosions. *See also p83.*

Spring

Festival de Música Electroacústica 'Primavera en La Habana'

Information: Laboratorio Nacional de Música Electroacústica, Calle 17 #260, esquina I, Vedado (830 3983/lnme@cubarte.cult.cu). **Venues** Basílica Menor de San Francisco de Asís, Sala Teatro del Museo Nacional de Bellas Artes. **Date** mid Mar; even-numbered years.

The festival is organised by Juan Blanco, Cuba's most famous exponent of electro-acoustic music. International participants include American, Latin American, Asian and European avant-garde musical minimalists. More recently, the festival has started to experiment with DJs, techno and performance arts, as well as audio-visuals.

Festival 'Los Días de la Danza'

Information: Julián González Toledo, Consejo Nacional de las Artes Escénicas (CNAE), Calle 4 #257, entre 11 y 13, Vedado (830 4126/cnae@min.cult.cu). **Venues** Gran Teatro de La Habana, Teatro Mella, Teatro Nacional. **Date** 23-29 Apr 2007; annual.

A yearly showcase for Cuban dance companies of all genres and abilities, plus international dance groups. A good seven days of new talent-spotting.

Primero de Mayo

Venue Plaza de la Revolución. **Date** 1 May. **Map** p254 D9.

May Day parades celebrating International Workers' Day are a must on any socialist country's calendar. The routine? Get up at the crack of dawn, apply sunblock, watch the stream of workers enter the Plaza de la Revolución, listen to Fidel's speech and wave a paper Cuban flag.

Festival Internacional de Guitarra de La Habana 'Leo Brouwer'

Information: Alexis Vázquez, Instituto Cubano de la Música (ICM), Calle 15 #452, entre E y F, Vedado (830 3503-6/alexisv@icm.cu). **Venue** Teatro Amadeo Roldán. **Date** 8-13 May 2007; even-numbered years. **Map** p254 B10.

Organised by Cuba's multi-talented composer and guitar maestro Leo Brouwer, who is also conductor of the National Symphony Orchestra, this festival and competition has a large international following.

Feria Internacional del Disco 'CUBADISCO'

Information: Ciro Benemelis Durán, Instituto Cubano de la Música (ICM), Calle 15 #452, entre E y F, Vedado (832 8298/www.cubadisco.icm.cu). **Venue** Pabellón Cuba. **Date** 19-27 May 2007; annual. **Map** p254 B12.

Festival Internacional de Ballet. *See p141.*

Now into its second decade, Cubadisco is the island's largest commercial musical event – both a fair and festival – and covers all genres within the Cuban music world. Pabellón Cuba is the main venue but concerts by Cuba's best musicians take place all over the city. A daily programme is published.

Festival de Raíces Africanas 'Wemilere'

Information: Dirección Musical de Cultura de Guanabacoa, Calle Independencia #321, entre San Andrés y San Juan Bosco, Guanabacoa (97 9776/9187/dmcgbcoa@cubarte.cult.cu). **Venues** throughout Guanabacoa. **Date** to be confirmed.

If you've had a run of bad luck or desire something specific, Cubans will advise you to visit the little town of Guanabacoa. And it's worth the ferry trip across the bay to discover the pulse of Afro-Cuban religions too. Each year the week-long Wemilere (meaning 'party') is dedicated to a visiting country from the African diaspora, with live music, dance, workshops, lectures, art exhibitions and a craft fair. Some of the carnival-type dancing can border on the cheesy, but you can usually find plenty of real deal Afro-Cuban music and dance too. It used to be held in late November each year, but will probably not take place in 2007 and will switch to May from 2008.

Summer

See also p142 **CubaDanza**.

Salón Internacional de Arte Digital

Information: María Santucho, Centro Cultural Pablo de la Torriente Brau, Calle Muralla #63, entre Oficios e Inquisidor, La Habana Vieja (861 6251/centropablo@cubarte.cult.cu). **Venue** Centro Cultural Pablo de la Torriente Brau, Fototeca de Cuba, Museo Nacional de Bellas Artes, various galleries. **Date** 18-24 June 2007; annual.

Digital artists, designers and photographers from all over the world get together every year to exchange experiences and show their print and audio-visual art. Exhibits fill various galleries and museums and, in some cases, are even on show in the street. In addition to the exhibitions, there are theoretical discussions, papers, talks and awards.

Festival Internacional 'Boleros de Oro'

Information: José Loyola, UNEAC, Calle 17 #351, entre G y H, Vedado (832 0395/www.uneac.com). **Venues** Teatro América, Teatro Amadeo Roldán, Teatro Nacional, UNEAC. **Date** 19-24 June 2007; annual.

A week-long event with performances by famous bolero singers, groups and orchestras of *filin* (a word literally derived from the English 'feeling') from Cuba, Latin America and Spain, plus lectures and competitions. Boleros are famous for their lyrics of love and loss, so bring a hankie. Note that some events also take place in Santiago de Cuba. In 2006 the event was dedicated to Colombia.

Carnaval de La Habana

Venues all over Havana. **Date** July/Aug, but varies.

'Life is a carnival,' sang Cuban singer Isaac Delgado. Less now than before, sadly – one of Havana's biggest attractions has become a bit touch and go. In 2002 the carnival was cancelled to channel money into schools; in 2003 it was postponed to coincide with the anniversary of the founding of Havana. In 2006 it was cancelled due to Castro's serious health problems. The sad truth is that, even when it comes on time, it isn't the flamboyant spectacle it once was. Having disappeared during the Special Period, the carnival's latter-day reincarnation is but a shadow of the pre-1990s three-tier-float days, although the government has pledged improvements. If it does go ahead, expect cheap beer, smelly portaloos and brawls, and keep an eye on your belongings.

Festival Nacional del Humor 'Aquelarre'

Information: Centro Promoción del Humor, Calle A #601 altos, entre 25 y 27, Vedado (830 3708/3914). **Venues** Teatro América, Teatro Fausto, Teatro Mella, Teatro Nacional. **Date** 1st half July; annual.

Cuban humour relies heavily on stereotypes – gay men, mothers-in-law, people from the east of the island – and slapstick. It can also be topical and cutting at times, but the delivery is so rapid and the understanding of Cuban life required so advanced that you'll miss a lot if you don't have excellent Spanish and local knowledge. *See also pp159-71.*

Festival Internacional de Rock 'Caiman Rock'

Information: Dirección Nacional de la Asociación Hermanos Saíz (AHS), Pabellón Cuba, Calle 23, entre M y N, Vedado (832 3511-3/ahsinternacional @ujc.org.cu). **Venues** Anfiteatro de Marianao, Salón Rosado de La Tropical. **Date** 18-22 July 2007; odd-numbered years.

Cuba isn't usually associated with rock, but *roqueros*, as fans are known, are surprisingly numerous in Havana. Don't expect subtlety from bands with names like Agonizer and Zeus (though perhaps Rice and Beans offer a more nuanced performance). International input comes mostly from Latin American countries.

Festival de Rap Cubano 'Habana Hip Hop'

Information: Dirección Nacional de la Asociación Hermanos Saíz (AHS), Pabellón Cuba, Calle 23, entre M y N, Vedado (832 3511/3/ahsinternacional @ujc.org.cu). **Venues** Anfiteatro de Alamar, Café Cantante (Teatro Nacional), Casa de la Música (Centro Habana), Casa de la Música (Miramar), Museo de la Música, Salón Rosado Beny Moré. **Date** 21-26 Aug 2007; annual.

This festival was once a patchy affair but the word is now well and truly out and the event has begun to attract an increasing number of hip hop artists from the United States, Latin America and Europe, as well as the cream of homegrown talent. Hip hop has hit the big time in Cuba in recent years, with over 1,000 outfits and an exuberant atmosphere surrounding performances. This popularity has attracted the inevitable government interest, and Cuban lyrics can only go so far. Some interesting raw expression does slip through, though – often in the chat of Cuba's fierce female rappers. The festival now includes DJs, graffiti artists, a colloquium at the Museo Nacional de la Música and a series of films. **Photo** *p141.*

Autumn

Festival Internacional de Música Popular 'Beny Moré'

Information: Dirección Provincial de Cultura de la Ciudad de La Habana, Centro Nacional de Música Popular, Calle G, entre Línea y 9, Vedado (831 1234/832 3503/icm@icm.cu). **Venue** Teatro Mella. **Date** 21-24 Sept 2007; odd-numbered years. **Map** p254 A9.

Dedicated to the legendary 'Bárbaro del Ritmo' – the man with the funny hat, crazy walk and intoxicating rhythms – this festival is organised by salsa star Isaac Delgado. Concerts are also held in Beny Moré's home town, Santa Isabel de las Lajas, Cienfuegos.

Festival de Teatro de La Habana

Information: Consejo Nacional de las Artes Escénicas (CNAE), Calle 4 #257, entre 11 y 13, Vedado (833 4581/desarrollo@cubaescena.cult.cu). **Venues** various theatres. **Date** to be confirmed.

If your Spanish language skills are up to the challenge, it's well worth exploring this 12-day theatrical festival, which features performances from international groups, plus workshops and lectures. The poster is always striking, well designed and plastered all over town. Note that the next event is likely to be in late September 2008, after which it will take place in even-numbered years.

Festival de La Habana de Música Contemporánea

Information: Guido López Gabilán (832 7121/teregav @cubarte.cult.cu). **Venue** Teatro Amadeo Roldán. **Date** 1-10 Oct 2007; annual. **Map** p254 B10.

This ten-day contemporary music fest puts Cuba's salsa and Latin jazz-only image to rest. The works of contemporary Latin American and European composers are performed by the island's maestros, a pot pourri of soloists, groups, and full orchestras.

Festival Internacional de Ballet

Information: Ballet Nacional de Cuba & Gran Teatro de La Habana, Calzada #510, entre D y E, Vedado (835 2948/bnc@cubarte.cult.cu). **Venues** Gran Teatro & other theatres. **Date** 2nd half Oct; even-numbered years.

The Festival Internacional de Ballet is prima ballerina Alicia Alonso's baby, and features her own Cuban National Ballet, along with companies and soloists from around the world (the Washington State Ballet and Alvin Ailey have both attended in the past). It also lures home Cuba's finest prodigals based abroad, such as Carlos Acosta and José Manuel Carreño. Each festival has a specific theme. **Photo** *p139.*

JO JAZZ

Information: Centro Nacional de Música Popular (CNMP), Avenida 1ra #1010, entre 10 y 12, Miramar (203 7667/mp@cubarte.cult.cu). **Venue** Teatro Amadeo Roldán. **Date** 2nd half Nov; annual. **Map** p254 B10.

Presenting the jazz stars of the future, JO JAZZ features the best of young (some extremely young) Cuban talent. There are several prizes to be won in the competition and one of the lucky musicians taking part gets a chance to cut an album with piano maestro Chucho Valdés.

Bienal de La Habana

Information: Consejo Nacional de las Artes Plásticas, Avenida 3ra #1205, entre 12 y 14, Miramar (204 2744/www.cnap.cult.cu). **Venues** Centro de Arte Contemporáneo Wifredo Lam, Parque Histórico Militar Morro-Cabaña, various other galleries. **Date** 1 Nov-1 Dec 2007; odd-numbered years.

This huge art festival has been rather erratic of late but it looks as if it's back on track. The Bienal gathers mostly Latin American and Caribbean artists, plus a sprinkling from the rest of the world, for exhibitions of contemporary art held all over Havana. Installation and related dance, music and theatre events, plus special film seasons in the first few weeks, also feature. *See also p151.*

Festival Internacional de Jazz 'Jazz Plaza'

Information: Alexis Vázquez Aguilera, Instituto Cubano de la Música (832 6769/www.festival jazzplaza.icm.cu). **Venues** Casas de la Cultura plus various theatres. **Date** 29 Nov-2 Dec 2007; odd-numbered years.

One of Havana's most famous music events, this jazz fest is organised by pianist Chucho Valdés and attended by la crème de la crème of Cuban and world jazz. Started in 1980 by Cuban jazzman Bobby Carcassés, the festival has attracted names from the US, Canada, Europe, Latin America and Australia, such as Dizzie Gillespie, Steve McCall, Max Roach, Kevin Haynes and Ronnie Scott. Hollywood film stars might turn up unexpectedly.

Festival de Rap Cubano 'Habana Hip Hop'. *See p140.*

O Céu de Suely won first prize at Havana's **Film Festival** in 2006.

Winter

For January's **Premio Literario Casa de las Américas**, *see p138.*

Festival Internacional del Nuevo Cine Latinoamericano

Information: Alfredo Guevara Valdés, Casa del Festival del Nuevo Cine Latinoamericano, Calle 2 #411, entre 17 y 19, Vedado (838 2854-64/ www.habanafilmfestival.com). **Venues** most cinemas. **Date** 4-14 Dec 2007; annual.

This has to be Havana's best-known and -organised festival. For the price of a pass (CUC 40), you can buy into the island's most glamorous event, with competitions, lectures and parties, and – at the heart of it all – ten days of non-stop cinema. Most films and documentaries are made in Latin America, but there is work from independent US and European directors too. Social events and hobnobbing is based at Havana's flagship Hotel Nacional; sit in the beautiful gardens and peruse your daily programme. Essential viewing. *See also pp146-50.*

Feria Internacional de Artesanía FIART

Information: Lisette Cartelle, Fondo Cubano de Bienes Culturales (204 6428/liset@fcbc.cult.cu). **Venue** Fortaleza San Carlos de la Cabaña. **Date** 9-17 Dec 2007; annual. **Map** p256 D16.

With this fair, one of the most colourful in Havana, the foundation acknowledges Cuban and foreign handicraft artists who use their art as a means of identity and cultural diversity. Lectures, exhibits, fashion shows, not to mention the handicrafts themselves, attract several thousand visitors each year; it's particularly good for buying interesting Christmas presents.

CubaDanza

Information: Miguel Iglesias, Danza Contemporánea de Cuba, Teatro Nacional, Calle Paseo, esquina Calle 39, Plaza de la Revolución (879 6410/www.cubarte.cult.cu). **Venue** Teatro Nacional. **Dates** 1st half Jan & Aug; annual. **Map** p254 D10.

A festival of modern dance classes, workshops and performances organised by Danza Contemporánea.

Feria Internacional del Libro de La Habana

Information: Iroel Sánchez Espinosa, Instituto Cubano del Libro (862 8091/presidencia@icl.cult.cu). **Venue** Fortaleza de San Carlos de la Cabaña. **Date** Feb; annual. **Map** p256 D16.

Every year the 11-day International Book Fair of Havana gathers thousands of participants and hundreds of publishing houses from around the world. It's a good way of buying books at reasonable prices, getting them signed by their authors, and enjoying book exhibits and outdoor concerts from some of the best Cuban bands.

Festival del Habano

Information: Eloisa Castellanos, Havanos, S.A. (204 0513 ext 566/habanos@habanos.cu). **Venues** Fortaleza de San Carlos de la Cabaña, Museo de Bellas Artes, Palacio de las Convenciones, Plaza de San Francisco. **Date** late Feb/early Mar; annual.

With its trade fair, seminars and trips to tobacco fields around Pinar del Río, this week-long annual cigar festival caters to both business people and dedicated cigar aficionados. The highlight is the CUC 400-a-head gala dinner where cigar-filled humidors autographed by Fidel are auctioned (the money goes to the Cuban health service), along with cigar-inspired artwork. Matt Dillon has been spotted here several times.

Children

Family fun, the old-fashioned way.

What Havana lacks in child-oriented amenities it more than makes up for in attitude. There may be none of the malls, cinema multiplexes, burger bars or theme parks that form the staple modern child's entertainment package, but with careful planning and an open mind, Havana can be a wonderful family destination. Aside from the risks of scrapes and sunburn, the city is very safe. Also, *habaneros* love children, and having one or two in tow can be a passport to aspects of local life you might otherwise miss.

ADMISSION

Under-12s pay little or nothing to get into museums and other sights. Children are usually allowed into bars and restaurants with parents, but discos are a no-no.

RISKS AND PRECAUTIONS

The heat in Havana at any time of the year can be hard on children, but the summer months are the hottest. Take light, cotton clothing and avoid synthetic fabrics. Include long-sleeved tops and cardigans as air-conditioning can be brutally high. Do your sightseeing in the morning and plan some down-time in the afternoon. Apply sunblock regularly and make sure everyone gets lots to drink. Children should drink only sealed, bottled water, or water that you can guarantee has been boiled, and avoid eating uncooked food and food sold on the street. Unfortunately, it's also a good idea to stay away from ice-creams from street stalls as water quality cannot be guaranteed.

Traffic is lighter in Havana than in most large cities but pedestrians do not have the right of way, so take extra precautions with children. Roads and pavements are often in a state of bad repair, so watch out for potholes.

There are very few public toilets in Havana and those that do exist are grim. Your best option is to duck into a nearby restaurant or hotel. Many toilets, even in restaurants, don't have toilet paper or even running water.

TRANSPORT

Avoid public buses (known as *guaguas*) – they are usually exceedingly hot, packed-in affairs that arrive after an interminable wait. The most convenient way to get around Havana as a family is by taxi; the newer fleet of mainly European cars usually have rear seat belts although earlier models might not.

A rental car is the best option if you plan on travelling outside of Havana. New cars with seat belts and airbags are available, as are four-wheel drives and people carriers. However, infant car seats are non-existent. For short trips around town, bicycle rickshaws (*bicitaxis*) and yellow *cocotaxis* are fun, open-air options.

If you're reluctant to take your expensive all-terrain buggy to one city where the pavements actually warrant it, then you can pick up a very rudimentary alternative in Havana. It would also be the ideal gift to leave behind for a Cuban family without their own.

WHAT TO TAKE

Pack a first aid kit with child-strength fever reducers, diarrhoea medicine, cold remedies, plasters and other medicines that are either not available or hard to find in Cuba. Basic baby necessities are available in Havana, but save yourself the hassle by packing nappies and baby wipes. Take plenty of sunblock, as well as lightweight raingear as sudden, torrential downpours occur frequently between May and October. It's a good idea to take books, small toys, crayons and paper; these things can be hard to find and are often poor quality.

Days out

La Habana Vieja

Most of the renovated streets and squares of the Old City are closed to car traffic, making it an excellent spot for families to explore on foot. Start in the **Plaza de Armas** (*see p56*), where the **Castillo de la Real Fuerza** (*see p57*) has good views from the tower and you can try a sustaining glass of *guarapo* (sugar cane juice) in the snack bar on the terrace. On the south side of the square, the **Museo Nacional de Historia Natural** (*see p57*) has child-friendly displays on the plants and wildlife of Cuba.

North of the museum, along Calle Tacón, is where a **crafts market** has been held for years; it was due to move to a new location in southern Old Havana as this guide went to press (*see p67*). In nearby **Parque José de la Luz y Caballero** between Calle Tacón and Avenida Céspedes, children can ride ponies for just a few pesos on weekend afternoons. Further along Tacón is the **Parque Infantil la Maestranza**, where sturdy toy trains, swings, slides and roundabouts are all positioned on a safe sandy base, making this activity playground ideal for a romp. The adjoining bouncy castle park is an equally good destination in which to let off steam.

Two of the museums worth taking in with children are the **Depósito del Automóvil** (*see p60*), with its vintage cars, and the **Maqueta de La Habana Vieja** (Scale Model of Old Havana; *see p65*). On the nearby Plaza Vieja is the **Cámara Oscura** (*see p63*), a rooftop observatory that projects the city on to a parabolic screen. After that, take a break at **La Taberna de la Muralla** (*see p110*), the beer hall opposite, while your kids run around the colonnades of the centuries-old buildings in the square. A short distance north of here is the **Casa de África** (*see p65*), where the displays relating to African and Afro-Cuban arts, crafts and religion offer a visually arresting diversion.

The **Aqvarivm** (*see p61*) features a riotous monthly (weekly in summer) children's event with Mamá Guajacona, a frenetic piscine puppet. At sunset, hire a horse-drawn carriage in **Plaza de San Francisco** (*see p58*).

Centro Habana

The **Museo de la Revolución** (*see p73*) is a good place for older children to learn something about Cuba's extraordinary recent history. On display in the yard you'll find fighter planes and army tanks. At the corner of Calles Espada and Vapor is the **Casa del Niño y la Niña**, a children's workshop with activities like music, chess and trips to the beach. You can also hire sports equipment here.

Vedado

The small natural history display at the university's **Museo de Ciencias Naturales Felipe Poey & Museo Antropológico Montané** (*see p82*) shows off various species indigenous to Cuba and has an area where children can pet stuffed animals. In Nuevo Vedado to the west is the **Jardín Zoológico de La Habana** (*see p89*). The landscaping is attractive but the animals are confined to small cages, which may come as a shock to children used to first-world zoos.

Miramar & the western suburbs

The **Maqueta de La Habana** (*see p92*), a vast and detailed scale model of the whole of Havana, gives a great sense of the layout of the city. A mezzanine gives a bird's-eye view that's useful for smaller children. Nearby, the **Acuario Nacional** (*see p92*) boasts a fine display of tropical fish and has dolphin and sea lion shows throughout the day; there's also a restaurant alongside the tanks.

Several miles further down Quinta Avenida, **Marina Hemingway** (*see p188*) is a complex with a bowling alley for kids over 12, a small amusement park and water games.

Eastern Bay & the Coast

Across the bay is the **Parque Histórico Militar Morro-Cabaña** (*see p95*). This vast military compound is a great place to learn about Havana's colonial history. The highlights are the lighthouse (Faro del Morro) and maritime displays at the Castillo de los Tres Reyes del Morro, plus the moats, ramparts and weaponry at the Fortaleza de San Carlos de la Cabaña. If you come in the late afternoon, stay on for the **Ceremonia del Cañonazo** (*see p138*) at 9pm every night, when soldiers fire a cannon from the battlements.

THE BEACHES

The beach is the obvious place to go for a jaunt out of town with children, and there are plenty of them within a 20-minute taxi journey of the city. Join the Cuban families at **Boca Ciega**, where the shallow waters are ideal for youngsters, though watch for any unexpected undertows. You can also hire out pedaloes, catamarans and kayaks here.

Further south

If you've had enough of the city, try spending a day in the huge parks on the south-western outskirts of Havana. You can get a taxi to take you but arrange for the cab to wait, and agree on a fare before boarding. The immense **Parque Lenin**, about 20 kilometres (12.5 miles) from Old Havana, has a range of amusements, including an old-fashioned fairground, with merry-go-rounds and a miniature train. Ponies and horses are available for rides within the park, and look out for the **rodeo** (*see p185*) at the weekend. On the Embalse Paso Sequito, an artificial lake within the park, you can rent a six-person rowing boat.

South of Parque Lenin is the **Jardín Botánico Nacional**, which has a variety of tropical and subtropical plants. To the west of Parque Lenin is the **Parque Zoológico Nacional**, more of a safari park than a zoo. It can be visited by bus or, for an extra CUC 5, an English-speaking guide can accompany you in your car.

For more information about all three parks, *see p55* **South parks**.

Baseball and ice-cream: a messy combination.

Entertainment

Musical shows, films, puppetry and clowns are presented throughout the city at weekends and often on other days too. Venues include: **Teatro Nacional de Guiñol** (*see p177*) for puppet shows; **Centro Cultural Bertolt Brecht** (*see p175*), **Teatro Fausto** (*see p176*), **Teatro Mella** (*see p177*) and **Museo de Arte Colonial** (*see p67*). Children's films are shown at **Cinecito** (*see p148*), **Chaplin** (*see p147*), **23 y 12** (*see p148*) and the Fundación del Nuevo Cine Latinoamericano's **Sala Glauber Rocha** (*see p148*). The annual Día de la Infancia is celebrated in the third week of July.

Feeding time

Most restaurants offer the typical Cuban meal: chicken or pork accompanied by rice, beans and a side salad. Other commonly available options are chips, hot dogs, pizza or *bocaditos de jamón y queso* (ham and cheese sandwiches). A few fast-food chains (Burgui, El Rápido) do exist, but quality is poor. As kids are welcome at most *paladares* opt for places offering home-cooked food in child-friendly environs. A sure-fire hit is Havana's ice-cream emporium **Coppelia** (*see p81*).

If you're travelling with younger children, try to stock up on lightweight snacks and drinks. Soft drinks and bottled water are sold everywhere but, when available, try fresh tropical fruit juices. In terms of milk, only UHT is available commercially. Some of the larger supermarkets stock baby food. At the **Centro Comercial Palco** (*see p125*) in Siboney, you'll find a well-stocked cold-cuts section with imported meats and cheeses, plus fresh baguettes, granola bars and other snacks. The **Pain de Paris** bakeries (*see p129*) are also a good source of bread, pastries and sandwiches. For a very Cuban experience, visit one of Havana's *mercados agropecuarios* or *agromercados* (farmers' markets; *see p130* **Living on the veg**), which is the only place you're likely to find a wide variety of fresh seasonal fruit and vegetables.

Shops

If you need children's clothes or toys, you can find them at **Hotel Comodoro** (*see p51*), **La Puntilla** (*see p125*) and **5ta y 42** (*see p125*).

Where to stay

In hotels, children under 12 often have to pay half the adult room rate, but if no extra bed is required they can sometimes stay for free. Some hotels offer formal babysitting, but if not, one of the chambermaids will usually look after the kids by arrangement. A hotel with a pool offers a respite from the dust and the heat, but even if yours doesn't have one, many of the upmarket hotels, such as the Riviera (*see p47*) and the Nacional (*see p48*), charge a fee or a minimum consumption rate (usually CUC 10-15), for non-guests. For more on swimming, *see p188*.

A *casa particular* (private home) is a good alternative for families, as there will often be two rooms available at the same time, and many rooms are furnished with two beds. Some *casas* may be slightly shabby, but they are invariably spotlessly clean and can usually provide hearty, home-cooked meals. They open a door to life in Cuba that tourists rarely see in hotels. The ideal is a *casa* with a yard or patio for shaded relaxing. Most households have pets.

Film

Movies and shakers.

Yara. *See p148.*

Forget modern multiplexes and classy art-house cinemas: going to the pictures in Havana is a down-to-earth affair. It's a chance for everyone, from film buffs to groups of noisy adolescents, to escape their harsh reality for a couple of hours. No matter if the air-conditioning is on the blink, the seats are broken or the image on screen is blurry and has a dodgy soundtrack. Nonetheless, Havana's film-goers are a clued-up lot with an interest in what they are seeing – cinematic information is plentiful: analysis precedes most films shown on TV and details of new releases are given in the local press.

EARLY CINEMA

Set up by a Frenchman arriving from Mexico, Havana's first cinema, the Cinematógrafo Lumière, opened its doors in 1897. While the 1930s and '40s were marked by the presence of Mexican and Argentinian influences, it was the intense stream of American movies that captured the locals' imaginations. By the pre-Revolutionary 1950s, Cuba was embedded with the aura of a mythical island paradise, thanks to Havana's blistering nightlife and the bevy of Hollywood stars who visited the island, living the high life while their films were shown in the new cinemas springing up around Vedado.

That all changed in 1959. **ICAIC** (Instituto Cubano del Arte e Industria Cinematográficos, at Calle 23 #1110, entre 8 y 10, Vedado), the umbrella organisation responsible for the production, exhibition and distribution of films in Cuba, was founded just months into the Revolution, bringing with it a new emphasis on expressing Cuban identity and creating a new type of less decadent cinema. US films vanished from the screens in favour of movies from the Soviet Bloc – both good and bad – and, in lesser quantities, France, Spain and Japan. It took a couple of decades for Cuba to begin to open up culturally, and for its people to have the opportunity to see films made outside Eastern Europe. The irony, of course, is that these days the average cinema-goer is now exposed to a heavy load of American blockbusters, albeit a couple of years out of date and often on cranky video projectors. But it's not all Bruce Willis.

WHO'S WHO

The 1960s were a golden era for the Cuban film industry. ICAIC nurtured some of the country's finest directors to date, such as its best-known filmmaker, Tomás Gutiérrez Alea. His *Memorias del subdesarrollo* (1968) and the later *Fresa y chocolate* (1993) were both groundbreaking films, the latter openly examining aspects of Cuban gay life. Other key directors flowering during this period were Humberto Solás, with *Lucía* (1968) and *Cecilia* (1982). The 1980s gave us Juan Carlos Tabío's delicious comedy *Plaff o demasiado miedo a la vida* (1988), Fernando Pérez with his debut fiction film *Clandestinos* (1987), plus Orlando Rojas with the visual impact of *Papeles secundarios* (1988). And then the walls tumbled down. The austerity of the Special Period meant less money for film making, and market forces reared their head.

The majority of recent Cuban films are co-productions with Spain and France. This has affected content to some extent: films have all too often become comedy versions of tropical kitchen-sink dramas, full of Cuban caricatures and clichés: sexy *mulatas*, *santería* trances, gossiping neighbours and wealthy foreigners. Luckily, though, there is fresh new talent emerging (*see p149* **Ones to watch**).

RESOURCES

For analysis and history of Cuban cinema, try ICAIC's sporadic Spanish-language *Cine Cubano* magazine. For programmes, film reviews and related articles, look out for the monthly *Cartelera* gazette, also in Spanish. The institute itself sometimes carries them, but try bookshops or second-hand book stalls for current or back copies of both. Visit www.cubacine.cu for a history of Cuban cinema. **ICAIC** (*see p146*) has an archive collection of films, but with perennial shortage of funding for its maintenance; alternatively, try the **Latin American Video Archive** (www.latinamericanvideo.org). ICAIC has begun releasing its best titles in DVD format. They can be found at the institute as well as in music shops and bookstores.

GOING TO THE CINEMA

Cinemas in Havana tend to be run-down. Vedado has some of the best movie houses, such as the **Riviera** (*see p148*), **Cine La Rampa** and the **Chaplin** (for both, *see below*). There are no multiplexes in Cuba and all the cinemas show one film at a time; that's not to say, however, that the same films are screened at all venues. Cinemas in Havana can be roughly divided into three categories: the 'art house' Chaplin cinema (and to a lesser extent La Rampa), where audiences behave how you would expect film lovers to; the vast **Yara** and **Payret** (for both, *see p148*), showing the latest releases and attracting groups of young courting couples; and the shabbier neighbourhood picture houses. Cuban film-goers generally prefer their foreign films subtitled rather than dubbed. However, outside the Chaplin and La Rampa cinemas, there can be no guarantee that films will be presented in their original language.

With the exception of the Chaplin and La Rampa, the relaxed atmosphere in Havana's cinemas seems to lead people to believe they're at home. So, be prepared for plenty of coming and going, and loud discussions about the film (sometimes this entertainment alone justifies the ticket price). Note also that most cinemas and video rooms have air-conditioning, although it might work only sporadically.

Cinemas charge in Cuban pesos and do not accept credit cards. Performances tend to start at 4.30pm and 9pm, with some late shows at weekends and children's films on Saturday and/or Sunday mornings. Most cinemas are open every day of the week.

Programmes usually change every Thursday, but check with individual cinemas. Each has a weekly city information sheet pinned up near the entrance. There's also a monthly bulletin available from newspaper kiosks. Many – but not all – cinemas in Havana show films on a continuous loop: you'll need to ask what time the showings are so as not to see the ending before the beginning. There's a 'no shorts, no flip-flops' dress code for men (which may or may not be enforced).

Cinemas

Major cinemas

Chaplin (Cinemateca de Cuba)

Calle 23 #1155, entre 10 y 12, Vedado (831 1011).
Map p253 C8.

This recently renovated cinema has a great sound system, an excellent and carefully chosen range of films, and appreciative audiences. Not surprisingly, it's a popular choice for premières, presentations and film festivals. The programme changes daily; the month's schedule is pinned up in the lobby, which also houses an art gallery and a counter selling books, videos and posters. Undoubtedly the best cinema in Havana.

Cine La Rampa

Calle 23 #111, entre O y P, Vedado (878 6146).
Map p254 B12.

Built in the second half of the 1950s, La Rampa retains some of its original atmosphere, although it's definitely seen better days despite recent repairs. During the Latin American Film Festival, the wall alongside its glamorous curved ramp is used to display film posters. La Rampa offers a new film each day, thematically devoted to the same director, actor or a genre; for instance, war films from Argentina, Cuba, USA, Mexico and the former USSR. Shows are from 4pm.

Payret

Paseo de Martí (Prado) #503, esquina San José, Centro Habana (863 3163). **Map** p256 D14.

The most important cinema in La Habana Vieja, although its current state suggests otherwise. On its left outside there's a bar (with prices in *moneda nacional*, except sodas and beers, which are charged in CUCs) and a café with few choices (CUCs); there are usually vendors outside hawking their wares: popcorn, home-baked peanuts and all sorts of sweets. There's no air-con, but two big fans go some way towards reducing the heat levels. The programme starts at 12.30pm, and there are midnight shows from Friday to Sunday.

23 y 12

Calle 23 #1212, entre 12 y 14, Vedado (833 6906). **Map** p253 C8.

This cinema used to show predominantly children's films (*see p145*), but now it also covers art-house movies and short films from young local directors. It's a rather small venue, so get there early to bag a seat (adult shows start at 8pm).

Yara

Calle L #363, esquina 23, Vedado (832 9430). **Map** p254 B11.

Built in 1949 by a TV mogul, this huge cinema is still one of Havana's landmarks, albeit without the cutting-edge technology it once boasted. All walks of life converge here, and it's a favourite spot for people-watchers, peanut sellers, customers from the Coppelia ice-cream parlour opposite (*see p81*) and habitués of the gay scene. It attracts a dolled-up, noisy Saturday night crowd (you might have to change your seat a few times), and has a similar programme to the Payret and Acapulco (but with a better location). There's a small art gallery in the foyer, plus a kiosk selling popcorn, drinks and Cuban videos – all in CUC. Programmes run continuously from 12.30pm, with late shows at midnight on Friday, Saturday and Sunday. **Photo** *p146*.

Other cinemas

Acapulco

Avenida 26, entre 35 y 37, Nuevo Vedado (833 9573). **Map** p253 D7.

The Acapulco's setting – in a once-affluent neighbourhood – means that a mainly quiet and respectful audience is guaranteed. It's comfortable, in fairly good condition and its foyer sometimes serves as a gallery and tearoom. For most of the year its programming is a mix of international and Cuban films, but during the Latin American Film Festival it shows Spanish and independent US films (although its out-of-the-way location doesn't help if you've got a tight agenda). **Photo** *p150*.

Actualidades

Avenida de Bélgica (Monserrate) #262, entre Ánimas y Neptuno, Centro Habana (861 5193). **Map** p256 D14.

Located slightly off the main tourist track – near the Bacardí building and the Museo de Bellas Artes – this small cinema does at least have air-conditioning. The films shown are mainly of the US action movie variety, but if that's not your thing, take note that the cinema is on the annual Latin American Film Festival roster, when it features more sophisticated fare.

Cinecito

Calle San Rafael #68, esquina Consulado, Centro Habana (863 8051). **Map** p255 D14.

Shows films for children at 4.30pm in winter, and 2.30pm in summer (10.30am at weekends throughout the year). The ultimate place to catch an Elpidio Valdés movie, the Cuban children's cartoon hero.

Cinematógrafo Lumière (La Maqueta de La Habana)

Calle Mercaderes #114, entre Obispo y Obrapía, La Habana Vieja (866 4425). **Map** p256 E15.

Inside the Maqueta de La Habana building – easily identified by its dark glass frontage – is the Cinematógrafo Lumière, a clear homage to the man who introduced cinema to the island. The programme includes two films daily, one at 2pm for children, which is free, and the other at 4pm for adults, which cost just one peso.

Metropolitan

Calle 13, entre 76 y 78, Playa (209 6715).

The Metropolitan's grand signage makes it easily recognisable in this mainly residential neighbourhood. Another cinema that's seen better days, it too plays its part on the Latin American Film Festival circuit. The venue's daily changing programme starts at 5pm (3pm in summer).

Riviera

Calle 23 #507, entre Presidentes (G) y H, Vedado (830 9564). **Map** p255 B11.

The Riviera's distinctive lettering stands out like a beacon along a not particularly pretty stretch of Calle 23. Programming yields a mixed bag: dubbed US action (yes, again) and run-of-the-mill films alternating with films previously on at the Yara – leftovers, you might say. Nonetheless, audiences always seem to enjoy themselves.

Sala Glauber Rocha

Fundación de Nuevo Cine Latinoamericano, Quinta Santa Bárbara, Calle 212, esquina 31, La Coronela, Marianao (271 8967/201 2104).

A modern cinema within the mansion where the late poet Dulce María Loynaz used to live, which now belongs to the Fundación del Nuevo Cine Latinoamericano (the cinema is one of the main venues for the Latin American Film Festival). Though it's slightly out of the way, set right in the middle of the Polo Científico (Biotech Research Zone), it's worth the trip for the lovely gardens alone. A bookstore and café are also on site. Films are shown twice a day from Tuesday to Sunday, with weekend screenings for children (call for times).

Ones to watch

Recent international successes have proved that Cuba's homegrown film talents are well on the way to critical acclaim – and some are already there. In particular, an ensemble of three short films, each with a distinctive style, by three thirtysomething filmmakers from Havana – Pável Giroud (*photo right*), Lester Hamlet and Esteban Insausti – made the international film community sit up and take note in 2004. *Tres veces dos* took the Silver Zenith prize at the Montreal Film Festival that year. The award is even more incredible when you consider the conditions involved in creating these works: the films were made on a shoestring budget – just US$13,000 – and with only seven days of filming.

Since then the trio has been busy. In 2006 Pável, one of the most in-demand video-clip makers in Havana, directed his first solo feature film, *La edad de la peseta* (*photo below*), about a ten-year-old growing up in 1950s Havana. The film was edited by the award-winning Hamlet, and premièred at the Toronto Film Festival. It went on to take the Coral (the highest prize) for best art direction and best photography at the Latin American Film Festival in Havana in December 2006.

Insausti, meanwhile, went on to make *Existen* (2006), in which mentally ill people on Havana's streets talk about the present and future of the island. It scooped Best Experimental Movie at the 2006 Latin American Film Festival. When budget allows, his next project, *Cuatro hechizos*, will follow four friends at the dawn of the Special Period who promise never to separate.

Away from these three, a clutch of other young filmmakers is gaining credibility on the international scene. These include Humberto Padrón, whose *Frutas en el café* (2005) follows the daily struggles of three *habaneras*, and Ismael Perdomo, whose *Mata que Dios perdona* (2006) is a sordid tale of loneliness. And fans of Beny Moré should check out Jorge Luis Sánchez's 2006 biopic about the late singer, entitled simply *El Benny*; the soundtrack is delightful. Also keep an eye out for Juan Carlos Cremata's *Viva Cuba* (2005), about two schoolmates who decide to run away together when one of their families is about to abandon Cuba for the US; the film claimed no fewer than 25 prizes around the world, including one at Cannes. Proof – if it were needed – that Cuba's film industry is looking as hot as the country's salsa dancers these days.

Salas de video (Video rooms)

With notable exceptions, video rooms are hot, humid and squashed, with postage stamp-sized screens. The films they show are usually a mix of old and new releases.

Centro Cultural Cinematográfico ICAIC

Calle 23 #1155, entre 10 y 12, Vedado (833 9278). **Map** p253 C8.

Havana's finest *sala de video*, facing the Chaplin cinema, with 32 supremely comfy seats, high-quality equipment and one screen, plus a good selection of Cuban and Latin American features and documentaries. Screening information is displayed on a board inside the main entrance. 'El Centro' also houses a bar and a shop selling Cuban videos and books, plus the Videoteca del Sur, a project set up to promote Latin American cinema, and an art gallery.

Charlot

Chaplin cinema, Calle 23 #1155, entre 10 y 12, Vedado (831 1101). **Map** p253 C8.

Seating 50, this video room is upstairs from the Chaplin (*see p147*). The Charlot always shows interesting films, often complementing the main cinema's fare, though there's often a queue. Don't forget to tell the ticket seller you want the *sala de video*.

Museo Nacional de Bellas Artes

Edificio Arte Cubano, Calle Trocadero, entre Zulueta y Monserrate, Centro Habana (861 0241/3858). **Map** p256 D15.

The quiet and calm **Acapulco**. *See p148.*

The restored building housing the Cuban art collection has a small Sala de Audiovisuales showing art-house movies, plus another for children's films. Quiet and with a calm atmosphere, it's a good place to finish an exploration of the museum (*see p72*).

Sala Caracol

Calle 17, esquina H, Vedado (832 8114). **Map** p254 B11.

A rather small video room inside the grand house of the National Union of Writers & Artists (UNEAC). Shows international art-house films on a loop, starting at 12.30pm. See *Cartelera* or phone the venue for details. It has a loyal following, so get there early.

Yara A, B, C

Calle L #363, esquina 23, Vedado (832 9430). **Map** p254 B11.

The three 30-seater upstairs rooms show a diverse selection of mainly US films. Arrive early and make sure you buy the right ticket. No air-conditioning.

Festivals

The film festival that makes the headlines is the annual **Latin American Film Festival** (Festival Internacional del Nuevo Cine Latinoamericano; *see p142*), held in December. It features worldwide independent films and documentaries, retrospectives and directors' presentations. Not to mention stars: Francis Ford Coppola, Robert De Niro and Matt Dillon have all shown up in the past.

The **Hotel Nacional** (*see p48*) is the epicentre of activities surrounding the festival. Just CUC 45 will buy a pass giving you access to a special mailbox in the foyer and entry to all cinemas and peripheral events. The festival website (www.habanafilmfestival.com) is a good source of information. Check with **La Casa del Festival** (Calle 2 #411, entre 17 y 19, Vedado, 838 2864/2854) for information.

Cine Pobre (www.cinepobre.com) is an annual festival in May for low-budget films and documentaries. It takes place in Gibara, Holguín, but is organised from Havana by veteran Cuban director Humberto Solás. The annual **Festival de Nuevos Realizadores** (www.cubacine.cu/muestrajoven) in February gives young filmmakers the chance to show their mettle. The **Festival Internacional de Documentales Santiago Álvarez in Memoriam** (www.cubacine.cu/festival santiagoalvarez) has been running for more than a decade in Santiago de Cuba, but is increasingly gaining attraction.

Embassies of different European countries have organised mini festivals for the past few years; France and Germany seem to be mainstays. Check with ICAIC (*see p146*) for information on all of these events.

Galleries

The city's beating art.

In the last decade or so, the explosion of tourism in Cuba has had a knock-on effect on the local art scene. Visitors are travelling to the island specifically to buy Cuban artworks and state-run galleries have been joined by commercial home-studios. Well-known names have even been getting in on the street-art act too (*see p154* **The writing's on the wall**).

Several years after the Revolution, Castro described the relationship between art and the new politics in the following enigmatic statement: 'Within the Revolution everything; outside the Revolution nothing.' The constraints of this statement were felt most heavily by artists in the 'grey years' of the 1970s, when increased ideological censorship led many to seek exile. But art in 21st-century Cuba is no longer being made solely about social themes and utopian ideals.

LISTINGS AND INFORMATION

There is often a hazy line between state-run and commercial galleries; we have listed a combination of both. Galleries are a growth area, so it's worth asking around for new additions. For more information on Cuban art and artists visit www.art-havana.com and www.cubarte.cult.cu; for plastic arts, visit www.cnap.cult.cu or www.sancristobal.cult.cu.

BIENAL DE LA HABANA

The most interesting time to see Cuban art is during the month-long **Bienal de La Habana** (*see p141*), an international contemporary art festival that is spearheaded by a team of curators from the **Centro de Arte Contemporáneo Wifredo Lam** (*see p152*).

BUYING ART IN CUBA

When buying art, antiques or collectibles, obtain the necessary permission to leave with your items. Cuba requires that you register your items at the **National Heritage Office** (*see p125*) and obtain a *certificado de exportación*. You must pay CUC 10 for every five objects. Art purchased from a state-run institution will usually already have its export stamp. When purchasing directly from artists, buy at least two days before leaving the country, to ensure you get the certificate (you may have to pick it up the following day). Bring the object and bill of sale (including title, date and medium) with you to the National Heritage Office.

La Habana Vieja

Old Havana – particularly around Calle Oficios – is a hotspot for galleries and artists' studios. Permanent non-commercial exhibitions of art can be found in **Casa Oswaldo Guayasamín** (*see p64*), **Casa de México** and **Casa Simón Bolívar** (for both, *see p65*).

Casa de los Artistas

2nd floor, Calle Oficios #6, entre Obispo y Obrapía. Zaida del Río (862 8986); Roberto Fabelo's Galería Suyú (861 2387/www.art-havana.com/fabelo); Ernesto Rancaño Vieties (862 6521); Pedro Pablo Oliva (863 6243); Ángel Ramírez (no phone). **Open** 10.30am-4.30pm Mon-Sat. **Map** p256 E15.

Despite its location off the tourist-filled Plaza de Armas, Casa de los Artistas is a serious art house. It is home to the galleries and workshops of five of the most famous contemporary Cuban artists alive today: Zaida del Río, Roberto Fabelo, Ernesto Rancaño Vieties and Pedro Pablo Oliva. Prices reflect this, starting around CUC 1,000.

Casa de Carmen Montilla

Calle Oficios #162, entre Amargura y Brasil (Teniente Rey) (866 8768). **Open** 9am-5pm Tue-Sun. **Map** p256 E15.

Centro de Arte La Casona. *See p152.*

Big Brother is watching you.

This charming gallery was established in 1994 by the Venezuelan artist Carmen Montilla. The quaint interior courtyard and the view from the second-floor are worth a peek, not to mention the impressive wall mural by leading Cuban ceramicist Alfredo Sosabravo. The focus of the space is on contemporary art (both permanent and commercial exhibitions), plus Cuban and Latin American sculpture.

Centro de Arte La Casona

Calle Muralla #107, esquina San Ignacio (861 8544/ www.galeriascubanas.com). **Open** 10am-5pm Tue-Sat. **Admission** free. **Map** p256 E15.

One of Havana's leading exhibition spaces, this prominent gallery was beautifully restored in 1979. Under the direction of art entrepreneur Luis Miret Pérez, La Casona is devoted in the main to solo exhibitions, but also has catalogues of leading contemporary Cuban artists. Artwork is sold here for anything from CUC 100 to CUC 5,000. The complex also houses the Tienda de Ediciones Artísticas (a small serigraphy shop) and the Galería Diago, specialising in Afro-Cuban folk art. **Photo** *p151*.

Centro de Arte Contemporáneo Wifredo Lam

Calle San Ignacio #22, esquina Empedrado (861 3419/wlam@cubarte.cult.cu). **Open** 10am-5pm Mon-Sat. **Admission** CUC 3; free under-12s. **Map** p256 D15.

Named after Wifredo Lam (1902-82), a Cuban painter with Afro-Chinese origins, this state-run cultural complex was inaugurated in 1983 for the study and promotion of the contemporary visual arts of Third World nations. It is now one of the country's most important galleries, and responsible for the organisation of the Bienal de La Habana (*see p141*), Cuba's major international art fair. While the centre's 1,250-piece permanent collection carries a sizeable number of Lam's lithographs and acrylic works, there are also temporary exhibitions from Cuba and beyond. The building also houses a bookshop, café, library, conference rooms and an interior courtyard; the whole complex was closed for restoration as this guide went to press, with work expected to be completed in late summer/early autumn 2007.

Centro de Desarrollo de las Artes Visuales

San Ignacio #352, esquina Brasil (Teniente Rey), Plaza Vieja (862 3533/avisual@cubarte.cult.cu). **Open** 10am-5pm Tue-Sat. **Map** p256 E15.

A state-run contemporary art centre devoted mainly to exhibitions of young emerging Cuban artists, although there are occasional exhibits by well-known international artists. At press time the building and its four galleries were undergoing wholescale renovation work, which was scheduled for completion by mid 2007.

Centro Pablo de la Torriente Brau

Calle Muralla #63, entre Oficios e Inquisidor (866 6585/www.centropablo.cult.cu). **Open** 8am-5pm Mon-Fri. **Map** p256 E15.

This independent non-profit centre established in 1966 now focuses on new media and audio-visual technology. The Centro Pablo, as it is locally known, organises a burgeoning annual digital art festival each June (*see p139*) and has played host to more than 70 *nueva trova* (modern folksong) concerts over the past decade or so.

Centro Provincial de Artes Plásticas y Diseño

Calle Oficios #362, esquina Luz (862 3228/3295/ cpap@cubarte.cult.cu). **Open** 9am-5pm Mon-Sat; 9am-1pm Sun. **Map** p256 E15.

This art centre houses two galleries featuring paintings, ceramics and drawings by Cuban artists. The house dates to 1732; the second floor has attractive marble floors and mahogany woodwork.

Estudio-Galería Los Oficios

Calle Oficios #166, entre Amargura y Brasil (Teniente Rey) (863 0497/www.ndominguez.com). **Open** 10.30am-5pm daily. **Map** p256 E15.

This is the studio-gallery of Cuban artist Nelson Domínguez. In keeping with an artist of this stature, his work – which includes painting, pottery, jewellery and sculpture – doesn't come cheap.

Fototeca de Cuba

Calle Mercaderes #307, entre Muralla y Brasil (Teniente Rey), Plaza Vieja (862 2530/www.cnap.cult.cu/insti2g.html). **Open** 10am-5pm Tue-Sat. **Map** p256 E15.

Established in 1986, the Fototeca de Cuba is the capital's leading photographic centre, containing the widest and most valuable archive of Cuban photos, plus temporary exhibitions. Its permanent exhibition – displaying the work of Cuba's photographic heroes such as Raúl Corrales, Alberto Korda, Osvaldo Salas, Ernesto Fernández and Mario García Joya – is the main reason for coming. There's also a shop selling postcards, photographic works and publications, Tuesday to Friday only. Also housed here is one of Havana's scarce communal darkrooms, so it's a good place to meet photographers.

Galería Forma

Calle Obispo #255, entre Cuba y Aguiar (862 0123). **Open** 9am-9pm daily. **Map** p256 E15.
One of the better of a half dozen commercial galleries on lively Calle Obispo, selling pottery, sculpture, jewellery and painting by Cuban artist-artisans across all artistic genres. Prices tend to be affordable but can go as high as CUC 1,000.

Galería Havana Club/ Museo del Ron

Calle San Pedro (Avenida del Puerto) #262, esquina Sol (862 4108/3832). **Open** *Museum & Gallery* 9am-5.30pm Mon-Thur; 9am-4pm Fri, Sat; 10am-4pm Sun. **Map** p256 E15.
This modern museum, part of the Fundación Havana Club complex, is dedicated to the making of the quintessential Cuban tipple. The second floor houses the Galería Havana Club, a decent set of spaces that sell work by Cuban and international artists. For the museum's bar, *see p119*.

Galería Manos/Asociación Cubana de Artesanos Artistas

Calle Obispo #411, entre Compostela y Aguacate (ACAA 866 6345/acaa@cubarte.cult.cu/Galería Manos 860 8577). **Open** 10am-5pm daily. **Map** p256 D/E15.
A state-run craft gallery on two floors, specialising in popular Cuban crafts – pottery, jewellery, leather goods, glass work and carvings.

Galería Víctor Manuel

Calle San Ignacio #56, esquina Callejón del Chorro, Plaza de la Catedral (861 2955/866 9268/vmanuel@fcbc.cult.cu). **Open** 9am-9pm daily. **Map** p256 D15.
This gallery contains a range of somewhat mainstream, yet often quite smart, pieces of Cuban art for sale, including paintings, wood carving, jewellery, pottery and crafts. Given its prime location and popularity, don't expect anything to come cheap.

Prado Art Walk

Paseo de Martí (Prado), entre Neptuno y Trocadero. **Open** noon-6pm Sat. **Map** p256 D14.
A three-block-long open-air exhibition of paintings by dozens of independent artists is set up every Saturday afternoon along El Prado. The work varies in quality – stooping to touristy renderings of '57 Chevys – but it's worth a look. Officially, the work is for exhibition and not for sale on site, though negotiating may be possible.

Taller Experimental de Gráfica de La Habana

Callejón del Chorro #62, off Plaza de la Catedral (862 0979/www.cnap.cult.cu/insti2k.html). **Open** 9.30am-4pm Mon-Fri. **Map** p256 E15.
Although printmaking in Cuba began in the 19th century, it wasn't until 1962 that this, Cuba's only engraving workshop, was established by Cuban artist Orlando Suárez. While the sight and smell of the workshop capture the attention, the small Galería del Grabado upstairs is not to be missed. It sells excellent, non-touristy prints, including etchings, lithographs, woodcuts and collagraphs.

Centro Habana

The **Museo Nacional de Bellas Artes** (*see p72*), housed in two buildings (Arte Cubano and Arte Universal), is the island's largest and most impressive permanent art collection.

Galería La Acacia

Calle San José (San Martín) #114, entre Industria y Consulado (861 3533). **Open** 9am-4.30pm Tue-Fri. **Map** p254 D14.
A high-end and well-stocked commercial gallery just across from the Capitolio building in Centro Habana dedicated to Cuban contemporary and avant-garde art. A chamber within the galleria is dedicated to the work of internationally renowned Cuban artist José Fuster (*see p155*). A good place to see who the up-and-coming hot artists are.

Vedado

Other than the galleries listed below, the **Casa de las Américas** (*see p83*) has two galleries that house both permanent and commercial exhibitions.

Espacio Aglutinador

Calle 25 #602, entre 6 y 8 (830 2147/aglutsan@cubarte.cult.cu). **Open** 10am-8pm daily. **Map** p254 C9.
Off-the-beaten-path Espacio Aglutinador opened in 1994 as Cuba's first independent exhibition space and is still run by co-founder Sandra Ceballos. The recently renovated space still plays a key role in showing artists left out of the official culture, as well as under-recognised older artists.

Galería Habana. *See p155.*

The writing's on the wall

Havana artwork ventures further than its myriad galleries. As with so much of Cuban lifestyle, some of the most arresting sights are to be found out on the streets, where kaleidoscopic murals unfurl along a wall or up the side of an apartment block, while vibrant political slogans in calligraphic technicolour turn a city stroll into an impromptu artfest.

Mural artistry is a well-established genre in Latin American art history, with artistic heavyweights like Mexican Diego Rivera still providing inspiration for today's artists. It's a tradition that the Revolution has put to good use: of the many gallons of paint employed to such ends much comprise extracts from speeches by Fidel and Raúl Castro, Che Guevara and other heroes. Slogans and catchphrases are often accompanied by iconic images of the men (rarely women) themselves. Artists are commissioned by a *barrio*'s CDRs (Defense Committees of the Revolution), with the Union of Young Communists co-ordinating work in public areas like roadsides.

While much of the political work is formulaic, originality shines through on more creative efforts. Commissioned by art bodies like the Fondo Cubano de Bienes Culturales, which also manages galleries countrywide, artists have much freer reign over what murals, sculptures and installations they can create. Artists can also approach the organisation and petition for commissions. Paint is provided for free or subsidised, and many materials are bought under the cover of a third party country.

The essence of Cuban murals is colour. Bold primary colours and oranges, pinks and other hues glow in the Caribbean sun. Symbolism is a recurring theme, with artists drawing extensively on patriotic motifs such as the national flag, shield and images of historic figures. Symbols and icons from Afro-Cuban religions are also popular.

In the last five years an urban graffiti style has started to emerge, and collaboration with foreign artists is also increasingly common. A trip to **Regla** (*see p97*) is rewarded with the 100-metre-long (328-foot) mural in the centre of the village showing off the best of Cuban and Brazilian artists. Eagle-eyed visitors will spot iconic images by British graffitist **Banksy**, including a ghetto rat on the corner of Obispo and Aguiar in La Habana Vieja, and cool animal stencils by the French graffiti collaborative **Mosko et Associés** in Centro.

To see homegrown artwork at its best, head to the ebullient **Callejón de Hammel** in Centro Habana (*see p77*). Work in progress started here in the 1990s when local artist Salvador González Escalona decided to give his neighbourhood a makeover. González's project was originally self-funded, driven by a desire to improve the appearance of his *barrio*, which was at the time one of the most run-down areas in Havana. Beginning with one small panel of plaster painted red, black and yellow high on a crumbling wall, murals, sculptures and installations have spilled out along the narrow street, while the nearby apartment blocks have also been painted. González's work combines strong use of Afro-Cuban imagery and colours with his own esoteric poems lettered in an elegant calligraphy. He and a team of apprentices regularly maintain and embellish the street, as well as running *rumba peñas* and a gallery (*see also p75* **Street beats**).

A word of warning, though: street art in Havana is a transitory pleasure. Even pieces that are little more than a year old assume the patina of decades in the corrosive sea air. Nothing is permanent on these city streets – so enjoy it while you can.

Fundación Ludwig de Cuba

Calle 13 #509, 5t° piso, entre D y E (832 4270/ 9128). **Open** 10am-4pm Mon-Fri by appointment only. **Map** p254 B10.

German Peter Ludwig founded this centre in 1995 to support young Cuban artists. Housed in the penthouse of a five-storey building, with a breathtaking view of Vedado, it hosts regular exhibitions of works by young Cuban and international artists.

Galería Ciudades del Mundo

Calle 25 #307, entre L y M (832 6062/dppfach@ceniai.inf.cu). **Open** 8.30am-5pm Mon-Fri. **Map** p254 C11.

This gallery belongs to the Urban Planning Institute of Havana and specialises in artwork in the fields of architecture, urbanism and ecology.

Galería Habana

Calle Línea #460, entre E y F (832 7101/habana@cubarte.cult.cu). **Open** 9am-5pm Mon-Sat. **Map** p254 A10.

One of Havana's longest-established galleries (founded 1962), this combination of state-run and commercial showplace exhibits the work of both Cuban and international artists in a host of forms – installations, paintings and sculpture. The gallery handles all the paperwork that allows you to leave the country with your new artwork, with prices ranging from CUC 100 to CUC 5,000. **Photo** *p153.*

Galería 23 y 12

Calle 23, esquina 12 (831 1810). **Open** 9am-5pm Mon-Fri; 10am-2pm Sat. **Map** p253 C8.

A state-run gallery that organises solo and group exhibitions of Cuban contemporary art. The small on-site shop sells prints, posters, engravings and suchlike. A similar gallery, Galería Servando, is just a block away on Calle 23 at the corner of 10th, but has no phone.

Sandra Ramos.

Cuban art is not just about the Revolution.

Galería Villa Manuela (UNEAC)

Calle H, entre 17 y 19 (832 2391/galeria_villa manuela@yahoo.es). **Open** 10am-5pm Mon-Fri. **Map** p254 B11.

Founded in 2004 by the National Union of Writers & Artists (UNEAC; *see p86*), this gallery exhibits some of the best contemporary Cuban artists.

Miramar & the western suburbs

Casa-Estudio de José Fuster

Calle 226, esquina 3A, Jaimanitas (home 271 3048/ agent 271 2932/www.art-havana.com/fuster). **Open** 9am-6pm daily.

Fuster has achieved international renown; here you can see the artist on his home ground. A long way out of town, but a fascinating excursion. A host of his works is also shown at Galería La Acacia (*see p153*).

Art Havana

Havana's private gallery-studios are home to some of the best artists in Cuba, many of international renown, so prices are likely to be in line with international trends.

The current roster includes printmaker **Abel Barroso** (830 4212, abelmeri@cubarte.cult.cu); **Ángel Delgado** (267 4090, adelgadof@yahoo.com), who uses unconventional materials; **Tania Bruguera**s (861 6855, estudio@tania brugueras.com), whose work takes in drawing, sculpture, video and performance; and **Sandra Ramos** (835 3027, sandraramos@cubarte.cult.cu), known for her sculptures and prints.

All visits are by appointment only; you can contact the artists directly, but a better bet is to go through **Art Havana** (www.art-havana.com), which organises tours for individual collectors or groups. Contact Sussette Martínez, the main curator, on 267 7989, or by emailing her on susyed@giron.sld.cu.

Gay & Lesbian

Cuba (increasingly) *libre*!

In terms of acceptance of gay culture and lifestyle, Cuba is probably the most easygoing of all Latin American and Caribbean countries. The worst that Cuban gays have to contend with nowadays is the type of police harassment common to most countries that allow for lax interpretation of public scandal laws.

Cuba's much-maligned AIDS policy of the late 1980s forced HIV patients into quarantine (this ended in 1993). But the reality is, because of good education and excellent public information about the disease, the island's HIV infection rate is one of the very lowest in the world – in spite of the famous Cuban libido. And while there is still an element of social stigma attached to homosexuality here, violence is rarely directed at gays and most people are happy to let others live their own lives.

After attempting to turn gay men, long-haired hippies and all manner of 'objectors' into 'real men' by sending them to work camps euphemistically called Military Production Support Units (UMAPs), the Revolutionary government went through a period of self-reproof. One by one homophobic laws were taken off the books, starting in 1975 with the overturning of a 1971 law preventing homosexuals from working in various professions. This was followed in 1979 by the decriminalisation of homosexuality (the same year as in Spain).

Homophobic rhetoric has now been eradicated from Cuban law – although the public scandal laws continue to be used by a largely unaccountable police force – and gay issues have made an entrance on to the public stage. The National Sex Education Centre (CENESEX) website has a very well-presented section on sexual diversity (www.cenesex.sld.cu/webs/diversidad/diversidad.htm) as well as open discussion on issues pertaining to police harassment of GLBT Cubans. There is now even a Gay Film Festival in Havana (albeit a very small one).

The international success of Tomás Guttiérrez Alea's 1993 film *Fresa y chocolate* about the attraction of an openly gay man for a young straight revolutionary did more for gay liberation in Cuba than anything else by breaking the taboo. Sonja de Vries's excellent 1994 documentary *Gay Cuba* recorded the ecstatic reactions of Cubans pouring out of the Yara cinema after watching the film ('What a friendship! I would love to have a friend like that!' – 'Are you gay?' – 'What, me? No way! Straight! Pure macho!'). More recently, a *Juventud Rebelde* newspaper article described the remorse a couple were experiencing for rejecting their gay son, and a case study of six same-sex couples was published by the University of Havana commenting on the fact that they had – unsurprisingly – very similar issues to couples of any sexual make-up.

This is not to say that there haven't been homophobic reversals in Cuba. A few years ago an unpleasant – and heavily criticised – editorial in a local newspaper, *Tribuna de La Habana*, openly attacked transvestites, and was responsible for the suppression of regular drag shows at the **Castropol** (*see p157*), and the temporary movement of the gay scene from the seafront Malecón to Calle 23 and Paseo. Happily, everyone is now back on the Malecón in force.

In public, holding hands might still be a little forward, but a kiss on the cheek and a manly hug is perfectly acceptable. Even transvestites and cross-dressers in full regalia can be seen out and about. In fact, one of the odd and contradictory aspects of macho culture in Cuba is the immense enjoyment of cross-dressing or transvestite shows.

The city of **Santa Clara** in the Central Provinces has a thriving gay scene, most of which is centred on the gay and lesbian nights at the Mejunje nightclub in the town centre (*see p204*). This is effectively the only official nightclub on the island with a gay theme.

WHERE TO GO

There are few specifically gay bars and clubs in Havana, and none that is state-backed. As a result, the gay scene is often played out on the street and at private parties. The **Yara** cinema (*see p148*) is the traditional night-time rendezvous for gay men, although there have been efforts by the police to move people along when things get crowded around 11pm. The scene then heads down **La Rampa** (the section of Calle 23 from the junction of Calle L to the seafront) to the Malecón and settles on the sea wall, where gay men and lesbians openly hang out in large numbers until dawn.

On Fridays and Saturdays there is almost always a gay and/or lesbian party somewhere. Just show up at the Yara around 10pm and ask.

Making new friends on the **Malecón**.

There will be cars ready to take you to the action for a few CUC. The gay fiestas used to be wild affairs held in anything from an old mansion in the middle of a wood to a 1950s beachside club, but things have changed due to the worsening economy and a concerted anti-drug campaign. Plus, the increase in male hustlers drives people away; the vast majority of the gorgeous men in their 20s at these parties are *jineteros* or *pingueros* (literally, 'penis guys'). It's fun to be around these stunners for a drink or two (on you), but remember it isn't always your fabulous body that's attracted them. The bulge in your trousers they're really after is no doubt the one made by your wallet.

PRACTICAL INFORMATION

As with so many things in Cuba, the gay scene is prone to sudden change for no apparent reason; you should therefore be prepared for any of the following venues to be closed at short notice and for other information, such as admission prices, to fluctuate (they're nebulous at the best of times for any venue in Havana, let alone gay ones). Some, but not all, venues have air-conditioning. In the ones that do, it's prone to breaking down or is turned up so high that your libido is seriously affected.

As well as the straightforward *homosexual*, you may also hear the terms *maricón* or *pato* (poof), *pájaro* or *loca* (queen), and *tortillera* or *tuerca* (dyke). It's best not to use these terms casually as they may cause offence.

For more on AIDS and STDs, including an anonymous helpline, *see p227.*

Bars, cafés & clubs

Many bars and cafés in and around Havana attract gay crowds without advertising themselves as gay. As always in Cuba, everyone's welcome.

Cafetería La Arcada

Calle M, esquina 23, Vedado (832 0677). **Open** 24hrs daily. **Admission** free. **Map** p254 B11.

This pleasant place – quite similar to the Cafetería 23 y P (*see below*) but more downmarket – has become a primarily male gay haunt at night.

Cafetería 23 y P

Calle 23, esquina P, Vedado (870 7631). **Open** 7am-3am daily. **Admission** free. **Map** p254 B12.

Close to the Yara cinema, this is a regular bar that has become a gay evening hangout simply because most of its clients happen to be, well, gay.

Castropol

Malecón #107, entre Genios y Crespo, Centro Habana (861 4864). **Open** noon-midnight daily. **Dance shows** 4-9pm Sun. **Admission** free. **Map** p255 C15.

Once a drag-show cabaret, this popular nightspot features a small, outdoor patio filled with tables and chairs crowded together, and an inside dance-floor (house, salsa and Madonna). The crowd is friendly and, best of all, there's no hustling. Tuesday and Thursday nights used to be for a mostly lesbian crowd, although Cubans don't tend to make a big deal about who is what. Now that the place has been refurbished it is, unfortunately, atracting a more mainstream crowd.

Night Club Tropical

Calle Línea, esquina F, Vedado (832 7361). **Open** 10pm-2am daily. **Admission** CUC 2. **Map** p254 A10.
A small and smoky (but now air-conditioned, at least) cellar offering different nights for different patrons. Club Tropical often attracts young, gay fashion victims, but is less ostensibly gay these days. Before paying the cover, find out what kind of night is in store for you by checking out the (very) young crowd milling about outside.

San Lázaro #8A

San Lázaro #8A, entre Paseo de Martí (Prado) y Cárcel, Centro Habana (no phone). **Open** 11pm-4am Thur-Sun. **Admission** free. **Map** p256 C15.
This house at the end of Prado at La Punta (the entrance to the Havana Bay), is the scene of regular Friday and Saturday night parties for a mostly young, male Cuban crowd. There's a drag show that can, ahem, drag on a little at one and a half hours. Drinks are CUC 1 a pop, and food is cheap. Very hot and steamy but relatively few hustlers.

Cruising

Cuba's public scandal laws seek to dissuade sex workers and those looking for casual public sex. Police officers have ample room to interpret these ambiguous laws however they see fit. Thus, even picking someone up in a park can lead to hassle. Any Cuban involved is likely to be treated as a hustler (which is often the case). It is certainly not illegal to meet and talk with someone on the street, but if you do this behind the bushes – even if your clothes are intact when a police torch lights up your evening – you will probably be taken down to the station and given a warning. Having said this, police intervention is fairly rare. Cruising action abounds in the locales below. And Christmas Eve midnight mass at the Catedral is another cruising opportunity, with what appears to be the entire gay/lesbian community out in force in the square in front of the cathedral.

At the ballet

Any good ballet (and in Cuba it's always good) attracts a large percentage of Havana's gay male population. You can find them in full force at the Sala García Lorca in the Gran Teatro de La Habana (*see p173*) in Centro Habana, and the intermissions offer great cruising opportunities. Prop yourself in the curve of the grand piano in the foyer, look gorgeous, cultured and uninterested, and wait.

At the beach

Playa Mi Cayito, some 30 minutes by car from Havana along the Playas del Este (*see p100*), offers a perfect backdrop: palm trees; blue, warm, clear water lapping on the shore; hour-glass fine sand; and plenty of same-sex couples sunbathing, with a plethora of bods to choose from on weekends. The easiest way to get there is to take a taxi (CUC 10-15 each way) from anywhere in Havana. Be sure not to go at the wrong time of year, though: summer officially ends with August and few Cubans go to the beach after September. There is a heavy police presence to dissuade sex workers, but at least the officers wear shorts these days.

At the cinema

Cine Payret (*see p147*), opposite the Capitolio in Centro Habana, offers the chance for old-fashioned back-row snogging. The film can be quite good too.

On the street

Not the most romantic setting, but there's plenty of action along Calle G (from Calle Línea to 23, and from the José Miguel Gómez monument at 27 and to the School of Dentistry). The seafront by Hotel Neptuno-Tritón (corner of Avenida 3ra and Calle 72) in Miramar is active but some way out of town.

Lesbian life

There are fewer hangouts for lesbians than there are for gay men in Havana, but a stroll along the Malecón close to La Rampa around midnight will reveal an increasing number of young women who are taking back a little of the street that the gay male population has overrun. Lesbian fiestas in Havana are less publicised affairs, with news travelling by word of mouth. And, unlike the male gay parties, they aren't riddled with hustlers.

Lesbians are far more 'out' in Cuba than just about anywhere else in Latin America. But this doesn't mean that they're as visible as Cuba's gay men, who are a cinch to spot. Butch dykes and femmes are around, of course, but lesbians tend not to dress to stereotype and so blend in with their heterosexual counterparts. There are many older – and a few younger – lesbian couples living openly in Havana, although they'd be hard put to do the same thing in the provinces. Don't come expecting New York or London, and you'll be pleasantly surprised.

Where to stay & eat

Most establishments in Cuba are gay-friendly, but we'd particularly recommend the following *paladares*: the **Decameron** (*see p115*), **La Esperanza** (*see p117*) and **La Guarida** (*see p113*). For a *casa particular*, try **Casa de Carlos y Julio** (*see p49*) in Vedado or **Casa de Eugenio y Fabio** (*see p44*) in Old Havana.

Music & Nightlife

Whether it's a Buena Vista Social Club-fuelled nostalgia trip, the alternative music scene or a glitzy salsa extravaganza, Havana always hits the high notes.

As clichéd as it sounds, music is everywhere in Havana. You'd literally have to tape your ears shut to escape the melodies of this city. Indeed, locals joke that Cuba is the only country in the world where you have to pay musicians not to play. Most bars and restaurants feature trios, quartets and septets; neighbourhoods are filled with the sounds of radios on full volume, *toques de santo* (religious ceremonies with drumming, singing and dancing), spontaneous rumba sessions and bands rehearsing. Even many *bicitaxis* are equipped with pedal-powered boom boxes. At night the Malecón, Havana's living room, is rammed with *habaneros* drinking rum and strumming guitars.

Even in their darkest hours Cubans have been able to create music – and quality music at that. The level of musical training here is remarkably high, and one of the consequences of the US embargo is that, rather than being overrun by American pop, Cuba has nurtured its own unique blends of African and European rhythms – from rumba to bolero, *chachachá* to *timba* – and kept its levels of creativity high. The unparalleled popularity of the Buena Vista Social Club has reminded everyone inside and abroad that music was always one of the country's leading exports, and authenticated Cuba's status as a musical powerhouse in the Americas, alongside the US and Brazil.

INFORMATION

Havana is filled with bars and clubs for dancing or just listening, and every night of the week you're guaranteed to find something of interest. The Spanish- and English-language *Cartelera* is a main resource for cultural listings, but it's patchy. In Friday's edition of *Juventud Rebelde*, a half-page cultural section provides details of the major weekend events. Check www.egrem.com.cu, the website of Cuba's main recording label EGREM, for details of venues under its management. Radio Taíno (FM 93.3) plays a blend of Cuban and world music, and broadcasts updates in English on music events.

There is a regular rotation of bands among the premier clubs, namely the two **Casas de la Música**, the **Piano Bar Delirio Habanero** and **Café Cantante**. These four venues are all managed by EGREM, which has access to the very best bands. Look out in particular for Los Van Van, Adalberto Alvarez y su Son, NG La Banda and Isaac Delgado. You will pay more to see these in-demand acts (CUC 15-25) but it's worth it. The main act will often not start until 11.30pm or later, but go early if you want a table. For further ideas on names to look out for, *see p162* **Broadening your musical Vistas**.

Some of the most renowned *timba* and traditional music bands play in Havana's upmarket hotels. The surviving Buena Vista Social Club members each play with their own ensembles, most commonly at the **Salón 1930 'Compay Segundo'** at the Hotel Nacional.

The Cuban government has also, in recent years, staged occasional free concerts by high-profile acts along the Malecón, just below the Hotel Nacional, and at the **Tribuna Antimperialista** (*see p83*). Audioslave, Rick Wakeman and Air Supply have all played there. These concerts are generally announced a day or two before the event, normally on Radio Taíno or Radio Ciudad.

The best Venues

For cutting edge acts

Café Cantante Mi Habana (*see p164*); **La Madriguera** (*see p168*).

For dancing with the locals

Centro Cultural El Gran Palenque (*see p165*); **Casa de la Cultura de Centro Habana** (*see p163*); **Piano Bar El Diablo** (*see p170*).

For a sense of history

El Gato Tuerto (*see p166*); **Salón 1930 'Compay Segundo'** (*see p168*); **Salón Rosado Beny Moré** (*see p171*).

For an unusual setting

Basílica Menor de San Francisco de Asís (*see p161*); **Casa del Tango** (*see p164*); **Callejón de Hammel** (*see p163*).

For *son*

Café Taberna (*see p161*); **Club Tikoa** (*see p166*).

Glossary

Bolero Born in Santiago, this is a romantic, heart-felt genre, usually sung by a soloist or harmony duo in the form of a ballad.
Filin An evolution of *bolero* and *trova, filin* (a transliteration of 'feeling') started in 1940s Havana as a Cuban response to American jazz singers like Sinatra.
Nueva trova This often politicised genre came about after the Revolution in 1959, when the government took several *filinista* singer-songwriters under its wing. Pablo Milanés and Silvio Rodríguez are the most famous exponents of this folk-tinged and emotionally charged genre.
Rumba Umbrella term for various forms of Afro-Cuban song and dance. *See also p66.*
Salsa Something of a catch-all term, this transnational genre is descended from Cuban *son* but borrows heavily from other styles, especially American jazz. Salsa dancing is also influenced by other Afro-Cuban forms, particularly rumba (for example, 'casino-style').
Son The mother of all Cuban music genres, *son* originated in the 19th century in the rural eastern provinces, a merger between Spanish verse-and-chorus forms and African vocals and percussion – the *clave* (two wooden sticks that beat syncopated rhythms), the *güiro* (a long, hollow piece of wood with ridges that are scraped with a hard stick), the maracas and the bongos. What really defines *son* are the off-beat bass (*marimbula*) and the *tres*, a small guitar-like instrument with three sets of double steel strings, used with or instead of guitar. Septet formats later added in a trumpet; the genre continues to evolve.
Timba A contemporary development of Cuban *son*-derived salsa that has become one of the dominant sounds on the island today. Driven by the uniquely Cuban way of whole-body dancing, it draws on Afro-Cuban folkloric dances and rhythms, especially rumba, and more modern genres such as rap and reggae.
Trova Originating with the singer-songwriters (troubadours, hence 'trova') of the eastern part of the island, who, in colonial times, would go from house to house singing ballads about love, women and the motherland. The genre developed from the guitar-and-singer structure of the Spanish-influenced *canción*.

If your budget is tight head for one of the places that charge in Cuban pesos (*moneda nacional*), or take in a matinée (always cheaper) at one of the larger clubs, such as the two **Casas de la Música** and **Café Cantante**; we have given admission prices in Cuban pesos if there's no alternative CUC charge.

Clubs open and close with frequency in Havana, and hours, cover charges and bills change often too, so it's always wise to call ahead to confirm who is performing and at what time. Also note that only the major venues take credit cards.

Cubans like to look cool when they go out and many places operate a strict dress code, so avoid wearing shorts, sleeveless shirts or sandals. Women should dress up to the nines if they don't want to stand out.

CLASSICAL MUSIC

Classical music isn't exactly the first thing that comes to mind in connection with Cuba. Yet the history of classical music on the island actually dates back a long way, to the mid 18th century, with the works of Esteban Salas (1725-1803) and, later, Juan París (1759-1845), who produced sacred, vocal and chamber music, based on European musical traditions. It was the 19th century that saw Cuban classical music developing a voice of its own. The first piece of work that did this was the *Contradanza San Pascual Bailón* (1803, anonymous), along with works by Manuel Saumell and Ignacio Cervantes in the mid 1800s, while the western world was going through its romantic nationalist period in music.

Rhythmic variety and richness were the main ingredients in the rapid evolution of Cuban classical music. Needless to say, the Spanish and African cultural traditions that shape Cuban culture inevitably permeated the work of Cuban classical music composers. In fact, not only did many of them use elements of the Cuban folkloric music for classical compositions but also produced popular as much as classical compositions. Gonzalo Roig (1890-1970), for example, won international acclaim for his Cuban operetta *Cecilia Valdés* (1932) and song 'Quiéreme mucho' (1911), while Ernesto Lecuona (1895-1963) became famous for his collection of Cuban *zarzuelas* and his compositions for piano.

By the mid 20th century Cuban classical music was well established in the international arena. The two main classical composers at the time were Amadeo Roldán (1900-1939) and Alejandro Garcia Caturla (1906-1940). They both followed the steps of composers such as Béla Bartók and Igor Stravinsky, yet achieved a contemporary compositional style of their own.

However, state art schools were a creation of the Revolution for the people and classical music was taught there from the beginning. Students were taught to praise the works of Prokofiev and Soviet Socialist Realism but equally to respect Mozart, Beethoven, Bach and Hector Villalobos. Classical music education became available for the people – as long as they have the required talent. However, like elsewhere in the world classical music came to be seen by many as an elite type of music and fell out of favour to an extent after the Revolution as it was considered bourgeois. The island had to import musicians and teachers from the Eastern bloc to keep its orchestras intact.

With the collapse of the Soviet Union, large crowds began to turn out for symphony concerts, even breaking down the doors of the Teatro Nacional to hear a Bach recital. Classical music, overlooked for 30 years, reminded people of better days. Young Cubans began to attend the conservatories again and the island is now involved in the task of creating home-grown symphony orchestras in every province.

Today there are two major venues for classical music in Havana: the **Teatro Amadeo Roldán** in Vedado, home of the National Symphony Orchestra; and the **Basílica de San Francisco de Asís**, home of Camerata Romeu, an all-female chamber ensemble. Other venues include **Iglesia de Paula**, home to prestigious ensemble Ars Longa, and the **Oratorio de San Felipe Neri**, which opened in February 2006. It's also worth trying to catch outdoor performances of the Municipal Band of Havana, which plays the more popular style of Cuban and Hispanic classical music on Fridays in the foyer of the Inglaterra Hotel or by Plaza de Armas.

FESTIVALS

For the best of Cuba's many music festivals, *see pp138-142*. The main agents for Havana events are **Paradiso** (Calle 19, #560, esquina Avenida C, Vedado, 832 6928/9538) and **Havanatur** (*see p191*).

La Habana Vieja

There's a multitude of touristy bars and cafés churning out the ubiquitous *Guantanamera* and hits from the Buena Vista Social Club in and around Calle Obispo, Plaza de Armas and Calle Tacón. If you want something a bit different, try the following.

Restaurants and bars with particularly good music include **La Mina** (*see p110*), **El Patio** (*see p110*), **Café París** (*see p120*) and **Bar Monserrate** (*see p119*). On Calle Obispo try **Casa del Escabeche** (corner of Villegas; two sets, at noon-7pm and 7pm-midnight), **Bosque Bologna** (*see p119*; two sets in summer, at noon-5pm and 7pm-midnight); **Bar la Dichosa** (corner of Compostela; two sets, at 1-6pm and 6pm-midnight), **Hotel Florida**, with its piano bar (*see p41*) and **Hotel Ambos Mundos** (whose rooftop bar has a Cuban night twice a week; *see p41*).

Other venue options include the **Museo Nacional de la Música** (*see p67*), with its small, narrow hall cherished by classical and jazz musicians alike; and the **Centro Pablo de la Torriente Brau** (*see p152*) near Plaza Vieja, which holds concerts by *trovadores* in its pretty courtyard area.

Basílica Menor de San Francisco de Asís

Calle Oficios, entre Amargura y Brasil (Teniente Rey) (862 9683/3467). **Open** *Museum* 9am-6.30pm daily. *Performances* 6pm Sat. Closed Aug. **Admission** CUC 10. **Map** p256 E15.

This imposing and peaceful basilica with fine acoustics hosts some of the most important classical concerts in Havana. Set in the square of the same name, the church is the home of the Grammy-nominated Camerata Romeu, an all-female chamber ensemble, and many other excellent soloists, groups and choirs ask to be booked here, among them Coro Exaudi and the ensemble Solistas de la Habana.

Café Taberna

Calle Mercaderes #531, esquina Brasil (Teniente Rey) (861 1637). **Open** noon-midnight daily. *Performances* 11am-4pm, 4-7pm daily. **Admission** free. **Map** p256 E15.

This restaurant, built on the site of Havana's very first café, opened in 1777. It is now a fine setting to enjoy some of the best *son* in town. The house bands are Son del Trópico, Sonido Son and the Septeto Matamoros (led by the grandson of famous composer Miguel Matamoros), who perform every day in two separate sets. They play as if there's no tomorrow and there's no cover charge. If you're not planning on visiting Santiago, the cradle of *son*, see it here instead. *See also p106.*

Casa de la Cultura de La Habana Vieja

Calle Aguiar #509, entre Brasil (Teniente Rey) y Amargura (863 4860). **Open** 8pm-midnight Tue-Sun. **Performances** phone for details. **Admission** 10 pesos. **Map** p256 E15.

This venue was recently taken over by new management, and was also relocated to a two-storey building in the heart of Jesús María, a troubled neighbourhood in Old Havana. But the Casa's newly appointed director Reynaldo Méndez Chenique seems to be aware of what the institution can do for the community. Tango and rumba feature through the week, sometimes with amateur musicians, sometimes with major acts.

Broadening your musical Vistas

Some people still think today's Cuban music scene can be summed up in four words: Buena Vista Social Club. The myth offered to the international public is that a foreign producer came to Cuba and discovered some aged stars past their prime, then launched them to the top of the charts. Not surprisingly, it's a myth that's not well received on an island that's proud of the quality of its musicians. While there's no denying that it was Wim Wenders' 1996 film that catapulted the BVSC musicians to international fame, they were already well-known major talents.

A decade on, however, the passage of time has resulted in the inevitable: between 2000 and 2006 five major members of the band – Compay Segundo, Rubén González, Manuel Licea ('Puntillita'), Ibrahim Ferrer and Pío Leyva – passed away, leaving a major question mark over its future.

But maybe the band has just entered a new phase. According to BVSC *timbales* player Amadito Valdés, 'with the death of the star musicians, maybe a cycle has come full circle... BVSC is heading towards another cycle of its evolution as the concerts and records of its remaining members bear out'.

In any case, there are plenty of remaining band members to continue the good work. As well as Valdés himself, there's Cachaito López, the only musician to have played on every track on every album of the BVSC series; Barbarito Torres, regarded by many as the best lute player in Cuba; trumpet player Manuel 'Guajiro' Mirabal, who has been spicing up the records of countless Cuban artists for more than 50 years; Grammy winner Manuel Galbán, a pianist, organist and arranger; and Jesús 'Aguaje' Ramos, who played trombone on all solo albums by Rubén González, Omara Portuondo and Ibrahim Ferrer. The list goes on. What has become clear is that the future of the BVSC project lies in the separate careers of these artists rather than in a collective effort. They do, however, try to play together in Cuba or abroad when the chance arises.

But what of new musical talents emerging from the island? There's plenty to look out for. Recent winners of the Gran Premio Cubadisco, the most important record industry event on the island, are Equis Alfonso (2005) and the collective Interactivo (2006) – all of whom are in their early 30s, with a long and promising future ahead of them (*photo right*).

Alfonso has a very impressive background indeed. He studied piano at the prestigious Amadeo Roldán Conservatory. In the 1990s he was part of the hip hop group Amenaza, and also formed the short-lived metal ensemble Habana. His parents, Carlos Alfonso and Ele Valdés, are founding members of Síntesis, a band that mixes progressive-rock with Afro-Cuban and urban sounds. Alfonso was a member of this outfit, and its Grammy-nominated album *Habana a flor de piel* boasts some of his arrangements.

Alfonso's solo career began in 1999 with *Mundo real*, followed by *X Moré* (2001), which was also nominated for the Grammy. In 2006 he won a Goya, the Spanish equivalent of the Oscar, for the soundtrack of the film *Habana Blues*.

Iglesia de San Francisco de Paula

Avenida del Puerto, esquina San Ignacio (860 4210). **Open** *Museum* 9am-7pm daily. *Performances* phone for details. **Admission** CUC 5-10. **Map** p256 F15.

The Iglesia de Paula is home to Cuba's prestigious early music ensemble Ars Longa, and hosts concerts most weekends, plus two big events every year: Septiembre Barroco and Festival Internacional de Música Antigua Esteban Salas. Newer acts dedicated to this ancient music are also beginning to emerge: look out for Ars Nova, Cantiga Armónica, Dúo Cáliz, El Gremio and Dúo Sonus in particular.

El Mesón de la Flota

Calle Mercaderes #257, entre Amargura y Brasil (Teniente Rey) (862 9281/863 3838). **Open** noon-midnight daily. *Performances* 9.30pm daily. **Admission** free. **Map** p256 E15.

Although it might not seem so at first glance, flamenco is very popular in Cuba. This place has a *tablao flamenco* (wooden stage), where dancers and musicians, such as the Havana Flamenco Company and Ecos, perform daily. *See also p109.*

Oratorio de San Felipe Neri

Calle Aguiar #412, entre Obrapía y Lamparilla (862 3243). **Open** 9am-6.30pm Mon-Sat. **Admission** CUC 5. **Map** p256 E15.

The opening of this concert hall is a result of the archaeological work being carried out in La Habana Vieja. Originally a church built in 1693, it was acquired two centuries later by a bank and remained a money vault until restoration began in the 1990s. The acoustics and the solemnity of the hall work best with classical piano concerts; check local press for details of what's on.

As a musician, eclecticism is a word that best describes Alfonso, and he doesn't shy away from the term. He sees this quality 'as a link with the creative spirit of the African slaves who reached the island centuries ago'. As an artist he understands the advantages of technology better than many of his peers. He writes, arranges and produces his records; he films and edits his own video-clips, and for *X Moré* he paid homage to Beny Moré by deconstructing and then sampling Moré's voice. Equis regards himself as a revolutionary 'but of my work and my music', he says, 'I have no limits'.

On the other hand, Roberto Carcassés, the undisputed leader of Interactivo, is regarded as a spiritual guru who believes the purpose of playing music is to find the legendary 'lost chord'. The project came about while recording the album *Yusa*, the debut of one of its female members, bassist and vocalist Yusa.

Since then the Interactivo name has established itself as an inspiring workshop. And right here lies the merit of Interactivo: all the musicians who embrace the concept (Carcassés himself, Yusa, singer-songwriter William Vivanco, techno-*timbero*, Francis del Río, female rapper Telmary Díaz and horn-player Julito Padrón, to name a few) already have reputable careers as artists and/or producers. In this case, the whole is indeed greater than the sum of its rather formidable parts.

They've been making beautiful noise since 2001, most notably since 2002 when they release *Wanted*, a demo that was later included in their official debut album *Goza Pepillo* (2005). After hearing their music, Brazilian musician and Grammy winner Lenine agreed to join them on stage in a sell-out concert at the Teatro Nacional in 2003.

The award received from Cubadisco in 2006 is all the more relevant not only because it was shared with the great jazz pianist Chucho Valdés, one of Cuba's most famous musicians. It's a gesture that serves as a symbolic passing of the torch, but it also seemed to be a statement from the organisers of the event that the future is already here – there's no need for outsiders to come and 'discover' it.

Centro Habana

The rooftop bar at the **Hotel Inglaterra** (*see p44*) is also worth a look, with free concerts from 9pm to 11pm daily.

Callejón de Hammel

Callejón de Hammel, entre Hospital y Aramburu (878 1661). **Performances** 8.30-11pm last Fri of mth; 10am-noon Sat (children); noon-3pm Sun. **Admission** free (donations welcome). **Map** p254 C12.

Artist Salvador González has turned this alley into a shrine to both *santería* and the power of artistic vision. Brightly coloured murals, objects and kiosks celebrate Afro-Cuban religions with cheerful serendipity. It's worth a visit to see the preservation of local traditions at a community level. Top rumba bands play here every week (in particular Clave y Guaguancó), and locals turn out to sing and dance. *See also p77 and p75* **Street beats**.

Casa de la Cultura de Centro Habana

Avenida Salvador Allende (Carlos III) #720, esquina Castillejo (878 4727). **Open** 8pm-1am daily. **Admission** free. **Map** p254 D12.

Centro's Casa de la Cultura is set in a distinctive run-down six-storey mansion. This popular venue has a varied cultural programme aimed primarily at local residents, which includes: bolero and *filin* music (first Sunday of the month), live jazz featuring the Bailadores de Santa Amalia (third Sunday of the month), blues and rock (last Friday of the month), plus weekly shows.

Casa de la Música de Centro Habana

Avenida de Italia (Galiano), entre Neptuno y Concordia (860 8296/862 4165). **Open** 10pm-4.30am Tue-Sun. *Performances* 11.30pm Tue-Sun. *Matinées* 4-7pm Thur-Sun, occasional other days. *Bar* 2pm-6am. **Admission** *Performances* CUC 5-25. *Matinées* 30 pesos. **Map** p255 D14.

Like its counterpart over in Miramar, this Casa de la Música franchise is managed by state record label EGREM and used as a launching pad for many of its artists. If you want to see the salsa bands that are currently making waves, check the programme as it's bound to feature the likes of Paulo FG, Bamboleo, Adalberto Álvarez and Manolito Simonet. *Reguetón* takes place on Thursday afternoons. Cover charges vary according to the status of bands.

Casa del Tango

Calle Neptuno #309, entre Águila y Italia (Galiano) (863 0097). **Open** 10am-8pm daily. *Performances* 5-7pm Mon. **Admission** free. **Map** p255 D14.

The Casa del Tango's owners, Wilki and Adelaida, have transformed their home into one of the more distinctive and eccentric music venues in Havana, offering visitors dance classes in tango and salsa, along with a floor show and dancing later on in the evening. The main room is a shrine to dance, packed as it is with old posters, sheet music and other memorabilia. **Photo** *p165.*

Casa de la Trova de Centro Habana

Calle San Lázaro #661, entre Gervasio y Padre Varela (Belascoaín) (879 3373). **Open** 8-10pm Thur-Sun. **Admission** free. **Map** p255 C13.

This club has fallen on hard times in the last few years. Nevertheless from Thursdays to Sundays it still features some very good soloists and small groups playing traditional *trova* and, more recently, bolero. You'll sometimes find comedy being performed, plus *nueva trova* singers.

Centro Andaluz en Cuba

Paseo de Martí (Prado) #104, entre Genios y Refugio (863 6745). **Open** 1pm-midnight daily. *Performances* 8.30-11pm Wed; 10pm-midnight Fri, Sat. **Admission** 60 pesos min consumption. **Map** p256 D15.

This former social club is part of a larger network of societies designed for local Spanish descendents. Nowadays it's dedicated almost entirely to flamenco, with performances from home-grown troupes like Ecos and Habana Flamenca.

Club Oasis

Paseo de Martí (Prado) #256, entre Trocadero y Colón (863 3829). **Open** 6pm-2am daily. *Performances* 10.30pm daily. **Admission** CUC 2 min consumption. **Map** p256 D14.

On the ground floor of the Arabic Union of Cuba (*see p73*), this nightclub comprises a large, dimly lit room hosting a floor show, karaoke, comedians and increasingly popular *reguetón*. The snack bar and restaurant on the premises are open from noon daily.

Vedado

As befits the grander environs of Vedado, the music and nightlife in these parts tend to centre on major hotels, as well as the headquarters of several national cultural institutions, housed in large, elegant former residencies and mansions. Nightclubs are scattered up and down Calle Línea.

Amanecer

Calle 15 #112, esquina O (832 9075). **Open** 10pm-3am daily. *Matinées* Tue-Sat 4-8pm. **Admission** CUC 3. *Matinées* CUC 1. **Map** p254 B12.

This comfortable club, with a capacity of 130, has a large bar and dancefloor. Evening shows start at 10pm daily, along with matinées from Tuesdays to Saturdays, which are devoted to bolero. Recently, on Thursdays, a DJ has been taking to the decks, spinning salsa, *reguetón* and house. Expect to hear recorded music before and after the show. Admission is always restricted to couples.

Cabaret Turquino

Habana Libre Hotel, Calle L, entre 23 y 25 (838 4011). **Open** 10pm-4am daily. **Admission** CUC 10. **Map** p254 B11.

The management returned to the formula that made this site so popular among generations of *habaneros*: a full-blown cabaret show plus a very popular band. Add some enchanting views to the mix and you can see why the venue is always packed. Because of its location, it is a favourite spot for hustlers.

Café Amor 'Karabalí'

Calle 23, entre O y N (832 6757). **Open** *Café* noon-4.30pm. *Club* 11pm-3am daily. *Performances* 11pm daily. **Admission** CUC 5. **Map** p254 B12.

A café by day, this club offers a floor show and live music at 11pm. Thursdays is for rumba, Fridays for hip hop, while on Saturdays a DJ spins music from the '70s and '80s.

Café Cantante Mi Habana

Teatro Nacional de Cuba, Avenida Paseo, esquina 39, Plaza de la Revolución (878 4273/5). **Open** 10pm-3am daily. *Performances* 5pm-midnight Mon-Fri, Sun; 4-8pm, 5pm-midnight Sat. *Matinées* phone for details. **Admission** CUC 5-15. *Matinées* 50-100 pesos. **Map** p254 D10.

This is one of Havana's best and most popular clubs and since it was taken over by EGREM the level of comfort and the credibility of artists have improved. It's almost always jam-packed in the afternoons, and shows feature hip hop, salsa, rock, pop and traditional Afro-Cuban music. These afternoon sessions are a must if you want to see up-to-date Cuban music. Days have different themes, so call ahead for details, and get there as early as possible. Major acts vie with one another to perform at the Café Cantante's night-time shows: big names from the world of salsa and *timba* play two separate shows, then a DJ plays the latest hits until 3am.

Casa de la Amistad

Avenida Paseo #406, entre 17 y 19 (830 3114/5 ext 117). **Open** 6pm-midnight Tue, Thur; 9pm-2am Sat, 5-11pm Sun. **Admission** CUC 3 (plus CUC 2 min consumption). **Map** p254 B9.

This beautiful 1920s mansion belongs to the mighty Instituto Cubano de Amistad con los Pueblos (ICAP, the state-run socio-cultural institution), and boasts a vast garden covered with tables and a dancefloor. The best night for live music under the stars is Tuesday's Peña Chan Chan, when old-timers such as the Orquesta América and the Septeto Habanero take to the stage. Other shows are sometimes offered on Mondays (boleros) and Saturdays (*noche cubana*). The Saturday cabaret show is notably cheap.

Casa de la Cultura de Plaza

Calle Calzada (7ma), entre 6 y 8 (831 2023). **Open** phone for details. **Admission** phone for details; usually free. **Map** p253 A8.

Although it no longer organises the Festival Jazz Plaza (*see p41*), this local cultural centre still plays host to sporadic live reggae, pop, rock, salsa and hip hop. During the week you can enjoy bolero, tango and *filin* as part of an international development programme (call ahead for details).

La Casona de Línea

Calle 11, entre D y E (832 5373). **Open** 8.30pm Sun. **Admission** 10 pesos. **Map** p254 B10.

This magnificent mansion is the headquarters of the legendary theatre troupe Teatro Estudio (*see p176*). Almost every Sunday night its courtyard hosts well-selected concerts by *trovadores*, singer-songwriters and young talents in the making. The stage is just a small concrete deck, and there are only a few plastic seats, so arrive early to bag a good place near the front or you'll be sat on the floor for the performance. As shows are usually publicised by word of mouth, phone the venue for more information.

Centro Cultural Cinematográfico ICAIC 'Fresa y Chocolate'

Calle 23 #1155, entre 10 y 12 (833 9278). **Open** 6pm-2am Fri-Sun. **Admission** CUC 5. **Map** p253 C8.

Situated across the street from the ICAIC (Cuban Film Institute; *see p146*), this lobby-turned-bar offers some weekend music as part of a bigger attempt to invigorate the cultural life of Calle 23 and environs. It all starts on Fridays with La Tanda, where *trovadores* of all generations and styles play music, mixing it with videos, poetry, literature and theatre. On Saturdays a blues band is followed by a comedy show, while on Sundays the Jazz Joven sees aspiring jazzists jam. The spot always has a nice and relaxed mood, frequented by artists and members of the film industry. There's a *sala de video* (video room) here too (*see p150*).

Centro Cultural El Gran Palenque

Calle 4, entre 5ta y Calzada (7ma) (833 9075). **Performances** 3-5pm Sat. **Admission** CUC 5. **Map** p254 A9.

El Gran Palenque is home to the world-renowned dance troupe Conjunto Folklórico Nacional de Cuba (*see p173*). The venue's Sábado de la Rumba (on Saturdays) is a pioneering event on the island and gives you the chance to see geniune Afro-Cuban dances and rituals. Performances come from members of the *conjunto* and invited guests. The mixed bill changes regularly and the atmosphere is almost always hot. Expect a strong, loyal crowd of Cuban regulars, hustlers included.

Centro Vasco

Calle 3ra, esquina 4 (830 9836/833 9354). **Open** *Bar* 10am-2.30am daily. *Restaurant* noon-midnight daily. *Performances* (Taberna Don Sabino) 8pm-2.30am daily. *Matinées* 3-7pm Tue-Sun. **Admission** *Tue-Sun* CUC 5 (couples only). *Matinées* (over 16s) CUC 1. **Map** p254 A9.

This is one of Havana's former Spanish social clubs that opened their doors to the general public while keeping its former name. It now offers music and various shows daily, including comedy, fashion and themed nights. The street-level balcony serves drinks and food during the day, and is especially packed if international football is on TV.

Club Imágenes

Calle C, esquina Calzada (7ma), (833 3606). **Open** 10pm-1.30am daily. **Admission** CUC 5 min consumption. *Fri-Sun* CUC 5 (incl CUC 3 towards drinks). **Map** p254 A10.

Shrine to dance: **Casa del Tango**. *See p164.*

Arts & Entertainment

Buena Vista legend Amadito Valdes.

The charming piano bar here makes the Club Imágenes a perfect venue for a date. The Hopper-like lighting ensures it is safe for solo drinkers too. Try the house cocktail: *crema catalana* with Havana Club Reserva (CUC 2).

Club Tikoa

Calle 23, entre N y O (830 9973). **Open** 10pm-3am Fri-Sun. *Matinées* 4-8pm Sun. **Admission** CUC 4-5. *Matinées* CUC 1. **Map** p254 B12.
Local people choose this venue for its modest prices and great location on La Rampa. They dance to the house band, which plays *son*, salsa, or rock covers. The Sunday matinée is heaven for baby-boomers, with recorded music from the '60s to '80s.

El Gato Tuerto

Calle O, entre 17 y 19 (833 2224). **Open** noon-3am daily. *Performances* from 10pm daily. *Restaurant* noon-4am. **Admission** CUC 3 min consumption. **Map** p254 B12.
This is a club with a strong tradition. During the wild nights of the 1950s it was one of the main haunts of the writers and singers credited with creating *filin*, among them César Portillo de la Luz, José Antonio Méndez and Elena Burque. After years of closure and abandon, it reopened in 1998 with a cool decor. These days it's a prominent venue for bolero, and the bill usually features first-rate artists who play three sets with interludes until 4am. Light snacks are served and there's a restaurant upstairs. The downstairs has a grand piano, a bar and seating for up to 80.

Habana Café

Hotel Meliá Cohíba, Avenida Paseo, esquina 3ra (833 3636). **Open** 8pm-2.30am daily. *Performances* 9pm (main band at 11.30pm) Thur-Sun. **Admission** CUC 10-15. **Map** p254 A9.
The decor at Habana Café is the closest thing you'll find to a Hard Rock Café venue. It's a pastiche that borrows heavily from the American 1950s, with cars, petrol pumps, a small plane hanging from the ceiling and pre-Revolutionary memorabilia. There's a floor show most nights before the major act begins. Thursday to Sunday nights feature renowned salsa names, such as Los Van Van, Bamboleo and Isaac Delgado. It's pretty expensive as Havana's venues go, but you could do a lot worse.

Humor Club Cocodrilo

Calle 3ra, entre 10 y 12 (837 5305). **Open** 10pm-3am daily. *Performances* 11.30pm. **Admission** CUC 4 Mon-Thur, Sun; CUC 5 Fri, Sat. **Map** p253 A6.
A comedy club with a comfortable ambience inside and peculiarly tacky decor outside. Not recommended unless your Spanish is excellent, however. A disco follows. Reservations have to be made in person at the venue between 9.30am and 4.30pm.

Hurón Azul (UNEAC)

UNEAC, Calle 17, esquina H (832 4551-3). **Performances** 5-8pm Wed; 10pm-midnight Sat. **Admission** CUC 5. *Wed* 40 pesos. **Map** p254 B11.
The home of the National Union of Writers & Artists is a grand old Vedado mansion, where a large veranda serves as a stage and its patio provides table seating. It's best known for La Peña del Ambia, a gathering on Wednesday afternoons, which features all types of music and dance traditions from around Cuba; on alternate Wednesdays *trova* and *son* are played. The place is jam-packed by 5pm, so arrive by 4.30pm if you want a table. Saturday night (entry from 9pm) is devoted to bolero, featuring the country's top soloists, such as Manolo del Valle, Ramón Fabián Veloz and Roberto Sánchez. **Photo** *p168*.

Jardines del 1830

Malecón, esquina 20 (838 3091/2). **Open** 10pm-2am Tue-Sun. *Matinées* 4-9pm Fri-Sun. **Admission** CUC 2-5. **Map** p253 A7.
A beautiful outdoor garden facing the sea, with a capacity of 200 people, a small stage and a dance-floor. Set behind an opulent restaurant, the club has fashion shows, dance reviews and music. Lately rock cover bands have been taking to the stage on Sunday matinées (4-9pm) and the admission is low. Note, however, that the loveliness of the setting is not usually matched by the quality of the entertainment, although Friday house nights are popular.

Jazz Café

Galerías Paseo, top floor, Calle 1ra, entre Paseo y A (838 3302). **Open** noon-2am daily. *Performances* 11pm-1am daily. **Admission** CUC 10 min consumption. **Map** p254 A9.
Havana's top jazz venue, this place has a splendid view of the sea, a relaxed atmosphere and Cuba's

Taste the rum and hear the band

More Vegas than Berlin, Havana's *caberet-espectáculos* are song and dance variety shows performed by G-stringed *mulatas*. With the state aware of their huge popularity with foreign visitors, the primary function of cabarets these days seems to be to fleece tourists. Dress regulations apply in most cabarets: avoid shorts, sleeveless T-shirts and sandals.

Cabaret Parisien

Hotel Nacional, Calle O, esquina 21, Vedado (873 4701 ext 129). **Performances** 10pm daily (doors open 9pm). **Tickets** CUC 35 (CUC 60 with dinner). **Credit** MC, V. **Map** p254 B12.

This beautiful, well-designed room is where Sinatra once sang for his mafia mates and molls. The show these days features a dance revue with a live band. The main company dances every day except Monday. Not half as good as the Tropicana, but half the price. Reservations recommended.

Cabaret Tropicana

Calle 72 #4504, Línea del Ferrocarril, Marianao (267 1717/0110). **Open** 8.30pm-1am daily (show 10-11.45pm). **Tickets** CUC 65-85 (incl bottle of rum & snacks). **Credit** MC, V. **Map** p252 F3.

Tucked away in the western neighbourhood of Marianao, this is the grandest of Havana's cabarets, with an outdoor theatre seating up to 800 and a smaller indoor space used when it rains. Opened in 1931 and hailed as the biggest nightclub in the world, the Tropicana has in its time played host to the likes of Beny Moré, Nat King Cole, 'Lucky' Luciano, Ernest Hemingway and Jack Nicholson. A spectacular, almost hallucinatory, revue is performed by over 200 dancers and singers, plus one of the best orchestras on the island. Sure, it's touristy as hell, but at least it's well executed. Make up your own mind as to whether the show is tackily sexist or infectiously sexy; it's pictured below.

Copa Room

Hotel Riviera, Malecón, esquina Paseo, Vedado (334051 ext 119). **Performances** 10pm Mon, Wed-Sun (doors open 9pm). **Tickets** CUC 10 Mon, Wed, Thur; CUC 25 Fri-Sun. Includes open bar after 11.30pm. **Credit** MC, V. **Map** p254 A9.

The Riviera was the last hotel built by mobster Meyer Lanksy before the arrival of Revolutionaries in Havana. Aptly, the room looks a lot like Vegas. It was formerly the renowned Palacio de la Salsa, fondly mentioned in many a salsa song. Regrettably the show isn't up to scratch these days. Still, some of Havana's finest groups perform at the weekends; Paulito FG is a regular.

Hurón Azul (UNEAC). See p166.

top jazz musicians: Habana Ensemble, Bobby Carcassés, El Greco and Diákara, to name but a few. Add in the minimum consumption entrance fee and you have one of the best deals in town.

Karachi Club

Calle K, entre 15 y 17 (832 3485). **Open** 10pm-3am daily. *Matinées* 4-8pm. **Admission** CUC 2. *Matinées* CUC 1. **Map** p254 B11.
This place offers a diverse music programme. Salsa bands used to play on Mondays, Wednesdays and Saturdays but as the audience has got ever younger the programme now features hip hop and *reguetón* on Tuesday and Thursday nights respectively. Weekend matinées take a trip back in time to the '60s and '70s.

La Madriguera

Quinto de los Molinos, entre Infanta and Jesús Peregrino (879 8175). **Performances** 8.30pm Sat, Sun (occasionally Fri). **Admission** 5 pesos. **No credit cards. Map** p254 D11.
A dilapidated cultural centre that's home to the youth cultural association Hermanos Saíz (part of the League of Young Communists), La Madriguera is located in an oasis of greenery tucked between two busy thoroughfares where Vedado meets Centro Habana. The mission of Hermanos Saíz is to promote young artists (it also runs the annual rap fest; *see p134*), and there always seems to be music of some kind being played. This is the site of individual and group rehearsals for emerging artists, and shows are produced on an irregular basis, so most of the time you'll have to take a chance. For this reason, it's best to phone ahead to check the schedule.

El Pico Blanco

Hotel St John, Calle O, entre 23 y 25 (833 3740). **Open** 10pm-3am daily. **Admission** CUC 5 Mon-Fri, Sun; CUC 10 Sat. **Map** p254 B12.
Previously a hotel dance room with live music daily and a disco afterwards, but now El Pico Blanco boasts a more varied programme that features comedy on Tuesdays and live music on Wednesdays; Thursdays are given over to bolero and *filin*, Fridays are Cuban night, with an entirely musical show, Saturdays are romantic night, while Sundays are given over to the musical show Ritmo Caribe. The amazing views of the bay and the city are a plus.

La Red

Calle 19, esquina L (832 5415). **Open** noon-3am daily. *Performances* 10pm-3am. **Admission** CUC 3. **Map** p254 B11.
A small subterranean bar with a variety of shows, including comedy, DJs, karaoke and live music (pop, salsa, rap, rock) at weekends. Not the best dancefloor in the world, though.

Salón 1930 'Compay Segundo'

Hotel Nacional de Cuba, Calle P, esquina 21 (836 3564/3567). **Open** 9.30pm Wed, Sat. **Admission** CUC 25 (CUC 40 with dinner). **Map** p254 B12.
This luxurious hall at the Hotel Nacional was *the* place to see the original Buena Vista Social Club in Havana a few years ago, and even though the big names of the Buena Vista Project have passed away, the remaining musicians are masters in their instruments and play with real zest. Among the artists often found here are 2006 Grammy nominees Los Hijos de Compay Segundo, Barbarito Torres and Amadito Valdés. All in all, one of the top venues to enjoy traditional Cuban music. Booking is recommended, and even with a ticket, don't count on arriving here half-an-hour before the show and getting a seat. Note that the show falls slightly short of the advertised two hours' performance time.

Salón Piano Bar 'Delirio Habanero'

Teatro Nacional de Cuba, Avenida Paseo, esquina 39, Plaza de la Revolución (878 4275). **Open** 10pm-6am daily. *Matinées* 3-7pm Sat, Sun. **Admission** CUC 10. *Matinées* 20-100 pesos. **Map** p254 D10.
This intimate bar with minimalist decor sits atop the National Theatre and boasts an astonishing view of the Plaza de la Revolución. Pay attention to the matinée schedule, as it enables you to catch some interesting up and coming fusion and hip hop groups, and because there's an option to pay in pesos, the audience is at least partly made up of locals. The

programme features *son*, smaller salsa bands, *trova* and vocal ensembles. The cover is CUC 5-15, depending on the artist, and drinks cost twice what they do in the afternoon. Still, the ambience is usually pleasant and the quality of the music is very high.

Salón Rojo

Hotel Capri, Calle 21, entre N y O (833 3747).
Open 10pm-4am daily. *Performances* 11.15pm.
Admission CUC 5; CUC 10 (incl dinner, 2 drinks).
Map p254 B12.

This luxurious hotel was one of the key spots for gambling back in the 1950s. In the '90s, when salsa and *timba* were very much in vogue, it was turned into a disco to attract tourists – and was then shut down again before reopening in 2003 as a cabaret venue. The *salón* now runs fashion shows, a major music act from 1am to 2am, plus comedy and recorded music afterwards.

Teatro Amadeo Roldán

Calle Calzada (7ma) #512, esquina D (832 5551).
Concerts *Main hall* 5pm Sun. *Sala Caturla* 8pm Thur-Sun. *Opus Bar* varies. **Admission** CUC 5-10.
Map p254 A10.

Fire destroyed this theatre in 1976 and a lack of resources delayed its restoration until the second half of the 1990s. It now boasts excellent acoustics for classical music, but other genres can sound a little flat. The theatre is the home of the National Symphony, which plays in the main hall every Sunday, and occasionally hosts world-class guitarist and composer Leo Brouwer. The theatre has another smaller hall, the Sala Caturla, with good acoustics. There are various special concerts throughout the year – mainly classical music, but rock, *trova* and jazz ensembles also feature. The Opus Habana bar on the top floor is a popular spot for drinks before and after shows; if you prefer a Mojito with your music you can watch the concert on the TV monitors in the bar. The main hall is also used for several prestigious festivals, including the Festival Internacional de Jazz (*see p141*) and Cubadisco (*see p139*).

Las Vegas

Calle Infanta #204, esquina 25 (836 7939).
Open 10pm-3am daily. *Matinées* 4-8pm.
Admission CUC 3. *Matinées* CUC 1/2.

Previously a bit sordid, the recently revamped Las Vegas now has a new management and a better, more varied programme. Thursday to Sunday nights are devoted to Habana mía, a conventional cabaret show. From Mondays to Wednesdays the dance troupe Sabor Caribe take charge. On Fridays the matinée is hosted by the poet Olga Navarro and her guests, usually good bolero singers. On weekends the matinée doubles its cover to CUC 2. We'd recommend the Afro-Cuban group Yoruba Andabo, who perform their dances and chants on Saturdays.

La Zorra y El Cuervo

Calle 23, entre N y O (833 2402/zorra@cbcan.cyt.cu).
Open 10pm-2am daily. *Matinées* 3-7pm Sat, Sun.
Admission CUC 10 (incl CUC 5 towards drinks).
Matinées CUC 3 (incl CUC 1 towards drinks).
Map p254 B12.

This jazz club – 'the Fox and the Crow' – is an institution in Havana and a pleasant, intimate room for live music. The monthly schedule offers a glimpse of the top artists of the Cuban jazz scene, and on some nights you can witness a casual jam. Weekend matinées – called Afternoons of Remembrance or Club de los tembas (*tembas* means middle-aged people) – comprise live bands, recorded music and videos all devoted to music from the '60s and '70s. It's also one of the main venues for Havana's international jazz festival in December. **Photo** *p171*.

Teatro Amadeo Roldán.

Friday night's all right

Blink twice and you may be forgiven for thinking that you're in a trendy Miami club. No, you're in Havana (or thereabouts), and it's a Friday night. The Friday night party is the place to be if you're part of the young Cuban nouveau riche set. The last thing you will listen to is traditional salsa. Only the latest techno and ambient jazz are on offer here as the trendy youth of Havana flit around talking into their mobile phones and posing over a Red Bull and vodka.

The Friday night party has managed to keep going for more than five years now, regularly changing location. The biggest parties were held in the fantastic location of the Morro castle, where literally thousands of people made up Cuba's biggest and trendiest party, complete with big screens flashing the latest video tracks. Quite how permission was obtained for this is a bit of a mystery, but the organisers must have some outstanding favours. In any case, things have moved on and for now the party seems to have settled on the bar above the Karl Marx theatre.

However, beware that this may well alter again, given that venues have changed over the years and have included Café Cantante, the rum museum, a social club in Tarará, the Riviera hotel and a host of other locations, so you should find someone in the know. Friday night parties have also migrated to Saturday nights too. Something of a misnomer, true, but though it's a different night and different place, it's the same people.

Miramar & the western suburbs

Ali Bar

Avenida Dolores, esquina Lucero, Arroyo Naranjo (55 8011). **Open** 9pm-2am Tue-Sun. **Admission** (couples only) CUC 5 (incl 2 drinks).

This cabaret was immortalised by Beny Moré, the legend of Cuban popular music, for being the hideout where he used to play with his orchestra at the end of his career. It's down in the south-western outskirts of the city and way out of the loop, but the release in 2006 of the biopic *El Benny* has drawn attention to the spot again, where bolero, love songs, salsa, 1960s, '70s and '80s music during the week sit alongside cabaret shows at the weekends. Nice ambience and good service – but too physically remote for some.

Casa de la Música de Miramar

Calle 20, esquina 35, Playa (204 0447). **Open** 10pm-3am daily. *Matineés* 4-8pm Tue-Sun. **Admission** CUC 10-20. *Matineés* CUC 5. **Map** p253 D8.

Housed in a beautiful Miramar mansion, Casa de la Música books the best stars of Cuban *son* and salsa: Adalberto Álvarez, Bamboleo, Manolito Simonet y su Trabuco, Pachito Alonso y sus Kini Kini, José Luis Cortés y NG La Banda. Highly recommended.

Club Ipanema

Hotel Copacabana, Calle 1ra, esquina 54, Miramar (204 1037 ext 6131). **Open** 10pm-2am Fri; 5-9pm, 10pm-3am Sat; 7pm-midnight Sun. **Admission** CUC 3 (incl 1 drink). **Map** p252 B3.

This agreeable club draws a large crowd on Saturdays and Sundays for Club de los Tembas, featuring music from the '60s and '70s, which is hugely popular with Cubans in their 30s and upwards.

Macumba Habana

Complejo La Giraldilla, Calle 222, esquina 37, La Coronela, La Lisa (273 0568/9). **Performances** 5-11pm Tue-Sun. **Admission** CUC 5 (with pre-recorded music), CUC 10 (with show) Tue, Wed, Sun; CUC 5 Thur-Sat.

It may be a long way from the centre of town, but Macumba Habana is a beautiful, stylish old mansion with a huge garden. It used to host major *timba* acts exclusively, but now the staff books pop/rock, *reguetón* and young emerging artists like Haydée Milanés and William Vivanco, targeting a much more demanding audience. If you eat before the show at one of the complex's restaurants the cover charge is waived. The orchestra starts at 6pm for three hours but the programme sometimes lasts till midnight. Phone ahead to see what's on so you don't go all that way for a fashion show. Dress smartly.

La Maison

Calle 16 #701, entre 7ma y 9na, Playa (204 1543/1585). **Open** 10pm-3am daily. *Performances* 10pm-1.45am daily. *Matinées* 4-8pm. *Piano bar* 10pm-6am daily. **Admission** *Performances* CUC 10. *Matinées* CUC 1. *Piano bar* CUC 5 (incl CUC 3 drinks) Sat, Sun. **Map** p253 B6.

Since the 1970s La Maison has been best known for its fashion shows, but these days it also has a small cabaret and a piano bar with comedians and karaoke. The Saturday and Sunday matinées feature two live sets from Los Kent, one of the first bands to play rock on the island.

Piano Bar El Diablo

Calle 35, esquina 20, Playa (204 0447/202 6147). **Open** 11pm-6am Tue-Sun. **Admission** CUC 10. **Map** p253 C6.

This club, next to the Casa de la Música, is smaller but also features some very good ensembles. The small dancefloor gets packed when popular *reguetón* acts such as Gente de Zona and Triángulo Oscuro play. A good opportunity for mixing with the locals.

Río Club

Calle A, entre 3ra y 5ta, Miramar (209 3389).
Open 10pm-3am Mon-Sat; 6pm-3am Sun.
Admission (couples) CUC 5. **Map** p253 A7.
Situated on a tranquil spot on the banks of the Río Almendares, this pleasant venue is housed in a lovely 1950s building with a capacity of about 200. There's a daily show that includes *reguetón*, plus a house music set afterwards. On Sundays the club hosts a show called La Casa del Cubano; it's very popular with Cubans, who go there prepared to dance wildly to anything.

Sala Atril

Avenida 1ra, esquina 10, Miramar (203 0801-5).
Open phone for details. **Admission** CUC 5.
Map p253 A6.
As part of the Karl Marx complex, this hall has its own entrance to the right of the theatre of the same name (*see below*). After functioning on and off for decades, this hall opened again in 2005 and soon became a favourite spot for arty types. After a session of video-clips, the main act begins to play between 11.30pm and midnight for more than an hour, with no intermission. Recorded music follows – mainly techno and *reguetón*. The venue attracts a kind of affluent, freewheeling young audience, who appear to be much more interested in dancing frantically than in listening quietly. Snack food, beers and other drinks cost more than most places. Nevertheless, it's always crowded.

Salón Bolero

Complejo Dos Gardenias, Avenida 7ma, esquina 26, Miramar (204 2353 ext 116). **Open** 10.30pm-1am Mon-Thur; 10.30pm-3am Fri-Sun. **Admission** CUC 5. **Map** p253 B5.
Along with El Gato Tuerto (*see p166*), this is Havana's best venue for bolero and *filin*. Some of the genres' greatest names have played here, and still do so, as part of an excellent roster. The complex is named after the song 'Dos Gardenias', written by the late, great bolero singer and composer Isolina Carrillo, and now a staple for any traditional bolero outfit. The Piano Bar presents a different show each day based on Cuban music. Dress smartly.

Salón El Chévere

Calle 49C y 28A, Kohly (204 4990/504 5162).
Open *Salón* 10pm-3am daily. *Snack bar* 10am-4am Thur-Sun. *Pool* 10am-6pm daily. **Admission** *Salón* CUC 10. *Pool* CUC 5. **Map** p253 D6.
An open-air disco nestling between a wall of rocks and the Río Almendares, in the middle of the Bosque de la Habana, with a wide range of classy acts. It's very popular with Cubans as a place to dance, but take a taxi or car there and back as it's a bit isolated.

Salón Rosado Beny Moré

Jardines de La Tropical, Avenida 41, entre 44 y 46, Playa (206 1281/2). **Open** 9pm-3am Mon, Fri, Sat. *Matinées* 4-8pm Wed-Fri; 1-8pm Sun. **Admission** CUC 5. **Map** p253 D5.
This was once *the* place to dance salsa. Lately the programme has broadened to welcome rock, *reguetón* and even techno concerts, but there's no set schedule aside from the 'grandparents' afternoon' on Sundays. There is a separate entrance and dance-floor for foreigners, but once inside you're free to go down to the Cuban section. It's still unruly and at times dangerous, so don't feel like you're a wimp if you want to stay relatively safe in the tourists' deck.

Teatro Karl Marx

Calle 1ra, esquina 10, Miramar (203 0801-05).
Open phone for details. **Admission** CUC 10-20.
Map p253 A6.
This theatre, run by the state for political events, has the largest audience capacity in Cuba (8,000). Aside from the fact it's rather cold and unattractive, and the security staff don't allow dancing, jumping or any such behaviour, it is probably one of the best-equipped venues in town. From time to time it hosts pop and rock concerts, by local big names like Carlos Valera, Pablo Milanés, Equis Alfonso and Buena Fe. Notable foreign acts to play here include the Manic Street Preachers in 2001, and Rick Wakeman and Air Supply in 2005.

La Zorra y El Cuervo. *See p169.*

Performing Arts

All Havana's a stage – and all its people players.

Gran Teatro de La Habana is the city's most prestigious venue. *See p174.*

Havana has a fertile performing arts scene. The city is home to one of the best ballet companies in the world and is the birthplace of many popular dances, as well as the Afro-Cuban dance traditions of the *santería*, Palo Monte and Abakuá religions. The city's theatre is equally diverse. As a visitor, you can discover some unique Cuban forms like the 19th-century *teatro Bufo*, or see how classics by Shakespeare, Sartre or Brecht can find thrilling new life in a Caribbean staging. There's also a bright pantheon of writers who have produced challenging, original theatre work, following in the steps of the late playwright Virgilio Piñera.

REVOLUTIONARY TACTICS

Cuban theatre has always had a rebellious side. On 22 January 1869, during the Ten Years War, audience members at the Teatro Villanueva began shouting anti-colonial slogans and waving Cuban flags. Spanish soldiers stormed the theatre and opened fire, killing dozens of people. The date of the massacre is now National Theatre Day, when the prestigious Villanueva prizes – Cuba's equivalent of the Tony or Olivier Awards – are awarded.

The 1959 Revolution triggered a boom in new companies and playwriting. While only 40 Cuban plays were performed in Havana between 1952 and 1958, 281 were staged in 1967 alone. One of the Revolution's first acts was to create departments for the various arts, including, for the first time, folkloric dance. Foreign companies toured the island, playing in schools, factories and sugar mills. Most plays written in the first five years following the Revolution focused on exorcising evils from the past rather than discussing the new social changes. But by 1965 playwrights had begun experimenting with new theatrical methods through which to express contemporary artistic and ideological concerns.

This shift in focus, however, ushered in the 'grey years' (1968-76): government retaliation against those questioning official dogma.

Homosexuality was labelled immoral, and antisocial and artists were censored for being 'alienated' from the aims of the Revolution. 1976 was a turning point, as the Ministry of Culture and **Instituto Superior de Arte** were established. The Instituto is the only university in Latin America to teach all the arts and was the training ground for the greats of today's theatre, among them Flora Lauten, Nelda Castillo, Carlos Díaz and Carlos Celdrán. However, many artists had already left the island and, after years of stagnation, it was hard to regain audiences.

In the post-Special Period era Abel Prieto, the minister of culture, has done much to put the city's performing arts scene back on its feet, although the obstacles are formidable. Salaries for all performing artists and technicians are low even by Cuban standards, and depend on what 'level' the authorities judge them to have reached. Supplies of material and technical resources are also scarce. Some companies receive support from foreign performing arts companies, embassies or charities.

But resources aren't the only problem. The Caribbean heat drains energy quickly. Public transport shortages mean that an actor can spend several hours a day travelling between home and rehearsal room. Even then, artists must still work under strict parameters; there is a definite 'white list' of writers (Martí, Lezama Lima) and a greyish-black list, made up of anyone critical of the Revolution (Reinaldo Arenas, Eliseo Alberto and, until he was awarded the 2000 Premio Nacional de Literatura, Antón Arrufat, Cuba's finest living playwright). Many of the artists who moved abroad have found new opportunities to fulfil their professional goals: these include the playwrights Joel Cano and José Triana, who currently live in Paris, director Víctor Varela (Miami), choreographer Marianela Boán (Philadelphia) and dancer Carlos Acosta, now resident in London.

DRAMA KINGS

Many plays staged in Cuba are text-heavy, extremely contextual and hard to penetrate. However, there are several companies worth seeing for the beauty and daring of their stagings. **Teatro Buendía** (*see p177*) is one: Flora Lauten's productions are unusual and often controversial. Also well worth catching is **Teatro el Público** (*see p178*), directed by Carlos Díaz, who manages to emphasise the erotic in any text he touches. A more popular writer/director, who focuses on the trials and tribulations of daily life, is Héctor Quintero. Another interesting director is Esther Cardoso at Gaia, while the work of ex-Teatro Buendía member Carlos Celdrán at Argos Teatro is truly astonishing, constantly searching deep into the human condition.

In terms of writers to look out for, Abelardo Estorino, Virgilio Piñera, Antón Arrufat and Alberto Pedro are/were the most distinguished chroniclers of the dramas of Cuban life; younger names include Nara Mansur, Abel González Melo and Lilian Susel Zaldívar de los Reyes.

LORDS OF THE DANCE

Dance in Cuba is really something special. The country has one of the world's most famous ballet companies (**Ballet Nacional de Cuba**; *see p179*) and, thanks to its Spanish and African roots, boasts a rich, unique history of popular dance, including such styles as rumba, mambo, *son*, *contra-danza*, *danzón*, *timba*, *chachachá*, *mozambique* and *pilón*.

Post-Revolutionary choreographers have focused on capturing national and ethnic values and integrating them with international dance codes. Ramiro Guerra's celebrated **Danza Contemporánea de Cuba** (*see p181*), which fuses modern, popular and folkloric styles, has been largely responsible for the development of modern dance in Cuba. Another key group is **Conjunto Folklórico Nacional de Cuba** (*see p179*), founded by the state in 1962, thereby giving African culture official status.

The future currently looks bright for Cuban dance. New companies are proliferating, with around 50 officially registered with the Consejo Nacional de las Artes Escénicas (CNAE). In summer 2006 the authorities showed their commitment to dance by opening the **Centro de Danza de La Habana**, giving offices to three of the top dance producers (DanzAbierta, Danza Combinatoria and former Tropicana director Santiago Alfonso).

TICKETS AND INFORMATION

Phone numbers (including official box office numbers) are provided below for theatres and companies, but note that operators are unlikely to speak English. In reality, few theatres have advance or reliable telephone booking facilities, so the best way to get information and tickets is to go to the theatre beforehand. Tickets for visitors are usually paid for in CUCs, while Cuban nationals pay in pesos; few theatres accept credit cards. Also note that ballet performances are the only ones that start punctually in Cuba.

Listings can be found in the free English-Spanish monthly guide *Cartelera* (*see p138*) or in *Entretelones*, published monthly by the CNAE and available online at www.cubaescena.cult.cu; or on TV shows *Hurón Azul* on Thursday evenings at 10.30pm, and *Sitio del Arte* on Monday evenings. Radio Taíno has a cultural listings show every day at 1.30pm; the daily *Granma* also has information. Dance listings and reviews can be found in *Danzar.cu*, published every three months. For general information on performing arts in Cuba, visit the state-run www.cubaescena.cult.cu.

Major venues

Gran Teatro de La Habana

Paseo de Martí (Prado) #458, entre San Rafael y San Martín (San José), Centro Habana (861 3077/5873). **Open** *Box office* 9.30am-5pm Tue-Sun. *Performances* 8.30pm Thur-Sat; 5pm Sun. **Tickets** CUC 5-20. **Map** p256 D14.

Havana's loveliest and most prestigious theatre was built by the megalomaniac Spanish governor Tacón, and was duly named the Teatro Tacón. The theatre, which seated 4,000 people and had 150 boxes, opened in 1846. Between 1907 and 1914, it was remodelled by Austrian architect Paul Belau, and the completed neo-baroque building opened with a spectacular production of *Aïda*. It now has various performance spaces, most importantly the 1,500-seater Sala García Lorca. Performers here have included actresses Sarah Bernhardt and Eleonora Duse, tenor Enrico Caruso and musicians Arthur Rubinstein and Sergei Rachmaninov.

The Gran Teatro stages performances by the Ballet Nacional de Cuba (*see p179*), the Ballet Español de La Habana, the Teatro Lírico Nacional de Cuba, Ballet Lizt Alfonso (*see p179*) and Danza Contemporánea de Cuba (*see p181*). The 120-seat Sala Antonín Artaud features experimental works, the 100-seat Sala Lecuona presents festivals of oral narrative, while the 509-seater Sala Alejo Carpentier has a more diverse bill. **Photos** *p172*.

Street theatre

Drama is alive and well in Havana, and we're not talking Shakespeare. Acting out the trials and tribulations of their daily lives is part and parcel of a *habanero*'s existence, and generations of them have honed skills that professional actors take years to perfect. You need only take a short walk around to see the following talents in practice:

● Talking as if to a large audience. *Habaneros* masterfully project their voices, whether calling from a sheet-festooned balcony to someone three stories below in a noisy street, or bellowing just as boisterously from the kitchen to someone in the living room three feet away.

● Due to Havana's unreliable communications infrastructure, the oral traditions of storytelling and gossip haven't been eroded as in many other countries. So stories are still acted out with all the vim and vigour of a Shakespearean play – even though it's just for the pleasure of a neighbour in your apartment block.

● By maintaining disquieting levels of eye contact, *habaneros* always make sure they grab one another's attention. This level of intensity is held just as strongly with acquaintances as with complete strangers.

● *Habaneros* use their bodies consciously and vigorously. Body language is essential in communication, with gestures and facial expressions often saying more than words.

● Revelling in human interaction and confrontation, whether it be the conflict and melodrama of the baseball enthusiasts at the *esquina caliente* (literally, 'hot corner'; *see p187*), the sultry romance at a *barrio* fiesta, or the semi-playful aggression of a street corner domino game.

● Like so many people in desperate situations, *habaneros* mock their personal and collective problems, turning suffering into humour. Theatre of the Absurd and Tragicomedy are well-known notions to them.

● *Habaneros* are experts in the art of improvisation. Adaptation is the key to life in a country where nothing can be taken for granted. When cookers are regularly made out of a breezeblock and copper wire, and satellite dishes are fashioned from tea trays, these players demonstrate on a daily basis that 'the show must go on'.

● Likewise, with luxury items so scarce, *habaneros* have learned to act using 'props', making what little is available take on a great significance in the theatre of life. So a bottle of home-made moonshine becomes the finest seven-year rum; and the simple act of meeting up to listen to music is the social event of the year.

● With its ramshackle buildings and the make-do-and-mend philosophy of its inhabitants, Havana is a piece of performance art in itself. It is at once ugly and beautiful, its story fascinating yet terrible. It must change and adapt itself on a daily basis, yet the façade remains ever the same. Havana subverts the very meaning of the word 'city' – and what better accolade for a piece of performance art is there?

Teatro Nacional de Cuba: ugly from the outside, but it's what goes on inside that counts.

Teatro Nacional de Cuba

Avenida Paseo, esquina 39, Plaza de la Revolución, Vedado (870 4655/879 6011/www.teatronacional.cult.cu). **Open** *Box office* 9am-5pm Tue-Sun. *Performances* 8.30pm Fri, Sat; 5.30pm Sun. **Tickets** CUC 5-10. **Map** p254 D10.

Opened in June 1959, this ugly construction was the first major building to be inaugurated after the Revolution. Today some of Cuba's best theatre and dance are performed here. The 2,500-seat Sala Avellaneda is an impersonal space used for large-scale dance and theatre productions. The 800-seater Sala Covarrubias was named after the playwright Francisco Covarrubias and is used by a range of theatre companies. The Noveno Piso (Ninth Floor) is a warehouse-like space that hosts avant-garde productions of theatre and dance, often by Argos Teatro. the Salón Piano Bar 'Delirio Habanero' (*see p168*) on the third floor overlooks the Plaza de la Revolución. In the basement, meanwhile, Café Cantante Mi Habana (*see p164*) – which is managed by the state music label EGREM – stages matinée performances and evening concerts.

Other venues

Casa de la Comedia

Calle Justiz #18, entre Baratillo y Oficios, La Habana Vieja (863 9282). **Open** *Box office* 1hr before performance. **Tickets** CUC 2. **Map** p256 E15.

Comedy was first performed here in 1778, but these days the Casa de la Comedia promotes new Cuban plays. Also known as the Salón Ensayo, it is the base for the company El Taller, directed by Rolando Dima. Afro-Cuban rituals are often held on its patio, and stand-up comedy shows are staged some Saturdays and Sundays at 7pm. This venue is at its most dynamic during theatre festivals.

Centro Cultural Bertolt Brecht

Calle 13, esquina I, Vedado (832 9359). **Open** *Box office* 1hr before performance. Closed until mid 2007. *Performances* 8.30pm Fri, Sat; 5pm Sun. **Tickets** CUC 5. **Map** p254 B11.

Founded in 1968, this cultural centre houses a 300-seat space called La Sala Alternativa and a smaller 150-seat basement café-theatre, Café Brecht. Most interesting of the companies that work here is Teatro Mío, directed by Miriam Lezcano, which often focuses on the work of playwright Alberto Pedro Torriente. Other resident theatre groups are: Pequeño Teatro de La Habana, directed by José Milián; Teatro del Círculo, directed by Pedro Ángel Vera; and Teatro D'Dos, directed by Julio César Ramírez. Children's shows are held here on Saturdays and Sundays at 10am, and there are regular comedy nights. The centre was closed for renovation as this guide went to press, and due to reopen later in 2007.

Cine Teatro Trianón

Linea #315, entre Paseo y A, Vedado (830 9648). **Open** *Box office* from 6pm Fri, Sat; from 3.30pm Sun. *Performances* 8.30pm Fri, Sat; 5pm Sun. **Tickets** CUC 5. **Map** p254 B9.

The Trianón is home to the company Teatro el Público (*see p178*), directed by Carlos Díaz, at the weekend. It doesn't have optimal conditions to host theatre at present, but improvements are underway. It is also home to a cinema, and is used as a venue for the International Film Festival in December.

Gaia

Calle Brasil (Teniente Rey) #157, entre Cuba y Aguiar, La Habana Vieja (862 0401). **Open** times vary phone for details. **Tickets** phone for details. **Map** p256 E15.

Gaia is an arts centre that was set up in 2000 as a not-for-profit collaboration between Cuban, British and international artists. It stages theatre and dance performances, workshops and exhibitions of works by young artists. Gaia Teatro, the centre's resident theatre company, has produced some interesting work: *Las cenizas de Ruth* was Esther Cardoso's radical reinterpretation of the biblical story. On the last Saturday of every month, the centre hosts a mask workshop for children in the morning, and, at 5pm, *Felices los normales*, a programme for Cubans with HIV/AIDS (participants come forward to tell an HIV-related story, which is then enacted by a group of professional actors and musicians).

Sala Teatro Adolfo Llauradó

Calle 11, entre D y E, Vedado (832 5373). **Open** *Box office* from 5pm Thur-Sun.**Tickets** CUC 5. **Map** p254 B10.

This 120-seat theatre opened in 2003 in the backyard of La Casona, a Vedado mansion. Today it is the home of the Teatro Estudio troupe, founded in 1958 by siblings Raquel and Vicente Revuelta, both major figures in Cuban performing arts. It has a varied theatre programme for both children and adults, and other cultural events are also held in the cosy, arty setting. Arrive early as it soon gets packed.

Teatro América

Avenida de Italia (Galiano) #253, entre Concordia y Neptuno (862 5416/teatroamerica@cubarte.cult.cu). **Open** *Box office* 9.30am-1pm, 2-5pm Wed-Sun; from 10am Sat, Sun. *Performances* 8.30pm Thur; 10am (children's show) Sat, Sun; phone for other times. **Tickets** CUC 10. **Map** p255 D14.

In the 1950s this art deco building was one of the country's most glamorous theatres, hosting performances by Latin stars like Beny Moré, María Félix and Pedro Vargas. It had a facelift in 2001, and now stages children's shows at 10am on Saturdays and Sundays, vaudeville and variety shows on weekend evenings, and comedy (*see p181*) on Thursdays.

Teatro Fausto

Paseo de Martí (Prado) #201, esquina Colón, La Habana Vieja (863 1173). **Open** *Box office* 2-8pm Tue-Sun. *Performances* 8.30pm Fri; 10am (children's show), 8.30pm Sat; 10am (children's show), 5pm Sun. **Tickets** CUC 5. **Map** p255 D15.

Run by the Centro Promotor del Humor, and directed by Iván Camejo, the Fausto is probably the best place in Havana for variety and comedy acts, as well as children's theatre. Look out for shows by the flamboyant writer, director and actor Héctor Quintero (who also presents at the Mella; *see right*).

Teatro Hubert de Blanck

Calle Calzada (7ma) #657, entre A y B, Vedado (830 1011/833 5962). **Open** *Box office* 6.30pm Fri, Sat; 3pm Sun. *Performances* 8.30pm Fri, Sat; 5pm Sun. **Tickets** CUC 5. **Map** p254 A9.

In 1947 this building was bought by the wife and daughter of Belgian musician Hubert de Blanck, who founded Havana's first music conservatory; they then turned it into a theatre. The long-running theatre group of the same name predominantly stages classics of the international theatrical canon, under the management of Orieta Medina. Productions have included *Cartero*, directed by Medina, and director Bertha Martínez' musical comedy *El tío Francisco y Las Leandras*. The theatre is the production house for Abelardo Estorino, Cuba's most prolifically performed living playwright.

Teatro Mella

Línea #657, entre A y B, Vedado (833 8696/ tmella@cubarte.cult.cu). **Open** *Box office* 2-6pm Tue-Sun. *Performances* 8.30 Fri, Sat; 5pm Sun. **Tickets** CUC 5-10. **Map** p254 A9.

Refurbished in 2000, this 1,500-seat theatre has a Gaudí-esque feel – a meringue-shaped balcony wraps around the auditorium. It's used for dance, folklore (home to the Conjunto Folklórico Nacional de Cuba; *see p173*), circus and variety shows, and for seasons of comedy and dance.

Teatro Nacional de Guiñol

Calle M, entre 17 y 19, Vedado (832 6262). **Open** *Box office* 1hr before performance. *Performances* 3pm Fri; 10.30am, 5pm Sat, Sun. **Tickets** CUC 3; CUC 2 children. **Map** p254 B11.

This is the home to Cuba's leading children's theatre and puppetry company. As well as performing in this space, it presents shows in public squares. Look out for performances of *El caballero de la mano de fuego*, written by Javier Villafañe.

Teatro El Sótano

Calle K, entre 25 y 27, Vedado (832 0630). **Open** *Box office* 5-8.30pm Thur-Sat; 3-5pm Sun. *Performances* 8.30pm Thur-Sat; 5pm Sun. **Tickets** CUC 5. **Map** p254 C11.

Home to the company Teatro Rita Montaner, named after one of the greatest Cuban divas of the 1950s, the repertoire at Teatro El Sótano includes work by Valle-Inclán. Comedy shows take place here on Thursday evenings.

Theatre companies

Havana's principal theatre companies are listed below; note that others are mentioned under their relevant performance venues.

Argos Teatro

Information: Calle Ayestarán #307A, esquina 20 de Mayo, Cerro (information 878 1883/5551/ www.argosteatro.cult.cu). **Map** p254 E10.

Argos was formed in 1996 by former Buendía member Carlos Celdrán – one of the most challenging directors working in Cuba – with the stated intention of 'creating a permanent laboratory for actors and students looking for a common language.' In

You'll see performances all around as you walk through the city. *See p174* **Street theatre**.

2006 Argos produced *Chamaco*, written by promising young Cuban playwright Abel González Melo, and *Stockman, un enemigo del pueblo*, to mark the centenary of Henrik Ibsen's death. Also in the group's repertoire is *Vida y muerte de Pier Paolo Pasolini*, a portrait of the eponymous film-maker's homophobic murder, and winner of the critics' prize for directing. Celdrán has produced acclaimed versions of Strindberg's *Miss Julie* and Brecht's *Baal*. Although some performances take place at the above address, most are held at the Noveno Piso at the Teatro Nacional (*see p175*). Look out for explosive performances by its three principal actors, Alexis Díaz de Villegas, Pancho García and José Luís Hidalgo. Many young actors and actresses have seen their talent grow at Argos under Celdran's direction – check for Zulema Díaz and Yailene Sierra (the latter currently with Teatro el Público; *see p178*).

El Ciervo Encantado

Information: Instituto Superior de Artes (ISA), Calle 120 #1110, entre 9 y 11, Miramar (switchboard 208 0017). **Tickets** free.

Founded in 1996, the Enchanted Deer is directed by Buendía graduate Nelda Castillo. A gutsy challenger of the status quo, hers is an anthropological theatre that seeks to create an exchange between actor and spectator. Highlights have been an expressionistic production of *Pájaros en la playa*, adapted from the novel by Severo Sarduy, and her witty use of cabaret and Cuban gestures in *¿De dónde son los cantantes?*, based on texts by Sarduy and the enfant terrible of Cuban letters, Guillermo Cabrera Infante. The company's latest production, *Visiones de la Cubanosofía*, was praised by both critics and audiences for its metaphorical exploration of the many-sided notion of 'Cubanness'. The company performs at the fine arts faculty at the ISA (*see p93*).

Estudio Teatral Vivarte

Information: Teatro El Sótano, Calle K #514, entre 25 y 27, Vedado (832 0630). **Map** p254 C11.

Directed by actress Antonia Fernández, another daughter of the Buendía company, this small company received state backing in 2002. It is currently building its own space on Avenida Carlos III; in the meantime, recent productions have taken place at the Teatro El Sótano; *see p176*.

Teatro Buendía

Calle 39, entre Loma y Bellavista, Nuevo Vedado (881 6689). **Open** *Box office* 2hrs before performance. *Performances* phone for details. **Tickets** phone for details. **Map** p253 D8.

Buendía is probably the best known – internationally, at least – of Cuba's theatre companies. Flora Lauten, its director, is the fairy godmother of Cuban theatre; everything she touches turns to dramatic metaphor. Lauten, the last Miss Cuba before the Revolution, formed the groundbreaking Buendía in 1985. It went on to become the most innovative, courageous and internationally successful Cuban theatre company of the 1990s. Committed to finding an autonomous voice, the company has benefited from contact with international masters such as Peter Brook, Enrique Buenaventura, Jerzy Grotowski, Santiago García and Eugenio Barba. The Buendía production of *Innocent Eréndira*, Gabriel García Márquez's tale of prostitution and rebellion, toured the world for five years, to great acclaim. Its complex, masked version of Peter Weiss's *Marat/Sade*, entitled *Charenton*, won a 2005 Premio Villanueva. The company performs in a Greek Orthodox church; the audience sits on hard, steeply raked benches, so bring a cushion. Also note that because of the small venue, spaces fill up quickly – arrive early (with or without ticket).

Danza Contemporánea de Cuba. See p181.

Teatro de la Luna

Teatro Nacional, Avenida Paseo, esquina 39, Plaza de la Revolución (information 879 6011/3558). **Map** p254 D10.

Works by the Teatro de la Luna have strong socio-political references and require excellent Spanish to be understood. The company is led by versatile young director, choreographer and actor Raúl Martín. His version of the late Alberto Pedro's play *Delirio habanero* is in repertory, as are his take on Pirandello's *Six Characters in Search of an Author*, and his adaptation of Virgilio Piñera's *Los siervos* and *Últimos días de una casa*. The company performs in either la Sala Covarrubias (*see p175*) or, more usually, in the compact Sala Teatro Adolfo Llauradó (*see p176*). It has also recently managed to secure its own venue, in the shape of the former Cine Pionero in Centro Habana (Calle San Lázaro, entre Espada y San Francisco).

Teatro el Público

Cine Teatro Trianón, Línea #315, entre Paseo y A, Vedado (830 9648). **Open** *Box office* 6pm Fri, Sat; 3.30pm Sun. *Performances* 8.30pm Fri, Sat; 5pm Sun. **Tickets** CUC 5. **Map** p254 B9.

The company is directed by Carlos Díaz, and in recent years has collaborated with the gay-taboo-busting *wünderkind* poet Norge Espinosa and actress Yailene Sierra, who first made her name in Benito Zambrano's critically acclaimed movie *Havana Blues*. Díaz proudly presides over an active repertoire that includes Espinosa's *Icaro* and international classics such as Fernando de Rojas's *La Celestina* and Tennessee Williams' *Glass Menagerie*. Carlos Díaz's stagings tend to be artistically controversial and guaranteed to spark debate in cultural circles: the female lead in *The Crucible* was played by a man, and there was no shortage of on-stage nudity in *La Celestina*.

Dance companies

Así Somos

Calle A #310, apto 7B, entre 3ra & 3ra A, Miramar (203 4276/lorna@cubarte.cult.cu). **Map** p253 A7.

Founder Lorna Burdsall was born in the US and trained at the Juilliard in New York under Merce Cunningham, among others. She fell for a Cuban Bacardí executive in New York and in 1955 moved back with him to Havana. After the Revolution, she was a founding member of Danza Nacional (now Danza Contemporánea, *see p181*). In 1981 she set up Así Somos with a group of graduates from the National School of Arts. Lorna is best described as an artistic magpie, assembling her work out of theatre, music, dance, masks and contemporary folklore. Her work has been performed in all of Havana's theatres, and internationally. These days, though, she prefers to stage performances in her living room, which fits 25 people.

Ballet Español de Cuba

Gran Teatro de La Habana, Paseo de Martí (Prado) #458, entre San Rafael y San Martín (San José), Centro Habana (861 3076/eduveiti@cubarte.cult.cu/cnae@min.cult.cu). **Map** p255 D14.

Direction of this Spanish dance company – founded in 1987 by Alicia Alonso with the name Conjunto de Danza Española – has been assumed by Alonso's protégé, Eduardo Veitía. Now renamed the Ballet Español de Cuba, the company's main styles are flamenco and the *escuela bolera* (combining popular Andalucían dances with ballet; also known as the *baile de palillos*). The company has worked with important figures in Spanish dance, such as Trini Borrul, Goyo Montero and Emilio Sagi. Notable productions are *El fantasma*, inspired by Gaston Leroux's *The Phantom of the Opera*, and *Danzando sueños*, a tribute to Cuba's most renowned painter

Wilfredo Lam (1902-82). Ballet Español de Cuba tends to perform at the imposing Gran Teatro de La Habana (*see p174*).

Ballet Lizt Alfonso

Calle Compostela #659, entre Luz y Acosta, La Habana Vieja (866 3688/9/www.balletliztalfonso.cult.cu). **Map** p256 E15.

This company, made up exclusively of female dancers, has a music ensemble play live at its shows, and also boasts a junior ballet, all under the general direction of Lizt Alfonso. It performs regularly at the Gran Teatro (*see p174*), but also tours extensively both inside and outside Cuba (so far, it's the only Cuban dance company to have performed on Broadway). It features a fusion of dance and musical influences, such as flamenco, ballet, popular Cuban dances and Afro-Cuban rhythms.

Ballet Nacional de Cuba

Calle Calzada (7ma) #510, entre D & E, Vedado (835 2946/www.balletcuba.cu). **Map** p254 A10.

A highlight of any trip to Havana is a performance by the Ballet Nacional de Cuba. The company's fusion of tropical passion, extraordinary physical power and Soviet discipline has made it as technically accomplished as any other. Ballet in Cuba was an entirely European notion until the mid 20th century. But in 1948 Cuban ballerina Alicia Alonso teamed up with her then-husband Fernando and his brother Alberto to open a company in Havana, the Ballet Alicia Alonso, which in 1961 became the Ballet Nacional de Cuba. Today the company has 97 works in repertoire, 26 of which were choreographed by Alicia. Cuban ballet dancers trained under Alonso's tutelage are now with several top US companies: look out for Lorna Feijó, her husband Nelson Madrigal and her sister Lorena Feijó, as well as Jorge Esquivel and José Manuel Carreño. Carlos Acosta, meanwhile, is a principal dancer with London's Royal Ballet (*see p180* **Man in tights**).

Performances are held at the Gran Teatro (*see p174*), whose interior competes with the world's great ballet stages. It's also possible to watch rehearsals during the week.

Codanza

Calle Fomento #202, entre Arias y Agramonte, 8010, Holguín (information 024 42 2234/sethlg@tauronet.cult.cu).

Catch this Holguín-based company if you can. Founded in 1992 and directed by Maricel Godoy, it uses a ballet base to build a style that mixes popular rhythms with theatre and comedy. It performs during dance festivals in Havana and Holguín, and also regularly tours Cuba.

Compañía de la Danza Narciso Medina

Cine Teatro Favorito, Calle Padre Varela (Belascoaín), esquina Peñalver, Centro Habana (878 2650/medinadanz@cubarte.cult.cu). **Performances** 3pm Sat, Sun. **Tickets** CUC 2-4. **Map** p254 E12.

Founded in 1993 by Narciso Medina, this contemporary dance group includes oriental and martial arts dance and movement in its performance style. The company has toured in the US, France and Japan, where it received the Grand Prix at Saitama for its best-known work, *Metamórfosis*.

Compañía Folklórica Cubana JJ

Centro Cultural Los Orishas, Calle Martí, esquina Lamas, Guanabacoa (94 7878/792 1338/johannesjg@cubarte.cult.cu.). **Performances** 8pm Fri. **Tickets** phone for details.

This company was founded by Johannes García, once the lead dancer of the Conjunto Folklórico Nacional de Cuba. It stages anything from large-scale productions to duets, and seeks to reflect Cuba's various cultural influences.

Compañía Rosario Cárdenas de Danza Combinatoria

Information: Centro de Danza de La Habana, Prado #111, entre Genios y Refugio (878 6765/rcrw@cubarte.cult.cu). **Map** p255 D15.

This company was founded as Compañia Danza Combinatoria in 1990 by former dancer Rosario Cárdenas, and added her name in 2003. Under her directorship, the small but well-established company takes a sensual, sculptural form of surrealism to the stage. Cárdenas applies mathematical principles to dance – permutation, combination and variation. She also applies the principles of painting composition, and borrows from Eugenio Barba's work and from the Abakuá religion. Cárdenas' 2006 production *La Stravaganza* used rubbish bags for costumes, and a combination of Vivaldi and live hard rock. Other shows to look out for include *Combinatoria en Guaguancó*, *Noctario*, *El ascenso* (winner of the 2004 UNEAC prize) and *Ouroboros*.

Conjunto Folklórico Nacional de Cuba

Calle 4 #103, entre Calzada (7ma) y 5ta, Vedado (830 3060/cfnc@cubarte.cult.cu). **Open** *Box office* from 2pm on performance days. *Performances* 3pm Sat. **Tickets** CUC 5. **Map** p254 A9.

Founded in 1962, the Conjunto Folklórico Nacional is one of Cuba's largest and best-known dance companies. Its current director is acclaimed choreographer Manolo Micler. Co-director (and founding member) Rogelio Martínez is a noted Afro-Cuban academic and writer/poet. The CNC is the flagship of the Revolution's missionary strategy to preserve the racial and traditional roots of Afro-Cuban culture. The company is still flourishing, with a repertoire of over 70 productions. These represent the full spectrum of Afro-Cuban dance and music, primarily consisting of dances representing the Yoruba deities, plus dances of Haitian origin and the full range of Cuban social and popular dances. It performs at Teatro Mella, with occasional outdoor spectaculars. Rumba is played every Saturday afternoon at 2.30pm (CUC 5) in El Gran Palenque, the courtyard attached to the company's home.

Man in tights

Hailed as the greatest ballet dancer performing today by critics from St Petersburg to New York, Carlos Acosta is a major figure in dance. Something of an icon at home, Acosta is an intriguing cultural phenomenon. He is one of the world's first black ballet superstars, and is also the first Latin American ballet superstar since Alicia Alonso. Additionally, he has built on Alonso's legacy in helping to destroy *machista* prejudices about ballet dancers, raising their status close to that of footballers in other Latin American countries (which is fitting, given that Acosta himself wanted to be a footballer when he was younger).

But above all Acosta is a phenomenal dancer: his jumps are stratospheric; his spinning-top pirouettes slow sensually to total stillness; and he effortlessly knots and un-knots his legs mid-leap. The combination of his athletic upper body and the grace of his movements has justifiably earned him comparisons with his two heroes, Rudolph Nureyev and Mikhail Baryshnikov.

Acosta's life-story is a classic rags-to-riches tale. Born in 1973, the son of a truck driver and the youngest of 11 children (most of them with different mothers), Acosta grew up in Los Pinos, a poor neighbourhood in southern Havana. Carlos's father sent him to ballet school at the age of nine, but Acosta played truant so much that the school expelled him – twice. At the age of 13, after seeing the Ballet Nacional perform for the first time, he was inspired. He studied hard in Pinar del Río and, aged 15, returned to the Escuela Nacional de Danza, and three years later joined the prestigious Ballet Nacional de Cuba, who packed him straight off to Italy to gain experience with the Turin Ballet.

Soon after he won the prestigious 1990 Prix de Lausanne, the English National Ballet contracted him, and his career seemed to be poised for take-off. But London weather and society jarred with Carlos, who soon became nostalgic for Cuba, and he began to-ing and fro-ing between the two countries, as well as New York's American Ballet Theatre.

Having conquered all the great classical roles, Acosta choreographed his first show, *Tocororo*, in 2003. It premièred in front of Fidel Castro at Havana's Gran Teatro and went on to play at Sadler's Wells in London. Named after Cuba's national bird, the production loosely tells Acosta's own life story, mixing an array of forms – Afro-Cuban dance, musical theatre, ballet, teatro Bufo, breakdance, rumba and contemporary dance. Critics were as complimentary about Acosta's lead performance as they were damning of his choreography, but the show returned to better reviews in 2004 and 2006.

In the past couple of years Acosta's career has gone from strength to strength. He even made it on to BBC Radio's *Desert Island Discs*, asking for a case of Havana rum as his luxury item. Among his most outstanding moments of 2006 he cites his debut of *Romeo and Juliet* with the Royal Ballet, dancing for the second time with the Opéra National de Paris (performing *La Bayadère de Nureyev*), and being given an honorary degree by London Metropolitan University. During the summer of that year he danced at three of London's major venues: the Royal Opera House, Sadler's Wells and the Coliseum.

But while some people might be ready to hang up their pointes by now, Acosta shows no sign of slowing down: as well as having his debut in the ballet *Spartacus* with the Bolshoi, he is working on a new show for Sadler's Wells, which should première in November/December 2007, and finishing his autobiography (to be published in late 2007 by HarperCollins), which he hopes will inspire a new generation of Cuban dancers (of which there is currently a noticeable dearth).

Acosta has also spoken of his desire to set up his own company in Havana. In the meantime, he returns to Cuba to perform, usually in the Gran Teatro, in collaboration with Danza Contemporánea (*see p181*). And while Acosta's heart may be in Cuba, it seems being in London may agree with him after all.

For more about Carlos Acosta, see his website www.carlosacosta.com.

DanzAbierta

Information: 881 7871/www.danzabierta.com.

DanzAbierta (meaning 'open dance') is Cuba's best-known contemporary dance ensemble on the international stage. Director Marianela Boán, former dancer/choreographer with Danza Contemporánea, has evolved as Cuba's answer to postmodernism in dance theatre. She mixes the gestures of everyday life with social and political comment and techniques. Boán was one of the main leaders of a new avant-garde, forming her own company in 1988 and pioneering investigations into gesture, corporeality and Cubanness to create what she called 'contaminated dance'. DanzAbierta's first productions revealed scrupulous research, a wide field of cultural reference and an effusively free style. Her best pieces in recent years include *El pez de la torre nada en el asfalto*, a witty reflection on the absurdities of the Special Period, and *El árbol y el camino*, in which five naked dancers portray a mythical tree. Boán moved to the USA in 2003, but continues to direct the company remotely through her partner Guido Gali.

Danza Contemporánea de Cuba

Teatro Nacional de Cuba, Avenida Paseo, esquina 39, Plaza de la Revolución, Vedado (879 6410/2728/ danzacontcuba@cubarte.cult.cu). **Map** p254 D10.
The powerhouse of Cuban contemporary dance, directed by former dancer Miguel Iglesias, is a true must-see for modern dance fans. The company was founded in 1959 by Ramiro Guerra, who initiated the evolution of a particularly Cuban approach to contemporary dance, drawing heavily on Afro-Cuban dance movement and rhythm, as well as popular Cuban dance forms. In 2003 the company teamed up with Cuba's best-known dancer, Carlos Acosta, to première his first choreographic effort, *Tocororo*, (*see also p180* **Man in tights**). Other recent shows are *Restaurante El Paso* by Julio César Iglesias, set to a Sonic Youth score; *El soñador* by Jorge Abril and *Compás*, a piece by the Dutch choreographer Jan Linkens. The company's main seat is at the Nacional, but it also holds performances at the Gran Teatro, among others. **Photo** *p178.*

Danza Teatro Retazos

Teatro Las Carolinas, Calle Amargura #61, entre Mercaderes y San Ignacio, La Habana Vieja (866 0512/860 4341/www.retazos.cult.cu). **Map** p256 E15.
Founded in 1987, Retazos is led by Ecuadorean choreographer Isabel Bustos, who creates a sensual, disciplined chaos of unusual physicalities. She describes her work as 'intimist' – that is, founded on an aesthetic of intimacy and emotion. The group's new base has two performing spaces: one colonial-style, outdoors, and in-the-round; the other modern, indoors and end-on.

Danza Voluminosa

Information: 262 0785/jmmasvoluminosa@yahoo.es.
This company, which celebrated its tenth anniversary in November 2006, has an interesting USP: all its dancers are unashamedly fat. The average weight of the troupe's performers is 15.5 stone (98 kilograms), with some tipping the scales at more than 20. But there's a serious side to it all: under director Juan Miguel Más, the company focuses on allowing overweight people to nurture their creative abilities and challenge stereotypes. Their best-known works are *Fedra* (a pastiche of the Greek Phaedra myth) and *Una muerte dulce* (*A Sweet Death*, in which a girl eats herself to death on sweets). They rehearse at the Teatro Nacional (*see p175*) but perform at locations throughout the city, including theatres, museums and squares.

Comedy

Comedy is popular in Cuba, providing a crucial safety valve for the real frustrations and absurdities of daily life. As a visitor, however, you may be left out in the cold. For a start, you need an excellent comprehension of Spanish to work out what's being said. In addition, there's a complex set of subtextual references, the most common being gestures indicating a beard to portray Fidel. Then there's the political incorrectness: jokes are often sexist (whores or unfaithful wives), racist (stupid, thieving negritos), or homophobic (mincing fags, *maricones*, devilish dykes, *tortilleras*).

That said, there is some good material out there. The best live comedy, mime and clown shows can be found at the **Festival Nacional del Humor 'Aquelarre'** (*see p140*), **Teatro Mella**, **Teatro América** and the **Teatro Fausto** (for all, *see p176*). Look out for stand-up comic Iván Camejo, whose company Humoris Causa is one of the best known and most risqué in Cuba. Another leading light is Mariconchi, who dresses up as a busybody woman to apply his acerbic wit to contemporary Cuban reality. He performs regularly at **Teatro América**'s Thursday comedy shows (*see p176*). Also look out for Pagola la paga, La oveja negra, and performers from the Matanzas ensemble **La seña del humor** and Santa Clara's **La leña del humor**. The best comics can be viewed on the TV shows *¿Jura decir la verdad?*, *Deja que yo te cuente* and *Punto G.*

Festivals

April is a bumper month for performing arts festivals in Havana. The annual week-long street dance festival **La Habana Vieja: Ciudad en Movimiento** sees over 500 international artists perform in inner courtyards of colonial mansions, or in the Plaza Vieja. Also starting in April is the **Festival 'Los Días de la Danza'** (*see p139*); the **Festival de Academias de Ballet**, with shows by students at the international ballet school; and the **Festival Elsinore**, with productions by students from the **ISA** (*see p93*).

The **Festival de Teatro de La Habana** (*see p140*) takes place in odd-numbered years in September, and the **Festival Internacional de Ballet** (*see p141*) in even-numbered years from the end of October. **Mayo Teatral** is a new festival of Latin American drama that takes place in May in even-numbered years, organised by the **Casa de las Américas**. **CubaDanza** (*see p142*) is a festival of modern dance organised by Danza Contemporánea every even-numbered year in January and August.

Sport & Fitness

Havana's sporting scene may be staging a financial comeback, but it's still on the ropes when it comes to performing.

Since the Revolution, sport in Cuba has played an integral role in the building of a healthy, moral society. The National Institute for Sport and Recreation (INDER) was formed in 1961 with a remit of promoting 'Sport for All' and developing world-class athletes. Today there are over 30,000 physical education teachers, and at least two specialist sports schools in every Cuban province.

Despite the immense wealth that professional sport generates around the world, Cuba has stuck to its principles of strict amateurism: money earned and won by Cuban sportsmen and women in international competitions goes into the state coffers. But balancing the need to survive economically with the ideals of the Revolution has taken its toll; sports facilities have generally deteriorated, and with the exception of a few top-class sportsmen and women, most Cubans earning a living from sport remain relatively poor. This has meant that gold medal winners and world champions do not (refreshingly) assume celebrity status.

However, when it comes to results, it is possible to point to a relative decline in top-level Cuban sport. Over the last four Olympic Games the country has dropped from fifth place at Barcelona in 1992 to 11th at Athens in 2004. Indeed, the 1992 Games can be seen to mark the country's sporting peak, in recent terms. Nonetheless, given the country's small population and limited resources, it's fair to say that it is punching above its weight.

In addition, almost two decades after the catastrophic loss of funding and resources provided by the Soviet Bloc, there are now signs that Cuba's sports scene is bouncing back, at least financially. Firstly, homegrown coaches and athletes are being farmed out to other countries – Cuban baseball players have played in the Japanese league, for instance, earning handsome revenue for the system. Secondly, international events offering large sums of prize money are also being targeted, with high hopes of success in the future. Here's hoping that the upwards trend continues.

GAMES WITH FRONTIERS

The Cold War and US–Cuban relations have often taken a toll on Cuba's international sporting profile. Although 1999 saw a historic match between the Baltimore Orioles baseball team and the Cuban national team – the first time a major league US baseball team had competed in Cuba – relations have since stuttered somewhat. In 2006 the US tried to prevent Cuba from competing in the inaugural World Baseball Classic. When it eventually relented, all attention turned to the possibility of defections – a big problem for Cuban sport. Sportsmen and women are frequently lured abroad, where celebrity and cash await. In 2001 there was a mass defection by most of the men's national volleyball team and in 2004 Kendry Morales fled Cuba in a motorboat and now plays for the Los Angeles Angels.

INFORMATION

The websites www.inder.co.cu, www.jit.cu, www.cubasports.com and www.cubadeportes.cu are all useful resources.

Spectator sports

The best sources for details of forthcoming events are the websites of the prominent sports institutions (*see above*). For information and help obtaining tickets for events, the tourist desks or PR (*relaciones públicas*) department of major hotels are good places to start.

The best newspapers for information on fixtures and results are *Juventud Rebelde* (www.jrebelde.cubaweb.cu) and *Granma* (www.granma.cubaweb.cu). You can also try the sports pages of www.radiococo.cu, particularly good for baseball, and www.radiorebelde.co.cu.

Baseball

A visit to a Cuban ballpark during the Serie Nacional de Béisbol (late October to April) or for the play-offs in April/May is a relaxing escape into baseball's innocent past, free of luxury boxes and giant electronic scoreboards. Matches are usually held all over Cuba on Tuesday, Wednesday, Thursday and Saturday at 9pm, and on Sunday at 1.30pm. The All Star game between East and West takes place in the middle of the season. Havana has two teams in the Serie Nacional, Metropolitanos and Industriales (or Los Azules, the Blues), the latter the most successful team in the league's history. The home ground for both teams is the **Estadio Latinoamericano**.

For a measure of how seriously Cubans take their baseball, and how fanatical they can be about it, head for Parque Central on the edge of La Habana Vieja. Here you can witness a daily gathering of baseball aficionados arguing passionately over the game (*see p187* ***Esquina caliente***). The best resource for Cuban baseball is the Federación Cubana de Béisbol Aficionado website (www.beisbolcubano.cu).

Estadio Latinoamericano

Calle Pedro Pérez #302, entre Patria y Sarabia, Cerro (870 6526/6576). **Games** 8.30pm Tue-Thur, Sat; 1.30pm Sun. **Tickets** CUC 1-3. **Map** p254 F10.

Basketball

The national basketball league (Liga Superior de Baloncesto or LSB) currently runs from November to January and consists of just six teams. The Havana team is Capitalinos; they can be seen in action at the **Sala Polivalente Ramón Fonst**. Occasional games are held at the **Coliseo de la Ciudad Deportiva** (*see p186*).

Sala Polivalente Ramón Fonst

Avenida de la Independencia, entre Bruzón y 19 de Mayo, Plaza de la Revolución, Vedado (881 1011/ 883 0781/2). **Games** 6.30pm Mon-Sat; 3pm Sun. **Tickets** CUC 1. **Map** p254 D10.

Boxing

Cuba has been the overall champion of the boxing competition at every Olympic Games in which it has competed since Munich in 1972 (with the exception of Montreal '76), completely dominating Athens 2004 with five golds, two silvers and a bronze. Former and current stars, such as Kid Chocolate, Teófilo Stevenson and Felix Savón, are national heroes. Boxers to look out for these days are Odlanier Solís Fonte and Guillermo Rigondeaux.

The Girardo Córdova Cardín International Tournament is Cuba's most prestigious competition (every April or May). There's also the annual Torneo Nacional de Boxeo por Equipo, an interprovincial team competition (September and November). International championships are held at the much bigger **Coliseo de la Ciudad Deportiva** (*see p186*). You can see budding Stevensons training and fighting at the **Arena Trejo**.

Arena Trejo

Calle Cuba #815, entre Merced y Leonor Pérez (Paula), La Habana Vieja (862 0266). **Open** 8am-7pm Mon-Fri. **Tickets** CUC 1. **Map** p256 F15.

Cycling

The **Velódromo Reinaldo Paseiro** is a purpose-built facility in eastern Havana constructed for the Pan-American Games in

Catch the Capitalinos in action at the **Sala Polivalente Romón Fonst**.

Come on you Reds!

In Cuba, the world's most popular sport has always had to compete with the nation's most fervently held obsession, baseball. Until relatively recently, football came way down the pecking order in the country's sporting priorities. But in November 2006 Cuba was placed 46th in the FIFA World Ranking, its highest position since the official rankings began, a leap of over 50 places in less than a year. There is still a long way to go – but at least Cuba is no newcomer to the sport.

The Asociación de Fútbol de Cuba is thought to have been in existence by 1907. This organisation spawned the first club, Sport Club Hatuey; one of the first games on record took place between Hatuey and a team of English sailors, on 14 February 1910. The following year, on 11 December 1911, the first official game on the island was held, between Hatuey and another newly formed Havana team, Rovers Athletic Club.

The national team came into existence considerably later, following the creation of the Asociación de Fútbol de Cuba in 1924, and played its first international match in 1930 against Jamaica (which it won 3-1). Cuba competed in the 1938 World Cup in France, the first Caribbean team to play in the tournament. They beat Romania in the opening round before being beaten 8-0 by Sweden in the quarter finals. That was Cuba's only showing in the World Cup to date.

The English influence on early Cuban clubs was superseded by an equally blatant Spanish connection: league winners included teams such as Deportivo Español, Real Iberia and DC Gallego. These clubs were generally run by businessmen or factory owners and were certainly privately owned until the Revolution, when, effectively, they were nationalised, along with everything else. Teams were reborn with names reflecting the priorities of the new Cuba, like Granjeros (Farmers), Azucareros (Sugar Workers) and Industriales (Industrialists), but these only lasted until 1978 when Cuban political boundaries and therefore the league were reorganised. Yet football continued to be ignored by the government.

Following the 1998 World Cup – which, significantly, was broadcast on television in Cuba – there has been a tangible change in football's popularity and success. Football is today far more visible in Havana, and throughout Cuba, than it was only ten years ago. Nowadays you're almost as likely to see kids kicking a ball around their street as swinging a bat and strides have been made towards becoming a more respectable force in the elite form of the game.

In 2002 FIFA donated US$400,000 to improving the training facilities and stadium infrastructure at the Estadio Pedro Marrero (*see p185*) in Havana. Then, in 2005, the competition format of the national league changed, from a US-style play-off system to a league style that was more in tune with the rest of world football (*see below*). Having qualified for the last three CONCACAF Gold Cups, the regional biennoial tournament for North America, Central America and the Caribbean, things are looking up for the national team too.

Yet the standard of football in Cuba still lags way behind almost every other Latin American country: playing surfaces for many league games are still substandard; the lack of spotlights at most 'grounds' means the league has persisted with mid afternoon kick-off times (far from ideal in the sweltering sub-tropical climate), and the national team will need to test themselves more regularly against tougher opponents.

Cuba can, however, already claim world champion status in one area of football: Erick Hernández, a Cuban footballer, now holds the world record for the most headers in 30 seconds – 146.

1991. Major events to be held here include the Vuelta a Cuba (Tour of Cuba) every February (vueltacuba@hotmail.com); get in contact with the **Comisión Nacional de Ciclismo** or directly with the velodrome for information about other events.

Comisión Nacional de Ciclismo

Avenida Monumental Km4.5, Villa Panamericana (95 3776/1286/panaci@enet.cu).

Velódromo Reinaldo Paseiro

Avenida Monumental Km4.5, Villa Panamericana, Habana del Este (information 95 3776/68 3776). **Open** 8.30am-5.30pm Mon-Fri. **Tickets** CUC 1.

Football

In recent years the quality of Cuban football has risen, though it's still light years away from the standard of the top South American teams. The

Havana team, Ciudad Habana, nicknamed Los Rojos ('the Reds'), have traditionally been one of Cuba's four strongest teams, along with Pinar del Río, Ciego de Ávila and Villa Clara. The competition format was changed in 2005 to ensure the best teams played one another more often. The national league runs from October to February. Havana games are held at the **Estadio Pedro Marrero**. *See also p184* **Come on you Reds!**

Estadio Pedro Marrero

Avenida 41 #4409, entre 44 y 46, Marianao (209 5428). **Matches** 3pm Wed, Sat. **Tickets** CUC 1.

Martial arts

Cuba has achieved impressive results in the martial arts, taking home six judo medals, three wrestling medals and one tae kwon do medal from the Athens Olympic Games in 2004. In Havana you can watch martial arts at the **Sala Polivalente 'Kid Chocolate'**, the **Sala San Isidro** and the **Sala Polivalente Ramón Fonst** (*see p183*).

Sala Polivalente 'Kid Chocolate'

Paseo de Martí (Prado), entre San Martín y Brasil, Centro Habana (information 861 1548/862 8634/ 861 1547). **Open** varies. **Tickets** CUC 1. **Map** p256 E14.

Sala San Isidro

Calle San Isidro, La Habana Vieja (861 7242). **Open** 8am-6pm Mon-Fri. **Tickets** CUC 1. **Map** p256 F14.

Rodeo

Rodeos take place on occasional Sundays at the stadium in **Parque Lenin** (*see also p55* **South parks**), while fairs are held in July, November and February. Lively **Feria Agropecuaria de Rancho Boyeros** (Rancho Boyeros Farmers' Fair) is held close to Havana's José Martí Airport, and hosts monthly rodeos. At the same venue, usually in March or sometimes February, is the annual Feria Internacional Agropecuaria (FIAGROP), with an international rodeo competition.

Feria Agropecuaria de Rancho Boyeros

Avenida de la Independencia (Avenida de Rancho Boyeros) #31108, Boyeros (683 4536). **Open** 10am-10pm daily. **Admission** CUC 5. **Tickets** vary.

Volleyball

Volleyball was quick to develop in Cuba. The national male team rose from nowhere to win the bronze medal at the Olympic Games in Montreal in 1976, while the women's team were crowned world champions two years later. Called Las Morenas del Caribe, the team held every major international title at one point.

Unfortunately, Cubans rarely get to see the women's team play at home, but they do pack the **Coliseo de la Ciudad Deportiva** to admire the men's team in action in the FIVB Liga Mundial de Voleibol (FIVB World Volleyball League). The Intercontinental

Street football.

Round of the league, the best time to catch the team in Cuba, is usually held in July and August. Sometimes matches are held at the **Sala Polivalente Ramón Fonst** (*see p183*).

Coliseo de la Ciudad Deportiva

Avenida de la Independencia (Boyeros), esquina Vía Blanca (648 5000). **Open** 8am-5pm Mon-Fri. **Tickets** CUC 1-3. **Map** p253 F7.

Active sports

Public sports facilities are few and far between in Havana. However, if you don't mind playing on relatively low-grade facilities there are plenty of options, with informal games of baseball, football, outdoor squash (*cancha*) or basketball taking place in neighbourhoods throughout the city. If you bring your own basketball, football or gloves and bats, you're virtually guaranteed to attract willing players.

Some of the popular sites are the dilapidated **Complejo Deportivo José Martí** on the Malecón in Vedado (entrance at the corner of Calles H and 5ta), where there are basketball courts, outdoor squash courts, a concrete five-a-side football pitch and a baseball field; the **Estadio Juan Abrantes** (Calle Ronda, esquina Avenida de la Universidad, Vedado), where there's an athletics track, several basketball courts and games of football; and the **Ciudad Deportiva** (*see above*), which has every kind of sports field and pitch.

Visitors can also pay to use **Club Habana** (*see also p94*), a luxurious private members' club on the coast to the west of the city, where facilities include tennis courts, a large swimming pool, a fitness centre with a gym and sauna, a lovely beach, yacht hire, scuba-diving excursions and other watersports facilities.

Club Habana

Avenida 5ta, entre 188 y 192, Jaimanitas (204 5700). **Open** 7.30am-9pm daily. **Admission** *Monthly membership* CUC 150. *Daily rate* CUC 20 Mon-Fri; CUC 30 Sat, Sun; free under-14s.

Cycling

If you fancy getting out of the city, contact the **Club Nacional de Cicloturismo**, which organises cycling trips in the countryside, and also promotes ecological bike tours. For more information on cycling in Havana, contact the **Comisión Nacional de Ciclismo** (*see p223*); and for bicycle hire *see also p223*.

Club Nacional de Cicloturismo

Information: Transnico, Lonja del Comercio, Calle Amargura #2, esquina Oficios, La Habana Vieja (866 9954/0170). **Open** 9am-5pm Mon-Fri; 10am-3pm Sat, Sun. **Map** p256 E15.

Fishing

Fishing fanatics flock to Cuba to try their luck with the huge number of fish that swim in the Gulf Stream. The country hosts numerous major fishing competitions, the most famous of which is the annual Ernest Hemingway International Marlin Tournament in May or June. Other important international competitions include the Curricán Tournament in April, the Blue Marlin Tournament in August or September and the Wahoo Tournament in November or December. For information, contact Club Náutico Internacional Hemingway (204 6653/1689) or Marlin SA (204 6848/1150-57), both at Marina Hemingway.

You can charter a boat for sport fishing from **Marina Hemingway** and **Marina Tarará** (for both, *see p188*). To go ocean fishing, you have to bring your passport and check out with the coastguard and immigration at Marina Hemingway. It's also important to know which fish can be eaten; barracuda can be contaminated with a highly venomous coral toxin.

Islazul

Main office: Calle 19 #710, esquina Paseo, Vedado (832 0571-9). International tourism: Calle 3ra, esquina Avenida de los Presidentes (G), Vedado (832 5152/www.islazul.cu). **Map** p254 B9.

Fitness

There are two types of gym in Havana: hotel gyms with facilities used predominantly by foreign tourists; and local public gyms, used almost exclusively by Cubans – but staff can usually arrange an informal price of CUC 1-2. Both types of gym generally have ageing running/step machines, although hotel gyms tend to have better weights rooms.

Golf

Cuba's best golf course is the 18-hole **Varadero Golf Club** (*see p199*). Closer to Havana is the **Club de Golf Habana** (Havana Golf Club).

Club de Golf Habana

Calzada de Vento Km8, Capdevila, Boyeros (649 8918). **Open** 8.30am-dusk (earlier in winter) daily. **Fees** *Non-members* CUC 20 for 9 holes; CUC 30 for 18 holes. *Club hire* CUC 10. *Caddie hire* CUC 5 for 9 holes. **Lessons** CUC 10 for 30mins.

Horse riding

The Centro Nacional de Equitación (also known as the Club Hípico) offers riding lessons and pony rides in **Parque Lenin** (*see p55*). Riding lessons are also available at the **Feria**

Esquina caliente

A unique aspect of Cuban baseball culture is the '*esquina caliente*' (literally 'hot corner'). In Parque Central in Old Havana (or at the corner of 23 and 12 in Vedado), you will see a group of men of all ages arguing and gesticulating excitedly. It's easy to confuse this commotion with a social disturbance, but when you get closer, you will find that it is simply Cuban baseball fanatics gathering to argue fervently about the recent performance of their favourite teams and the inside scoop on the players. Several people yell at the same time, puffing up their chests and trying to tower over their debating opponents, creating a cacophony of voices and waving arms. Never does it come to blows, though. Rather, it's testament to the place that baseball holds in the hearts of Cubans.

Agropecuaria de Boyeros (Avenida de la Independencia #31108). If you're in Santa María del Mar, ask at the **Club Atlántico** (Hotel Atlántico, Avenida de las Terrazas, 97 1085) about hiring a horse. If you've got small kids, more leisurely riding is available at **Parque de Anfiteatro** (*see p67*) in La Habana Vieja.

Running

The **Comisión Marabana**, in conjunction with **Cubadeportes**, organises a schedule of competitive runs throughout the year. The blue ribbon event is Marabana, the Havana Marathon and accompanying Half Marathon, 10km and 5km runs, which takes place in November. Entry costs are between CUC 60 and CUC 70; it's worth noting that there is a discount if you apply early.

Other key running events include the International Terry Fox Race (5km/3 miles) every February, which raises funds for cancer research; the Ultra Marabana (98km/62 miles) in April; the Mother's Day Race (5km/3 miles) and the Clásico Internacional Hemingway race (10km/6 miles) in May; and the Olympic Day Mini Marathon (4km/2.5 miles) in June.

The **Estadio Panamericano**, **Estadio Pedro Marrero** (*see p185*) and at the **Ciudad Deportiva** (*see p186*) all have athletics tracks.

Comisión Marabana

Ciudad Deportiva, Vía Blanca, esquina Boyeros, Apartado 5130 (648 5022/41 0911/marabana @inder.co.cu).

Cubadeportes

Calle 20 #710, entre 7ma y 9na, Miramar, Playa (204 0945/www.cubadeportes.cu).

Estadio Panamericano
Carretera Vieja de Cojímar Km1.5, Habana del Este (95 4140). **Open** 8.30am-5.30pm Mon-Fri; 8.30am-2pm Sat. **Admission** CUC 1.

Sailing & boating

Marina Hemingway offers mooring for up to 100 yachts in four parallel, six-metre-deep, specially designed waterways. Boat owners aren't required to make mooring reservations (although it's advisable). Call the control tower on VHF16, VHF72 or VHF77 to announce your vessel's arrival. The marina authorities organise an international amateur sailing regatta, the Regata Corona Internacional, usually held in June and open to all. Yachts and motorboats can be rented out at the marina.

Other services available include sailing and boat rides along the shore (around CUC 22 an hour), and trips with snorkelling, swimming, fishing and lunch included (adults CUC 45, children CUC 25, minimum six people). To the east of the city, next to the Playas del E ste, **Marina Tarará** has 50 berths (1.5 metres deep), each with water and electricity hook-ups. The marina has a variety of vessels for hire, including motorboats, yachts, dinghies and pedal boats. Note that Cuban citizens are not allowed to accompany a foreigner on motor yachts or sailing boats. The only exception to this rule is the Corona sailing regatta.

Marina Hemingway
Calle 248, esquina 5ta, Santa Fe (209 7270/7928/ comercial@puertomh.cha.cyt.cu).

Marina Tarará
Calle 7ma, esquina 25, Vía Blanca Km19, Playa Tarará, Habana del Este (96 0242).

Scuba diving

Cuba's crystal blue waters and beautiful coral reefs entice both amateur and professional divers from around the world. **La Aguja Centro de Buceo**, **Centro de Buceo Tarará-Mégano**, **Gaviota** and **Havanatur** offer attractive packages at good prices. It's also worth trying the **Comodoro** hotel (*see p51*). Shipwrecks can be explored off the Barlovento shore to the west of Havana, or at Cojímar in Habana del Este (*see p98*).

Equipment is good quality and instructors are trained to international standards. To take part in a diving trip, all divers require an international scuba licence. Lessons and initiation dives for beginners are also available.

La Aguja Centro de Buceo
Marina Hemingway, Avenida 5ta, esquina 248, Barlovento (204 1150 ext 2119).

Centro de Buceo Tarará-Mégano
Vía Blanca Km19, Playa Tarará, Habana del Este (96 0242/97 1462).

Gaviota
3rd floor, Edificio La Marina, Avenida del Puerto #102, La Habana Vieja (866 6777/gaviota@ gaviota.gav.tur.cu).

Havanatur
Complejo Neptuno-Tritón, Avenida 3ra, esquina 70, Miramar, Playa (201 9800/havanatur@ cimex.com.cu).

Swimming

Some of the best pools in Havana can be found in the upscale hotels, such as the **Meliá Cohíba** (*see p48*), **Meliá Habana** (*see p49*), **Occidental Miramar** (*see p50*), **Nacional** (*see p48*), and **Saratoga** (*see p46*). Other swimming alternatives include the **Complejo Turístico La Giraldilla**, a leisure complex in the western reaches of the city, and the pool at the **Marina Hemingway** (*see above*).

Note that, while it might look enticing, the sea off the Malecón is badly polluted and there are sharp rocks beneath the surface.

Complejo Turístico La Giraldilla
Calle 222, esquina 37, La Coronela, La Lisa (273 0568/0569). **Open** noon-midnight daily (swimming pools 10am-6pm). **Admission** CUC 5; CUC 2 concessions; free under-6s.

Tennis & squash

The Cuban tennis team train at the six tennis courts (*canchas de tenis*) at the **Eastadio Panamericano** (*see above*) in eastern Havana. The tennis federation (*see p182* **Information**) can help co-ordinate accommodation and transport at decent rates. The following hotels have courts that can be used by non-guests. Squash and tennis: **Occidental Miramar** (*see p50*); tennis only: **Meliá Habana** (*see p49*), **Nacional** (*see p48*). The courts at the **Estadio Panamericano** are also for hire. It's best to bring your own balls and strings. At **Club Habana** (*see p186*) and Occidental Miramar you can get lessons from a tennis pro for around CUC 5 per hour.

Watersports

The coast near Havana has facilities for watersports such as jetskiing, kayaking and water-skiing. Try **Club Habana** (*see p186*), **Marina Hemingway** (*see above*), **Marina Tarará** (*see above*) and hotels in the Playas del Este.

Trips Out of Town

Features

Parque Josone, Varadero. *See p197.*

Getting Started

Tips to help you find your own bit of paradise.

Varadero. *See p197.*

To visit Havana without seeing something of the rest of Cuba would be a great shame. Beyond the capital lie cities, villages and beaches not yet transformed by mass tourism. Houses, farms and mountain slopes remain much as they were decades ago.

Cuba is made up of huge, diverse landscapes, and it would take months to cover the country (and its islands) entirely. The following chapters cover the highlights.

One of the most manageable trips from Havana is to Pinar del Río Province, in particular the charming village of **Viñales**, famed for its *mogotes* (limestone rock formations) and lush landscape, and the **Las Terrazas** biosphere reserve. The rest of the province is poorly served by public transport, but if you have a car, **María La Gorda**, on Cuba's western tip, is scuba heaven.

Varadero, a two-hour drive east of Havana, is a cinch to get to. This popular beach resort, with its all-inclusive hotels (and little else), may not be everyone's cup of tea, but if you're after some beach time you can't go far wrong here. There are hotels for all budgets.

Perfectly preserved colonial **Trinidad** is an essential stop on any tour of Cuba. Its setting, between lush mountains with waterfalls and forest trails and the Caribbean coast, couldn't be more spectacular. On the downside, the small town is gradually becoming overrun by camera-wielding tourists, so try to visit out of season.

Santa Clara and Cienfuegos are not as impressive as Trinidad in architectural terms, but they do offer insights into provincial town life. **Santa Clara** has a vibrant, sociable feel, while bayside **Cienfuegos** is more subdued.

The big trip, however, is without doubt **Santiago de Cuba**, the country's second city, at the eastern end of the island. It's a long way from Havana, granted, but it's worth the journey for its vibrant music and dance scenes and impressive mountain scenery.

For a map of Cuba, *see p246.*

LISTINGS

Note that most museums charge a nominal fee of CUC 1-3 for entry, and that few establishments other than the large, more upmarket hotels will accept credit cards.

Travelling around Cuba

Expect the unexpected when it comes to public transport. Petrol shortages and breakdowns can create last-minute problems, although the Víazul bus network is generally very reliable, and petrol shortages are now much rarer thanks to the increased imports from Venezuela. The Víazul timetable can be viewed online at www.viazul.com; tickets are best booked in advance at the bus station in Nuevo Vedado or through a branch of Infotur. For Havana's bus stations, *see p221*.

By air

Most domestic flights within Cuba leave from Terminal 1 of José Martí International Airport. **Cubana** (officially Cubana de Aviación) covers many destinations within Cuba, including Cienfuegos, Santiago de Cuba and Varadero. However, its flights, while usually the cheapest available, are prone to delays and provide little comfort. Cubana's most central office is on La Rampa in Vedado (Calle 23, #64, entre O y P, Vedado, 834 4173/4949, www.cubana.cu). A generally more expensive but more comfortable option is **Aerocaribbean**, which covers Holguín, Santiago de Cuba and Cayo Coco. Its office is in the Cubana office in Vedado (870 4965).

By bus

Tourists are encouraged to use the big Víazul buses, which are kitted out with air-conditioning, video screens, toilets and refreshments. You pay in CUC, but prices are reasonable. The Astro company serves the same destinations, but only has two seats per service reserved for foreigners (and none on the Varadero service); it's slightly cheaper, and buses are now air-conditioned. For Havana's bus stations, *see p221*.

By rail

There are daily departures from the central train station in Havana (Estación Central de Ferrocarriles; *see p220*) to all Cuba's major towns. Tickets can be bought in CUC in person at least an hour before your train departs, or before 7pm if you're travelling at night. For details of the electric train between Havana and Matanzas, *see p96*.

Tourist agencies

The following state-run tourism companies variously offer excursions, activities and hotel and tour bookings around Cuba, including full packages out of Havana. If you don't have the time to roll with the uncertainties of independent travel – of which there are many in this country – you'd do well to arrange a trip in advance. Most of these organisations also have branches around the country for making local arrangements. For further ideas, including activity holidays, *see p235* **Specialist package holidays**.

For sources of tourist information, *see p234*.

Asistur

Paseo de Martí (Prado) #208, entre Trocadero y Colón, La Habana Vieja (866 4121/867 1315 24hr service/www.asistur.cu). **Open** 9am-4.30pm Mon-Fri. **No credit cards. Map** p256 D14.
Services include medical care, legal help, travel documents, air and hotel reservations.

Cubamar

Calle 3, entre 12 y Malecón, Vedado (832 1116/831 0008/www.cubamarviajes.cu). **Open** 8.30am-5.30pm Mon-Fri; 8.30am-2pm Sat. **Credit** MC, V. **Map** p253 A8.
Specialist youth and nature tourism, with campsites, villas and nature trails.

Cubanacán

Calle 17A, entre 174 y 190, Siboney, Playa (208 8666/www.cubanacan.cu). **Open** 8am-5pm Mon-Fri. **Credit** MC, V.
Runs hotels and restaurants, three marinas, scuba centres, health tourism facilities and a travel agency.

Cubatur

Calle 23, esquina L, Vedado (833 3569/www.cubatur.cu). **Open** 8am-8pm daily. **Credit** MC, V. **Map** p254 B11.
Services include guides, hotel reservations, excursions, custom-made programmes, organisation of events and conferences, car rentals and plane tickets.

Gaviota

Avenida 49 #3620, esquina 36, Reparto Kohly, Playa (204 4781/www.grupo-gaviota.com). **Open** 8am-8pm Mon-Fri. **Credit** MC, V. **Map** p256 E16.
As well as owning hotels, marinas, restaurants and shops, Gaviota also runs a travel agency.

Havanatur

Edificio Sierra Maestra, Avenida 1ra, entre 0 y 2, Miramar (204 7416/www.havanatur.cu). **Open** 8.30am-4.30pm Mon-Fri. **Credit** MC, V. **Map** p253 A7.
Havanatur's main reservations office, offering full travel services including tailor-made packages.

Infotur

Calle Obispo #524, entre Bernaza y Villegas, La Habana Vieja (863 6884/www.infotur.cu). **Open** 9.30am-1pm, 2-6.30pm daily. **No credit cards. Map** p256 D15.
Sorts out excursions, hotel bookings, museums plus aninternet, fax and postal service. Infotur also sells maps and posters.

Pinar del Río Province

These mountains and nature reserves are not far from Havana geographically, but they're a world away atmospherically.

The *mogotes* of **Valle de Viñales**: among Cuba's most outstanding scenery. *See p194.*

Pinar del Río offers neatly packaged and relatively accessible day trips from the capital. This is one of the most rural provinces in the country, its fertile earth perfect for cultivating a wide variety of crops, including sugar cane, citrus and coffee, and ideal for growing tobacco.

The showpiece valley of Viñales, is, like all the province's other highlights, situated away from the major population centres. Bypass altogether the provincial capital, Pinar del Río city. Most of the places worth visiting are hidden within the Cordillera de Guaniguanico mountain range, which runs down the centre of the province, forming its backbone. Beyond the mountains, in the far west, the land flattens out as it nears the coastline on the Península de Guanahacabibes, a great place for scuba diving.

Las Terrazas

Just beyond Havana Province, 80 kilometres (50 miles) from the capital, approachable from both the *autopista* (Km51) and the Carretera Central (*see p196*), is the first of Pinar del Río's biosphere reserves – **Las Terrazas**. This rural community project and tourist complex takes its name from the terraces dug out of the hillsides during the late 1960s: as well as restoring the ecosystem – damaged by years of deforestation by 19th-century French coffee planters – the project aimed to provide the impoverished local *campesinos* with access to better housing, education and medical services. Some 50 per cent of those now living in Las Terrazas are involved in tourism.

There is a CUC 4 charge per person for entering the reserve, payable at the toll gate on the only road into Las Terrazas. There's a huge amount to see and do here: hiking, swimming under the cascades of the San Juan river, boating on the lake, guided nature walks, cycling, horse riding, visiting ruins and even a Canopy Tour of the community along cables suspended above the village. The helpful **Rancho Curujey information office and Ecology Research Centre** (082 57 8700/8555) within the complex should be your first port of call, and if you're going to stay, the project is centred around the eco-friendly **Hotel Moka** (*see p193*).

The complex also contains a lakeside cottage where Las Terrazas' most famous contemporary son, the late singer Polo Montañez, lived. It's now the **Peña de Polo** and displays his gold and platinum discs. There's also a small museum with the skeleton of a *cimarrón* (runaway slave), plus a library and a cinema. Wandering among the cottages and apartment buildings, peeking in at the artists' studios and workshops, the set-up here does feel rather contrived. But whether tourist trap or genuine Cuban community, this is a successful project and one-third of the income is reinvested in its upkeep.

UNESCO designated the area as a biosphere reserve in 1985. It's home to the *zunzuncito* (the world's smallest humming bird); Cuba's national bird, the red, white and blue *tocororo*; the planet's tiniest frog, about the size of a thumbnail; and a huge variety of stunning flora.

Walks on all the designated hiking routes and nature trails are chargeable, at Rancho Curujey (*see p192*), and must be led by a guide, at a cost of around CUC 10 per person, with additional costs for other activities. It's worth a slight detour to visit Cafetal Buenavista (no phone), a restored coffee plantation abandoned by its French owners and now a living museum.

Where to stay & eat

Perched on the wooded slopes overlooking the village is the 'ecological' **Hotel Moka** (Carretera de la Candelaría Km51, 082 57 8600, reservas@commoka.get.tur.cu, doubles CUC 80-110), which has a grill and restaurant serving international food. There's a CUC 3 cover for non-residents using the swimming pool.

There are two restaurants in the village: **La Fonda de Mercedes** (main courses CUC 4.95-7.50), which serves Creole food in a patio setting; close by is **El Romero** (main courses CUC 5-12), arguably the best vegetarian restaurant in Cuba; there are several others within the reserve, including **El Bambú** on the banks of the San Juan river and the **Casa del Campesino** at the Hacienda Unión, a ruined colonial coffee plantation.

Soroa

Some 80 kilometres (50 miles) west of Havana and close to Las Terrazas is **Soroa**, located in the small valley of the Río Manatiales. Founded as a French colonial coffee plantation in the 19th century, it was originally famous for its orchid gardens, waterfall and medicinal baths. In the 1940s Tomás Felipe Camacho, a lawyer from the Canary Islands living in Havana, decided to turn his Soroa summer residence into a shrine to his youngest daughter, Pilar, who had died in childbirth. The 3,500-square-kilometre (1,350-square-mile) park on the slopes of the Guaniguanico mountain range is home to 6,000 species of ornamental plants, trees and flowers, including an orchid garden (CUC 3) with 700 species of orchids, 110 of them indigenous to Cuba. The best time to visit is between November and March, but the area's microclimate ensures that there are always some orchids in bloom. An international event on growing and tending orchids is held in March (even-numbered years; contact emujica@vrect.upr.edu.cu for details).

Cross the road and follow the path, which eventually becomes stone-stepped, down to the 22-metre-high (73-foot) **Arco Iris** waterfall (CUC 3, free for guests of nearby hotels). There's a pool, and a marvellous view of the valleys and sea from the top of the waterfall. Nearby are medicinal baths offering mud treatments and massage. Nature and bird walks take in visits to coffee plantation ruins, the Loma de Vigía observation point, the charcoal makers' pit and a slaves' stone mine. Villa Soroa (*see below*) can arrange walks and horse riding.

Where to stay & eat

Villa Soroa (Carretera de Soroa Km8, Candelaría, 085 52 3534/3556, www.hotelescubanacan.com, doubles CUC 45-55) has a 49-cabin air-conditioned complex set in the grassy area around a swimming pool (CUC 3 non-residents). There are some self-catering villas with swimming pools near the orchid garden (doubles CUC 70-80), plus a five-bedroom mansion (CUC 85-100) close to the **Castillo de las Nubes** restaurant (main courses CUC 4-8). **La Caridad** campsite (no phone) is located in the woods close by, and is very basic.

Further west

About eight kilometres (five miles) along the road from Soroa is the *paladar* **El Trebol** (also known as El Ranchón). You can't miss it as it's on a main junction, set back slightly from the road. It offers basic Cuban fare in generous portions, all in Cuban pesos. There are also a few *casas particulares* scattered along the way.

Moving westwards, 120 kilometres (80 miles) from Havana is the **Balneario San Diego de los Baños**, a natural spa for the relief of arthritis, rheumatism and skin problems. Legend has it that its fame spread after the mineral springs cured a slave of his leprosy. Its waters have been used since 1700; and the Spanish developed it into a spa in 1891. In the 1980s it was developed into a resort for health tourism. It's looking a little worn these days.

What a dive

Tips and notes on getting wet

● Though equipment is frequently of a high standard, it's advisable to bring your own gear if you can (at least a wetsuit), as some of the equipment available for hire is old and falling apart.

● No centres are PADI recognised as it's a US organisation, but PADI qualifications are recognised, as are those issue by BSAC (British Sub Aqua Club).

● Steel tanks, not aluminium ones, are used, which are heavier so you need much less additional weight.

● In all cases it's cheaper and easier to pre-book dive packages from Havana-based tour operators or your home country (*see p188*).

● On María La Gorda, expect to find pristine coral and a wide variety of sponges, huge canyons and tunnels, breathtaking drop-offs, walls, ledges, overhangs and coral heads. The only downside is the lack of significant marine life, though you will see the odd sea turtle, barracuda, grouper, scorpion fish, stingrays, moray eels, crabs and lobsters, and plenty of smaller stuff on the shallower reefs, such as gobies, anemones and Christmas tree worms. For the diving centre, *see p196*.

● Cayo Levisa is another picture postcard spot; however, because the island is not protected geographically, diving is often suspended because of the wind and the waves. Local operators encourage you to pre-book dives, but it's better to ring the diving centre (*see p196*) ahead to establish whether a trip is planned and pay when you get there. Stunning coral formations and the fact that you will have the reef to yourself are the big draws. Huge brain, star and fan corals shelter the small but beautiful marine life including grouper, parrot, scorpion fish, and crabs and lobsters.

Health programmes are offered as packages with accommodation across the road at the **Hotel Mirador** (*see below*).

Around five kilometres (three miles) west along the Carretera Central is **Parque Nacional La Güira**. The 220-square-kilometre (85-square-mile) park is now sadly neglected, but worth a visit just to wander among the ruins of a once-handsome mansion with sculpted gardens. Cross the bridge and descend through the forest to the lake and river. Apart from the birds it shelters (migratory species as well as native birds), the forest is also the habitat of the Creole deer, a species on the verge of extinction.

At La Güira's northern edge, 16 kilometres (ten miles) from the Carretera Central and located among the pine groves, is the **Cueva de los Portales**, where Che Guevara made his headquarters during the 1962 missile crisis. The cave contains the original furniture.

Where to stay & eat

The **Hotel Mirador** (Calle 23 final, 082 77 8338, www.islazul.cu, doubles CUC 32-41) is located right next to the spa. Built in 1948, it was refurbished in 1994 and hosts birdwatchers and spa users. The pretty grounds feature a small pool and lovely compact gardens. Rooms are adequate. The hotel serves a passable buffet (CUC 8) and has a grill and snack bar.

Valle de Viñales

The **Valle de Viñales** lies 25 kilometres (15 miles) north of Pinar del Río city along the 241, a sound but winding and narrow road. The valley and its village are nestled among the Sierra de los Órganos, the section of mountain range lying west of the Sierra del Rosario, with breathtakingly verdant landscapes, featuring *mogotes* – tree-covered limestone knolls. The limestone bedrock has been steadily moulded by underground rivers, creating huge caverns in the area. UNESCO has declared the area a Natural World Heritage Site and it's easy to understand why. The two best viewing points are from **Hotel Jazmines** (*see p195*) and **Hotel La Ermita** (*see p195*).

Alternatively, if you want to enjoy the area's natural beauty close-up, you can hike up **Dos Hermanos**, the area's most famous *mogote*, five kilometres (three miles) west of the town of Viñales. There are also guided tours around several caves in the vicinity. Three kilometres north of the village is the 140-metre-long (467-foot) **Cueva de San Miguel**; it takes about five minutes to explore, is a bit slippery (wear sensible shoes) and costs CUC 1 to enter. The entrance area has a bar and a late-night show every Saturday. On the other side, at the cave's exit, is **Palenque de los Cimarrones**, a reconstruction of an escaped slaves' settlement.

There is a restaurant here aimed at tour groups and an Afro-Cuban show usually accompanies lunch. Two more kilometres along the road from the village is a much bigger cave, the **Cueva de los Indios** (08 79 6280), where for CUC 5 you get to explore the first 400 metres (1,300 feet) on foot, then take a 10-20-minute boat ride along the underground river.

The other major tourist attraction in Viñales is the **Mural de la Prehistoria**. Che Guevara was apparently responsible for commissioning Cuban painter Leovigildo González (one of Diego Rivera's pupils) to execute the huge mural on the cliff face in 1961. It costs CUC 1 to see the mural at close quarters. But just as pleasant is meandering around the pretty little village of Viñales, with its wooden church, bookshop, craft shop, art gallery, museum and Casa de la Cultura (with nightly events).

Where to stay & eat

Hotel Los Jazmines (Carretera a Viñales Km25, 08 79 6205, www.hotelescubanacan.com, doubles CUC 65-77) is probably the area's best-known hotel, with lots of facilities (horseback trekking, restaurant, two bars, poolside grill bar, disco, shops) and archetypal views of the valley. Food in the first-floor restaurant is adequate (main courses CUC 4.50-9).

For somewhere a bit more tranquil, and with more spacious grounds, **Hotel La Ermita** (Carretera de La Ermita, Km1.5, 08 79 6071/6100, www.hotelescubanacan.com, doubles CUC 60-69) is pleasant, clean and only 20 minutes' walk from town; facilities include tennis courts and a swimming pool. Its sloping lawns are surrounded by the 62 rooms in two-storey blocks with red-tile roofs. The restaurant serves an assortment of Creole food (main courses CUC 5-20). All the other accommodation options are in the village and on the valley floor.

Seven kilometres (4.5 miles) north of Viñales village, just beyond the Cueva de los Indios, is **Rancho San Vicente** (Carretera Puerto Esperanza Km33, 08 79 6201/6221, www.hotelescubanacan.com, doubles CUC 48-58). This spa and ecotourism complex has 54 rooms in pine cabins set in sloping, grassy grounds around a swimming pool. The restaurant (main courses CUC 5-9) is small and tastefully decorated. The most economical state-run place to stay is **Campismo Dos Hermanas** (Carretera de Moncada Km3, 08 79 3223, cabins CUC 15), a well-maintained and good-value basic cabin site in the shadows of two *mogotes*.

In Viñales village there are no hotels but there are around 200 *casas particulares*, most of them simple bungalows and often with very little to distinguish one from another. If you arrive in the village at lunchtime or before, you shouldn't have any problem getting a house on spec, but by dark, especially in peak season, most places are booked up, so ring in advance if you expect to arrive late in the day. Most places charge CUC 15-20 in low season and up to CUC 25 in high season. Recommended are **Villa La Familia** (Calle Salvador Cisnero #66, 08 79 3372), opposite the Víazul bus stop; and **Villa Magdalena** (Calle Rafael Trejo #41, esquina Ceferino Fernández, 08 79 6029).

Most of the restaurants in Viñales are in the hotels and at the tourist attractions. The restaurant at the **Cueva de los Indios** (08 79 3202, main courses CUC 4-6) serves à la carte Creole fare during daylight hours, as do the restaurants at the **Palenque de los Cimarrones** (08 79 3203, main courses CUC 5-8) and the **Mural de la Prehistoria** (08 79 3394, main courses CUC 9-15).

El Bambú. See p193.

Soroa's orchid garden. *See p193.*

Paladares are not permitted in Viñales. The only proper restaurant in the village is the **Casa de Don Tomás** (08 79 3114, main courses CUC 4.50-12.50), a beautiful colonial house built in 1889. It has a good atmosphere, tasty Cuban food including lobster, and friendly service.

Cayo Levisa

With five kilometres (three miles) of unspoiled beaches, sand banks, coral reefs and crystal waters, Cayo Levisa is pretty much paradise – and official policy is to keep it that way. Take the road leading northwards from Viñales to Palma Rubia (or, if you're coming from Havana, take the Circuito Norte through Bahía Honda and La Palma). A ferry leaves for Cayo Levisa at 10am (and at 11am in high season). The fare (return trip only), including cocktail, costs CUC 20 (CUC 27-40 with lunch). The ferry returns at 5pm, but speedboats can take you back at other times for a CUC 10 fee. The key has a diving centre (contact via the hotel; *see below*), which offers scuba courses, plus facilities for kayaking, sailing and snorkelling. The **Hotel Cayo Levisa** has accommodation in the form of bungalows or wooden cabins (082 77 3015, www.hotelescubanacan.com, doubles CUC 71-80). The restaurant has a short menu of Cuban and international food, and holds candlelit dinners three times a week.

Península Guanahacabibes & María La Gorda

The **Guanahacabibes** nature park, along the westernmost point of the peninsula, is a biosphere reserve and the country's largest forested area. It's home to a profusion of flora and fauna – including turtles, wild deer and migratory birds – plus underground caverns and over 100 lakes. Stop at the reserve's **Estación Ecológica** (082 75 0366) for information on exploring the reserve beyond the main road. There is no charge for entering the reserve on the main road, but driving or walking beyond it must be done with a guide, on an organised excursion arranged through the Estación Ecológica. Prices are currently negotiable. **María La Gorda** is regarded as the finest diving spot in Cuba, with an amazing diversity of sealife in the surrounding reefs, but also for its quiet isolation. The well-run diving centre here (contact them via the Villa María La Gorda; *see below*) offers diving courses and excursions (CUC 35, with discounts for pre-booked packages), equipment hire, snorkelling, excursions for non-divers and other sports facilities. Everything on the peninsula is charged for in cash and there is no bank or bureau de change.

Where to stay & eat

Opposite the Estación Ecológica, in front of the meteorological headquarters, are four very basic double rooms (CUC 9), though there are plans to close them down. For further information call 082 75 0366. **Villa María La Gorda** (082 77 8131/3072, doubles CUC 86) has 56 rooms, some lining the beachfront and the rest in attractive pine cabins set in woodland. The cost of a room here includes breakfast and dinner at the buffet restaurant (which for anyone not staying the night costs CUC 15). Lunch can be bought at the resort's other restaurant, which serves half-decent pizzas and sandwiches. This area's charm lies in its isolation, so remember to bring anything you may need (there is a grocery shop but it's very small and stock extremely limited).

Getting there

For travel information to Cayo Levisa, *see above*.

By bus

From Havana, both Víazul and Astro go to the centre of Viñales village via the provincial capital (fares CUC 12 and CUC 8 respectively; journey time 3.5hrs).

By car

From Havana, there's a good six-lane *autopista* that terminates in Pinar del Río city. Or there's the more scenic route along the Carretera Central (CC). Or else the Circuito Norte (CN) travelling inland along the coast west. It's a three-hour drive from the city of Pinar del Río to María La Gorda, along the Carretera San Juan, taking in the Vuelta Abajo tobacco fields.

By rail

A slow train bound for Pinar del Río city leaves La Habana Vieja train station every other day, calling in at San Cristóbal, the nearest station to Soroa and Las Terrazas, and arriving after more than five hours.

Varadero

A peach of a beach and spots of lavish luxury... but no place for culture vultures.

Varadero seems to disappoint and delight in equal measure. It is the biggest resort complex in the Caribbean, equipped with over 14,000 hotel rooms – an ever-increasing figure – many in all-inclusive luxury hotels. But some visitors complain that this is a generic beach resort that could just as easily be any holiday haven in the world. Others spend a few days here and find it a great place to unwind in the day, on the extraordinarily perfect beach, but not such a good place to wind up at night, with few decent nightclubs and no real centres of activity.

Few visitors argue over the stunning setting. Varadero town, in Matanzas Province, marks the western end of the Hicacos Peninsula, a 22-kilometre (14-mile) finger of land blessed with crystal-clear aquamarine waters and a fine white-sand beach running almost its entire length. The northern, ocean-facing side is lined with hotels of varying degrees of luxury; the side facing the Bahía de Cárdenas is where the majority of the local population lives. At the eastern end, beyond the town, are the mega-resorts, tourist towns with every available amenity, but where the sense of being in Cuba is completely lost, as the beach is exclusively for hotel guests and the only locals are the staff.

Although Cubans have been spending beach holidays in Varadero since the 19th century, things really took off in the 1930s, when American tycoon Irénée Dupont bought a huge chunk of this paradise and began to build on it. Others followed suit, and the area soon became to Havana what the Hamptons are to New York. Varadero today is more akin to the Costa del Sol than the Hamptons. As for the presence of Cubans nowadays, it is true that they are, at least in peak season, outnumbered by foreign tourists and also true that they are not permitted to stay in some of the hotels. However, the occasionally heard claims, usually made by non-Cubans, that nationals are not allowed on the beach here or are banned from holidaying in Varadero are, frankly, ridiculous. There are plenty of hotels in the town area with both Cuban and foreign guests and several hotels exclusively for Cubans, while the beach itself is a free-for-all, other than at the far eastern end.

Varadero isn't particularly well tailored to independent travellers. Similarly, aside from live music performances in some nightclubs and many hotels, there's not much in the way of local culture. If your main stay is in Havana, you can easily visit Varadero on a one-day excursion. However, sunrise and sunset are both spectacular enough to make it worth staying a night. Check weather reports if you plan to visit during hurricane season (September to November).

Sightseeing

Varadero is all about the beach and for a taste of a more authentic Cuba you should head for the nearby towns of Cárdenas and Matanzas. On the peninsula itself one of the most pleasant places in town is the lush green of **Parque Josone**, off Avenida Primera between Calles 56 and 58. It's a spacious, well-trimmed park, with tree-shaded paths, an artificial boating lake, a medium-size swimming pool (CUC 3) and some excellent restaurants (*see p198*).

The **Museo Varadero** (Calle 57, entre 1ra y Playa, 045 61 3189) is charming if unextensive. The history section has artefacts from the pre-Columbian period to the present. The **Delfinario** (Autopista Sur Km12, 045 66 8031, closed Mon, CUC 15) holds dolphin shows daily.

Mansión Xanadú. *See p199.*

A neatly packaged half-day trip from the town is to an area known as **Punta Francés**. Here the **Varahicacos Ecological Reserve** has been established, a protected square mile (three square kilometres), incorporating a small cave network complete with ancient writings and a 500-year-old cactus tree. Trails through the wood thicket and scrub-covered reserve are well marked, but you will need to pay CUC 3 for one of the multilingual guides to get the most out of your visit or to enter one of the two caves (*see below*). If you go early in the morning or just before sunset, you will see a variety of birds including numerous migratory birds from Canada, the US and Cuba's northern keys.

One trail leads to the **Cuevas de los Musulmanes**, where an indigenous burial ground was found. Another cave is filled with hundreds of bats. The reserve lays claim to the oldest cactus tree in Cuba – perhaps in Latin America – and the only completely natural beach in Varadero. There's nowhere to buy food, however, unless you're staying at one of the surrounding all-inclusive hotel complexes, so it's worth bringing a packed lunch.

Where to eat

Except for the all-inclusives, most hotels have decent restaurants and snack bars open to the public. The eastern end of town, between Calles 54 and 64, and nearby Parque Josone is the only area with concentrations of places to eat.

Las Américas

Mansión Xanadú, Autopista Sur Km7 (045 66 7750). **Open** noon-10.30pm daily. **Main courses** CUC 12-45. **Credit** MC, V.

This classy seafood specialist has a great wine list and some of the best food on the whole peninsula, served in an elegant colonial-style dining room. For the hotel, the gorgeous Mansión Xanadú, *see p199.*

La Campana

Parque Josone, Avenida Primera, entre 56 y 58 (045 66 7224). **Open** noon-11pm daily. **Main courses** CUC 7.90-24.90. **Credit** MC, V. **Map** p199 ❶

An old rustic stone and wood building serving typical Cuban cuisine in a relaxed atmosphere. The food is well prepared, with classics such as *ropa vieja.*

Dante

Parque Josone, Avenida Primera, entre 56 y 58 (045 66 7738). **Open** noon-11pm daily. **Main courses** CUC 4.50-12. **Credit** MC, V. **Map** p199 ❷

A delightful location next to the lake in Parque Josone, with a veranda perched over the water, this Italian restaurant serves decent pastas and pizzas.

La Mallorca

Avenida Primera, entre 61 y 62 (045 66 7746). **Open** noon-11pm daily. **Main courses** CUC 3.30-24.90. **Credit** MC, V. **Map** p199 ❸

Great-value paella and a laid-back ambience are the draws at this unremarkable roadside building.

Pizza Nova

Plaza América, Autopista Sur Km7 (045 66 8585). **Open** 11am-11pm daily. **Main courses** CUC 4.85-19.60. **Credit** MC, V.

The best Italian restaurant in Varadero, with sea views from its pleasant balcony.

El Retiro

Parque Josone, Avenida Primera, entre 56 y 58 (045 66 7316). **Open** noon-11pm daily. **Main courses** CUC 5.50-28. **Credit** MC, V. **Map** p199 ❹

Lobster tops the Creole cuisine menu at El Retiro; it's served in seven different ways. Set in an elegant residence, the best tables are on the balcony.

Nightlife

Most of the all-inclusive hotels in Varadero have their own disco – or some form of evening entertainment – and some of these are open to non-guests. The best of these is **La Bamba** at

the Hotel Tuxpán on the Avenida de las Américas. Within half a kilometre of here, on the same road, are **Habana Café** and **La Rumba**, the two biggest and swishest nightclubs in Varadero.

Shopping

Plaza América (Autopista Sur Km7) is the only shopping mall in Varadero and the best place for upmarket clothing as well as cigars, souvenirs, books and music. The biggest range of arts and crafts is at the outdoor market on Avenida Primera between Calles 15 and 16. The Casa del Habano at Avenida Primera between Calles 63 and 64 sells a wide selection of cigars.

Sports

Varadero is one of the best spots in Cuba for watersports. Most hotels offer their own aquatic sports, boats, equipment and instructors. But if yours doesn't, or you're on a day trip, **Marina Gaviota** (Autopista Sur, 045 66 7755), **Marina Chapelín** (Carretera Las Morlas Km12, 045 66 7565/7550), **Diving Centre Coral** (045 66 8063) and the **Barracuda Diving Centre** (Avenida 1ra, esquina 58, 045 61 3481/66 7072) all offer snorkelling trips out on the keys, deep sea fishing and diving. **Boat Adventure** (Marina Chapelín, Carretera Las Morlas Km12, 045 66 7565/7550, CUC 39 per person) lets you pilot your own Aqua-Ray on a two-hour adventure. **Varasub** (Avenida Playa, entre 36 y 37, 045 66 7027, CUC 35) offers a 90-minute trip on a semi-submerged sub.

Varadero is also home to the **Varadero Golf Club** (Carretera Las Américas Km8.5, Autopista Sur, 045 66 7388, www.varadero golfclub.com), the best in Cuba, and the only one with an 18-hole course.

Where to stay

Varadero has over 50 hotels, and standards vary hugely. The budget options are scattered around the town, with the most upmarket mega-complexes isolated at the eastern end of the peninsula up to ten kilometres (6.2 miles) from the town centre. As most of the peninsula is no more than 500 metres wide, and considerably narrower in places, all hotels are within walking distance of the beach and many are right on the beach itself. Most hotels in Varadero are billed as 'all-inclusive' or 'ultra all-inclusive' (and other variations on the theme), but it's best to check beforehand to find out what this actually includes, besides room, meals, beach and pool. For example, some include all nautical sports, others only the non-motorised ones. Most include a wide variety of entertainment, sports and other activities. Some even include excursions. Note that in low season some hotels can be quite empty, so the hotel disco may close early, and some of the activities advertised in the brochure may not take place.

Expensive

Mansión Xanadú

Autopista Sur Km7 (045 66 7388/8482/fax 045 66 8481/info@varaderogolfclub.com). **Rates** CUC 120-160 single; CUC 150-210 double. **Credit** MC, V.

Unique among the upmarket options in Varadero, this former mansion now houses the best rooms on the peninsula. Each of has its own distinct look and character, from art deco to rococo, and all strike a great balance between comfort and refinement. Communal spaces include a sleek attic bar with great views and one of the finest restaurants in Varadero. As the hotel is run by the Varadero Golf Club there are discounts on green fees. **Photo** *p197.*

Meliá Paradisus

Punta Francés (045 66 8700/fax 045 66 8705/ www.solmeliacuba.com). **Rates** CUC 395-635 double. **Credit** MC, V.

This stunning all-inclusive is mind-bogglingly luxurious and packs in a jaw-dropping variety of features and facilities. The rooms, all 429 of them suites, are spacious, comfortable and tasteful, and surrounded by well-tended gardens. There are eight restaurants, three bars, two pools, tennis courts, a gym, sauna and jacuzzi, beauty parlour and a captivating lobby with gangways around a set of ponds.

Meliá Varadero

Autopista Km7 (045 66 7013/fax 045 66 7012/ www.solmeliacuba.com). **Rates** CUC 130-255 per person. **Credit** MC, V.

One of Varadero's chicest all-inclusives. The highlight is the cavernous seven-storey central atrium filled with lush tropical vegetation and a little network of waterways. The main buffet is excellent, as are the three à la carte restaurants. The grounds, featuring two pools and pristine gardens, are situated atop a low rocky headland with ocean views.

Tryp Peninsula Varadero

Punta Hicacos (045 66 8800/fax 045 66 8805/ www.solmeliacuba.com). **Rates** CUC 150-255 per person. **Credit** MC, V.

The sheer scale of this vast complex – like the expansive oceanfront lagoon it borders – is its most striking feature. There's enough space for almost 600 rooms, most of them in Hollywood-style mansions. The Tryp is the best-equipped hotel on the peninsula for families: the area set aside for kids is fantastic, with a large, shallow pool at the heart of an adventure playground, complete with mini castle and a fabulous ship-shaped climbing frame.

Mid-range

Hotel Club Tropical

Avenida Primera, entre 21 y 22 (045 61 3915/fax 045 61 4676/www.hotelescubanacan.com). **Rates** CUC 57-69 single; CUC 102-112 double. **Credit** MC, V. **Map** p198 ❶

Compared to some of the nearby and only slightly cheaper high-rise hotels, this beachfront establishment is soft on the eye and gets even better once you're inside, making a room here a relatively good deal. The interior pool terrace has a pleasantly private feel, shrouded by palm trees and walled in by the balcony-clad accommodation blocks.

Mercure Cuatro Palmas

Avenida Primera, entre 60 y 64 (045 66 7040/fax 045 66 8131/www.accorhotels.com). **Rates** CUC 120 per person. **Credit** MC, V. **Map** p199 ❷

The best-looking hotel in the town area, this is one of the only places that combines style, grace and comfort with a convenient location, right in the heart of the restaurant district. The main hotel facilities are provided in attractive, arched, red-tile roof buildings. They surround an attractively landscaped pool area with direct access to the beach. Many rooms, however, are housed separately in three blocks on the opposite side of Avenida Primera. There's a gym, sauna and nautical centre but no scuba diving.

Perfect beaches line the peninsula.

Budget

Hotel Dos Mares

Calle 53, esquina Primera (045 66 7510/fax 045 66 7499/www.islazul.cu). **Rates** CUC 47-57 double. **Credit** MC, V. **Map** p199 ❸

It may be low on facilities but the Hotel Dos Mares is high on character and charm. This Spanish-style country villa, along with its partner hotel down the road, the Hotel Pullman, looks a little out of place in a beach resort but is no worse off for it. The subterranean bar and restaurant are both great places for a skulk and have a relaxed air about them. On the downside, rooms are cramped.

Hotel Herradura

Avenida Playa, entre 35 y 36 (045 61 3703/fax 045 66 7496/www.islazul.cu). **Rates** CUC 58-67 double. **Credit** MC, V. **Map** p199 ❹

Varadero's cheapest beachfront hotel is a simple semi-circular four-storey building, practically in the water. Rooms are in pairs with shared living rooms, kitchenettes and ocean-facing balconies, ideal for double-dating couples. A pleasant terrace has views over the water, but the food here is sub-standard.

Hotel Pullman

Avenida Primera, entre 49 y 50 (045 66 7510/fax 045 66 7499/www.islazul.cu). **Rates** CUC 47-57 double. **Credit** MC, V. **Map** p199 ❺

This adorable, simple little roadside hotel may not have a great location (although it is still only a stone's throw from the beach), but it's the perfect antidote to the noisy entertainment programmes laid on at so many of its rivals. With only 16 rooms, a neatly trimmed front garden patio, a dinky restaurant and a toy castle look about it, the Pullman is a pleasingly down-to-earth, laid-back option.

Villa La Mar

Avenida Tercera, entre 28 y 30 (045 61 4515-24/fax 045 61 2508/www.islazul.cu). **Rates** CUC 34-40 single; CUC 48-58 double. **Credit** MC, V. **Map** p198 ❻

Villa La Mar is cheap but it isn't nasty; there is, however, a low-grade 1960s look and feel to this hotel, though the clunky buildings here are in marginally better nick than some neighbours (like the Mar del Sur). There's no shortage of space and the palm-studded, fairly extensive landscaped gardens help to smooth off the rough edges.

Villa Sotavento

Avenida Primera, esquina 13 (045 66 7132/fax 045 66 7229/www.islazul.com). **Rates** CUC 48-70 double. **Credit** MC, V. **Map** p198 ❼

Dotted around the local neighbourhood between beachside Camino del Mar and Avenida Primera, the houses of Villa Sotavento work well for small groups. Houses vary in size and style but most are handsome pseudo-colonial constructions with communal areas like dining rooms and receptions but no kitchens. Guests can use the pool and all other facilities at the nearby Hotel Acuazul.

Resources

Hospital

Clínica Internacional de Varadero, Avenida Primera, esquina 61 (045 66 7710/1). **Map** p199.

Internet

Cybercafé, Avenida Primera, entre 39 y 40 (no phone). **Open** 9am-7pm Mon-Sat. **Map** p199.

Police station

Calle 39, entre Primera y Autopista Sur (emergencies 116). **Map** p199.

Post office

Avenida Primera, esquina 36 (no phone). **Open** 8am-6pm Mon-Sat. **Map** p199.

Tourist information

Cubatur, Calle 33, esquina Avenida Primera (045 66 7216/7/www.cubatur.cu). **Open** 8.30am-8.30pm daily. **Map** p198.

Getting there

By air

Varadero's Juan Gualberto Gómez airport (045 61 3016) lies 25km (16 miles) to the west of Varadero, plus a further 20km (12.5 miles) to the easterly end. There are no public service buses linking the airport with Varadero. A taxi should cost CUC 20-25.

By bus

The Vía Blanca dual carriageway goes from Havana to Varadero (CUC 2 toll for cars and motorbikes). Buses arrive at the small Terminal de Omnibuses on Calle 26 (Víazul 045 61 4886; Astro 045 61 2626). Astro's Varadero service is only for Cubans. Víazul buses to Havana (CUC 10) leave three times a day (8am, 12pm, 6pm): they take around 3hrs. There are also direct bus links with Trinidad and Santa Clara.

By car

Take the Vía Blanca dual carriageway, part of the larger Circuito Norte, all the way, cutting through the city of Matanzas en route (*see p208*).

By rail

The nearest railway stations are in Cárdenas, 18km (11 miles) to the south-east, and Matanzas, 42km (26 miles) to the west; it's not easy to get here by train.

Getting around

The Hicacos Peninsula isn't very walkable. The main road is the Autopista del Sur, which extends from the eastern mainland bridge to the peninsula's east. The main drag in Varadero is Avenida Primera. Taxis can be pricey (roughly 50¢ per kilometre); pick one up at one of the hotels, or call them directly (Transgaviota 045 61 9761; Taxi OK 045 61 4444). Most hotels rent out bicycles and scooters. An open-top double decker bus (9am-9.30pm; CUC 5 day pass with unlimited rides) takes an hour to complete its circuit. Or for CUC 10 per person you can take a horse-drawn coach.

The Central Provinces

Stunning scenery and pretty cities form the bulk of Cuba's mid-section.

Villa Clara Province

Santa Clara & around

One of the largest and liveliest cities in central Cuba is the capital city of Villa Clara province, **Santa Clara**. As in most colonial-era cities, Santa Clara's municipal life is centred around a public square; in this case it's the **Parque Vidal**, as sociable and animated a square as you will find in Cuba. Along its borders are grand buildings housing government offices, the public library, a not-so-grand hotel and various cultural institutions. Among these is the **Museo de Artes Decorativas** (042 20 5368, closed Tue), displaying art and furniture from the colonial era and one of the city's most coherent and complete museums. On the same side of the square is the **Teatro La Caridad** (042 20 5548, closed Mon), a 19th-century theatre whose stately, austere exterior belies a more opulent interior; guided tours are available.

Santa Clara was the scene of one of the most significant events of the Revolution: Che Guevara was the leader of the rebel column that took the city in 1958, after a battle that effectively spelled the end of Batista's rule in Cuba. The city is now a mecca for worshippers of Che and there are several monuments around the outer neighbourhoods where the famous rebel is commemorated. A huge statue of him, the **Monumento a Che Guevara**, towers over the entrance to the city at Avenida de los Desfiles on Plaza de la Revolución. The statue is inscribed with an emotionally charged letter from Che to Fidel when he left Cuba, which makes interesting reading for Spanish speakers.

This is where most visitors to Santa Clara come to pay tribute to Che and is the city's most engaging visitor attraction. Below the statue is the hero's mausoleum, which also houses the remains of the other Latin American guerrillas who died with him, and the **Conjunto Escultórico Memorial Ernesto Che Guevara** (042 20 5878, closed Mon). The museum contains displays on Che's involvement in the Revolution, and some of his personal belongings.

Elsewhere in the city there are other shrines to Che, such as the **Monumento a la Toma del Tren Blindado** (042 20 2758, closed Sun); it is the spot where, on 28 December 1958, 18 guerrillas, led by Che, used a bulldozer to attack one of Batista's trains containing 408 heavily armed troops. Four carriages – now containing related displays – of the derailed train and the bulldozer have been preserved. A few blocks north of the monument is **El Che de los Niños**, a life-size bronze statue by Casto Solano showing a striding Che holding a young child.

Where to eat & drink

The dining scene in Santa Clara is surprisingly poor for a city of this size, hampered by a law forcing all but one *paladar* (Sabor Latino) to offer standing-room only premises. For cheap meals or quick snacks there are plenty of

Monumento a la Toma del Tren Blindado.

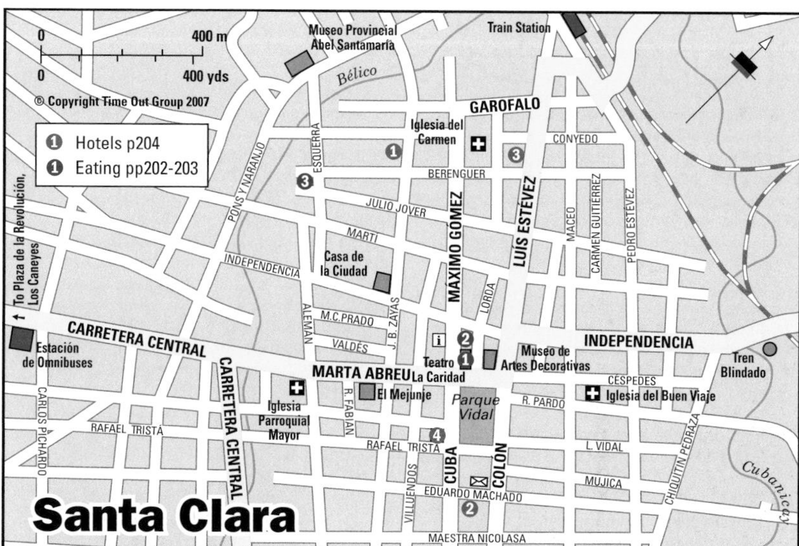

pizzerias charging in Cuban pesos, as well as a **Coppelia** ice-cream parlour (Calle Colón #9, entre Mujica y San Cristóbal, 042 206426, closed Mon). The hotels also offer food to non-guests: the best offer, an all you can eat buffet for CUC 12, is at Los Caneyes (*see p204*).

For drinking, there is a concentration of places on and off the section of Independencia that runs within a block of the Parque Vidal.

La Concha

Carretera Central, esquina Danielito (042 21 8124). **Open** 11am-midnight daily. **Main courses** CUC 1.25-13.50. **Credit** MC, V.

This place, a little out of the centre, is certainly the most polished restaurant in town, but in terms of atmosphere it's one of the most sterile too. The food, on the most varied and comprehensive menu in the city, is affordable despite being one of the few places charging in CUCs, and includes pizzas, pasta, seafood and the house special: rice, chicken and vegetables served on a clay plate.

La Marquesina

Parque Vidal, esquina Máximo Gómez (042 21 8016). **Open** 11am-1am daily. **No credit cards**. **Map** p203 ❶

Most nights this bar on the main square is buzzing with punters and attracts a lively mix of tourists and locals, as well as plenty of tourist-seeking-locals.

1878

Calle Máximo Gómez #8, entre Parque Vidal y Independencia (042 20 2428). **Open** 8.30am-10.30 am; noon-2.45pm; 7-10.45pm daily. **Main courses** CUC 2-5. **No credit cards**. **Map** p203 ❷

In terms of food quality this is the best of a bad bunch among the state-run restaurants, but the typical *comida criolla* does represent good value. The dignified yet slightly rough-edged colonial residence is atmospheric and there is a welcoming backyard patio. Prices are officially in national pesos, but you can pay in convertibles.

Sabor Latino

Calle Esquerra #157, entre Julio Jover y Berenguer (042 20 6539). **Open** noon-midnight daily. **Main courses** CUC 10-15. **No credit cards**. **Map** p203 ❸

The best meals in the city centre are served at this, the only proper, legal *paladar* in Santa Clara. The huge, carefully presented platters include lobster, shimp, chicken and pork dishes; the proud chefs are happy to tailor meals to your specific requests.

Nightlife

Santa Clara is pretty lively after dark. On weekend nights the square becomes the social hub for both young and old. The only other spot with a buzz is the pedestrianised section of Independencia, a block away from the square. There are several bars and cafés hereabouts, along with the city's slickest nightclub, **Club Boulevard** (Calle Independencia #219, entre Maceo y Pedro Estévez, 042 21 6236, closed Mon).

There are one or two isolated centres of activity elsewhere, the best being **Club Mejunje** (Calle Marta Abréu #107, entre Alemán y Juan Bruno Zayas, no phone), a

The great escapes

Villa Clara Province has some blissful keys (*cayos*) within easy reach of its northern mainland coastline. These miniature islands come complete with powdery white sand and translucent blue water, providing ample space for living out your paradise island dreams in relative isolation. A 48-kilometre (30-mile) causeway (*pedraplén*) was built between 1989 and 1999 out of the small port of Caibarién to the Archipiélago de Sabana-Camagüey, with a view to developing the keys. A fully blown holiday resort is now emerging on them as hotel development continues slowly but steadily – eventually somewhere in the region of 100,000 hotel rooms are to be spread between Cayo Santa María, Cayo Ensanchos, Cayo Las Brujas and Cayo Francés. After ecological problems were inflicted by the Cayo Coco causeway further along the coast, the causeway out of Caibarién has been built differently to allow the free movement of tidal waters.

There are currently four hotels in this cluster of keys. The newest and swishest is the **Royal Hideaway Ensenachos** (042 35 0300, www.royalhideawayensenachos.com, doubles CUC 320) with over 500 rooms, while on Cayo Santa María there are the **Hotel Sol Cayo Santa María** (042 35 0200, www.solmeliacuba.com, doubles CUC 175-220) and the **Hotel Meliá Cayo Santa María** (042 35 0500, www.solmeliacuba.com, doubles CUC 210-280), both luxury all-inclusives run by Sol Meliá, which share 11 kilometres (seven miles) of white sand beaches between them.

For a more subtle – and cheaper – resort, Gaviota-operated **Villa Las Brujas** (042 35 0199, doubles CUC 70-85) on Cayo Las Brujas comes recommended. Attractively designed modern cabins are arranged along a ridge with sea views. There's a restaurant and a quiet stretch of sandy beach that's usually free of music.

music and cultural centre with a bohemian feel, and the focus of Santa Clara's gay scene, although it's not a gay club as such.

Where to stay

There's a high standard and large number of *casas particulares* in Santa Clara, with a good concentration within a block or few of the central Parque Vidal. Hotels are thin on the ground, and for a decent level of comfort you'll need to head for the outskirts of the city.

Los Caneyes

Avenida de los Eucaliptos, esquina Circunvalación (tel/fax 042 20 4512/042 21 8140/www.hotelescubanacan.com). **Rates** CUC 45-50 single; CUC 50-55 double. **Credit** MC, V.

There are more than 90 well-kept rooms at Los Caneyes, and they are housed in attractive Taíno-style thatched cabins spread around a peaceful woody area. There's a pool, jacuzzi, shops and a decent restaurant. You'll need your own transport or a taxi to get to the centre.

Casa de Eva y Ernesto

Calle JB Zayas #253a, entre Berenguer y P Tuduri (042 20 4076/nestyhostal@yahoo.es). **Rates** CUC 15-25. **No credit cards**. **Map** p203 ❶

The architect owner's personal touches, like the spacious spiral staircase, are all over this *casa particular*, which features a double room and a fantastic open-plan apartment for rent. Great for self-caterers.

Casa Mercy

Calle Eduardo Machado #4, entre Cuba y Colón (042 21 6941/omeliomoreno@yahoo.com). **Rates** CUC 15-25. **No credit cards**. **Map** p203 ❷

This well-run *casa particular*, with two spick and span double rooms and a neat little upstairs terrace just for guests, strikes a great balance between reliable professionalism and hospitable warmth.

Hostal Señora Cary

Calle Luís Estévez #203 bajos, entre Berenguer y Conyedo (042 20 3229/5628). **Rates** CUC 15-25. **No credit cards**. **Map** p203 ❸

There is just one room (with two single beds) for rent at this compact and clean *casa particular*. The spiral staircase at the back of the house leads up to a roof terrace with good views.

Hotel Santa Clara Libre

Parque Vidal #6, entre Marta Abreu y Tristá (042 20 7548-51/fax 042 20 2771/www.islazul.cu). **Rates** CUC 29 single; CUC 36 double. **Credit** MC, V. **Map** p203 ❹

This 1950s high-rise is the only hotel in the city centre, conveniently placed on the central square. Rooms are poky and fairly basic, but many enjoy great views over the city (although the most spectacular views are from the rooftop bar).

Villa La Granjita

Carretera de Malezas Km2.5 (042 21 8190/1/fax 042 21 8149/www.hotelescubanacan.com). **Rates** CUC 38-42 single; CUC 50-55 double; CUC 75 suite. **Credit** MC, V.

Located well beyond the city limits, this cabin complex enjoys a natural setting, featuring a trim, landscaped pool area. Much of the large half-grassy, half-wooded site has been pleasantly untampered with. Rooms are in two-storey rustic lodges.

Tourist information

Havanatur

Calle Máximo Gómez #13, entre Boulevard y Alfredo Barreras (042 20 4001/2). **Open** 8.30am-noon, 1-5pm Mon-Fri; 8.30am-12.30pm Sat. **Map** p203.

Getting there

By bus

Astro and Víazul buses arrive at the Terminal de Omnibuses Nacionales (042 29 2113/4), located on the corner of Carretera Central and Calle Oquendo, in the west of the city (a CUC 2-3 taxi ride from the centre). Astro buses (CUC 18) to Havana leave at 6.30am, 9.30pm and 9.40pm and take about 4.5hrs. Víazul buses (CUC 21) leave at 9.30am, 3.30pm and 8pm and take 4hrs.

By train

Santa Clara's railway station (042 20 3256/2896) is on the Parque de los Mártires in the northern part of town, but you have to go across the park to Calle Luís Estévez Norte #323 to book. There are two departures daily for Havana (CUC 10). The journey takes about 5hrs.

Cienfuegos Province

Cienfuegos

Reaching out into the calm waters of a huge enclosed bay, with a waterfront promenade, broad avenues beautifying its leafy southern neighbourhoods and some sumptuous colonial architecture, **Cienfuegos** is one of the prettiest, most laid-back large cities in Cuba. Founded in 1819, much later than many provincial capitals, by French settlers, as opposed to Spanish, this distinct history imbues the city with a sense of newness and gracefulness,

especially in the Punta Gorda district to the south, where mid 20th-century Miami is evoked in the open-plan layout.

If you only have time for one sight, make it the intriguing **Palacio del Valle** (Calle 37, esquina 0, 043 55 1226) at the very tip of Punta Gorda. This magnificent Moorish-looking palace was built in 1917 and is the most intricately styled and designed construction in Cienfuegos. A drink on the roof bar or a meal at the restaurant (*see p207*) are the best ways of enjoying the building's ornate interior.

The city's other main district is the colonial centre, known as Pueblo Nuevo, centred around **Parque Martí**. Bordering this main square are numerous important buildings, among them the **Catedral de Nuestra Señora de la Purísima Concepción** (043 52 5298, closed to tourists Sun, free). Founded in 1869, the cathedral boasts lovely stained-glass windows from France.

Also on the square are the **Teatro Tomás Terry** (043 51 3361), one of the city's cultural landmarks (guided tours are available); the **Museo Provincial** (043 54 9722, closed Mon); the grandiose **Ayuntamiento** (City Hall); and several centres for art and culture including the Casa de la UNEAC and the Fondo de Bienes Culturales, which displays art.

Outside of the city, some 20 kilometres (12.5 miles) to the east, is Cienfuegos' famed **Jardín Botánico** (043 54 5115), which contains more than 2,000 species of plants.

Another popular trip is the **Castillo de Jagua** (no phone), at the mouth of the Bahía de Cienfuegos. The 17th-century fortress can be reached by ferry from the wharf in Cienfuegos at Calle 25, esquina 46 (remember to check return ferry times).

Where to eat & drink

There are just two legal *paladares* in Cienfuegos and only one of them (El Criollito) keeps reliable opening hours. There are a large number of eateries charging in national pesos on and around the intersection between Avenida 54 and Calle 37, and these are the best places for eating out on a tight budget but none can compete for quality of food or surroundings with the best of the CUC-charging restaurants. The best places for drinks are the hotels and restaurants, although there are a couple of small bars to be found on and around the main square and Avenida 54.

Café Cienfuegos

Club Cienfuegos, Calle 37, entre 8 y 12, Punta Gorda (043 51 2891 ext 112). **Open** noon-11pm daily. **Main courses** CUC 4-30. **No credit cards.**

Housed in the swankily restored former Yacht Club, where there is also a seafront terrace ideal for sipping Mojitos, this is effectively one restaurant split into two locations. The elegant, high-ceiling upstairs dining room knocks the socks off the soulless downstairs cafeteria, but they both have the same seafood, pork, beef and vegetarian paella menu.

Cienfuegos city centre. *See p205.*

El Criollito

Calle 33 #5603, entre 56 y 58 (043 52 5540). **Open** noon-11pm daily. **Main courses** CUC 8. **Credit** MC, V. **Map** p205 ❶

The strip lighting doesn't lend this front-room *paladar* a particularly warm atmosphere, but the three main dishes – chicken, pork and fish – are tasty enough and served with generous side orders.

El Embajador

Avenida 54, esquina 33 (043 45 1108). **Open** 10am-6pm Mon-Sat. **No credit cards. Map** p205 ❷

A cool, subdued and comfortable little bar at the back of a cigar shop that's just right for a daytime break or an early-evening rum.

1869

Hotel Unión, Calle 31, esquina 54 (043 55 1020). **Open** 7am-9.45am; noon-2.45pm; 7-9.45pm daily. **Main courses** CUC 7.50-21. **No credit cards. Map** p205 ❸

Formal without being posh, 1869 is one of the most pleasant and stylish restaurants in Cienfuegos. The Cuban cooking is above average, if a little heavy.

Palacio del Valle

Calle 37, esquina 0, Punta Gorda (043 55 1226/ 3021/5). **Open** *Restaurant* noon-10pm daily. *Bar* 10am-10pm daily. **Main courses** CUC 7-13. **Credit** MC, V.

The resplendent dining hall in this magnificent city landmark certainly makes for a ritzy location. The seafood menu is nothing more than satisfactory, although the lobster is good value. The rooftop café-bar has splendid views of the city and bay.

Nightlife

Most nightspots are in Punta Gorda, where there are several open-air music venues. The best of them for live music is **Casa de la Música** (Calle 37, entre 4 y 6, 043 55 2320, closed Mon), which gets going at about 10.30pm. With a smaller capacity but a more regular live music schedule is **Club Cienfuegos** nightclub (Calle 37, entre 8 y 12, 043 51 2891). Other than on and around Parque Martí, the place with the most action in the colonial part of town is **Club El Benny** (Avenida 54 #2904, entre 29 y 31, 043 55 1105), a smart couples-only nightclub.

Where to stay

Casas particulares in Punta Gorda, in the south of the city, tend to have gardens and be more spacious, but often lack the colonial character of many of the houses in the Pueblo Nuevo section of the city. Other than the three hotels in the city, there are the **Club Amigo Rancho Luna** (Carretera Rancho Luna Km18, 043 54 8012, www.hotelescubanacan.com, singles CUC 55-65, doubles CUC 70-80) and the more intimate **Faro Luna** (Carretera Rancho Luna Km18, 043 54 8030, www.hotelescubanacan.com, singles CUC 55-65, doubles CUC 70-80) on the nearby coastline, which offer seafront accommodation within 20 kilometres (12.5 miles) of town.

Casa de la Amistad

Avenida 56 #2927, entre 29 y 31 (043 51 6143/ casamistad@correosdecuba.cu). **Rates** CUC 20-25. **No credit cards. Map** p205 ❶

A unique place to stay thanks mostly to the lively, eminently sociable elderly couple who run this large, eclectically decorated and furnished *casa particular*. Leonor is fond of cooking vegetarian dishes.

Chico

Avenida 14 #5306, Playa Alegre, Punta Gorda (043 51 5397). **Rates** CUC 20-25. **No credit cards.**

This bungalow *casa particular*, owned by an elderly couple, in a quiet corner of Punta Gorda, right next to a tiny and very scrappy beach, has two reasonably equipped rooms and a neat little covered terrace out the back.

Hotel Jagua

Calle 37 #1, entre 0 y 2 (043 55 1003/fax 043 55 1245/www.gran-caribe.com). **Rates** CUC 60-74 single; CUC 85-105 double; CUC 125-150 suite. **Credit** MC, V.

The block-building of this four-star hotel is nothing special, but the location is attractive and tranquil, near the tip of Punta Gorda on the edge of the bay. Facilities include a pool, restaurants and a cabaret.

Hotel Unión

Calle 31, esquina 54 (043 55 1020/www.hoteles cubanacan.com). **Rates** CUC 90 double; CUC 100-170 suite. **Credit** MC, V. **Map** p205 ❷

Beautifully restored and well located, this colonial building is by far and away the best option in central Cienfuegos. It has 49 rooms, a beautiful swimming pool, plus a gym, restaurant and rooftop bar.

Palacio Azul

Calle 37, entre 12 y 14, Punta Gorda (043 55 5828/ www.hotelescubanacan.com). **Rates** CUC 47 single; CUC 50 double. **Credit** MC, V.

Perfectly located for easy access to Punta Gorda nightlife, this magnificent neo-colonial mansion has a conversely down-to-earth atmosphere with well-appointed, spacious and characterful rooms.

Tourist information

Cubatur

Calle 37 #5399, entre 54 y 56 (043 55 1242/www. cubatur.cu). **Open** 9am-noon, 1-6pm Mon-Fri; 9am-noon Sat. **Map** p205.

Havanatur

Avenida 54 #2906, entre 29 y 31 (043 55 1613/ 1393). **Open** 8.30am-5.30pm Mon-Fri; 8.30am-noon Sat. **Map** p205.

Getting there

By bus

All buses arrive at the bus station on Calle Gloria, between 56 and 58 (043 51 5720). Astro buses to Havana (CUC 17) leave four times a day (6.15am, noon, 4.15pm and 7.30pm) and take 5hrs. Víazul buses (CUC 21) leave twice a day (8.15am, 1pm) and take about 4hrs.

By train

The railway station is across the road from the bus station (043 52 5495). In theory the service to Havana (CUC 16) runs once a day, but it's not very reliable.

Sancti Spíritus Province

Trinidad

Trinidad was among the first seven villas, or towns, to be established in Cuba, founded as the Villa de la Santísima Trinidad on the site of a small Indian settlement in 1514. It wasn't until the 19th century that it became one of the most prosperous cities on the island, when sugar cane became the principal crop in the nearby valley, the Valle de los Ingenios, creating great wealth for the landholders and enabling them to build the fine homes in the city that have lasted to this day. The Wars of Independence against Spain (1868-78, 1895-8) took a heavy toll on this area, and by the time they were over, neighbouring Cienfuegos and Matanzas provinces had become the hub of the sugar trade. Trinidad remained in a time warp. No longer a bustling commercial centre, though now one of the most visited towns on the island, it has maintained its charm and elegance through the centuries.

The city, with its red-tiled roofs, cobblestone streets, stained-glass arches and intricately designed wrought-iron grated windows, was declared a World Heritage Site by UNESCO in 1988. It is one of Cuba's premier tourist attractions, with daytrippers arriving by the coachload to see this intact relic of Spanish colonial times, and although it remains unspoilt physically, there is a slight sense that it has become a bit over-run by visitors. For this reason, there is an extra appeal to visiting Trinidad in low season.

The city's museums and churches are concentrated around the delightful **Plaza Mayor** (**photo** *p210*). Here you can sit on one of the park benches, in the shade provided by a canopy of bougainvillea, and watch the daily life of the town. As tourism takes a hold over this small town, hustlers are increasing in numbers and persistence, and it can be a drain on the visitor. The **Iglesia Parroquial de la Santísima Trinidad** (0419 3368, closed to tourists Sun) on the north-east side of Plaza Mayor was the main parochial church of Trinidad until 1814, when it was destroyed by a storm. The church was rebuilt in 1892 and resumed its former role. Today it is important for the relics it contains, such as the 1713 Cristo de la Vera Cruz (Christ of the True Cross).

As befits a historic city, Trinidad has a number of museums, housed in the former homes of the landed aristocracy. On the Plaza Mayor itself, the Palacio del Conde Brunet is now the unmissable **Museo Romántico** (Calle Echerrí, esquina Simón Bolívar, 0419 4363, closed Mon), its beautifully restored rooms perfectly laid out with outstanding pieces of colonial-era furniture; the former home of Sánchez Iznaga has become the **Museo de Arquitectura Colonial** (Calle Desengaño #83, closed Mon).

The **Museo Municipal de Trinidad** (Calle Simón Bolívar #423, esquina Callejón de Peña, 0419 4460, closed Fri) is located a block below the square in a mansion that once belonged to the Borrell family. The highlight of this museum is the tower with picture-postcard views.

The **Museo Nacional de la Lucha Contra los Bandidos** (Calle Echerrí, esquina Piro Guinart, 0419 4121, closed Mon, Sun) portrays the history of the five-year-long battles between local rebel forces and counter-Revolutionary insurgents (*bandidos*) hiding out in the surrounding Escambray mountains after 1959. Exhibits include photos, authentic objects and parts of a US U-2 spy plane that was shot down in the area. The museum is housed in the former San Francisco de Asís convent, a block north of Plaza Mayor. The bell tower of the convent, something of a symbol of the town, is often open to the public. From here you will have a breathtaking view over Trinidad and down to the coast.

Where to eat & drink

Considering its size and villagey feel, Trinidad has a surprising number of restaurants, most of them in fine colonial mansions. For snacks head for **Las Begonias** café, on the corner of Gutiérrez and Simon Bolívar, which is also something of a social hub for young locals and travellers. There are three legal *paladares* in Trinidad, all offering relatively good-value food. If you stay in a *casa particular*, your hosts will almost certainly offer you meals. The restaurant in the **Iberostar** hotel (*see*

Trips Out of Town

p210) serves a fantastic but very expensive CUC 35 buffet dinner and CUC 20 set-menu lunches.

Going out for a drink in Trinidad, especially after dark, is no party. There are two or three isolated bars and walking around hoping to discover somewhere is usually a fruitless experience. It's worth checking during the day that something is going on at one of the spots and then settling in for the night once you get there – otherwise you'll do a lot more walking than drinking.

Estela

Calle Simón Bolívar #557, entre Márquez y José Mendoza (0419 4329). **Open** noon-10pm daily. **Main courses** CUC 8-10. **No credit cards**. **Map** p209 ❶

Some of the best meals and heartiest portions in the city are dished up at this down-to-earth, verdant backyard *paladar* in the historic centre. Classic Cuban home cooking at its best.

El Jigue

Calle Villena, esquina Piro Guinart (0419 6476). **Open** 10.30am-10.30pm daily. **Main courses** CUC 5-24. **Credit** MC, V. **Map** p209 ❷

A rustic appeal complements the elegance here, the wooden shutters, uneven floor and iron railings on the windows in slight contrast to the chandeliers and carved-wood furniture. Standard Cuban dishes and good value set-meals served at less than CUC 8.

Sol y Son

Calle Simón Bolívar #283, entre Frank País y José Martí (no phone). **Open** noon-11pm daily. **Main courses** CUC 7-15. **No credit cards**. **Map** p209 ❸

An impressive *paladar* that puts most state restaurants in Trinidad to shame. Professional service, excellent Cuban food, ample helpings and a wonderful plant-filled neo-colonial location. Avoid the one or two non-Cuban dishes, like the pasta.

Taberna La Canchánchara

Calle Villena, esquina Piz Girón (0419 6403). **Open** 9.30am-8pm daily. **No credit cards**. **Map** p209 ❹

The speciality at this sociable drinking spot, located in a narrow colonial courtyard, is a cocktail made of rum, honey, lemon and water, from which the tavern takes its name. In addition to the drinks, it's also good spot for live music in the day.

Trinidad Colonial

Calle Antonio Maceo, esquina Colón (0419 6473). **Open** 9am-10.45pm daily. **Main courses** CUC 4-22. **No credit cards**. **Map** p209 ❺

The widest choice of dishes that you can find among the state restaurants is here at the Trinidad Colonial, in the most aristocratic of the old buildings housing those restaurants. Lobster, shrimp, various fish dishes, beef and pork are cooked with a reasonable variety of ingredients including rum and hot sauce. This large building also contains one of the best and most authentic colonial-style bars in Trinidad.

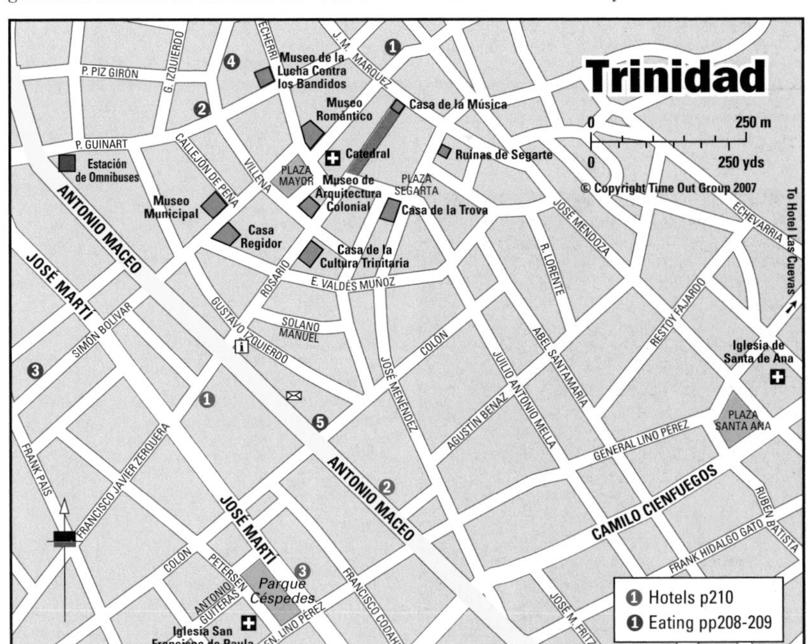

Nightlife

The Discoteca Ayala (0419 6133, closed Mon), known locally as **La Cueva**, occupies a huge cave and is certainly Trinidad's most novel night out, but it struggles to attract the crowds who usually head for the **Casa de la Música** (Calle Zerquera #3, 0419 6622), more specifically the small open-air plaza halfway up the broad staircase leading up to it. This and the smaller **Casa de la Trova** (Calle Echerrí #29, no phone), a block east of the Plaza Mayor, are the two best spots for live music. Nearby, the courtyard at the **Ruinas de Segarte** (Calle José Menéndez, esquina Márquez) has a mixed bill of traditional music and Afro-Cuban dance.

Where to stay

Despite the endless stream of tourists visiting this small city, there are only two hotels in Trinidad, with several more down on the nearby **Península de Ancón** (*see p211*). There are, however, countless *casas particulares*. It is worth ringing ahead if staying at a house in Trinidad, as your hosts will often meet you at the bus station to prevent the swarm of insistent hosts and *jineteros* waiting there from poaching their guests.

Casa Tamargo

Calle Zerquera #266, entre José Martí y Antonio Maceo (0419 6669/felixmatilde@yahoo.com).
Rates CUC 20-25. **No credit cards**. **Map** p209 ❶
With well over a decade of experience, the owners of this *casa particular* run a tight ship, and keep their delightful house in great shape. There's a smart dining room and leafy, trim central patio.

Plaza Mayor in Trinidad. *See p208.*

Hostal Colina

Calle Antonio Maceo #374, entre Lino Pérez y Colón (0419 2319/zulenaa@yahoo.com.es). **Rates** CUC 25-30. **No credit cards**. **Map** p209 ❷
A truly outstanding *casa particular*, run by two sisters. The hotel-standard rooms with stained-glass windows over the doors are at the back of the modern half of the house, while the 1830-built colonial half has been beautifully restored to its original splendour, replete with period furnishings. To top things off there's a fantastic outdoor bar.

Hostal Digna Aguila Ibargollin

Calle Frank País #476, entre Fidel Claro y Santiago Escobar (0419 4301/manuelca2@hotmail.com).
Rates CUC 20-25. **No credit cards**.
The highlight at this *casa particular*, owned by an elderly couple, is the lovingly kept and designed mezzanine backyard, with a neatly enclosed patio and a *bohío*-roof covered bar complete with rocking chairs. The two double rooms for rent are simple.

Hotel Las Cuevas

Finca Santa Ana (0419 6133/4/fax 0419 6161/ www.hotelescubanacan.com). **Rates** CUC 50-59 single; CUC 65-75 double; CUC 87.75-101.25 triple; CUC 90 suite. **Credit** MC, V.
A 15-minute walk from the historic centre, this tidy complex spread around a hillside offers seclusion and serenity in simple but sufficiently equipped concrete cabin bungalows, most of which have great views. There's a pool, a good restaurant and nightly music and dance shows on the terrace.

Iberostar Grand Hotel Trinidad

Calle José Martí #262, entre Lino Pérez y Colón, Parque Céspedes (0419 6073-5/fax 0419 6077/ recepcion@iberostar.trinidad.co.cu). **Rates** CUC 135-210 single; CUC 190-270 double. **Credit** MC, V. **Map** p209 ❸
Opened in 2006, this superb luxury colonial conversion is the classiest place to stay in the whole province. Every space is a highlight, from the dignified smokers' lounge and the grand buffet restaurant to the splendid central patio enclosed by stone arches, and the 40 sumptuous rooms.

Tourist information

Cubatur

Calle Zerquera, entre Antonio Maceo y Gustavo Izquierdo (0419 6314/www.cubatur.cu).
Open 9am-7pm daily. **Map** p209.

Getting there

By bus

Buses from other provinces arrive at the bus terminal (0419 4448) on Calle Piro Guinart #224, between Antonio Maceo and Izquierda. Astro buses leave every other day for Havana (CUC 21) and take six hours. Víazul buses go twice a day (CUC 25); journey time around five hours.

By car

The *autopista* cuts right through the middle of these central provinces and takes you within 6km (3.5 miles) of the centre of Santa Clara. For Cienfuegos and Trinidad, take the Circuito Sur, which runs down from the *autopista*, just inside the western Cienfuegos provincial border, to the southern coastline, cutting right through both cities before it heads back up to the middle of the island joining up with the Carretera Central.

By train

The railway station (0419 3348) is located on the south-western edge of town, on General Lino Pérez, although it only serves destinations in the nearby area, such as the Valle de los Ingenios (*see below*).

Around Trinidad

Valle de los Ingenios

Sweeping through the hills north-east of Trinidad, towards Sancti Spíritus, the **Valle de los Ingenios** (Valley of the Sugar Mills) was the most important sugar-producing area in colonial Cuba, and has been declared a UNESCO Cultural Heritage Site. Its 65 archaeological plots include the remains of numerous mills, with parts of their machinery and many tools and utensils still intact. You will also find the remains of manor houses, a slave hamlet, warehouses, infirmaries and a bell tower.

The key site within the valley is Manaca Iznaga, one of the most important sugar mills during the 19th century. The best-preserved parts of the complex are the slaves' quarters, the buildings that served as warehouses, and the 43.5-metre (145-foot) Manaca Iznaga tower, which you can climb for a view of the entire valley. The old mansion of the Iznaga family has been fitted out with a bar and restaurant.

The most interesting way to see the valley is on the delightful 1919 steam train that runs between Trinidad and Guachinango (CUC 10 or CUC 21 with lunch; reservations with Cubatur; *see p210*). The train stops at the ruins of the Magua mill, and again for lunch at Manaca Iznaga. The train departs at 9.30am and comes back at 3pm. The regular train costs a fraction of the price.

Topes de Collantes

Twenty kilometres (12.5 miles) north of Trinidad – and surrounded by a totally different type of landscape filled with giant ferns, moss, lichens, pine and eucalyptus trees – the road winds up the mountains of the Escambray to the **Topes de Collantes** hotel and health resort.

The huge **Kurhotel** (042 54 0180, doubles CUC 45-50) offers natural therapies and usually needs to be booked in advance with a programme of treatment; **Los Helechos** (042 54 0330-05, doubles CUC 45-50) and the bungalows of **Villa Caburní** (042 54 0330, doubles CUC 45-50) are the other two hotels open to foreigners. The whole complex has a rather jaded air, and is hardly the luxury health farm many visitors might be expecting.

Treks, available to non-residents for between CUC 3 and 6.50, are the highlight of a visit to the area, but for a guided walk you need to book in advance with the travel agents in Trinidad (*see p210* Cubatur). The most popular trail is to the 62-metre (207-foot) waterfall known as **Salto del Caburní**, with a small pool suitable for bathing. The path is challenging (allow three hours, plus swimming time), but well signposted, and worth the sweat (though avoid the path after rain).

For information on the trails and anything else around Topes de Collantes, visit the **Centro de Información** (042 54 0219) at the heart of the resort. Note that this area is only accessible by car or private taxi from Trinidad.

Península de Ancón

South of Trinidad – a short taxi ride from the centre of town – the **Península de Ancón** is caressed by the warm blue-green waters of the Caribbean, and is a good spot for watersports. Most of the peninsula is covered in scrub, but the coastline is attractive and at the far end the beach is a pretty good spot to relax.

The 279-room **Hotel Ancón** (0419 6120/3-9, www.hotelescubanacan.com, doubles CUC 100-120) is on the best section of beach – right at the tip of the peninsula. This hotel, a typical piece of Soviet-style concrete-block architecture, isn't pretty to look at from the outside but the rooms aren't bad. Staff can arrange watersports, including scuba diving around the sunken ships along the coast.

The newest addition to Playa Ancón's accommodation options is the swanky **Hotel Brisas Trinidad del Mar** (0419 6500-07, www.hotelescubanacan.com, doubles CUC 130-160), a decent all-inclusive resort designed in pseudo-colonial style, and decked out in bright colours.

Alternative accommodation can be found nearby at the **Hotel Costasur** (0419 6174, www.hotelescubanacan.com, doubles CUC 55-70) on Playa María Aguilar, further down the coast. Built in 1975, it has 111 rooms in the main building and two newer extensions, plus 20 rooms in duplex bungalows. There is a pool and a narrow stretch of sandy beach.

Santiago de Cuba

Cuba's second city has a music scene second to none and a character all of its own.

Musical myths about Cuba come alive in Santiago: the centre echoes with the rhythms of *son*, rumba, salsa, *trova* and bolero and there really does seem to be a band playing on every corner. The country's second city, located some 950 kilometres (600 miles) from Havana at the opposite end of the island, is as remote from the capital in character as it is in distance. The distinctly small-town atmosphere in the narrow streets of the colonial centre belies the city's size, while the local rhythmic accent, relative lack of new development, lower number of foreign visitors and the emphatically natural setting all serve to distinguish it.

The city started life in 1515 at the mouth of the Río Paradas, as the third villa built by Diego Velázquez (*see p12*). The settlement soon moved to its present location and became Cuba's capital city until it was supplanted by Havana in 1607. As one of the nearest points on Cuba to the rest of the Caribbean island nations, Santiago was the recipient of various waves of immigration. The first African slaves in Cuba were brought here; French colonists fleeing from neighbouring Haiti settled here, and Jamaicans often made the short trip.

Santiago has often been an incubator of revolution, having played a key role in the revolutions of both 1898 and 1959. One of the major historical attractions of the Revolution, the Moncada Barracks, is located here.

The city is noted for its hospitality and the warmth of its people, but it has become a prime hustling spot in recent years. The colonial centre, though hilly, is most easily explored on foot. As with all cities in Cuba, streets in Santiago have pre- and post-Revolution names, with the newer names the ones used on street signs and in this guide.

Santiago is hottest in July – and not just temperature-wise, as this is festival month. Rum flows in rivers, and the city throbs with music and dancing. Each *barrio* competes with its costumes, music and dancing before judges to win bragging rights for the year. The Carnival party stretches over a week towards the end of July and coincides with the national celebration of 26 July – the date of Castro's attack on the Moncada Barracks in 1953 (*see p214*). Indeed, the original attack by Fidel and his companions was set on this date to ensure the guards would be in no fit state to fight.

There's also a pre-Carnival party, the **Festival del Fuego** every year in early July. Contact the Casa del Caribe on 022 64 2285 or caribe@cult.stgo.cult.cu.

Carnival time in Santiago.

Sightseeing

Parque Céspedes

Parque Céspedes is the city's main square and is an eclectic mix of colonial and modern architecture. On the west side of the square is the oldest house in Cuba, completed in 1530. The site is now known as the **Museo de Ambiente Histórico** (Calle Félix Peña #612, entre Heredia y Aguilera, 022 65 2652, closed Sun), and is crammed with Cuban furniture from the 16th to 18th centuries.

On the south side of the park is the provincial cathedral, the white **Catedral Nuestra Señora de la Asunción** (Calle Heredia, esquina Félix Peña, closed Mon). It has been rebuilt four times due to an unfortunate series of disasters, from earthquakes to pirate attacks; the current structure dates from 1818. On the General Lacret side of the cathedral is the **Museo Arquidiocesano** (022 62 2143, closed Sun), its two small atmospheric rooms heaving with religious artefacts gathered mostly from the city's churches and the cathedral itself.

On the north side of the square is the **Ayuntamiento**, the town hall, a 1940s reconstruction of a 1783 design. Fidel Castro gave his victory speech from the balcony on 2 January 1959, after the defeat of Batista.

Around Parque Céspedes

Calle Heredia runs along the southern side of Parque Céspedes at the foot of the cathedral, and is lined with craftspeople and artists selling paintings, woodwork and musical instruments. It is also home to numerous cultural sites, the most famous of which is the **Casa de la Trova** at No.206 (*see p216*), a symbol of Santiago's deep-rooted musical culture. Further along, the **Museo del Carnaval** (Calle Heredia #303, esquina Pío Rosado, 022 62 6955) traces the history of Santiago's famous carnival (*see p212*). Folkloric dance performances sometimes take place here at 4pm.

A block north is the **Museo Emilio Bacardí** (Calle Pío Rosado, esquina Aguilera, 022 62 8402), the grand building housing the personal collection of the famous industrialist Emilio Bacardí Moreau, founder of the rum dynasty. The museum's collection includes a 19th-century printing press, items relating to slavery and an array of old weapons, as well as an interesting art gallery on the second floor.

South-west of Parque Céspedes is the **Museo de la Lucha Clandestina** (Calle General Rabí #1, entre Diego Palacios y San Carlos, 022 62 4689, closed Mon). This beautifully restored colonial building was once a police station and is now devoted to telling the story of Frank País and other local revolutionaries. Back towards

Sorting the men from the boys: street chess in Santiago's **Parque Céspedes**. *See p213*.

Parque Céspedes, proceed one block east of Padre Pico along Bartolomé Masó where, on the corner of Corona, you'll find the **Balcón de Velázquez**, a fortified platform with spectacular views. Four blocks east along Calle Bartolomé Masó, at No.358, is the **Museo del Ron** (022 65 1873, closed Sun), which explains the rum-making process and displays more than 100 different bottles of Cuban rum.

Cuartel Moncada & Museo Histórico 26 de Julio

No visit to Santiago is complete without a visit to the **Cuartel Moncada** (Moncada Barracks), where Fidel launched his first (and unsuccessful) attack on the Batista regime on 26 July 1953. Part of the building has been turned into the **Museo Histórico 26 de Julio** (Calle General Portuondo, esquina Moncada, 022 62 0157, closed Mon). The site is located a few blocks north of the **Coppelia** ice-cream stand, just off the Avenida de los Libertadores. The museum provides insight into the pre-Revolutionary period in Cuba from 1953 to 1959. Tours in English are available on request.

Plaza de la Revolución

From the turning for the Cuartel Moncada it's about a kilometre north on Avenida de los Libertadores to the Plaza de la Revolución, where, at the junction with Avenida de las Américas, General Antonio Maceo, one of the foremost revolutionaries of the 19th-century Wars of Independence and a native of Santiago, is honoured. The monument consists of a gargantuan bronze statue of the general on horseback, surrounded by huge iron machetes rising from the ground at different angles. The **Museo Antonio Maceo** (022 64 3053/3712) is housed below the monument, and features holograms of artefacts from the general's role in the Wars of Independence.

Reparto Vista Alegre

A kilometre east of the centre, connected to it by the Avenida Victoriano Garzón, is the former high-class neighbourhood of Vista Alegre, a great place for an aimless wander around its broad, leafy and subdued avenues lined with 1940s and '50s mansions. There are one or two specific sights here providing some focus for a visit. The **Centro Cultural Africano Fernando Ortiz** (Avenida Manduley #106, esquina 5ta, 022 64 2487, closed Sun), also known as the Casa de África, depicts the rich African heritage of Cuba. The area is home to the **Casa de las Religiones Populares** (Calle 13 #206, esquina 10, 022 64 3609, closed Sun), with displays on religious practices in Cuba, especially *santería*.

Castillo del Morro

Some 16 kilometres (10 miles) south of the centre is the impressive **Castillo del Morro** (022 69 1669), atop the bluffs over the entrance to Santiago Bay. The best part of the tour is a visit to the **Museo de Piratería** (022 69 1569) inside the castle, which explores the pirate attacks made on Santiago in the 16th century. A cannon-firing ritual, similar to the one in Havana (*see p138*), takes place every evening at sunset. There's a good restaurant on the site (022 69 1576; main courses CUC 8-10), best visited when the sun is setting over the mountains and sea.

Where to eat

Santiago is no place for foodies, but there are a few decent restaurants. All the hotels have restaurants, the best of which are at the Meliá Santiago and Casa Granda (for both, *see p218*).

La Casona

Meliá Santiago de Cuba, Avenida de las Américas, esquina M, Reparto Sueño (022 68 7070). **Open** 7-10am, 7-10pm daily. **Main courses** CUC 20. **Credit** MC, V.

Nirvana if you want to stuff yourself silly or just fancy an alternative to Cuban food. The huge all-you-can-eat buffet dinner includes quail and liver among the wide meat selection, good-quality pastas, a decent salad bar and even soft, unstale bread!

Don Antonio

Plaza Dolores (022 65 2205). **Open** 11am-11pm daily. **Main courses** CUC 2.70-17. **No credit cards. Map** p213 ❶

Classic Cuban cuisine in the smartest restaurant on the square. It also has the most comprehensive menu, with fish, lobster, beef, pork and chicken.

Las Gallegas

Calle San Basilio #305, entre General Lacret y Hartmann (022 62 4700). **Open** noon-11pm daily. **Main courses** CUC 8. **No credit cards. Map** p213 ❷

One of the only legal *paladares* in the colonial centre, Las Gallegas is a great spot to eat and watch people on the street. The speciality is lamb, with chicken and pork making up the rest of the menu.

La Isabelica

Meliá Santiago de Cuba, Avenida de las Américas y M, Reparto Sueño (022 68 7070). **Open** 7-11pm daily. **Main courses** CUC 11-50. **Credit** MC, V.

The finest dining in the city is at this intimate and formal hotel restaurant, where dishes like grilled lobster, chateaubriand in béarnaise sauce and curried chicken breast with plum and pineapple are served.

La Maison

Avenida Manduley #52, esquina 1ra (022 64 1117). **Open** noon-10pm daily. **Main courses** CUC 5-14. **No credit cards**.

An elegant whitewashed mansion with a fancy restaurant in the rear and a café out front almost suffocated by lush vegetation. The Cuban food is nothing to write home about, it's just good wholesome Creole cooking.

Salón Tropical

Calle Fernández Marcané #310, entre 9 y 10 (022 64 1161). **Open** 5pm-midnight Mon-Fri; noon-midnight Sat, Sun. **Main courses** CUC 4.60-7.50. **No credit cards.**

Without question the best, most professionally run *paladar* in Santiago, set on a pretty, suburban roof terrace with fantastic views and an outdoor grill. The varied menu includes liver, kebabs, chicken, fish and pork; the cooking is both subtle and simple.

ZunZún

Avenida Manduley #159, esquina 7ta (022 64 1528). **Open** noon-10pm daily. **Main courses** CUC 6-21. **No credit cards**.

A classy restaurant attempting to serve Cuban haute cuisine – not entirely successfully – this place does at least break the local mould, with dishes like beef in red wine sauce and shrimp in garlic butter. It's set in a 1940s mansion, with tables on the veranda.

Where to drink

Many of the music venues (*see p216*) are good places for a drink, while places operating only as bars are few and far between. The **Museo del Ron** (*see p214*) also has a slick little bar.

Bar Cachita

Hotel Libertad, Calle Aguilera #652, Plaza de Marte (022 62 7710). **Open** 10am-2am daily. **No credit cards. Map** p213 ❶

A popular rooftop bar with fabulous views of the east of the city, but a very limited drinks selection.

Santiago's **Tivolí** district.

Santiago 1900

Calle Bartolomé Masó #354, entre Pío Rosado y Hartmann (022 62 3507/9698). **Open** noon-11pm daily. **No credit cards. Map** p213 ❷

The table-service café-cum-bar upstairs at the former Bacardí family mansion, split between two balcony terraces, is a nice relaxing spot for a drink. Avoid the restaurant downstairs, though.

Arts & entertainment

Music

The music scene in Santiago is world-class. Most major venues are within a 15-minute walk from the main square, and cover is cheap (CUC 1-3), so if you're not impressed you can simply move on. Much of what you will hear around town is *son*, the style that originates from the countryside around Santiago.

The **Casa de la Trova** (Calle Heredia #206, 022 62 3943/2689) is the city's premier music venue. There are usually several shows during the course of the day and night in the Salón Principal (closed Mon), where the headline acts stage their performances and doors open for the main event around 9pm. Outside on **Patio de Virgilio** (closed Mon) there are daytime shows (3-7pm), and sometimes a night-time show too, which usually starts at 8.30pm.

Hotel Casa Granda (*see p218*) has a veranda overlooking the main square. Early evenings feature live music, with some very good groups performing everything from *son* to doo-wop. Drinks are a tad expensive but you're in pole position. The roof terrace has panoramic views and hosts occasional concerts.

The **UNEAC** headquarters (Calle Heredia #266, esquina Pío Rosado, 022 65 3465, free), across from the Museo del Carnaval, is a cultural centre hosting art exhibitions and poetry readings as well as an irregular schedule of varied live music, including everything from hip hop, rumba and salsa to folkloric dance.

Los Tejadas (Calle Heredia #304, entre Porfirio Valiente y Pío Rosado), also known as the Casa de Artex, is based in the small courtyard of a restored colonial building. It's a beautiful spot to listen to music under the open sky. Nearby **Coro Madrigalista** (no phone), in the alleyway between Calle Heredia and Calle Aguilera, is a funky community club (named after the choir that rehearses here) offering music from 9pm Monday to Saturday. The quality of performers is uneven, but admission is only CUC 1. Events are posted outside. Half a block from the other side of Parque Céspedes, there's more open-air fun to be had at **Bar Claqueta** (Calle Félix Peña #654, entre Heredia y Bartolomé Masó), which is open 24 hours.

The **Casa de la Música** (Calle Corona #564, entre Aguilera y José A Sacó, 022 65 2227/2243) is one of the slicker (or, depending on your point of view, tackier) live music venues, attracting a lively crowd and where live salsa and *son* performances are followed by a disco.

Everyone knows Patio de la Música Tradicional Cubana as **Los Dos Abuelos** (Calle Pérez Carbo #5, Plaza Marte, 022 62 3302/3267). It's a lovely colonial-style music club – an open-air venue with tightly-packed seating for 40 – featuring many of the same groups that appear at the Casa de la Trova.

Casa de las Tradiciones (Calle Rabi #154, entre Princesa y San Fernando) is a true neighbourhood haunt. This venerable club in the Tivolí area is open from 9pm and features nothing but *son* and *trova*, with some very good bands and plenty of guest artists sitting in. Being a little off the main tourist circuit saves this small venue from being overrun with foreigners. Definitely worth the trek.

One other musical event of note is the annual Festival de la Trova, held in mid March, hosted by Eliades Ochoa of Buena Vista Social Club fame, and his own touring band Cuarteto Patria.

When it comes to clubbing, the most popular venue in Santiago is **Discoteca Club Tropical** (Autopista Nacional Km1.5, 022 68 7020, closed Mon), at the Cabaret Tropicana venue (*see p217*), where the DJs play a lively mix of salsa, *reguétón* and techno. The local authorities have shut the place down on occasions on account of sex tourism, hence the couples-only rule. You'll have to negotiate the scrum at the gate, but be persistent and you'll eventually be admitted – though you may need to make up a 'couple' with one of the young Cubans waiting in line.

Back in the centre there's **Club 300** (Calle Aguilera, entre Hartmann y General Lacret, 022 65 3532), a tables and chairs affair with a dance floor. Attracting a younger local crowd who like their music loud and flashy is **Discoteca La Iris** (Calle Aguilera #617, entre Monseñor Barnada y Paraíso, closed Mon, Tue), just off Plaza Marte. It's a throwback to the early days of disco, with strobe lights and pounding beats. The downstairs café is open 24 hours.

Dance

The world-renowned **Ballet Folklórico Cutumba**, considered by many to be the island's best folkloric dance company, has its home at **Casa del Estudiante** (Calle Heredia #204, 022 62 7804). The colonial building hosts occasional performances, plus rumba and salsa events at odd times during the week. **Casa del Caribe** (Calle 13 #154, 022 64 2285), a cultural

Making use of a tropical rainstorm.

centre in Vista Alegre, also puts on interesting Afro-Cuban folkloric events, generally on Thursday nights and Sunday afternoons. It's best to call ahead to see what's cooking, but it's nearly always worth attending.

A different kind of dance experience is to be had at **Cabaret Tropicana** (Autopista Nacional Km1.5, 022 64 2579, closed Mon). This popular open-air venue has seating for up to 800 people and fills to capacity in high season. Choreographer Ernesto Arminan has created a panorama of Cuban history through music and dance. The costumes are exquisite, the dancing exciting and the band excellent. Worth the steep admission (CUC 20 Tue-Fri, CUC 30 Sat, Sun).

Where to stay

There is a surprisingly small number of decent hotels in the centre of town, so you should book as far in advance as possible. There is, however, no shortage of *casas particulares*, with a big concentration within five or six blocks on all four sides of Parque Céspedes. Breakfast is generally offered (costing extra) and it's a good idea to accept, as few places besides hotels serve food before noon.

Casa Colonial Maruchi

Calle Hartmann #357, entre General Portuondo y Máximo Gómez (022 62 0767). **Rates** CUC 15-25. **No credit cards. Map** p213 ❶

This sociable *casa particular*, run by the affable and hospitable Maruchi, can't be beaten for character in Santiago de Cuba, and scores highly for style and comfort too. An alluring central garden patio has a resident peacock. The brick-wall bedrooms have en suite bathrooms.

Casa de Nercy y Oscar

Calle Sánchez Hechavarría #560, entre Mayía Rodríguez y San Augustín (022 65 2192/ oscarmontoto@yahoo.com). **Rates** CUC 15-25. **No credit cards. Map** p213 ❷

The two well-equipped rooms at this comfortable *casa particular* are effectively mini-apartments, and one of them is particularly spacious. The *casa*'s attractive roof terrace affords great views over the bay and mountains.

Casa de Señora Vilma Cerrero

Avenida Victoriano Garzón #332, entre 2da y 3ra, Reparto Santa Bárbara (022 65 6981). **Rates** CUC 15-20. **No credit cards.**

This *casa particular*, set on one of the city's main arteries, has plenty of outdoor space, including a roof terrace and jungle garden.

Casa de Señores Aida y Ali

Calle José Antonio Saco #516, entre Mayía Rodríguez y San Augustín (022 62 2747/65 3891/lperez@medired.scu.sld.cu). **Rates** CUC 15-25. **No credit cards**. **Map** p213 ❸

A homely *casa particular* a block from Plaza Dolores. There are two good rooms; the more comfortable of them, up on the pleasant roof terrace, comes with a kitchenette. The roof also provides sweeping views.

Gran Hotel

Calle José Antonio Saco #312, esquina Hartmann (022 65 3020/ana@ehtsc.co.cu). **Rates** CUC 26 single, CUC 32 double. **No credit cards**. **Map** p213 ❹

Just around the corner from the Parque Libertad, this is very much an old-school Cuban hotel, with a practical and straightforward flavour. Though you will get better facilities and rooms at some of the other hotels listed here, this is definitely the cheapest hotel open to foreigners.

Hostal San Basilio

Calle Bartolomé Masó #403, entre Pío Rosado y Porfirio Valiente (022 65 1702/fax 022 68 7069). **Rate** CUC 46. **Credit** MC, V. **Map** p213 ❺

The eight well-appointed rooms at this delightful little hotel are huddled round two patios. Pleasant blend of colonial charm and refined comfort.

Hotel Las Américas

Avenida de las Américas y General Cebreco, Reparto Sueño (022 64 2011/2695/fax 022 68 7075/comerc@hamerica.hor.tur.cu). **Rates** CUC 44-53 single; CUC 58-69 double. **Credit** MC, V.

If you fancy a more subdued location than that offered by the town centre hotels, but can't stretch to the Meliá Santiago de Cuba over the road, this is the place for you. There's a decent pool, musical evening entertainment and internet access.

Hotel Casa Granda

Calle Heredia #201, esquina General Lacret, Parque Céspedes (022 68 6600/3021-4/fax 022 68 6035/comercia@casagran.gca.tur.cu). **Rates** CUC 67-96 single; CUC 78-112 double. **Credit** MC, V. **Map** p213 ❻

Among the hotels in the town centre, this grand old colonial beauty is by far the most upmarket and best equipped; it arguably has the best location too, though the noise of the main square may be a put-off. The roof terrace has views of the bay.

Hotel Libertad

Calle Aguilera #652, Plaza de Marte (022 62 7710/reservas@libertad.tur.cu). **Rates** CUC 32-38 double. **Credit** MC, V. **Map** p213 ❼

A small yet spacious hotel with a pleasant lobby, a rooftop bar with great views and enough colonial charm to make it a real bargain. Poor food though.

Meliá Santiago de Cuba

Avenida de las Américas, esquina M, Reparto Sueño (022 68 7070/fax 022 68 7170/www.solmelia.com). **Rates** CUC 115-133 double; CUC 165 suite. **Credit** MC, V.

On a broad, leafy avenue in a laid-back part of the city, the Meliá is by far the flashiest option in Santiago. There are three good restaurants and a fantastic pool area, along with all the facilities you'd expect from a five-star hotel.

Resources

All the big hotels have tour company desks for flights and further hotel reservations.

Hospital

Clínica Internacional de Santiago de Cuba, Avenida Raúl Pujol, esquina Calle 10 (022 64 2589).

Internet

Centro de Llamadas Internacionales, Calle Heredia, esquina Félix Peña, Parque Céspedes. **Open** 8.30am-7.30pm daily. **Map** p213.

Police station

Calle Corona, esquina Sánchez Hechavarría (emergencies 116). **Map** p213.

Post office

Calle Aguilera, entre Plaza Dolores y Donato Mármol (no phone). **Open** 8am-4pm Mon-Sat. **Map** p213.

Tourist information

Cubatur, Calle Heredia, esquina General Lacret (022 68 6033/www.cubatur.cu). **Open** 8am-8pm daily. **Map** p213.

Getting there

By air

International and domestic flights come into Aeropuerto Internacional Antonio Maceo (022 69 1052/3), located 5km (3 miles) south of the city. There are more than a dozen flights a week to Havana (CUC 100) and the journey takes 1-2.5hrs.

By bus

Interprovincial buses arrive at the Astro terminal (022 62 3050) on Carretera Central and Yayaró, near Plaza de la Revolución. Tourist buses pull into the Víazul terminal (022 62 8484/6091) next door. Both companies run daily services to Havana. The journey takes about 15hrs (Astro CUC 42; Víazul CUC 51).

By car

Driving to Santiago from the west, the motorway (*autopista*) gets you as far as the Sancti Spíritus-Ciego de Ávila provincial border; then take the Carretera Central down to Palma Soriano in Santiago de Cuba province. From here there is a 5km (3 mile) stretch of road linking up to the 50km (30 miles) of autopista that will take you into the city.

By rail

The railway station (022 62 2836) is on Avenida Jesús Menéndez, north-west of the city centre. Standard trains to and from Havana run every other day (CUC 30). There is also a deluxe train, Locura Azul (also known as the *tren francés*), departing on alternate days for CUC 42. Journey time is around 14 hours.

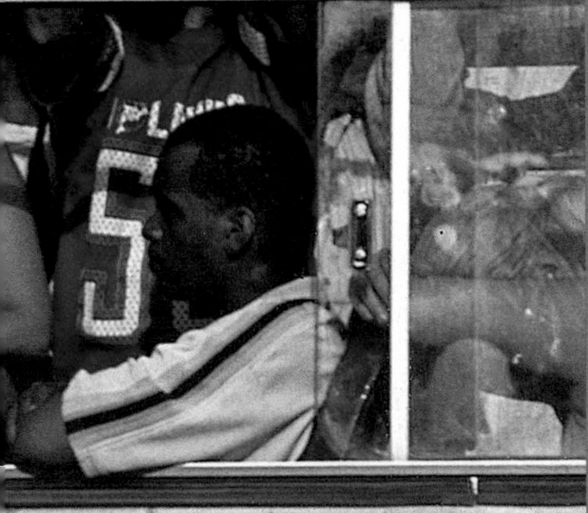

Directory

Features

A ***camello***. *See p221.*

Directory

Getting Around

Arriving & leaving

By air

Flights to Havana arrive at **Aeropuerto Internacional José Martí** (switchboard 649 5777, information 266 4644). The airport is 25 kilometres (16 miles) south-west of central Havana and has five terminals, with no interconnecting transport apart from taxis. Domestic flights use Terminal 1; charter flights from Miami and New York arrive at Terminal 2; most other international flights arrive at the large, modern Terminal 3 (flight information 266 4133/33 5754); Terminal 4 serves the military; Aerocaribe flights come into a fifth terminal. Terminal 3 has a 24-hour tourist information desk with English-speaking operators (266 4133). There is a bureau de change and several car rental desks (*see p222*).

There is no public transport directly to or from the international terminals, but it's easy to get a taxi. The journey into town takes 30 minutes and costs around CUC 13-16. The taxis lined up immediately outside Terminal 3 are the most expensive. Cheaper rates can be found by calling or picking up a Panataxi or other tourist taxi (*see p222*). Some tourist agencies run minibuses into town for tour groups, which independent travellers can often use for a charge.

Public buses (*see p221*) run from the domestic terminal to Vedado and Parque de la Fraternidad in Old Havana but, due to the distances between terminals, this service is useful only if you have arrived on a domestic flight at Terminal 1.

There are direct flights to Havana from Europe, Canada, the Caribbean and Central and South America, many of which are run by the country's national airline **Cubana de Aviación** (*see below*). Cubana flights are sometimes the cheapest available but they can be unreliable and are often heavily overbooked, so be sure to confirm your return flight at least 72 hours in advance of departure time.

From the UK, Cubana scheduled flights to Havana via Holguín depart from London Gatwick twice a week, on Wednesdays and Saturdays. A better option is **Virgin Atlantic** direct (twice a week from Gatwick; 08705 747747, www.virgin-atlantic.com), while other choices include **Iberia**, via Madrid (in the UK 0870 609 0500, in Havana 204 3444/5, www.iberia.com), **Air France**, via Paris, (in the UK 0870 142 4343, in Havana 833 2642, www.airfrance.fr), **Martinair** (in Havana 833 3730, www.martinair.com), **Air Jamaica**, often direct (in the UK 020 8570 7999; in Havana 833 2448, www.airjamaica.com) and **Air Europa** (in the UK 0870 777 7709, in Havana 204 6904, www.air-europa.com).

There are no direct flights to Cuba from Australia, New Zealand or the USA (the planes coming in from Miami, Los Angeles and New York are not for tourists, they are for licensed travellers and Cuban Americans; *see also p232* **US citizens travelling to Cuba**). Cubana runs scheduled services from Toronto and Montreal in Canada, from Cancún and Mexico City in Mexico and from several Caribbean, Central and South American airports. Nassau in the Bahamas is a handy stopover for people connecting from the US. If you're flying from the Caribbean, try **Air Jamaica** (*see above*) or **Aerocaribe** (www.aerocaribe.com.mx), and from Mexico, try Aerocaribe or **Mexicana de Aviación** (www.mexicana.com.mx).

All foreign visitors departing from Cuba on international flights are charged a CUC 25 departure tax. This must be paid at either of the designated counters between the check-in areas and passport control – so make sure you keep some CUCs. For details of customs regulations in and out of Cuba, *see p225*.

If you need to change your departure date, you must go in person to the relevant agency. Most charge a fee for this, depending on the type of ticket, starting from CUC 100. Check regulations with your booking agency before you leave Cuba, and if you are told you have a flexible ticket, bring a letter with you, if possible, to confirm this.

Cubana de Aviación

Havana office *Calle 23 #64, entre P y O, Vedado (836 4950/204 6679/www.cubana.cu).* **Open** 8.30am-4pm Mon-Fri; 8.30am-noon Sat. **Map** p254 B12.

London office *Unit 50, Skyline Village, Limeharbour Road, E14 9TS (020 7537 7909/booking line 020 7536 8178 10am-4pm).* **Open** *Phone line* 9.30am-4.30pm Mon-Fri.

By sea

There are no international scheduled ferry services to Havana and, due to the US embargo, few cruise ships visit Cuba as part of their itinerary. Cruise ships that do call in at Havana dock at the **Terminal Sierra Maestra** (Avenida San Pedro #1, La Habana Vieja, 862 3024 ext 129).

By rail

There are daily departures from the central train station in Havana to all major towns in the country (and vice versa). Tourists must pay for tickets in convertible pesos (CUC). The regular train from Havana to Santiago, for example, costs CUC 30 single (you can never buy return tickets on buses or trains) and takes about 16 to 18 hours. Conditions are basic: no air-conditioning, no buffet and bad toilets; on the plus side you can expect spacious carriages and a friendly, bustling atmosphere.

The *rápido* train is faster (taking about 12 hours to Santiago), has air-conditioning (take something warm to wear as temperatures can be less than tropical) and better toilets. Also take plenty of food and drink with you and be prepared for delays. Unfortunately, although train journeys are a great way to see the country, many rail lines are old and dilapidated and Cuba does not have a particularly good rail safety record.

Reserve tickets by phone or go in person at least one hour before departure and before 7pm if you're leaving during the night. Don't forget you'll have to show your passport for any type of travel transaction. For details of the national rail network and services, *see p190*. For information on the Hershey electric train that runs between Havana and Matanzas, *see p96*.

Estación Central de Ferrocarriles

Calle Arsenal, esquina Egido, La Habana Vieja (862 1920/861 2959/866 3320). **Map** p256 F14.

By bus

Modern, relatively luxurious, long-distance **Víazul** buses, and the sometimes older and less reliable **Astro** buses, depart from the national bus station (*see below*), as well as from the Víazul terminal in Nuevo Vedado, and travel to destinations around the country. For general information on bus travel in Cuba, *see p190*.

You can book with Víazul by phone, but you should pay for your ticket one day before your trip and always arrive at least half an hour before departure time. The buses are very punctual. Astro doesn't have a booking system for foreigners, and only two places are reserved for tourists on each bus – so get there at least an hour prior to departure time.

Fares are reasonable; for example, travelling Havana–Viñales by Astro takes around three hours and costs CUC 10. The same journey by Víazul takes about the same time and costs CUC 12.

There are also a number of well-organised bus agencies operating for tourists, including **Transmetro** (830 6584), **Panatrans** (881 1013) and **Panautos** (55 5456/5559-67), which run excursions and trips for tourists. These buses can also be hired for group travel. Contact major hotels for further information.

Astro (Asociaciones de Transportes por Omnibus)

Terminal de Ómnibuses Nacionales, Avenida de la Independencia (Rancho Boyeros) #101, Vedado (870 9401/ 879 2456). **Open** 24hrs daily. **Map** p254 D10.

Víazul

Avenida 26, esquina Zoológico, Nuevo Vedado (870 3397/811 1413/882 0645/www.viazul.com. **Open** 24hrs daily. **Map** p253 E7.

Getting around Havana

Buses

Before the Special Period, Havana's buses (*guaguas*, pronounced 'wa-was') efficiently served the whole city. But fuel shortages, lack of spare parts and general inefficiency during the 1990s left the whole system on the brink of collapse. The situation has improved a lot in the last few years, but most buses are still subject to massive overcrowding, which can make even the shortest journey a daunting undertaking. During rush hours (7-9am and 4-6pm), the struggle to get on and the crush of passengers can be hard work. Unless you're travelling long distances, it's usually quicker and more pleasant to walk, although bussing around is very cheap as all fares, even for tourists, are in fractions of a peso.

Transmetro rents out charter buses to companies to ferry their employees, although they do sometimes pick up individuals.

Ómnibus Metropolitanos is the main provider. Its *ruteros* (standard city buses, 40 Cuban¢ flat rate) and *taxibuses* (one Cuban peso) run non-stop services between the city and the bus and train stations. Much of the system's overload is carried by the *metrobuses*, lumbersome and highly unattractive converted articulated trucks that have two humps, hence their more common name: camels (*camellos*). *Camellos* carry up to 300 passengers and cover marginally longer distances, with a 20¢ flat rate. *Habaneros* call them X-rated buses because they often contain 'bad language, violence and sex'. The 'violence' is usually nothing more than pushing and shoving, while the 'sex' is usually limited to a spot of groping, made easy by the extreme proximity of your fellow passengers. It's an uncomfortable way of travelling and is not for the faint-hearted.

Contrary to appearances, queues (*colas*) operate religiously at most bus stops (*paradas*), so it is very important to ask for *el último* (the last in the queue) and board the bus directly after that person. Once on the bus, keep a very close eye on your belongings (crowded buses are fertile ground for pickpockets) and, importantly, make your way to the exit at the back of the bus as soon as possible to avoid missing your stop.

Most buses run at least hourly during the day and slightly less often between 11pm and 5am. The more popular routes (the P1 and P4, for example; *see below*) run every 15-30 minutes, sometimes more frequently. There are special night buses, less frequent, between midnight and 5am. There are neither route maps nor timetables for local buses but the front of each bus normally displays the route number and destination. (*camellos* are prefixed by the letter M). Many of the *camellos* converge on Parque de la Fraternidad in La Habana Vieja. Other useful places to pick up buses are Parque Central in Centro Habana and La Rampa (Calle 23) in Vedado.

Two examples of popular routes, useful for longer journeys, are the P1 and P4. The **P1** runs from Miramar to the San Miguel del Padrón district, along Avenida 3ra via Línea in Vedado to Infanta in Centro Habana. The **P4** runs from the roundabout on Avenida 5ta and Calle 164 in Playa (called El Padadero de Playa) via Calles 23 and 26 in Vedado, and Reina and Galliano in Centro Habana and finally to La Habana Vieja.

Taxis

Although much of Havana (and especially La Habana Vieja) is best explored on foot, taxis are a very useful and relatively cheap way to travel between neighbourhoods. There are plenty to choose from, although they are harder to find in less-visited areas. Just stand by the side of the road and flag one down. Sounds simple, but there are so many and various options that it can be very confusing.

Official tourist taxis (*turistaxis*) are modern cars with the taxi signs on the roof. The cheapest rates are offered by **Panataxi** (*see p222*), which can in theory be booked by phone (55 5555), though they never seem to answer. Rates within the city are not negotiable and meters start at CUC 1, with each kilometre charged at 45¢ (night-time rates are about 20% higher). Prices for long distances can be negotiated, and, depending on the type and size of car, can compare favourably to the cost of hiring a car. The second cheapest tourist taxi service is **Habanataxi** (*see p222*).

Cheaper than the tourist taxis are the black and yellow Ladas of the **Empresa Provincial de Taxi**. These vehicles are state-owned but privately operated and are not permitted to take foreigners. If you are on your own and don't look too obviously like a tourist, you might be able to flag one down, but phone bookings are only accepted for Cubans going to and from hospital. If they are running on a set route (on a main road from one area to another), you will normally pay ten Cuban pesos for any destination along that route, but if you want to go off-route or door to door you will need to negotiate a price before you get in.

Many of the large 1950s US-made vehicles (*máquinas*) with a cardboard 'taxi' sign on the dashboard are licensed in Cuban pesos and are not permitted to take tourists. The rate is fixed at ten pesos for set routes with negotiable prices for anything else. They travel a set route and can be found rumbling along Avenida 3ra in Playa, along Línea or Calle 23 in Vedado, mostly going to and from La Habana Vieja. They are also found at specific places (such as bus terminals), where they set off only when they have a full load.

There are also numerous illegal taxis, often driven by underpaid

Cuban professionals, trawling the streets and waiting outside hotels. Both permit-holding and illegal drivers can usually be hired for half a day for about CUC 20. Drivers may be fined if caught with a foreigner in the car, but many are willing to take the risk. With any non-metered taxi, always agree the price before you get in and don't be afraid to bargain, although don't be insensitive about this, as taxis are pretty cheap and it is seen as bad manners for a foreigner to barter just for the sake of it.

Aside from all the normal tourist taxis you can hail a ***cocotaxi***, a small three-wheeled scooter that looks like a scooped-out orange, with a bright yellow cab (the black ones are for Cubans only and charge in Cuban pesos). These fun taxis are now found as far out as Miramar and charge a flat CUC 1 rate plus 50¢ per kilometre (but check approximately how much your journey is going to cost beforehand as they don't have meters). You can try ordering a *cocotaxi* by phone (873 1411) and they can also be hired to ferry you around for CUC 7-8 an hour. They're not the safest method of transport, so just use them for shorter jaunts.

For another uniquely Cuban experience look out for the beautifully maintained, pre-Revolution classic American cars used as official tourist taxis. **Gran Car** (41 7980) has a fleet of models in tip-top condition. These gorgeous cars can be hired either as taxis for short runs, or with a driver by the hour (CUC 25-30) or the day (CUC 125-150), with fixed prices for trips out of town (a one-day return to Viñales, for instance, costs from CUC 326, and the same to Varadero beach costs from CUC 166). Contact Gran Car or the main hotels for details.

Tourist taxi companies

Fénix 866 6666
Habanataxi 648 9086/9090
Micar 204 2444/204 5555
OK Taxis 877 6666
Panataxi 55 5555
Rex (limousine service, most expensive) 642 6074
Transgaviota 33 9780

Other forms of transport

Rickshaw-style tricycles, known as *bicitaxis*, are a very pleasant way of roving the streets of La Habana Vieja and Centro Habana. They are cheaper than tourist taxis and a far more relaxing way of covering short distances. Expect to pay one CUC per ride within La Habana Vieja but always agree this before mounting.

Horse-drawn carriages can be picked up at various tourist spots in La Habana Vieja for a 50-minute tour of the Old City or a 50-minute tour of 'New Havana' (including Plaza de la Revolución). Reservations cannot be made by phone, but you can find them from 10am onwards outside of hotels Inglaterra and NH Parque Central (for both, *see p44*), in the Plaza de San Francisco and in front of the Capitolio (*see p72*), as well various other places around the city. Each tour costs around CUC 30 for two people or CUC 40 for four people. The *cochero* (driver) will also provide a normal taxi service to wherever you want to go. For more information contact Fénix (861 9380).

Driving

Traffic travels on the right in Cuba. Speed limits, which are rigorously enforced, are 20kph (12.5mph) in driveways and car parks; 40kph (25mph) around schools; 50kph (31mph) in urban areas; 60kph (37mph) in rural areas; 90kph (56mph) on paved highways; and 100kph (62mph) on the motorway. Any traffic fines you incur (from CUC 10 to CUC 30, depending on the infringement) must be paid within 15 days. Check details with your car rental agency.

Driving can be useful for venturing out of the city, but isn't recommended in Havana itself. As well as missing out on the pleasure of walking the streets or being driven in the back of a classic American car, visiting drivers are likely to find themselves horribly confused by the city's warren of one-way streets. The volume of traffic is increasing all the time and Havana now has noticeable rush-hour traffic, as well as many dangerous potholes.

Many *habaneros* drive quite recklessly and are inclined to make unpredictable manoeuvres. The use of indicators and brake lights isn't particularly widespread, so watch out for surprise stops (sometimes breakdowns), often in the middle of the road, and unannounced turns in fast-moving traffic. Cyclists present a further hazard as they also observe few rules of the road and often ride two or three (and an electric fan) per bike. If you can, avoid driving around La Habana Vieja, much of which is pedestrianised.

Due to its history of serious transport problems, Cuba has become a country of hitchhikers; many tourists are surprised to find that the overwhelming majority of hitchhikers in Havana are women. If you're driving in or outside the city, it is much appreciated if you stop to give lifts to people. Just be careful to keep your belongings in sight, as some might be tempted.

Car hire

None of the international car hire companies has offices in Cuba, so visitors are reliant on the national providers (for all, *see p223*). For quality, security and comfort choose **Rex**, then **Habanautos**. But the cheapest is **Micar**, then **Habanautos**. With the rise in tourism, the demand for hired cars in Cuba sometimes outstrips the supply. In high season (December to April) it may be wise to reserve a car before you arrive, although this can only be done 15 days in advance. Once in Havana, most hotels have a car hire desk or can help you make arrangements. The main car rental companies have offices all over the city and in the arrivals area of Terminal 3 at the airport; some are open 24 hours daily.

To rent a car, you must be at least 21 years old, with one year's driving experience, and must hold a valid national driving licence or an international driving permit.

Renting a car is the easiest way to see the country, but it's not cheap. Unless you're looking for a long-term hire, prices don't vary much. Most companies charge between CUC 50 and CUC 100 per day, plus a deposit of CUC 200-300. The fee and deposit must be paid in advance by cash, credit card (not one issued by a US bank) or travellers' cheques. Rates include unlimited mileage, but insurance, fuel and parking are extra. On hiring the car you'll be charged CUC 1.10 a litre (cash) for a tank of petrol (check that it's full), but don't expect a refund for any fuel remaining in the tank when the car is returned. You'll be offered insurance (payable in cash) either covering accidents but not theft (CUC 10-12 per day) or covering all risks except loss of radio and spare tyre (CUC 15 per day). Any additional drivers are normally charged a flat fee of CUC 10-15 each or CUC 3 per day. If you don't fancy driving yourself around, some companies also provide chauffeurs, for which you'll pay a daily rate, plus room and board if you're away overnight. Keep your hire agreement with you until you return the car or you'll be charged a CUC 50 penalty.

If you are involved in an accident or have something stolen from your car, you'll need to obtain a police report (*una denuncia*) in order to make an insurance claim. Allow plenty of time to do this as police work can be extremely slow. Hire cars can be poorly maintained, so try to get a new vehicle and always check it carefully. A test drive is a good idea. Make it clear if you want seat belts in the back as many cars don't have them.

Cubacar 273 7233/272 2146/ 273 2277/www.cubacar.info
Havanautos 203 9658/9805/ 9347/www.havanautos.com
Micar 204 2444/3437/ micar@colombo.cu
Transtur 838 3995-6

Breakdown services

Your car hire company should deal with all breakdowns and repairs. Check that your hire contract includes this information, plus emergency numbers, and call them first in case of any accident or emergency. In addition to this, repair services, but not recovery services, are provided by a branch of **Oro Negro** at Avenida 5ta #12001, esquina 120, Playa (208 6149), between 8am and 7pm Monday to Saturday. There are other branches, open 8am-4.30pm, at Avenida 7ma, esquina 2, Miramar (204 1906); Avenida 13, esquina 84, Playa (204 1938); Calle 114, esquina Cujae (267 6815), near the airport; and at Calle 17, esquina 12, in Vedado (833 9238).

If your broken-down car needs towing, call the very professional 24-hour Mercedes Benz subsidiary of **MCV Servicios SA** (260 7521 ext 2). They will charge nothing to get to the car, and 80¢ per kilometre to tow it to wherever you want to go.

Fuel stations

Servi-Cupet (SC) and **Oro Negro** (ON) both have several 24-hour petrol stations in the city (ON at Almendares, by the tunnel, Avenida 7ma, Miramar; SC at the corner of Malecón and Paseo, Vedado). Various grades of petrol are sold. It is illegal to put anything but *especial* in hired cars (95¢ per litre at time of writing). Do follow this rule, otherwise you may get the attendant into trouble and damage the car. Local petrol stations, which require special vouchers and charge in Cuban pesos, often run out of fuel and don't carry *especial*. Avoid buying black market fuel from individuals on the street – it not only harms the car but puts you and other people at risk; a well-publicised crackdown on illegal petrol sales in 2006 makes this even riskier now.

Parking

There are no parking meters on the streets of Havana and, although you have to avoid places where the pavement is painted yellow, it is unusual – thanks to the relatively low numbers of vehicles – to have difficulties finding a parking space. Car theft can be a problem, so it's advisable to use designated hotel car parks (*parqueos*) with a guard (*custodio*). These charge from 50¢ an hour, with overnight fees of CUC 1 (for non-hotel guests). There are car parks opposite the hotels Sevilla, Nacional, Habana Libre and Meliá Cohiba, among others (for all, *see pp36-51*). Illegally parked cars are subject to fines and may be towed.

Campervans

For a Cuban-style Route 66 experience, hire yourself a big, new, luxurious campervan and take to the open road. One week in this six-person roadster will set you back CUC 1,106, plus CUC 40 for a full tank of petrol and a refundable deposit of CUC 400. The price includes insurance and, if your budget won't stretch for the week, the daily cost is CUC 158 all in.

Campingcar

Calle 3ra, entre 12 y Malecón, Vedado (tel/fax 833 7558/cubacamper@ enet.cu). **Map** p253 A8.

Cycling

Cycling became a necessity due to the fuel shortages during the Special Period and remains a very common mode of transport, despite widespread potholes, copious fumes and the perils of sharing the road with the average unpredictable *habanero* motorist. Most Cubans use cumbersome Chinese bikes, although mountain-style bikes are becoming more common.

Punctures are inevitable given the state of the roads, and repair workshops are numerous throughout the city (look for the '*Ponchera*' sign). A puncture repair job costs ten Cuban pesos. There are scores of bicycle parking places (*parqueos*) where you pay one or two pesos to leave your bike in the charge of an attendant. You should still secure it well. These *parqueos* are crucial as you can never safely leave your bike on the street, even if you have a good lock. Spare parts and tools are scarce, so bring whatever you might need with you if you are travelling with your own bike. Contact the **Comisión Nacional de Ciclismo** (95 3776/1286/panaci@enet.cu; *see also p184*) for further information.

If you are travelling to the eastern side of the bay or to the eastern beaches, you can take the handy **Ciclobus**, which transports you and your bike through the tunnel from Parque El Curita (two blocks behind the Capitolio building on Calle Dragones) in La Habana Vieja. The fare is 40¢ one way.

Bicycle hire

Although you can very easily arrange to borrow a bike from a Cuban for a few days (expect to pay around CUC 2-3 a day), you can also hire one from **Orbe** (*see below*) for CUC 2 an hour or CUC 12 for 24 hours. You must leave your passport or copy of it, and a deposit. Also try major hotels for bike hire. Your alternative is to pick up a second-hand bike from the Cuatro Caminos market (*see p78*) for somewhere between CUC 20 and CUC 40, which be cheaper than hiring one.

The Club Nacional de Cicloturismo Gran Caribe (*see p184*) will provide bikes for those taking part in one of its cycling tours. For spectator cycling events, *see p183.*

Orbe

Edificio Manzana de Gómez, Calle Obispo, entre Agramonte (Zulueta) y Avenida de Bélgica (Monserrate), Centro Habana (860 2617). **Open** 9am-4pm Mon-Sat. **Map** p256 D14.

Motorbikes & scooters

Groovy little scooters can be hired from **Rumbos** outlets; they are a great way to get around the city. You can find branches in Parque Central, Calle Galiano #401 at the corner of San Rafael in Centro Habana or on Avenida 3ra at the corner of 30, Miramar (204 5491). Most major hotels also have outlets. Prices are around CUC 10 for an hour, CUC 13 for two hours, or CUC 24 for the day. If you hire for a number of days or weeks, prices drop significantly. Take good care on the roads, watch out for heavy downpours, patches of oil, potholes and the unpredictable manoeuvres of Cuban drivers.

Walking

As a pedestrian, keep a lookout for *bicitaxis* and *cocotaxis* when you cross the street, as they tend to come whizzing out of nowhere. Otherwise, walking is one of the most pleasant ways of enjoying Havana, especially in the city's denser areas, such as La Habana Vieja or Centro Habana, where walking is more practical. Distances between areas in Havana are relatively large.

The Malecón – the city's seaside promenade, connecting La Habana Vieja, Centro Habana and Vedado – makes for a lovely walk.

We've included street maps for most major tourist areas at the back of this guide; a more extensive one by Ediciones GEO is available at tourist offices around town.

Resources A-Z

Addresses

In Cuba (and in this guide), addresses state first the street name, then the number (#), followed by the two cross streets (*entrecalles*) between which the building is situated. Thus, an address given as Calle Oficios #6, entre [or e/, or e/n] Obispo y Obrapia, will be found on Calle Oficios, between Calle Obispo and Calle Obrapía. If a building is on or near the corner (*esquina*) of two streets, both streets are given, but the street where the entrance is located tends to be given first. So the Depósito del Automóvil, Calle Oficios #13, esquina Jústiz, will be on Calle Oficios at the corner of Calle Jústiz. (This address could also be given in a shorter form, ie Calle Oficios y Jústiz.) A street name followed by 's/n' indicates that the building has no street number. Residential addresses sometimes specify *altos* (upper floor), *bajos* (ground floor) or *sótano* (basement) in their address, or use *primer piso* (first floor), *segundo piso* (second floor) and so on.

Some street names in the city centre were changed after the Revolution, but *habaneros* are inclined to use the old and new names indiscriminately. To make matters worse, the words *calle* (street) and *avenida* (avenue) are often omitted entirely in directions or an address; even *habaneros* sometimes confuse the two. Hence, Cubans often give directions that refer to well-known landmarks, not streets.

We have given the new name of streets with the old name in brackets. Most maps follow this practice. Here is a list of streets with two names, with old names in brackets. Agramonte (Zulueta); Aponte (Someruelos); Avenida Antonio Maceo (Malecón); Avenida de México (Cristina); Avenida de Bélgica (northern half) (Monserrate); Avenida de Bélgica (southern half) (Egido); Avenida del Puerto (Avenida Carlos Manuel de Céspedes and Calle San Pedro); Avenida de España (Vives) Avenida de la Independencia (Rancho Boyeros); Avenida de Italia (Galiano); Avenida de los Presidentes (G); Avenida Salvador Allende (Carlos III); Avenida Simón Bolívar (Reina); Brasil (Teniente Rey); Calzada (7ma); Capdevila (Cárcel); Enrique Barnet (Estrella); Leonor Pérez (Paula); Línea (9na); Máximo Gómez (Monte); Padre Varela (Belascoaín); Paseo de Martí (Paseo del Prado); San Martín (San José).

Attitude & etiquette

Cubans are generally very warm and friendly, and usually well disposed towards tourists. As a foreigner you will often be expected to pay for Cuban friends if you go out eating or drinking with them as they simply won't have the money to pay or chip in. If you want to pay, you can help avoid an uncomfortable situation by saying *yo invito* (it's my treat), which can then be accepted or refused. Of course, many Cubans assume that foreigners are rich (which relatively speaking, they are). However, many others find this situation intensely embarrassing and like to help pay whenever they can. A good thing to do together is to go to the movies or the theatre, both of which cost only a few Cuban pesos at most.

While Cubans often address those whom they don't know as *Compañero/Compañera* (comrade), it's more appropriate for foreigners to use *Señor/Señora/Señorita* with strangers. When you don't know an adult, always use *usted* rather than *tu* 'you'. Both women and men greet females and children, even those they don't know well, with one kiss on the cheek and much affection. Men tend to shake hands with other men.

Everyday life for a Cuban demands an enormous amount of patience. As a tourist you may easily feel frustrated by things that don't work (*no funciona*), that take a very long time, or aren't in stock (*no hay*), as well as the pandemic lack of customer service. Try to relax, and remember that people here are struggling. It pays to be firm in some situations, but losing your temper will usually make things worse. A charm offensive is the best strategy. Cubans are known for their laid-back ways of dealing with difficulties, so unless you want to end up seriously stressed out (or to stress them out), your best bet is just to adapt and go with the flow.

Tourists of darker skin or of Latin appearance are more likely to suffer harassment from the police. Such visitors are often taken for Cuban and so might be asked to show their passports to gain access to hotels or other places where Cuban citizens might normally be approached. On the other hand, these same visitors avoid lots of the day-to-day hassles (panhandling, touting, etc) that many other foreigners experience.

You will also note if you are staying or moving around in La Habana Vieja (men and women alike) that you will often be approached by persistent people selling cigars, promoting restaurants or rented rooms, or by young people working as prostitutes. These are known as *jineteros* (literally 'jockeys', 'riding' on the backs of tourists). While this is almost never aggressive, it can be extremely wearing. Moreover, you could leave Cuba with a very one-sided impression indeed. Life is tough here, for some more than others, and necessity, unfortunately, breeds all manner of behaviour. Try to get out to the less touristy areas in order to leave Cuba with a more balanced impression.

Travel advice

For up-to-date information on travel to a specific country – including the latest news on safety, security, health issues, local laws and customs – contact your home country government's department of foreign affairs. Fro restrictions specifically applicable to US citizens, *see also p232* **US citizens travelling to Cuba**.

Australia
www.smartraveller.gov.au

Canada
www.voyage.gc.ca

New Zealand
www.safetravel.govt.nz

Republic of Ireland
www.foreignaffairs.gov.ie

UK
www.fco.gov.uk/travel

USA
www.travel.state.gov

Business

Cuba remains politically committed to socialism and the state continues to control all but some very small businesses. However, opportunities in Cuba abound and increasing numbers of suppliers and investors come to do business here every year. Joint ventures have meant the development of big business, especially in tourism, mining, power generation and biotechnology.

In the past, many business visitors have entered Cuba on tourist visas. Now, if you are coming to research business opportunities, you need to apply to the Cuban embassy in your country and ask for an A7 visa (in theory this can be issued on the spot). If you're actually coming to do business, a business visa (*visa de negocio*) will theoretically take between ten and 14 days to process. A journalist visa (*visa de periodista*) will take a minimum of six weeks. You can apply independently, although it's more usual to opt for sponsorship or partnership through an appropriate Cuban company, organisation or institution. Bear in mind that visa regulations can change at short notice, so it's always crucial to check with the Cuban embassy in your country of origin with plenty of time before setting off.

Those visiting Havana for any purpose should remember that annual trade fairs and international summit meetings, as well as the usual peak tourist season, can make it hard to book flights and hotels for the dates you require. *See also p236* **When to go**.

Business services & facilities

There are several hotels offering facilities for the business visitor, including meeting rooms, internet facilities and some secretarial or translation services. These include hotels NH Parque Central (*see p44*), Nacional (*see p48*), Meliá Cohíba (*see p48*) and Meliá Habana (*see p49*).

Representatives at your embassy can usually advise on commercial services available locally, and fax services may be available there for a small fee. If you need Spanish-language support during your stay, **ESTI** (Centre for Translation and Interpreting Services) can provide a translation and/or interpreting service. For more on internet access, *see p227*.

ESTI *Calle Línea #507, entre D y E (entrance on Calle 11), Vedado (833 3978/www.ecn.org/asicuba/cuba/esti.htm).* **Open** 8.30am-5pm Mon-Fri. **Map** p254 A10.

Customs

Things are always changing in this department, so check if in doubt. Incoming visitors over the age of 18 are permitted to bring the following items into Cuba: unlimited quantities of money (though you must declare any amount over CUC 5,000); personal effects; gifts worth up to CUC 50; ten kilograms of medications; three bottles of alcoholic beverages; 200 cigarettes or 50 cigars or 250 grams of tobacco. The import of food, plant and animal products and telecommunications equipment is subject to restrictions. Banned items include narcotics, obscene publications, explosives, weapons (except for licensed hunting weapons) and video recorders. Coming in with a laptop and/or mobile phone will not be a problem but don't consider bringing a computer or other telecommunication equipment. Officials may suspect that you intend to sell them in Cuba, and they could be held in customs until your departure.

Departing visitors can export cigars up to the value of CUC 2,000 (with a sales invoice); 23 cigars (without a sales invoice); and six bottles of rum. For restrictions on the export of art and antiques, *see p125*, and for allowances for US citizens, *see p232* **US citizens travelling to Cuba**. For more detailed information, go to www.aduana.islagrande.cu, the Cuban embassy in your country (*see p235*) or your embassy in Havana (*see below*).

Disabled

Havana is not an easy place for disabled travellers. There are very few amenities or services for people with physical disabilities, and the potholed streets and pavements make moving around very challenging for travellers in wheelchairs or with mobility difficulties. Several of the more expensive hotels (such as Meliá Cohíba, Hotel Nacional, NH Parque Central and Hotel Panorama) claim to have proper facilities, although these may not always meet international standards.

Drugs

There are some recreational drugs available in Havana, but penalties for illegal drug use are very severe. In response to evidence of trafficking by tourists, there has been a widespread clean-up and a fervent anti-drug campaign, which includes keeping a special eye on suspicious tourists. Most foreigners in Cuban jails are there for drug-related offences.

Electricity

The national grid operates on 110-volt, 60AC, as in the USA and Canada. European-managed hotels may have a 220-volt system, or even a combination of both, so check the voltage before plugging in your appliance. Two-pin plugs of the American flat pin type and screw-type light fittings are used. Visitors from the UK and the rest of Europe will need to bring an adaptor. Faulty wiring and sockets are common.

Despite improvements in the electricity supply system, which earned 2006 the title 'Year of the Energy Revolution', Havana is still subject to unexpected electricity blackouts (*apagones*), so do pack a good pocket torch along with some spare batteries. Bigger hotels tend to have their own back-up generators.

Embassies & consulates

Australia and New Zealand do not have diplomatic or consular representatives in Cuba, so those countries are represented by the Canadian and British embassies respectively. The Australian and New Zealand embassies in Mexico can provide consular assistance to their nationals in Cuba. The USA is officially represented by the US Interests Section in Havana.

For the Cuban embassy and consulate in Britain, *see p235*.

British Embassy

Calle 34 #702-704, entre 7ma y 17, Miramar (204 1771/consular fax 204 8104/commercial fax 204 9214/www.britishembassy.gov.uk/cuba). **Open** 8am-3.30pm Mon-Fri. **Map** p248 C4.

Canadian Embassy

Calle 30 #518, esquina 7ma, Miramar (204 2516/fax 204 2044/www.havana.gc.ca). **Open** 8.30am-5pm Mon-Thur; 8.30am-2pm Fri. **Map** p253 B5.

United States Interests Section

Calzada, entre L y M, Vedado (833 3551-9/emergencies & after hours 833 3032). **Open** 8.30am-5pm Mon-Fri. **Map** p254 A11.

Emergencies

In emergencies of any sort (illness to lost luggage), 24-hour assistance agency **Asistur** (*see p226*) is a good first contact. In serious cases contact your embassy (*see above*).

Asistur

Calle Prado #208, entre Colón y Trocadero, Centro Habana (office 866 4499/emergency 866 8527/ 8339/8087/www.asistur.cu).
Open *Office* 8.30am-5pm Mon-Fri. *Emergency phone lines* 24hrs daily.
Map p256 D14.
Asistur deals with insurance claims, arranges replacement documents and helps with financial problems.

Emergency numbers

Ambulance *(emergencia médica) 838 1185/2185*
Ambulance *(via Clínica Cira García) 201 2811-4*
Fire Brigade *105*
Poison Control Centre *(Centro Nacional de Toxicología) 106*
Police *867 7777*

Health

The public health system is rightly held up as one of the Revolution's greatest achievements. Statistically, the number of doctors, dentists, clinics and hospital beds per capita is impressive, although due to lack of funds, the condition of much of the equipment and facilities has been deteriorating badly in recent years. What is lacking in equipment and medicines, though, will often be more than made up for by the care shown by most hospital and neighbourhood health centre staff.

At 75 years for men and almost 80 years for women, life expectancy in Cuba is on a par with that of the US. Many tropical diseases have been eradicated, including typhoid, diphtheria, tetanus, polio and hepatitis A. Mosquitoes are not malarial but can be a nuisance, so bring plenty of repellent with you. There have also been occasional outbreaks of mosquito-borne dengue fever in Cuba; the latest cases were in Havana and Santiago de Cuba in 2006. At the time of writing, houses were being fumigated in Havana once again. However, Cuba's health system has proved itself competent in dealing with cases that occur.

Random checks have been carried out by some of the embassies and the results apparently confirm that the city's water supply is safe to drink. However, many Cubans boil their water as giardia and other parasites are very common. You are highly advised to do the same (ten minutes minimum) or stick to bottled water, which is readily and cheaply available in restaurants, *paladares* and shops. Avoid street food or drink containing water, such as soft drinks with ice cubes or ice-cream. In remote areas, it's a good idea to carry water-purifying tablets or a drinking bottle fitted with a filtration system.

Accident & emergency

In a medical emergency, call your neighbours, all the ambulance numbers and a taxi, as, for whatever reason, emergency services (*see above*) have been known not to answer. Minor accidents can be dealt with at the city hospitals that cater for foreigners (*see below*).

Before you go

You're only required to have a yellow fever vaccination if you're arriving in Cuba directly from a country where there is endemic yellow fever and cholera, or from a country declared infected by the WHO. Otherwise, no other vaccinations are strictly required for travel to Cuba. However, the UK Department of Health recommends vaccinations for hepatitis A, polio and typhoid. You might also want to consider a hepatitis B vaccination. All travellers should have had booster injections for tetanus and diphtheria within the last ten years, and ensure that their measles, mumps and rubella immunisation is complete. Children under 12 should be immunised against TB as a precaution. Check with your doctor before you go. Pregnant women should also check with their doctors which vaccines are safe before being immunised.

Some vaccinations require you to have an initial injection, then a follow-up shot a few weeks later, so make sure you leave enough time for both before your trip; a vaccination course should be started around eight weeks before travel.

For further information on health issues, consult the **Travel Doctor** website, www.traveldoctor.co.uk.

Complementary medicine

The impact of the US blockade and the sudden end to Soviet aid in the early 1990s meant that Cuba was forced to develop alternative medicines and techniques (known as *medicina alternativa* or *medicina verde*). These are now used in virtually all health centres. There is particular interest in acupuncture, acupressure, massage and suction treatment, as well as the so-called *medicina verde*: herbalism, homeopathy and honey remedies.

Alternative remedies are available from **Farmacia Ciren** (Calle 216, esquina 13B, Playa, 271 5044, ext 803). This outlet also provides information on practitioners of complementary therapy. There are also two homeopathic pharmacies in Vedado: Calle 23, esquina M (830 9797, open 8am-6pm Mon-Sat), and Línea, esquina 14 (830 9325, open 8am-4pm Mon-Sat). The international pharmacies (*see p227*) all carry a modest selection of herbal remedies. Most neighbourhoods also have a herb shop (*yerbero*).

Contraception

Condoms (*preservativos*) are widely and very cheaply available, but they're mostly Chinese in origin, unreliable, and about as sensual as a rubber glove. It's advisable to bring your own condoms or any form of contraceptives you might need.

Dentists

Dental treatment at any of the hospitals for foreigners (*see below*) is of a good standard and no more expensive than it would be in the private clinic in Britain.

Doctors

In addition to the doctors at the international hospitals, most four- and five-star hotels have a 24-hour doctor on site. First consultations at hotels cost around CUC 25 during the day, and around CUC 55 after 5pm. Daytime follow-up consultations are around CUC 20.

Hospitals & clinics

Havana has a large number of hospitals, mostly reserved for Cubans, though some are designed to attend to foreign patients as well. The last ten years have also seen the development of a network of hospitals and clinics catering exclusively to foreigners. Most of these are based in and around Havana and other tourist areas. In addition to emergency care, many offer advanced treatment in practically every sphere of health: orthopaedic surgery, neuro-rehabilitation, dentistry, cancer treatment, hypertension, cardiology, various kinds of eye surgery, geriatric conditions and plastic surgery. Some have achieved international recognition, such as **CIREN**, where groundbreaking work has been done on Parkinson's disease, nervous system conditions and spinal injuries affecting both adults and children.

As well as offering emergency and specialist treatment, some clinics are aimed at relatively healthy (and wealthy) people who simply want to improve their quality of life. The four-star **La Pradera**, for example, is specifically promoted as a hotel-cum-health resort.

English-speaking staff are available at most institutions that deal with foreigners. Nevertheless, language can sometimes be a barrier, and knowing a few words of Spanish or taking a fluent friend with you will always help.

Centro Internacional de Restauración Neurológica (CIREN)

Avenida 25 #15805, entre 158 y 160, Cubanacán (273 6003/ www.ciren.cu/ihome.htm).
The International Centre for Neurological Recovery (CIREN) specialises in neurological and neuromuscular disorders, and also offers dental services, holistic treatments and a full range of plastic surgery.

Centro Internacional de Salud La Pradera

Calle 230, entre 15a y 17, Siboney (273 7467/www.cuba.cu/pradera.
This clinic offers a wide-ranging health and beauty programme, including massage, mood therapy, waxing and dietary advice. In 2000 its most famous patient was footballer Diego Maradona, who checked in to recover from his cocaine addiction.

Clínica Internacional Cira García

Calle 20 #4101, esquina 41, Miramar (204 2811-4/4300-09/ www.cirag.cu). **Map** p253 B6.
Exclusively for foreigners, this state-of-the-art clinic offers a broad programme of treatment that includes more than 40 types of plastic surgery (a full nose job, for instance, costs CUC 1,710, including a five-night stay). It's also the best place to seek emergency and dental treatment. Generally speedy, efficient and attentive.

Hospital Cimeq

Avenida 216, esquina 11B, Siboney (271 5022).
A rather grim-looking but above-average hospital where ministry officials, some other Cubans and foreigners are treated.

Hospital Hermanos Ameijeiras

Padre Varela (Belascoaín), esquina San Lázaro, Centro Habana (877 6077/www.cubasolidarity.net/infomed). **Map** p255 C13.
This hospital is for Cubans, but has designated areas for patients paying in CUCs, with a wide range of treatments.

Pharmacies

Local pharmacies open either on *turnos regulares* (8am-6pm Mon-Fri; 8am-noon Sat) or less common *turnos permanentes* (24 hours daily). You'll find these all over Havana but unless you have a very simple complaint their stock may not be of much use. There are also several international pharmacies in Havana, which supply a comprehensive range of medication in CUC. Note that the Hotels Plaza, Comodoro, Habana Libre, Meliá Cohíba, Nacional, Parque Central, the Cira García Hospital and Marina Hemingway all have small pharmacies, and there is a 24-hour pharmacy (266 4105) at the airport (Terminal 3). For complementary medicine and supplies *see p226.*

Centro Internacional de Retinosis Pigmentaria Camilo Cienfuegos *Calle L #151, entre Línea y 13, Vedado (833 3599).* **Open** 24hrs daily. **Map** p254 B11.

Farmacia Casa Bella *Avenida 7ma #2603, esquina 26, Miramar (204 7980).* **Open** 8am-8pm daily. **Map** p253 B5.

Farmacia CIREN *Avenida 25 #15805, entre 158 y 160, Cubanacán (271 5044).* **Open** 8.30am-5.30pm Mon-Fri; 9am-12.30pm Sat.

Farmacia del Clínica Internacional Cira García *Ground floor, Clínica Internacional Cira García, Calle 20 #4101, Miramar (204 2880).* **Open** 24hrs daily. **Credit** MC, V. **Map** p253 C6.
This well-stocked pharmacy is located in an impressive hospital for foreign patients.

Farmacia Internacional Miramar *Avenida 41 #1814, esquina 20, Miramar (204 4350).* **Open** 9am-8.45pm daily. **Credit** MC, V. **Map** p253 C6.

Prescriptions

Due to the relative difficulty in getting hold of medication in Cuba, be sure to bring with you any prescription drugs you may need during your stay, plus aspirins and the usual holiday medications (*see also p235*). For contraception information, *see p226.*

STDs, HIV & AIDS

STDs such as herpes and gonorrhoea are fairly common in Cuba, but syphilis and AIDS are rare. Bring condoms from home – and use them.

Cuba's initial radical programme for treating HIV-positive Cubans – essentially quarantining them in sanatoria – was widely criticised as repressive. In its defence, the Cuban government had at least taken steps to control a disease about which little was known, and the sanatoria themselves gave good levels of care. Policies are very different today: the sanatoria provide optional housing for people living with HIV and AIDS, but also operate as outpatient clinics and support centres. The island now has labour legislation protecting HIV/AIDS carriers, education in schools and safe sex advertising. Cuba currently has one of the world's lowest infection rates.

Lineayuda

830 3156. **Open** 9am-9pm Mon-Fri.
This anonymous helpline is an important source of information about STDs, especially AIDS.

ID

Visitors should carry a photocopy of their passport around with them at all times. You'll need the passport itself when you want to change money, use travellers' cheques, draw out cash using a credit card, or pay for something with a CUC 50 or CUC 100 note.

Insurance

Visitors are highly recommended to take out private travel insurance for their trip to Cuba. A good policy should cover flight cancellation, theft, loss of life and medical charges. Health insurance is particularly advised, since the cost of medical services adds up quickly, even in Cuba. Make sure you are covered for hospitalisation, nursing services, doctors' fees and repatriation.

Internet

Public internet facilities are quite widely available, though are usually expensive and very slow – and very popular, as neither the majority of Cubans or foreign visitors have access to home computers. This means *colas* (queues). In view of this, and the frustratingly slow connections, allow plenty of time and *paciencia* (patience). The good news if you're a night bird is that some of the outlets are open 24 hours. And if you come with a laptop, the more modern hotels – such as the Meliá Habana (*see p49*), Meliá Cohíba and the Nacional (for both, *see p48*) – allow you to link up to the net from your room. Cuba's phone company, **ETECSA**, has two subsidiary internet service providers: **Unidad de Negocios** (881 6666, www.etecsa.cu) and **CITMATEL** (204 3600, www.citmatel.cu/internet2.php).

Internet access

Cibercafe Capitolio (Capitolio building, La Habana Vieja, 862 0485, CUC 5 per hr) is very central and one of the less expensive venues.

ETECSA has internet access for CUC 3 per half hour at its offices: Calle Habana #406, esquina Obispo, La Habana Vieja; Calle Aguila, esquina Dragones, Centro Habana; and at the Lonja del Comercio near the port (*see p61*). They also offer use of phones, PCs and fax.

Almost all mid-range to upmarket hotels have internet access (usually available to non-guests). Try hotels Meliá Cohíba, Inglaterra, Nacional, Habana Libre, NH Parque Central, Meliá Habana and Santa Isabel (*see pp35-51*). Hotel internet centres usually have shorter queues (if any), but you pay for the privilege, with prices up to CUC 12 per hour. At Hotel Inglaterra it is CUC 3 per 30 minutes.

For residents, there are internet services by the hour, starting with a base of around 20 hours per month. The fee is normally between CUC 3 and CUC 5 per hour. This service is offered by **CITMATEL**, Avenida 47 s/n, entre 18A y 20, Miramar (204 3600/comercial@citmatel.cu).

For a review of useful websites about Cuba, *see p239*.

Language

For Cuban-Spanish words and phrases, *see p237*.

Legal assistance

As a first point of call, visitors should contact their consulate (*see p225*) or **Asistur** (*see p226*). The **Consultoria Jurídica Internacional** also specialises in legal help for foreigners.

You can also visit **Bufetes Internacionales** (Avenida 5ta #16202, esquina 162, Playa, 66 6824/204 6749) or **Bufete Especializado de la Notaria del Ministerio de Justicia** (Calle 23, Edificio #501, sótano, esquina J, Vedado, 832 6813/besnet@ceniai.inf.cu). All these services are very professional, but go early as queues tend to form at the crack of dawn.

Consultoria Jurídica Internacional

Calle 16 #314, entre 3ra y 5ta, Miramar (204 2490/cji@cji.get.cu). **Open** 8.30am-noon, 1.30-4.30pm Mon-Fri. **Map** p253 B6.
Other locations: Casa 1, Calle 26, entre 3ra y 5ta, Miramar (206 9549); Casa 2, Calle 22 #108, entre 1ra y 3ra, Miramar (204 5691).

Libraries

Most of Cuba's libraries are poorly stocked and international books are thin on the ground. Libraries of any size, national or local, only offer reference, not lending, services. Even so, take your passport with you.

Biblioteca Nacional de Cuba 'José Martí'
Avenida Independencia, esquina 20 de Mayo, Plaza de la Revolución, Vedado (55 5442-4/www.bnjm.cu).
Open 8am-6pm Mon-Sat.
Map p254 D9/10.
Havana's main library occupies 16 floors. To obtain a library card, bring as many documents as you can in the way of university ID card, diplomas, certificates and proof of educational qualifications. A fee of 1-2 Cuban pesos is charged for the card.

Biblioteca 'Rubén Martínez Villena' *Calle Obispo #59, entre Oficios y Baratillo, Plaza de Armas, La Habana Vieja (862 9037-9).* **Open** 8.15am-7.45pm Mon-Fri; 8.15am-4.15pm Sat. **Map** p256 E16. This library now has multimedia facilities, making it easily Cuba's most modern library, although it's woefully short on books.

Instituto de Literatura y Lingüística *Avenida Salvador Allende (Carlos III) #710, esquina Castillejo, Centro Habana (878 6486).* **Open** 8am-4.30pm Mon-Fri; 8am-1pm Sat. **Map** p254 D12. Probably the best source of novels and non-Spanish texts in Havana.

Lost property

Lost property is *objetos perdidos/extraviados* in Spanish. Airport Terminal 3 has a *reclamaciones* counter open 24 hours daily (642 6172). If you leave something in a taxi, call the taxi office (*see p221*) as soon as possible and be persistent in asking staff to try to track it down.

Media

Unfortunately, and depressingly, it is not what is said, but what is not said, in Cuban press, television and radio that allows us to understand how the country operates. Supporters of the government argue that in the face of external threat from the north it is only prudent to aim for maximum consensus at home. The result is censorship or, to be more precise, self-censorship, which has created silences and gaps and ruled out the possibility of unbiased and accurate reporting. What is published tends to be trite and mediocre, so divorced from everyday experience that it can be wildly unrealistic.

Television

The above is particularly the case with television. Evening news broadcasts on foreign affairs are frequently negative: everything happening abroad is bad, while in contrast all things local are good. Coverage of domestic crime is almost non-existent. Cubans have to rely on word of mouth ('Radio Bemba') for information about what is really going on in the country.

However, some of the more outstanding intellectuals and journalists manage to excel in their ability to analyse. Round table discussions focusing on world and national developments have been broadcast since the time of the Elián González affair in 2000. These are often, but not always, the tedious exchanges that you might expect.

You may not get a chance to pick up more than one Cuban television station while you're here, as most hotels' local reception is minimal, limited to CNN (Spanish and English), HBO and perhaps international versions of Spanish, German, French and Chinese channels. Beyond the hotels, however, there is a choice of five channels in Havana: **Cubavisión**, **Telerebelde**, **Canal Educativo 1 and 2**, and **Canal Habana**, which took to the air in 2006. Cubavisión has a mix of programmes, but its highest ratings are undoubtedly the nightly soap operas and the Saturday night movies. Telerebelde specialises in sport and documentaries, while both of the educational channels offer documentaries and Open University-style classes for children and adults on a wide variety of subjects.

Press

The two main national dailies, *Granma* and *Juventud Rebelde*, comprise only four sheets of paper (eight pages) each. Even a cursory glance reveals that views opposing the official line are not published.

If a genuine forum for critical debate exists within the written press then you are most likely to find it in journals and periodicals. **Bohemia**, **Unión**, **Temas**, **Unión**, **Orbe** and **Tricontinental** are cultural and semi-intellectual publications that provide the kind of in-depth reporting and analysis on matters that are not generally covered in the daily press.

If you do want to keep up with current events during your stay in Cuba, then some of the larger hotels, such as the Habana Libre, Nacional, Meliá Cohíba and Comodoro, stock some international press, although usually Spanish- rather than English-language newspapers.

Bohemia Articles on literature, politics, culture, science, economics and sports.

Cuba Absolutely *www.cubaabsolutely.com.* Independent cultural, business and economic review in English, French and Spanish editions.

Cubarte Calling itself the 'portal of Cuban culture', this trimestral publication covers everything from Cuban theatre to art to music.

La Gaceta de Cuba Covers theatre, photography, cinema and the arts.

Granma *www.granma.cubaweb.cu.* The news bulletin for the Cuban Communist Party. Turgid and often self-righteous in tone. Weekly versions are available in English, French and Portuguese.

Juventud Rebelde *www.jrebelde.cubaweb.cu.* The Young Communist League (UJC) daily. Has more room for manoeuvre than Granma, so some of the articles have spark. The Sunday edition often publishes work by well-known international writers such as Gabriel García Márquez, James Petras and Eduardo Galeano.

Música Cubana This UNEAC (Cuban Union of Writers and Artists) publication comes out quarterly and carries articles on the leading figures and trends within Cuban music.

Orbe *www.prensa-latina.cu.* Features well-written articles on international affairs, science, economics, culture and sports.

Trabajadores *www.trabajadores.cubaweb.cu.* A weekly published by the CTC, the Central Trade Union co-ordinating body. Surprisingly, one of the more interesting periodicals.

Tribuna de La Habana *www.tribuna.islagrande.cu.* News and events in Havana.

Tricontinental *www.tricontinental.cubaweb.cu.* Published in Spanish by OSPAAAL (Organisation of Solidarity of the Peoples of Asia, Africa and Latin America); articles tend to focus on political matters related to the three aforementioned continents.

Unión Published by UNEAC, this journal comprises articles on Cuban and foreign writers and artists.

Radio

Radio has traditionally been something of a hot potato in Cuban politics. Fidel, Che and their Revolutionaries launched Radio Rebelde in 1957 from the mountains to lambaste Fulgencio Batista's regime and publicise their own cause. These days their only opposition comes from **Radio Martí**, the voice of the Miami anti-Castro throng. There are some 70 radio stations currently operating in Cuba.

Radio Enciclopedia *www.radioenciclopedia.cu.* Plays mostly instrumental music.

Radio Habana Cuba *www.radiohc.cu.* Broadcasts worldwide in nine languages on the shortwave and covers current affairs and cultural events from a strictly Cuban government perspective. See the website for frequencies.

Radio Progreso offers music and light entertainment.

Radio Rebelde *www.radiorebelde.com.cu.* Broadcasting music, sports, news and nightly programmes.

Radio Reloj *www.radioreloj.cu.* Offers round-the-clock news bulletins (broadcast in a deadpan voice) on national and international events to the accompaniment of a highly irritating clock ticking and beeping away in the background.

Radio Taíno targets mainly tourists and is broadcast in Spanish and American English. The tone is reminiscent of the worst commercial radio you can think of, but without the commercials.

Money

Cuba has two currencies: the convertible peso (CUC) and the Cuban peso. However, virtually every transaction you make in Cuba will be in convertible pesos. From 1993 until November 2004 US dollars were also legal tender. (The ban was imposed because the US fined a Swiss bank $100 million for conducting business with Cuba in US dollars, forcing the island away from that currency.)

European suppliers operating in Cuba have recently started to quote prices in euros. Use of the currency is limited at present to the big tourist resorts, such as Varadero and Guardalavaca, but is likely to become more widespread.

Note that if you bring US dollars into the country, a 10% commission is charged for changing them to CUCs (there is no fee for changing other currencies such as euros, Canadian dollars and British pounds; *see also p230* **Banks**). Make your life simple and come with non-US tender. Travellers' cheques are worth considering if you would otherwise be walking around with large amounts of cash on you, but your stay will be less frustrating if you can limit the number of times you have to seek out a bank. If you do bring travellers' cheques, remember to take your passport with you as ID when changing them up (or when drawing out money against a credit card). It's quite likely that you'll also need the original receipt for your travellers' cheques – it's certainly best to take it along with you.

Many foreign visitors paying in CUCs – that is, the vast majority – are surprised by how much money they end up spending in Cuba. Moreover, unlike many Latin American countries, there is not really a bargaining culture in Cuba; you may be able to negotiate on long-distance taxi fares, or the price of objects sold in crafts markets, but elsewhere you will be expected to pay the quoted price.

Before you leave Cuba, change most of your money back before you get to the airport, as you're not allowed to take it out of the country. Remember to keep enough money for minor purchases and your departure tax of CUC 25 (per person).

Pesos convertibles

Pesos convertibles (Cuban Convertible Pesos, or just convertible pesos) are designated CUC ('say-ooh-say'). They are also known as *divisas* or by the slang term *chavitos*. Many people use the word peso to refer to both Cuban and convertible pesos, and, the dollar symbol ($) is often used to denote both types of peso. The context should tell you whether a price is in low-value Cuban pesos or the much higher-value convertible pesos.

As we went to press, the exchange rate was CUC 1.16 (or about 24 Cuban pesos) to the euro but, of course, check before you go.

The currency circulates as notes of one, three, five, ten, 25, 50 and 100 pesos, and coins of five, ten, 25 and 50 centavos (¢), and one peso.

Carry CUCs in low denominations, as many places will not be able to give change, and take your passport (or a photocopy) if you intend to pay with a CUC 50 or 100 note.

Pesos cubanos

The Cuban peso (or CUP) is known simply as the peso, or *moneda nacional* (national currency). At press time it had an exchange rate of 24 pesos to one CUC. Each peso is divided into 100 centavos (¢). Notes are available in denominations of one, three, five, ten, 20 and 50 pesos; coins start at one centavo, followed by five centavos, ten centavos, 20 centavos, one peso and three pesos.

Although you'll pay for nearly everything in the city in CUCs, it's always useful to have a handful of Cuban pesos for buses, taxis and street stalls, fruit and vegetable markets (*agromercados*), peso restaurants and cinemas. You'll probably use pesos more if you go outside Havana. The export of local currency is restricted to 100 Cuban pesos and 200 convertible pesos.

ATMs

You can use most major foreign credit cards (Visa, MasterCard), but due to the American embargo you will not be able to use a US-issued card in Cuba. There are now many more holes in the wall in Havana. Key locations include:

La Habana Vieja corner of: Aguiar and Empedrado; Brasil (Teniente Rey) and Oficios; Cuba and O'Reilly; O'Reilly and Compostela.

Centro Habana corner of: Padre Varela (Belascoaín) and San José; San José and Monserrate; Infanta and Manglar; also at Plaza de Carlos III (*see p124*).

Vedado corner of: J and 23; 23 and P; Línea and M; also at Edificio FOCSA (*see p84*) and Hotel Habana Libre (*see p47*).

Miramar corner of Avenida 5ta and Calle 112.

If you have any problems you can go to the **National Card Centre** (FINCIMEX, Centro Nacional de Tarjetas de Crédito, Calle 23, esquina M, Vedado, 838 4444/4180/4189). Staff will ring your card centre free of charge and even help you access your current statement.

Banks

Banks in Havana will exchange foreign currency into convertible pesos and are the only places that cash travellers' cheques, but beware of paying commission when you buy and being charged again when you cash the cheques. Furthermore, though it is possible to withdraw money over the counter in a Cuban bank, they will run the transaction in US dollars, thus adding a ten per cent charge, in addition to a three per cent credit card charge.

Life is much simpler in Cuba with cash (plus a credit card as back-up). Branches of the Banco Financiero Internacional, Banco Internacional de Comercio and Banco Metropolitano will let you withdraw cash against a credit card (as long as it's not issued by a US bank). You can also now use credit cards at some CADECAs (*see below*) and at the big hotels.

Bureaux de change

CADECA (short for *casa de cambio*) exchange offices are found throughout Cuba – in tourist areas, shopping centres and next to many *agromercados* (food markets). Rates are usually in line with bank rates, service is reliable and the queues are often shorter. As well as exchanging money and travellers' cheques, they will also break larger convertible peso bills. You can withdraw convertible pesos using your credit card at most CADECAs (open daily from 8.30am to 6pm), including the following, though we've heard rumours that this may change:

La Habana Vieja corner of Obispo and Compostela; Obispo, between Cuba and Aguiar; Lonja del Comercio (*see p61*).

Vedado corner of 23 and L; corner of Línea and Paseo; Hotel Nacional (*see p48*), Hotel Habana Riviera (*see p47*).

Aeropuerto Internacional José Martí Terminal 3.

Most hotels can change money; they normally cash up their tills at 6pm.

Credit cards

Credit cards issued by US or US-affiliated banks are not accepted anywhere in Cuba. Non-US credit cards are accepted in a few shops and restaurants and in almost all tourist hotels. Credit card withdrawals can be made at some banks between 9am and 3pm Monday to Saturday (be prepared to queue) and in some CADECAs (*see above*). Alternatively, the bank at the Hotel Nacional (*see p48*) is open 8am-8pm daily.

In this guide we have only included credit card information in listings for chapters where they are most useful.

Natural hazards

See p226 **Health**.

Opening hours

Opening hours are variable; the times below are just guidelines. Allow plenty of time to get things done.

Banks 8.30am-3pm Mon-Fri.

Government offices 8.30am-12.30pm, 1.30-5pm Mon-Fri.

Fruit & vegetable markets (*agromercados*) 8am-6pm Tue-Sat; 8am-noon Sun.

Shops 10am-5.30pm Mon-Sat; some are also open 10am-1pm Sun.

Police stations

All crimes should be reported immediately, in person, to the **Policia Nacional Revolucionaria** (PNR). There is a police station in every district and, sometimes, a policeman on every street corner. The headquarters of the PNR is on Calle Tacón, opposite the Parque Arqueológico, in La Habana Vieja, but for emergencies call 106 and for information call 867 7777.

Postal services

Cuba's postal service (Correos de Cuba) is still snail-pace slow, generally unreliable and rife with petty theft. Letters posted in Cuba can arrive in Europe any time between two weeks later and never; the rule is, if you really want something to arrive at its destination, don't post it. It's best to rely on people you know travelling in and out of Cuba to carry letters and parcels for you. This is also the safest way to receive mail (there are no reliable poste restante services here either). If you do want to send a letter from Cuba (and whatever you do, don't include any money or anything else of value inside the envelope), it costs 75¢ from a local post office.

Urgent communications should be sent as emails from hotels as faxes aren't always reliable. Packages or documents can be sent by the costly but reliable **DHL** courier service (Calle 26, esquina 1ra, Miramar, 204 1578/comercial@dhl.cutisa.cu). A small package (up to 50 grams) costs CUC 39 to the United States, Canada and Mexico, or CUC 49 to the UK.

Telegrams

Telegrams are expensive, but given how unreliable regular postal services are in Cuba, they're a useful bet for short, important messages. Go to any post office and fill in a form; the words will be counted and you pay in CUCs; it can be surprisingly expensive.

Religion

Since the early 1990s, freedom of religion has been part of the Cuban constitution. Notionally, the majority of those who practise religion in Cuba are Roman Catholics. In reality, however, many Cuban Catholics are actually followers of the Afro-Cuban religion *santería*, which combines Catholicism with Yoruba beliefs. For more on Cuba's religious practice, *see p99* **Having faith**.

Islam

Casa de los Árabes

Calle Oficios #16, entre Obispo y Obrapía (861 5868). **Open** 9am-5pm Tue-Sat; 9am-1pm Sun. **Admission** free. **Map** p256 E15.

A small mosque – the only one in Cuba – provides religious services; the prayer room contains a copy of the Koran and other religious objects. *See also p60.*

Judaism

See also p80.

Casa de la Comunidad Hebrea/Synagoga Beth Shalom (Conservative)

Calle I, entre 13 y 15, Vedado (832 8953/www.chcuba.org). **Open** 9.30am-4pm Mon-Fri. *Services* phone for details. **Map** p254 B11.

Centro Hebreo Sefaradí

Calle 17 esquina E, Vedado (832 6623/judiosefarad@yahoo.com). **Open** phone for details. **Services** 7pm Fri, Sat. **Map** p254 B10.

Sinagoga Adath Israel de Cuba

Calle Acosta #357, esquina Picota, La Habana Vieja (861 3495/adath @enet.cu). **Open** 8am-7.30pm Mon-Sat; 8am-10am Sun. **Services** (Tora) 8am, 6.30pm daily. **Map** p256 E14.

Protestant

Catedral Episcopal de La Santísima Trinidad

Calle 13 #876, esquina 6, Vedado (833 5760/episcopal@ip.etecsa.cu). **Open** 9am-4pm Mon-Wed, Fri; 11am-7pm Thur; 8am-3pm Sat; 9am-1.30pm Sun. **Services** noon Mon-Sat; 9.30am, noon Sun. **Map** p254 B9.

Primera Iglesia Presbiteriana-Reformada de La Habana

Calle Salud #222, entre Campanario y Lealtad, Centro Habana (862 1219/1239/www.prccuba.org). **Open** 9.30am-noon, 2-5pm daily. **Services** 9am-noon, 2-5pm Mon, Wed, Fri. **Map** p255 D13.

Safety & security

Cuba has some of the lowest crime statistics in the Americas, but theft from luggage during baggage handling is common, so make sure you remove all valuables and lock suitcases before check-in.

A few years ago La Habana Vieja was notorious for petty theft from tourists, but the increased presence of police on many street corners in this area, as well as in Vedado and some of Centro Habana, has greatly diminished the problem.

Nevertheless, pickpockets are still about, so use common sense: don't flash cameras, jewellery or wallets. Violent crime against tourists is rare, though not unheard of. If you are the victim of a robbery, you should contact the police immediately (*see p230*) – you need a police statement in order to make an insurance claim.

Smoking

In 2005 the Cuban government announced the introduction of anti-smoking laws on the island. These were aimed at prohibiting people from lighting up in public places, such as hospitals, theatres, schools and offices. In hotels and restaurants, these regulations are inconsistently enforced, but many do now have designated smoking areas. The habit remains popular, though, with cigarettes available for Cubans on the *libreta* (ration book).

Study

Studying in Cuba is a growing market. However, the bureaucracy of arranging to study in Cuba can be very difficult. One way to ease your passage through the bureaucracy is to find someone who has gone through the maze and come out successfully at the other end. The red tape is best left to specialist organisations. If you do choose to enrol directly while you're in Cuba, the choice of courses on offer can be wider and cheaper than at home.

You can start by going directly to a number of institutions, depending on your study interest. Good places include the **Universidad de La Habana** (*see p233*), **Instituto Superior de Arte** (ISA; *see p93*), **Escuela Internacional de Cíne y Televisíon** in San Antonio de los Baños (Apartado Aereo 40/41, Finca San Tranquilino, Carretera Vereda Nueva km4, 38 3152) and **Escuela Nacional de Ballet** (Calle 120 #1110, entre 9na y 13, Cubanacán, Playa, 202 5678).

Student visas

Study in Cuba is possible with a tourist visa (*see p234*), but you'll have to leave the country every two months and re-enter, which can be a hassle and expensive. To stay in Cuba longer, you'll need to apply for a student visa. Do this as quickly as possible as paperwork can take an age. If you're exceedingly organised and enrol on a course at a well-established institution before you arrive in Cuba, the school will do the paperwork for you and you'll be able to apply for a student visa from the Cuban consulate in your home country. More often than not, however, students will have to do all the paper-pushing themselves once they are in Cuba.

Student visas are issued by the educational institution's Department of International Relations, or by the Dirección de Posgrado in the case of the University of Havana. For your application you will normally need six passport photos, CUC 80, a valid tourist card, a valid passport and a copy of the licence certificate of your residence in Havana. Foreign students must live either in university accommodation (limited availability) or in a *casa particular* that has an official licence. Don't be tempted to live in an unlicensed place as both you and the landlords could find yourselves in trouble.

Once you've got a student visa, remember that you must give two weeks' notice to International Relations (Relaciones Internacionales) and pay CUC 25-45 before leaving the country. In an emergency it's possible to leave at shorter notice for a bit more cash (normally CUC 50).

Long-term study

The easiest route is to enrol at a university in your home country that offers a year in Cuba as part of the study programme. For some years, universities such as Essex and London Metropolitan University in the UK and Buffalo (in the USA), among others, offer interesting study programmes in Cuba in the fields of language, business and culture.

Cuba has also become a popular destination for medical students, with Havana's Latin American School of Medicine currently the educational home of 7,200 students from some 24 countries. Despite the constant shortage of medicines, students are attracted to Cuba by its excellent healthcare reputation and the hands-on teaching methods. Cuban medical students deal with patients from the second year of their course, in contrast to most European medical students. Excellent Spanish is required to study medicine here.

Language courses

One of the more popular ways to study Spanish in Cuba is to enrol at the University of Havana, which offers language and grammar courses for all levels, plus classes on Cuban culture and film. You'll need to do an introductory test and courses run for two to four weeks (CUC 200/250 respectively), with classes daily from Monday to Friday. Longer courses are also available.

However, note that while previously it was possible to do short-term courses (30 days or less)

US citizens travelling to Cuba

Contrary to popular opinion, it isn't illegal for US citizens to travel to Cuba. The 'travel ban' is actually a restriction on financial 'transactions related to travel to, from, and within Cuba'. It is illegal for US citizens to spend money in Cuba. There are exceptions to the ban, but special licences must be obtained from the US government, and tourism is expressly excluded as legitimate grounds for obtaining a licence.

The current regulations regarding travel to Cuba stem from laws covering the wider economic embargo, first imposed on the country by the US in 1962. Subsequent legislation has included the Cuban Democracy Act of 1992, granting the US Treasury Department the authority to impose fines of up to $50,000 on those who violate the ban. In 1996 the Cuba Liberty and Democracy Solidarity Act (the Helms-Burton law) required all travel to Cuba to be licenced by the Office of Foreign Assets and Control (OFAC), a division of the US Treasury Department. In the past few years the US Congress has, in response to hard lobbying from agribusiness interests, attempted to weaken or repeal the travel ban, but President Bush has promised to veto any such legislation. Indeed, in October 2006, the US set up a task force to pursue embargo violators more aggressively.

Two categories of visitor don't require an OFAC licence: Cuban nationals are allowed to visit close family members once every three years; and those on a 'fully hosted' trip, where a third-party not subject to US jurisdiction pays for all expenses, are also exempt. US Customs officers have the authority to ask US citizens for proof that they didn't pay for anything on their trip. A word of caution, however: US Customs officers seem to have considerable leeway in deciding what constitutes a 'transaction'.

OFAC licences enable a US citizen to spend money on the island, as long as it's not for a commercial purpose. Under a 'general licence' journalists, government officials and certain researchers don't require written government permission. Americans usually travel to Cuba under 'specific licence'. Potential visitors must apply in writing to OFAC. Only those attached to educational institutions, research facilities and private foundations are eligible. In 2003 President Bush eliminated a whole category of 'specific licences', those by which museums, religious groups and cultural organisations could sponsor trips. Now, the only type of educational exchanges permitted are those by students enrolled in a degree programme at an accredited institution.

Be that as it may, Americans are travelling to Cuba in record numbers, many going illegally and entering via a third country. Customs officers in Cuba will generally not stamp American passports. But the Bush administration is on to this. If you do travel illegally, don't immediately board a flight home after returning from Cuba to a third country. US Customs officials have been known to visit airports in Canada and observe who transfers from flights from Cuba on to US-bound flights. Since Bush took office, well over 1,200 Americans have received letters from OFAC threatening fines of up to $50,000. If such a letter lands on your doorstep, write back within 30 days and request a hearing. Note that these restrictions are subject to change: check before you travel. Also note that the Cuban government requires that US citizens obtain a visa (tourist or otherwise). *See p234*.

Useful addresses

Center for Constitutional Rights

666 Broadway, 7th floor, New York, New York 10012 (212 614 6464/info@ccr-ny.org).
This organisation has a Cuba Travel project and gives legal information. Also distributes the publication *Advice for Travelers to Cuba*.

Marazul

800 223 5334/www.marazulcharters.com.
Operates charter flights from Miami and New York and can assist in obtaining Cuban visas.

National Lawyers Guild

143 Madison Avenue, 4th floor, New York, New York 10016 (212 679 5100/ nlgo@nlg.org).
This group campaigns against the ban. It also has a lawyer referral network.

OFAC

US Department of Treasury, 1500 Pennsylvania Avenue NW, Treasury Annex, Washington DC, 20220 (202 622 2480/www.treas.gov/ofac).
The best source for up-to-date information.

with a tourist visa, at present a student visa is required. To obtain one you should contact the director of the post-graduate department of the University of Havana (dpg@uh.cu) at least three weeks days prior to your intended arrival date. You will then be able to collect your student visa at the Cuban consulate in your country. Any foreign national studying in Cuba is required to stay at a university residence, tourist resort or at a licensed private rental home.

If you're after more flexible schedules, try the **Instituto Superior de Artes**. This music and art college has a very dedicated Spanish language faculty and will do its utmost to find a course to suit the language needs and length of stay of every potential student. Prices average about CUC 9 per three-hour class. Foreign art, music, drama and dance students at all levels are also accepted on a short-term basis at this prestigious college. Foreign students interested in a full-time course (CUC 2,500 per year) must sit an entrance examination. *See also p234* **Specialist package holidays**.

Instituto Superior de Artes (ISA)

Calle 120 #110, entre 9na y 13, Cubanacán, Playa (208 8075/ 9771/vrri@isa.cult.cu).

Universidad de La Habana

Postgraduate Department/ International Relations, Calle J, entre 25 y 27, Vedado (832 4245/831 3751/ dpg@comuh.uh.cu). **Open** *Sept-July* 8am-3.30pm Mon-Fri. *Aug* 8.30am-1.30pm Mon-Fri. **Map** p254 C11.

Telephones

The phone system has been greatly improved in Havana since a programme of digitalisation was introduced in 1994, but the incidence of wrong numbers, crossed or dead lines (usually when it rains), phones being out of order and other problems is still frustratingly high. Many *habaneros* do not have a phone, but then it's customary to take the number of a neighbour who will either yell for the person you want or take a message. Foreigners living longer term in a *casa particular* and sharing the phone line with their landlords will need to organise a very clear system of answering and taking messages as the latter is not a Cuban speciality.

Phone charges are still very cheap on peso lines and Cubans are used to talking extensively by phone. People may simply pick up the phone in a friend's house and make a call.

Dialling & codes

To call Havana from overseas, first dial your international access code (0011 from Australia; 011 from Canada; 00 from New Zealand; 00 from the UK; 011 from the USA), followed by 53 (for Cuba), 7 (for Havana), and finally the six- or seven-digit number (or eight, if it's a mobile). All mobile numbers in Havana begin with the prefix 5 (so if you're calling a mobile from abroad, you don't need the 7). Within Havana, to call from a landline to a mobile, prefix 05 to the number; to call from mobile to mobile, prefix 5 to the number.

Some destinations have a range of possible telephone numbers. We give them in the form 838 1234-6: this means the final number could be 4, 5 or 6 – all three will put you through.

We've checked all the phone numbers in this guide, but numbers are highly prone to change. ETECSA normally provides a recorded message for three months after a number change. If you are unsure of a number change, ask a friend, ring 0 for the operator or 113 for directory enquiries; the lines are usually busy but you might get lucky and get through.

Making a call

To call a number outside of Havana, first dial 0, followed by the city code. You can find city codes in any telephone directory; we also include a list below.

You can make an international call from a private phone but only through the international operator (bilingual, dial 12) and by reversing the charges. Then you can speedily (it's expensive) get your family or friends to phone you back.

To make a direct international call you will need to go to a hotel (a very expensive option) or, the more economical choice, to a staffed phone kiosk (*see also below* **Public phones**).

International codes include: Australia 43; USA 1; New Zealand 64; UK 44 (after the international code, drop the initial zero of the area code). Dial 119 first to get an outside line. The cost of international calls is high, starting at around CUC 2.45 per minute to North America and going up CUC 4-5.85 per minute for much of the rest of the world. Foreign charge cards cannot be used in Cuba.

Cuban area codes

(dial 0 first if you're inside Cuba)

Holguín 24
Matanzas 45
Pinar del Río 82
Sancti Spíritus 41
Santa Clara 42
Santiago de Cuba 22
Trinidad 419
Varadero 45
Viñales 8

Cuban operator services

Directory enquiries 113
International enquiries 09
National operator 0
Phone repairs 114

Public phones

There are four kinds of public telephone in Havana: convertible peso coin phones, Cuban peso coin phones, convertible peso card phones and Cuban peso card phones. They are found all over the city, but trying to make a call can be an irritating experience. The most widespread are convertible peso phones, which charge 15¢ for a three-minute call. Peso phones charge just five centavos for three minutes, but are not that common in tourist areas, are very often out of order and don't offer an international service.

You can make local, national and international calls and buy both Cuban and convertible peso phone cards at staffed ETECSA cabins. The Cuban peso cards cost five or ten pesos, the convertible cards (also available in hotels and some shops) are available in denominations of 10, 25 and 45.

Telephone directories

The Havana phone directory is updated every year, although numbers can change rapidly. Many entries are only listed by category, which can make looking for individual venues problematic. For instance, you might try to look for a restaurant under *restaurante* when it's actually been classed as a *cafetería*. Note, too, that while private domestic numbers are listed in the directory, private enterprises, such as *paladares*, are not.

Mobile phones

There is currently just one mobile phone company on the island: **Cubacel** (www.cubacel.cu), which which has an office at José Martí Airport (Terminal 3, open 10am-10pm daily) and at the Miramar Trade Center (Edificio Barcelona (bajos), Avenida 5ta, esquina 76, Miramar, open 8.30am-7.30pm daily). Alternatively, some of the larger hotels can arrange a deal through their business offices.

Cubacel has roaming agreements with many countries, so you may be able to use your own phone here. Coverage is national for US and tri- or quad-band handsets, although at the time of writing, older European single- and dual-band phones would only work in the Havana, Matanzas and Pinar del Río areas. If you are planning a longer visit or do not have your own mobile, you can open a temporary account with Cubacel to obtain a Cuban SIM card, or rent a temporary phone.

Be warned, though, that the cost of using a mobile phone in Cuba is phenomenally high, starting with a flat fee of CUC 111 (though there are periodic special offers) to activate the phone, followed by a monthly fee of CUC 10-40 (depending on services purchased) or a pre-paid card costing from CUC 20. Calls to landlines are charged on top of this at a rate of 60¢ per minute within Cuba (56¢ at night), CUC 2.70 per minute to North America, and around CUC 6 per minute to Europe. If you run out of credit on your phone, you'll have to call the office to arrange for more before being reconnected.

At present all mobile phone numbers in Havana begin with a 5; *see also p233*.

Faxes

Faxes can be received in most of the big hotels for only CUC 1 (sometimes less) per page but are costly to send to Europe, at around CUC 4 per minute.

Time

Cuba is five hours behind Greenwich Mean Time and therefore equivalent to Eastern Standard Time (New York and Miami). Daylight saving time runs from May to October.

Tipping

Whatever your financial situation may be at home, all tourists are relatively wealthy compared with the average Cuban, so if you get good service, tip accordingly. Tip five to ten per cent in restaurants and cafés unless a service charge is included in the bill. In hotels leave a one CUC bill for your cleaner on the pillow every morning if you can, or, if you are in a *casa particular*, hand over a few extra CUC when you leave if you have been satisfied with the service. Alternatively, you can leave hard-to-come-by items such as toiletries. Porters who help you with your luggage and tourist taxi drivers usually get one CUC.

Toilets

Public toilets are wretched places, and rare. Fortunately, most hotels and restaurants will let you use theirs. Some have attendants who should be tipped from 10¢ to 25¢. Most don't have paper.

Tourist information

Before you go

Tourism in Cuba is governed by the **Ministerio de Turismo** (Calle 19 #710, Vedado, 833 4202/0545/ www.cubatravel.cu). State tourist agencies such as Cubanacán, Cubatur and Havanatur (for all, *see p191*) represent Cuba abroad. US citizens should contact representatives of these organisations in Toronto or Montreal, Canada.

Cuban Tourist Board *154 Shaftesbury Avenue, London WC2H 8JT (020 7240 6655/cuba touristboard.london@virgin.net/ tourism@cubasi.info).* **Open** 10am-5pm Mon-Fri.

Bureau de Tourisme de Cuba *Suite 1105, 440 Boulevard Rene Levesque Ouest, Montreal H2Z 1V7 (514 875 8004).*

Cuban Tourist Board *Suite 705, 55 Queen Street East, Toronto M5C 2R6 (416 362 0700).*

In Havana

The government tourist bureau, **Infotur**, runs tours in Havana and to other parts of Cuba. It has five information offices in the city. In addition, most hotels have a tourist information desk where staff arrange package tours and provide information and maps. The desks in the lobby of the Hotel Habana Libre (*see p47*) are particularly good; the one at the airport is open 24 hours a day. In general it can be difficult to get clear, precise information on events and venues in Cuba. For publications on festivals and events in Cuba, *see p138*.

Agencia de Viajes San Cristóbal

Oficios #110, entre Lamparilla y Baratillo, La Habana Vieja (866 9585). **Map** p256 E15.

The official cultural travel agency for Habaguanex, the commercial wing of the City Historian's Office, can make bookings for Habaguanex hotels and organises some of the best guided tours. It can also arrange specialised tours beyond Havana.

Infotur

Calle Obispo #524, entre Bernaza y Villegas, La Habana Vieja (866 3333/obispodir@cubacel.net). **Open** 10am-6pm daily. **Map** p256 D15. **Other locations**: Terminal 3, Aeropuerto Internacional José Martí (266 4094); Avenida 5ta, esquina 112, Miramar (204 7036); Carretera del Rocío, Km3.5, Arroyo Naranjo (66 4396); Avenida Las Terrazas, entre 11 y 12, Playas del Este (97 1261).

Visas & immigration

Tourist cards & visas

All foreign visitors to Cuba require a passport (valid for at least six months beyond their departure from Cuba), an onward or return air ticket and a tourist card (*tarjeta de turista*). Tourist cards will be issued automatically if you book a package tour. Independent travellers can buy tourist cards from the travel agent or airline when they purchase their ticket or at the check-in desk before they board the plane to Cuba.

The Cuban consulate in London will also issue you a tourist card for £15 on presentation of a photocopy of your passport and booking confirmation for your trip from a travel agent. Most airlines won't allow passengers without a tourist card to board the plane in the first place.

On arrival, immigration officials will stamp your tourist card with the date of your arrival and it's then valid for four weeks from that date.

Hang on for dear life to your tourist card, as you'll need it to leave the country. A replacement costs CUC 25 (and can be a lot of hassle to organise) and in addition to the cost you may be delayed by some bureaucratic wrangling, which is problematic if your flight is about to depart. You're expected to give details on the tourist card of your intended address for at least the first two nights of your stay in Cuba. Enter the name of a state hotel or a licensed *casa particular* where you are staying. Certainly do not leave this section blank, or you could have your passport confiscated until you have booked approved hotel accommodation at the airport tour desk.

If you intend to stay in Cuba for a longer period, or you're travelling on business or for journalistic purposes, you'll need a special visa. Applications should be made through a Cuban consulate at least a month in advance of your trip.

Specialist package holidays

Dance

The best dance holidays package tuition with visits to clubs where you can dance the night away to the best of Cuba's salsa or *son* orchestras. The following British companies organise dance packages: **Salsa Caribe** (020 8985 1703, www.salsacaribe.co.uk); **Key to Cuba** (07767 313168, www.key2cuba.com); and **Club Dance Holidays** (01293 527722, www.danceholidays.com).

Spanish language

Language learning can often be combined with other activities. Edinburgh-based **Caledonia Languages Abroad** (0131 621 7721-3, www.caledonialanguages.co.uk) offers Spanish and salsa holidays in Santiago, with home-stay half-board accommodation, and other dancing and cultural trips. Its long-established Spanish courses, for all levels, operate in Santiago and Havana all year round. The Faculty of Modern Languages at the **Universidad de La Habana** (*see p233*) also runs various Spanish courses, some of which include music and culture modules.

Music & culture

AfroCubaWeb (www.afrocubaweb.com) runs dance, music and percussion trips with the **Conjunto Folklórico Nacional de Cuba** in Havana (*see p173*) and the **Conjunto Folklórico Cutumba** in Santiago.

Miscellaneous

In Cloud 9 (0870 242 4036, www.incloud9.com) specialises in tailor-made travel to Cuba, and can organise language, dance and music tuition. **Travelwelcome** (020 8681 3613, cubawelcome@enet.cu) is strong on sailing and fly-fishing trips. Scuba-diving enthusiasts should contact experienced diver Diana Williams at **Scuba en Cuba** (01895 624100, www.scuba-en-cuba.com) about tailor-made trips and packages.

If fly-drive is more your thing, get in touch with Bob Mortimer at **Rooms in Cuba** (020 8133 8807, roomsincuba@googlemail.com) for assistance on trips and accommodation.

For package holidays, try **Virgin Holidays** (0870 220 0088, virginholidays.co.uk) or **Captivating Cuba** (0870 887 0123, www.captivatingcuba.com).

Cuban Consulate in the UK

167 High Holborn, London, WC1V 6BA (0870 240 3675/www.cubaldn.com). Holborn tube. **Open** 9.30am-12.30pm Mon-Fri.

Extending your stay

If you want to extend your stay in Cuba beyond the four weeks designated on your tourist card, you have to go in person to the immigration office (Control de Extranjeros) with your passport and tourist card, before your first tourist card runs out. It's best to go there as near to 8.30am as you can. Take evidence of your official holiday residence even if only for the previous night. You'll rarely encounter any problems. It will cost you CUC 25 and must be paid using stamps of the same value, available from Banco de Comercio or Banco Financiero Internacional found all over Havana (*see p230* **Banks**).

Control de Extranjeros

Ministerio del Interior, Calle Factor, esquina Final, Tulipán, Nuevo Vedado (881 5294/883 9591). **Open** 8.30am-noon Mon-Fri. **Map** p253 E8.

Cubans & naturalised citizens

As far as the Cuban government is concerned, anyone who was born in Cuba is Cuban – even if they have since become a naturalised citizen of another country. However, visitors who fall into this category still require an entry permit (called an *autorización de entrada*) to re-enter the country. Alternatively, or additionally, they can also apply to the nearest Cuban diplomatic office for a *vigencia de viaje* (travel authorisation), which allows them to visit Cuba as often as they like within a two-year period.

US visitors

For details of regulations governing visitors to the island from America, *see p232* **US citizens travelling to Cuba**.

Weights & measures

The metric system is compulsory in Cuba. However, fruit and veg are sold by the pound in *agromercados*. Temperature is given in Celsius (°C).

Water

See p226 **Health**.

What to take

Clothes

Lightweight, loose-fitting clothes, preferably made of cotton, will help to keep you cool and fresh in the heat and humidity. Don't forget, though, that the temperature can drop considerably in the winter, so pack a warm sweater and a light jacket too. The former is also crucial for those arctic air-conditioner moments. Pack a sun-hat to protect you from the strong sun, and an umbrella for regular tropical downpours. Cubans like to dress up when they go out for the evening, so ladies, remember your heels and something glamorous for Havana's nightlife.

Medical supplies

Many day-to-day medical supplies are not readily available in Cuba. In addition to prescription medicines, you should bring the following: Antihistamine tablets/cream

Antiseptic wipes and cream
Aspirin/paracetamol
Bandages/plasters
Contraceptive pills/condoms
Diarrhoea preparation
Multi-vitamins
Rehydration salts

Other essentials

Adaptor; ear plugs; lighter; locks for luggage; mosquito repellent; photocopies of documents; sun-cream; torch (flashlight) and some spare batteries.

Useful extras

Candles; cigarette papers/rolling tobacco; cotton buds; dictionary (English-Spanish); envelopes; pens and pencils; pen-knife (in your hold luggage, not hand luggage); sanitary towels (these are available, but you won't be able to choose which brand you buy) or tampons; teaspoon; umbrella; water-purifying tablets.

When to go

High season in Cuba lasts from November to April and July to August. During this time hotels are at their busiest and most expensive, with most places fully booked at Christmas, New Year and Easter. Room rates tend to be 20 to 40 per cent lower at other times of year, but as most Cubans take their holidays in July and August, beaches are packed in high summer. Many hotels in Havana are fully booked for the Día de Rebeldía Nacional in July and during trade shows such as the Feria Internacional de La Habana (FIHAV) in early November. If you want to visit at these times, book flights and hotels as early as possible.

Public holidays

On the following days most shops, museums and businesses are closed.
Día de la Liberación (Liberation Day) 1 Jan
Día de los Trabajadores (May Day) 1 May
Día de Rebeldía Nacional (Celebration of the National Rebellion) 25-27 July
Inicio de la Guerra de Independencia (Anniversary of the start of the First War of Independence) 10 Oct
Navidad (Christmas) 25 Dec

Climate

Cuba is located in the tropics and has two distinct seasons: summer (May to October), which is hot and wet, and winter (November to April), which is slightly cooler and drier. Gulf Stream currents warm the waters around the island, while the north-east trade wind known as *la brisa* cools the city throughout the year. Humidity rarely falls below 70 per cent and can reach an enervating 90 per cent.

Two-thirds of the annual rainfall (132cm; 52in) falls between May and November, usually as short, sharp showers but also during occasional heavy and prolonged storms. Some years Cuba is suffers a dry period (*la sequía*) lasting three to five months. Otherwise, December, February, March and April are the driest months of the year. There is an average of eight hours of sunshine per day throughout the year. *See also below* **Average temperatures**.

Bear in mind that from May to October the weather is very hot and humid indeed, with the very hottest period usually being August and September.

August to October is official hurricane season in Cuba, and while overall they rarely cause much damage or destruction, the island has been particularly hard hit in recent years by Charles (August 2004), Dennis (July 2005), Katrina (August 2005) and Wilma (October 2005). Cuba has been lauded for its education, early-warning system and early evacuation programmes, all of which undoubtedly minimised the loss of life. If an electrical storm brews up while you are out and about, most likely during the summer months, keep away from the royal palm trees, which tend to attract lightning. For weather information, pick up a copy of *Granma* (*see p228*), which prints daily weather forecasts. There are also regular weather reports in Spanish on Cuban TV.

Average temperatures

	High (C/F)	Low (C/F)
Jan	25/78	17/63
Feb	26/79	17/63
Mar	27/82	18/66
Apr	28/84	20/68
May	30/87	21/71
June	31/88	23/74
July	31/89	23/74
Aug	31/89	23/74
Sept	31/88	23/74
Oct	29/85	21/71
Nov	27/82	20/69
Dec	26/79	18/65

Women

Although it's a macho country, Cuba is, on the whole, much safer for women than many other Caribbean countries. However, a woman of whatever age, travelling on her own, should be prepared to cope with stares, *piropos* (comments) and even proposals of marriage. Some Cubans want to escape their harsh conditions and would marry you tomorrow in order to do so. If it bothers you, wear a ring on your wedding finger and if necessary invent a tall, dark husband.

Although many Cuban women wear short skirts and a lot of lycra, some foreign women prefer to wear less revealing clothes in an attempt to avoid unwanted attention. If you are harassed by a Cuban man, make it clear if you're not interested and he is likely to get the message. Flirting is a national pastime and is normally very playful.

If you do need help or advice, contact the **Federación de Mujeres de Cuba** (Paseo #260, entre 11 y 13, Vedado, 552771, mccu@ceniai.inf.cu). Originally set up to implement the equality laws of the Revolution, the Federación now promotes the interests of women.

Working in Havana

If you're planning on working in Cuba, you can apply for a visa from the Cuban consulate in your home country (*see p234*). You'll need to know the name and details of the business or organisation that is sponsoring your stay and allow at least three weeks for your application to be processed. Journalists and students (*see also p231*) require special visas to enter the country; these are also available from the local consulate.

Vocabulary

Like other Latin languages, Spanish has different familiar and polite forms of the second person (you). Many young people now use the familiar *tú* form most of the time; for foreigners, though, it's always advisable to use the more polite *usted* with people you don't know, and certainly with anyone over 50. In the phrases listed here all verbs are given in the *usted* form. Cuban Spanish is notably different from Castilian Spanish in some of its vocabulary (such as *carro* rather than *coche* for car), and also in its tendency to drop final letters of words and also the 'd' from the final 'ado' of words. It's rare to come across a Cuban who speaks fluent English, though many, in Havana at least, speak a few words. For food- and drink-related vocabulary, *see p104*.

Pronunciation

c before an **i** or an **e** is soft, like **s** in **s**it.
c in all other cases is hard, as in **c**at.
g, before an **i** or an **e**, and **j** are pronounced with a guttural **h**-sound that does not exist in English – like **ch** in Scottish lo**ch**, but much harder.
g in all other cases is pronounced as in **g**et.
h at the beginning of a word is normally silent.
ll is pronounced almost like a **y**.
ñ is like **ny** in ca**ny**on.
z is always the same as a soft c, like s as in **s**it.
A single **r** at the beginning of a word and **rr** elsewhere are heavily rolled.

Basics

hello *hola*; **hello** (when answering the phone) *hola, diga*
good morning, good day *buenos días*; **good afternoon, good evening** *buenas tardes*; **good evening** (after dark), **good night** *buenas noches*
goodbye/see you later *adiós/hasta luego*
please *por favor*; **thank you** (very much) *(muchas) gracias*;
you're welcome *de nada*
do you speak English? *¿habla inglés?*
I don't speak Spanish *no hablo español*
I don't understand *no entiendo*
what's your name? *¿cómo se llama?*
speak more slowly, please *hable más despacio, por favor*
wait a moment *espere un momento*
Sir/Mr *señor* (*sr*); **Madam/Mrs** *señora* (*sra*); **Miss** *señorita* (*srta*)
excuse me/sorry *perdón*
excuse me, please *oiga* (to attract attention; literally 'hear me')
OK/fine/(or to a waiter) **that's enough** *vale*
where is... *¿dónde está...?*
why? *¿porqué?*, **when?** *¿cuándo?*, **who?** *¿quién?*, **what?** *¿qué?*, **where?** *¿dónde?*, **how?** *¿cómo?*
is/are there any... *¿hay...?*
very *muy*; **and** *y*; **or** o
with *con*; **without** *sin*
open *abierto*; **closed** *cerrado*
what time does it open/close? *¿a qué hora abre/cierra?*
pull (on signs) *tirar*; push *empujar*
I would like... *quiero...* (literally, 'I want...'); **how many would you like?** *¿cuántos quiere?*
I like *me gusta*;
I don't like *no me gusta*
good *bueno/a*; **bad** *malo/a*;
well/ badly *bien/mal*;
small *pequeño/a*; **big** *gran, grande*;
expensive *caro/a*; **cheap** *barato/a*;
hot (food, drink) *caliente*; **cold** *frío/a*
something *algo*; **nothing** *nada*
more/less *más/menos*
the bill/check, please *la cuenta, por favor*
how much is it? *¿cuánto es?*
do you have any change? *¿tiene cambio?*
price *precio*; **free** *gratis*
discount *descuento*
bank *banco*; **to rent** *alquilar*;
(for) rent, rental *(en) alquiler*;
post office *correos*; **stamp** *sello*;
postcard *postal*;
toilet *los servicios*

Getting around

airport *aeropuerto*; **railway station** *estación de ferrocarriles*; **car** *carro* or *coche*; **bus** *guagua* or *rutero* (general terms for a city bus); *autobús* (air-conditioned tourist bus), *camello* (pink articulated bus); **train** *tren*
a ticket *un billete*; **return** *de ida y vuelta*; **bus stop** *parada de autobús*;
the next stop *la próxima parada*
excuse me, do you know the way to...? *por favor, ¿sabe como llegar a...?*; **left** *izquierda*; **right** *derecha;* **here** *aquí* or *acá*; **there** *allí*; **straight on** *recto*; **to the end of the street** *al final de la calle*;
as far as *hasta*; **towards** *hacia*
near *cerca*; **far** *lejos*

Accommodation

do you have a double/single room for tonight/one week? *¿tiene una habitación doble/para una persona para esta noche/una semana?*
where is the car park? *¿dónde está el parking?*
we have a reservation *tenemos reserva*
an inside/outside room *una habitación interior/exterior*
with/without bathroom *con/sin baño*; **shower** *ducha*
double bed *cama de matrimonio*;
with twin beds *con dos camas*
breakfast included *desayuno incluído*
air-conditioning *aire acondicionado*;
lift *ascensor*; **swimming pool** *piscina*

Time

morning *la mañana*; **midday** *mediodía*; **afternoon/evening** *la tarde*; **night** *la noche*; **late night/early morning** (roughly 1-6am) *la madrugada*
now *ahora*; **later** *más tarde*
yesterday *ayer*; **today** *hoy*;
tomorrow *mañana*; **tomorrow morning** *mañana por la mañana*
early *temprano*; **late** *tarde*
delay *retraso*; **delayed** *retrasado*
at what time...? *¿a qué hora...?*
in an hour *en una hora*
the bus will take 2 hours *el autobús tardará dos horas*
at 2 *a las dos*; **at 8pm** *a las ocho de la tarde*; **at 1.30** *a la una y media*
at 5.15 *a las cinco y cuarto*;
at 22.30 *a veintidós treinta*
Monday *lunes*; **Tuesday** *martes*; **Wednesday** *miércoles*; **Thursday** *jueves*; **Friday** *viernes*; **Saturday** *sábado*; **Sunday** *domingo*
January *enero*; **February** *febrero*; **March** *marzo*; **April** *abril*; **May** *mayo*; **June** *junio*; **July** *julio*; **August** *agosto*; **September** *septiembre*; **October** *octubre*; **November** *noviembre*; **December** *diciembre*
spring *primavera*; **summer** *verano*; **autumn/fall** *otoño*; **winter** *invierno*

Numbers

0 *cero*; **1** *un, uno, una*; **2** *dos*; **3** *tres*; **4** *cuatro*; **5** *cinco*; **6** *seis*; **7** *siete*; **8** *ocho*; **9** *nueve*; **10** *diez*; **11** *once*; **12** *doce*; **13** *trece*; **14** *catorce*; **15** *quince*; **16** *dieciséis*; **17** *diecisiete*; **18** *dieciocho*; **19** *diecinueve*; **20** *veinte*; **21** *veintiuno*; **22** *veintidós*; **30** *treinta*; **40** *cuarenta*; **50** *cincuenta*; **60** *sesenta*; **70** *setenta*; **80** *ochenta*; **90** *noventa*; **100** *cien*; **1,000** *mil*; **1,000,000** *un millón*.

Further Reference

Books

Fiction & literature

Barclay, Juliet and Sera, Xiomara *Miri and the Magic Door* (2006). A lovely illustrated children's book, about a young girl's adventure with a pirate in Havana.

Bush, Peter (editor) *The Voice of the Turtle: a collection of Cuban short stories translated into English* (1998). The short story is a strong genre in Cuba and this collection gives a good overall picture, spanning over a century.

Cabrera Infante, Guillermo *Tres Tristes Tigres* (*Three Trapped Tigers*; 1998). A sharply comic novel of pre-Revolutionary Havana in which the hedonistic city itself is a protagonist.

Carpentier, Alejo *Los pasos perdidos* (*The Lost Steps*; 1953). It is in this novel that the great Cuban writer develops his theory of Magic Realism.

García, Cristina *Dreaming in Cuban* (1992). The young Cuban-American writer García explores the theme of families divided by politics and the Florida Straits through three generations.

Greene, Graham *Our Man in Havana* (1958). Set on the very eve of Castro's Revolution, the darkly comic novel evokes Havana in the 1950s through the misadventures of a vacuum-cleaner salesman turned reluctant spy.

Guillén, Nicolás. Guillén was the Revolution's official poet and has been widely translated. Apart from his political poems, Guillén is best known for his very rhythmical Afro-Cuban works, which have often been set to music.

Gutiérrez, Pedro Juan *Dirty Havana Trilogy* (2002). Interlinked stories from Havana's underground. Strong, unforgiving language makes it a powerful read.

Hemingway, Ernest *The Old Man and the Sea* (1952). This tale of a local fisherman's epic struggle won Hemingway the Nobel Prize for Literature in 1954. Hemingway dedicated the prize to Cuba's patron saint. Try also *Islands in the Stream* (1970), which is based on the author's experiences hunting Nazi submarines, and *To Have and Have Not* (1937), an exciting account of illegal trade between Havana and Florida.

Hijuelos, Oscar *The Mambo Kings Play Songs of Love* (1989). Cuban-American novel about the world of Cuban musicians playing in New York in the 1950s. Won the Pulitzer Prize in 1990.

Iyer, Pico *Cuba and the Night* (1995). An ambivalent love story set in the dark days of 1980s Havana.

Juan Castellanos, Ernesto *John Lennon in Havana: with a Little Help from My Friends* (2005). The story of the ban of the Beatles and rock in Cuba in the 1960s and '70s.

Lezama Lima, José *Paradiso* (*Paradise*; 1966). Lezama Lima is the giant of 20th-century Cuban literature. This, his only novel, gives a richly detailed picture of Havana through the eyes of a sensitive young protagonist growing up in the city.

Piñera, Virgilio. Best known as a playwright, particularly of absurdist drama, Piñera is one of Cuba's most important writers, although not much of his work has been translated.

Sarduy, Severo *¿De dónde son los cantantes?* (*From Cuba with a Song*; 1967). Explores Cuba's identity through Spanish, African and Chinese roots. Sarduy left Cuba and lived in Paris for many years before he died of AIDS in 1993.

Non-fiction

Arenas, Reinaldo *Antes que anochezca* (*Before Night Falls*; 1992). The autobiography of the Cuban dissident and homosexual. Arenas was persecuted and imprisoned in Cuba and finally abandoned the island in 1980 for New York. Suffering from AIDS, Arenas committed suicide in 1990.

Anderson, John Lee *Che Guevara: a Revolutionary Life* (1997). A weighty and exhaustive biography of the Revolutionary hero.

Barclay, Juliet *Havana: Portrait of a City* (1996). A well-written history by the local historian, with photos and illustrations, of the development of Havana from the early 16th century to the late 19th century.

Block, Holly *ArtCuba: the New Generation* (2001). A beautifully presented review of contemporary Cuban art by over 60 artists.

Cabrera Infante, Guillermo *Mea Cuba* (1995). Banned in Cuba for its strong condemnation of Castro, this collection of essays and memoirs presents a personalised account of the literary/political scene during the early years of the Revolution.

Fuentes, Norberto *Hemingway in Cuba* (1984). A key account of the author's life in Cuba.

González-Wippler, Migene *Santería: the Religion* (1994). Plenty of interesting information on Afro-Cuban religion.

LaFray, Joyce *¡Cuba Cocina!* (1994). Cuban cooking served up in all its glory.

Martí, José. Anyone hoping to understand Cuba needs some knowledge of Martí's poems, essays and letters. Martí wrote prolifically and his works are collected in over 30 volumes, most of which have been translated into English.

Matthews, Herbert *Revolution in Cuba* (1975). A sympathetic analysis by the *New York Times* journalist.

Miller, Tom *Trading with the Enemy: a Yankee Travels through Castro's Cuba* (1992). Part travelogue, part social analysis, Tom Miller's astute comments on Cuba in the 1990s make for one of the best recent books about the island.

Roy, M *Cuban Music* (2002). Comprehensive exploration of the origins, politics and key figures of Cuban music.

Smith, Stephen *The Land of Miracles* (1998). Tales of touring Cuba in an American car.

Szulc, Tad *Fidel: A Critical Portrait* (1986). An excellent biography of the Revolutionary leader.

Thomas, Hugh *Cuba, or the Pursuit of Freedom 1726-1969* (1971). Historian Hugh Thomas's scholarly history of the island is over 30 years old now, but is still probably the standard work. You could also try Thomas's more recent and equally definitive *The Cuban Revolution.*

Film

See also p149 **Ones to watch**.

Buena Vista Social Club (Wim Wenders 1999). Nostalgic documentary focusing on the elderly stars of the phenomenally successful album by the same name.

Comandante (Oliver Stone 2003). Oliver Stone interviews Fidel Castro with intriguing (but not ground-breaking) results.

Fresa y chocolate (*Strawberry and Chocolate*; Tomás Gutiérrez Alea and Juan Carlos Tabío 1993). Taboo-breaking film about the trials and tribulations of a homophobic Revolutionary student.

Lista de espera (*Waiting List*; Juan Carlos Tabío 1999). Tabío's debut, this comedy drama follows a group of travellers waiting at a run-down Cuban transit station for a bus.

Memorias del subdesarrollo (*Memories of Underdevelopment*; Tomás Gutiérrez Alea 1968). Follows a man whose family flees to Miami in 1961. A seminal work within the Spanish-speaking world.

Miel para Oshún (*Honey for the Goddess*; Humerto Solas 2001). The tale of a Cuban who was taken to the US as a child and returns decades later to look for his mother.

La muerte de un burócrata (*Death of a Bureaucrat*; Tomás Gutiérrez Alea 1966). A black comedy about the absurdities of Cuban bureaucracy.

Suite Habana (Fernando Pérez 2003). Powerful silent film following the lives of several *habaneros*.

Music

See also p162 **Broadening your musical Vistas**.

Artists

Buena Vista Social Club *Buena Vista Social Club* (1997). The Ry Cooder-backed album featuring a group of Cuban old-timers, which became nothing short of an international sensation. Surviving members of the group can often be seen playing venues in Havana and internationally.

Clave y Guaguancó *Noche de la Rumba* (1999). Cuba's foremost group to specialise in Afro-Cuban music has been around for over 50 years.

Delgado, Issac *Con ganas* (1993). An early album from Cuba's salsa/*timba* superstar.

Irakere *The Best of Irakere* (1978). Just one of many albums by this Grammy award-winning supergroup, founded by Chucho Valdés in 1973.

Milanés, Pablo *Serie Millennium 21* (1999). A double compilation CD set of classics from the famous *nueva trova* singer.

Papa Noel & Papi Oviedo *Bana Congo* (2002). Slick, highly listenable collaboration between veteran Congolese singer Papa Noel and Cuban *tres* player Papi Oviedo.

Orishas *A lo cubano* (2000); *Emigrante* (2003); *El Kilo* (2005). One of the hottest Cuban groups in recent years, Orishas blends hip hop, harmonies and percussion to impressive effect.

Rodríguez, Silvio *Días y flores; Unicornio; Rabo de Nuve*. One of Cuba's most prolific singer-songwriters on the *nueva trova* scene. A specialist in emotionally intense lyrics and moving ballads, Rodríguez's early acoustic albums are considered to be his best. Songs are often loaded with pro-Revolutionary ideology.

Segundo, Compay *Antología* (1995). This compilation of Compay's greatest songs is a good introduction to one of Cuba's all-time greats. Compay was part of the famous Buena Vista Social Club project.

Los Van Van *Llegó… Van Van* (2000). This multi-piece orchestra is one of Cuba's most popular long-standing groups. Inventors of the *songo* rhythm, Los Van Van won a Grammy in 2000 for best salsa group.

Yusa *Yusa* (2003). Up-and-coming singer with a soulful contemporary Cuban flavour.

Los Zafiros *Bossa Cubana* (reissued 1999). Los Zafiros was a pop sensation in the 1960s, with its rich harmonies and doo-wop choruses. *Bossa Cubana* contains some irresistible tunes.

Compilations

Antología del Bolero – Colección Tributo
This CD provides an excellent introduction to the complexities and variety of bolero music.

Fiesta Cubana: El Bolero
Another compilation CD, this one contains some of the giants of Cuban bolero music, including Beny Moré, Frank Domínguez and Bola de Nieve.

Rapsodia Rumbera
This compilation of rumba music includes works in all the major styles. Many of the great rumba musicians are featured on the CD, including Chano Pozo, Malanga, Nieve Fresneda and Tío Tom.

Cantos de Santería
A fascinating and mystical CD, this is one of the only recordings available dedicated to the religious music of *regla de ocha* or *santería*, the Christian/African synthesis religion still practised in Cuba and South America.

Vivencias – Charanga Típica de Guillermo Rubalcaba
A rich and complex recording of the music of the piano virtuoso Guillermo Rubalcaba, this CD combines internationally known orchestral works with waltz classics and more intimate pieces.

Websites

www.afrocubaweb.com
This up-to-date site draws together a vast array of information on themes such as culture, politics, literature, music, dance and theatre to celebrate the influence of African culture on Cuban life.

www.cuba.cu
This basic website – in Spanish only – isn't much to look at, but has useful links to other sites.

www.cubaabsolutely.com
This website is packed with useful information and interesting articles by local experts. It also lets you download the latest Ernst & Young business report on Cuba.

www.cubaliteraria.cu
An extensive website, dedicated to Cuban authors and literature.

www.cubatravel.cu
Cuban portal for tourism in English, listing tour operators/agencies, embassies and tourist offices, including addresses and phone numbers.

www.cubaweb.cu
A good general internet portal for information and links to resources relating to Havana and Cuba, Cubaweb covers topics including news, tourism, business, the internet, government, trade, culture and events. The site is produced in both English and Spanish – so doubles as a study aid.

www.cubaweather.org
Climate statistics and commentary, plus weather forecasts for Cuba.

www.cult.cu
The Cubarte site, in English and Spanish, is a key resource for the traveller interested in the cultural and artistic life of the island. It contains extensive information on cinema, dance, music, books, prizes and events.

www.discuba.com
The website for the Cuban Music Shop offers a wealth of information on all styles of Cuban music and discographies of the major artists. Info on upcoming musical events, performances and concerts as well as information on cinema and video releases. Offers online shopping too.

www.dtcuba.com/eng
English and Spanish language website called the *directorio turístico de Cuba* (Cuban directory). Health, embassies, nightclubs, restaurants and more besides are covered in this comprehensive website.

www.granma.cu/ingles
The website for the official newspaper of the Cuban Communist Party, Granma provides state-approved news in five languages: Spanish, English, French, German and Portuguese.

www.prensa-latina.cu
Prensa Latina is a news agency with English-language information and articles about Cuba.

www.uscubacommission.org
For the traveller who likes their holidays to be liberally laced with politics, the US-Cuba Commission's site gives up-to-the-minute information on the latest developments in political relations between the US and Cuba.

Index

Note: page numbers in **bold** indicate section(s) giving key information on topic; *italics* indicate illustrations.

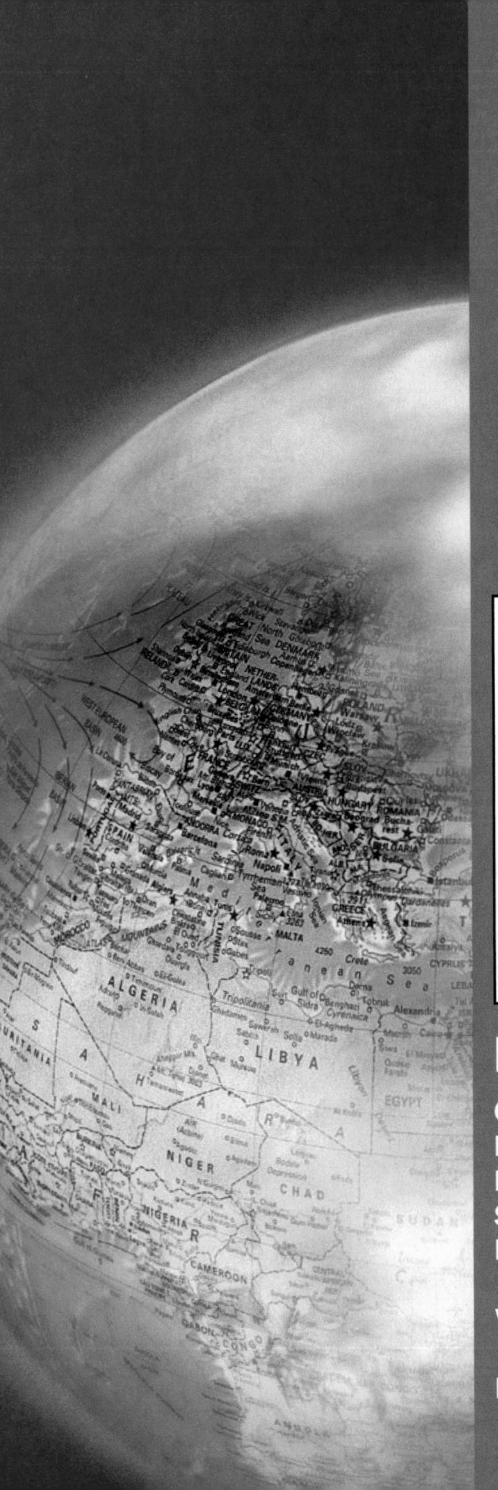

Legend	
Place of Interest and/or Entertainment	
Railway Station	
Park	
College/Hospital	
Beach	
Steps	
Area Name	VEDADO
Church	✚
Information	i
Post Office	✉
Hotel	1
Restaurant	1
Bar	1

Maps

Cuba

Gulf of Mexico
Straits of Florida
Andros Island
BAHAMAS
Cat Island
San Salvador
Great Guana Cay
Rum Cay
Anguila Cays
Great Exuma
Long Island
Samana Cay
Crooked Island
Long Cay
Ragged Island
Acklins Island
Archipiélago de Saban
Archipiélago de Camagüey
Cayo Las Brujas
Cayo Coco
Cayo Santa María
Cayo Sabinal
Havana
Mariel
Varadero
Matanzas
Cárdenas
Viñales
Artemisa
Pinar del Río
Golfo de Batabanó
Golfo de Guanahacabibes
Bahía de Cortés
María la Gorda
Nueva Gerona
Cayos de San Felipe
Isla de la Juventud
Archipiélago de los Canárreos
Cayo Largo
Península de Zapata
Cienfuegos
Remedios
Santa Clara
CUBA
Trinidad
Sancti Spíritus
Ciego de Ávila
Camagüey
Golfo de Ana María
Cayo Grande
Jardines de la Reina
Las Tunas
Holguín
Golfo de Guacanayabo
Bayamo
Manzanillo
Baracoa
Guantánamo
Santiago de Cuba
La Gran Piedra
Great Inagua
Windward Passage
HAITI
Jamaica Chann
JAMAICA
Kingston
Yucatan Basin
CARIBBEAN SEA
Cayman Islands
Cayman Brac
Little Cayman
Grand Cayman
Cayman Trench

CANADA
Winnepeg
Québec
Montreal
Ottawa
Minneapolis
Toronto
Boston
Detroit
Buffalo
Pittsburg
New York
Philadelphia
Chicago
Washington
Kansas City
St Louis
USA
Oklahoma City
Memphis
Atlanta
Charleston
Dallas
Houston
New Orleans
Miami
Havana
CUBA

0 100 miles
0 100 km

Havana Overview

Havana by Area
Estrecho de la Florida
Canal de Entrada
Bahía de La Habana
Ensenada de Atarés
EASTERN BAY & THE COAST
LA HABANA VIEJA
CENTRO HABANA
BARRIO CHINO
VEDADO
NUEVO VEDADO
CERRO
MIRAMAR & THE WESTERN SUBURBS
KOHLY
El Morro (Castillo de los Tres Reyes del Morro)
Fortaleza de San Carlos de la Cabaña
Castillo de San Salvador de la Punta
Estudiantes de Medicina
Máximo Gómez
Tunnel
Catedral
Museo de la Revolución
Museo Nacional de Bellas Artes
Memorial Granma
Edificio Bacardí
Parque Central
Capitolio
Gran Teatro
Real Fábrica de Tabacos Partagás
Palacio de Domingo Aldama
Casa de la Cultura
Convento de Santa Clara
Convento e Iglesia de Nuestra Señora de Belén
Estación Central de Ferrocarriles
Muralla de La Habana
Basílica Menor y Convento de San Francisco de Asís
Castillo de Atarés
AV CARLOS M. DE CÉSPEDES
SAN PEDRO
DESAMPARADOS
AV DEL PUERTO
DRAGONES
MÁXIMO GÓMEZ (MONTE)
MALECÓN
MALECÓN (AVE DE MACEO)
Monumento a Antonio Maceo
Convento Capilla de la Inmaculada Concepción
Torreón de San Lázaro
Iglesia Nuestra Señora Caridad del Cobre
Convento & Iglesia del Sagrado Corazón de Jesús
Casa de la Cultura de Centro Habana
ZANJA
AV SALVADOR ALLENDE (CARLOS III)
Estadio José M. Pérez
Casa Museo Abel Santamaría
Universidad de La Habana
Museo Napoleónico
AVENIDA WASHINGTON
Monumento al Maine
Pabellón Cuba
Edificio FOCSA
Cine Yara
Quinta de los Molinos
Museo de Historia Natural Montané
Cine La Rampa
(LA RAMPA)
Complejo Deportivo José Martí
Museo Nacional de la Danza
UNEAC
Monumento a Calixto García
Casa de las Américas
Iglesia del Sagrado Corazón de Jesús
Museo de Artes Decorativas
Agromercado
Teatro Amadeo Roldán
Teatro Mella
Galerías de Paseo
Casa de la Amistad
Parque Lennon
Casa de la Cultura de Plaza
ICAIC
Castillo del Príncipe
CALZADA DE ZAPATA
Terminal de Ómnibuses
Museo Postal José Luis Guerra Aguiar
Ministerio del Interior
Teatro Nacional
PASEO
BOYEROS
AV CARLOS M. DE CÉSPEDES
AV RANCHO BOYEROS
Palacio de la Revolución
Estadio Latinoamericano
CALZADA DEL CERRO
AV DE LA INDEPENDENCIA
Estación de Ferrocarriles 19 de Noviembre
Cementerio de Colón
Parque Almendares
Almendares
Bosque de La Habana
CALZADA DE PUENTES GRANDES
Ciudad Deportiva
AVENIDA 1RA
AVENIDA 3RA
AVENIDA 5TA
AVENIDA 7MA
Teatro Karl Marx
Museo del Ministerio del Interior
El Tocororo
La Maison
El Aljibe
1 km
0.5 mile
0
© Copyright Time Out Group 2007

Street Index

Miramar & the Western Suburbs
0 500 m
0 500 yds
© Copyright Time Out Group 2007
Hotel Comodoro
Hotel Meliá Habana
Embajada Rusa
Iglesia de San Antonia de Padua
To Náutico and Marina Hemingway
QUEREJETA
ALMENDARES
BUENAVISTA
LA CEIBA
Tropicana
5TA
7MA
1 Hotels pp36-51
1 Eating pp102-118
1 Drinking pp118-121

MALECÓN
AVENIDA 1RA
AVENIDA 3RA
AVENIDA 5TA
AVENIDA 7MA
MIRAMAR
Teatro Karl Marx
Maqueta de La Habana
Museo del Ministerio del Interior
Iglesia Santa Rita de Casia
La Maison
Tunnel
Casa de la Cultura de Plaza
VEDADO
LINEA
Almendares
Cira García Hospital
ICAIC
LA SIERRA
KOHLY
Parque Almendares
Cementerio Colón
See p254
LA TORRE
NUEVO VEDADO
Bosque de La Habana
AVE DE COL
TULIPAN
LOMBILLO
HIDALGO
Estación de Ferrocarriles 19 de Noviembre
ESTE
FACTOR
AVENIDA ZOOLÓGICO
RIZO
EMPIRIO
RECURSO
SANTA MARÍA
CALZADA DE PUENTES GRANDES
AVENIDA DE LA INDEPENDENCIA
CALZADA DEL CERRO
SAN CRISTOBAL
COLÓN
PRENSA
PRIMELLES
CHURRUCA
PEZUELA
INFANTA
SANTA TERESA
Ciudad Deportiva

9
10
11
12
A
B
C
D
E
F
Hotel Habana Riviera
Hotel Meliá Cohiba
Monumento a Calixto García
Casa de las Américas
MALECÓN
Complejo Deportivo José Martí
US Interests Section
Galerías de Paseo
Teatro Amadeo Roldán
Hotel Presidente
Tribuna Antimperialista
Teatro Mella
Iglesia del Sagrado Corazón de Jesús
Museo Nacional de la Danza
AVENIDA WASHINGTON
VEDADO
Edificio FOCSA
Monumento al Maine
Museo de Artes Decorativas
UNEAC
Hotel Victoria
Hotel Nacional
Parque Lennon
Casa de la Amistad
Agromercado
Cine Yara
Pabellón Cuba
Coppelia
AVENIDA DE LOS PRESIDENTES
PASEO
(LA RAMPA)
Hotel Habana Libre
Hotel St John's
Casa-Museo Abel Santamaría
Cine la Rampa
Hotel Vedado
See p253
Universidad de La Habana
Museo de Historia Natural Montané
CALZADA DE INFANTA
Museo Napoleónico
CALZADA DE ZAPATA
Castillo del Príncipe
Cementerio de Colón
Quinta de los Molinos
ZANJA
CENTRO
AVENIDA SALVADOR ALLENDE (CARLOS III)
Casa de la Cultura de Centro Habana
Ministerio del Interior
Terminal de Omnibuses Interprovinciales
AVENIDA CARLOS M. DE CESPEDES
PASEO
PLAZA DE LA REVOLUCIÓN
Museo Postal José Luís Guerra Aguiar
Memorial y Museo José Martí
Palacio del Gobierno
Convento & Iglesia del Sagrado Corazón de Jesús
AVENIDA RANCHO BOYEROS
AVE DE LA INDEPENDENCIA
Real Fábrica de Tabacos La Corona
Estadio José M. Pérez
CERRO
Estadio Latinoamericano
CALZADA DEL CERRO
MÁXIMO GÓMEZ (MONTE)
To Southern Havana